PENGUIN BOOKS

JOURNEY INTO RUSSIA

Laurens van der Post was born in Africa in 1906. Most of his adult life has been spent with one foot there and one in England. His professions of writer and farmer were interrupted by ten years of soldiering – behind enemy lines in Abyssinia, and also in the Western Desert and the Far East, where he was taken prisoner by the Japanese while commanding a small guerrilla unit. He went straight from prison back to active service in Java, served on Lord Mountbatten's staff, and, when the British forces withdrew from Java, remained behind as Military Attaché to the British Minister. Since 1949 he has undertaken several official missions exploring little-known parts of Africa. His independent expedition to the Kalahari Desert in search of the Bushmen was the subject of his famous documentary film and of *The Lost World of the Kalahari* (published in Penguins). His other books include *Venture to the Interior* (1952), *Flamingo Feather* (1955), *The Heart of the Hunter* (1961), *The Seed and the Sower* (1963), *Journey into Russia* (1964), *The Hunter and the Whale* (1967) and *A Story Like the Wind* (1972). All these books have been published in Penguins. His latest books are *A Far Off Place* (1974), (soon to be published in Penguins), *A Mantis Carol* (1975) and *Jung and the Story of Our Time* (1976).

Colonel van der Post, who is married, was awarded the C.B.E. for his services in the field.

JOURNEY INTO RUSSIA

Laurens van der Post

PENGUIN BOOKS

IN ASSOCIATION WITH THE HOGARTH PRESS

Penguin Books Ltd, Harmondsworth, Middlesex, England
Penguin Books, 625 Madison Avenue, New York, New York 10022, U.S.A.
Penguin Books Australia Ltd, Ringwood, Victoria, Australia
Penguin Books Canada Ltd, 2801 John Street, Markham, Ontario, Canada L3R 1B4
Penguin Books (N.Z.) Ltd, 182–190 Wairau Road, Auckland 10, New Zealand

—

First published by the Hogarth Press 1964
Published in Penguin Books 1965
Reprinted 1967, 1968, 1971, 1973, 1975, 1976, 1978, 1982

—

—

Made and printed in Great Britain by
Hazell Watson & Viney Ltd,
Aylesbury, Bucks
Set in Monotype Times

It would mean an enormous waste of wealth, labour and even human life but the strength of Russia and the secret of her destiny has always consisted to a great extent in the readiness and power to ignore the cost in obtaining a desired result.

From Waliszewski's PETER THE GREAT

Une révolution ne maintient sa victoire que par une technique opposée aux moyens qui la lui ont donnée. Et parfois même aux sentiments.

MALRAUX

For Ingaret

CONTENTS

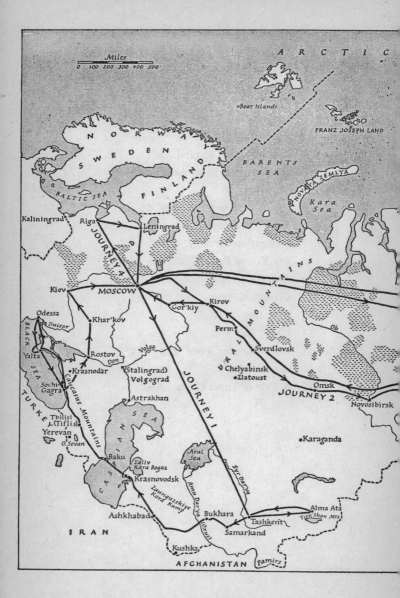

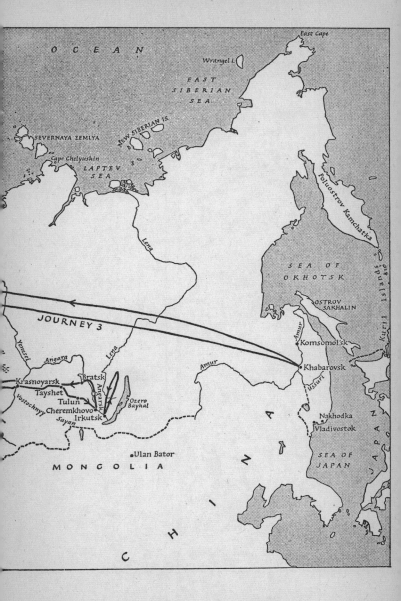

PREFACE

I AM not an expert on Russia and speak very little Russian. On my travels I had to rely a great deal on official guides and interpreters, though not so much as I had expected because I was amazed at the numbers of people I encountered who spoke either German, French, or, more especially, extremely good English to me. Therefore, what follows are no more than my impressions of the enormous physical scene of the Soviet Union, its history in so far as it still affects living issues and its peoples. My main justification for attempting even this much is that I have always been intensely curious about Russia; have been an ardent reader of Russian literature and history and now have accomplished what is perhaps the longest single journey through the Soviet Union undertaken since the war by someone who is not a Communist.

My chief regret is that I have been unable to be more specific about the people I met. For reasons into which I go fully in my account of the journey I believed it necessary in their own interests to camouflage their personalities and the incidents in which they were concerned. I realize that perhaps I may have been unduly fearful in my precautions but the impressions made on me by the Soviet system convinced me I had no option. I am sorry too that for the same reasons I could not be more explicit about my guides and interpreters. On the whole they served me well with good will, efficiency and sometimes great imagination. If they too are somewhat obscure in the account of my journey it is certainly not because I am ungrateful for the service they rendered me or that the service itself was inconsiderable.

Finally I have tried not to exceed my own experience. No one can travel through the Soviet Union alone as I did without being humbled by the realization of how little he has seen and can possibly know of so vast a country. Yet there is at the same time a similarity and continuity of character in the people who dominate the Soviet Union which encourages me to believe that one's slight experience can be more representative of the whole than it would

have been in many other countries of the world. However much
the physical nature of the land may change from the Polish
frontier to the Pacific one has the extraordinary sensation of always arriving at the point from which one had departed. In fact
the farther East I went the more Russian the scene and people
seemed to become.

I regret too that I cannot acknowledge all the many people who
helped me. Here I can only thank Harry Sions and Ted Patrick of
the distinguished American journal *Holiday* for commissioning
me to do the journey on their behalf; Sir Patrick Reilly, Britain's
former Ambassador to Moscow and an old friend of mine, for his
help and advice before setting out, and Bill Barker, the British
Minister in Moscow, and his wife Margaret for many reasons but
above all for giving me a home to go to when in need in Moscow,
and I owe an enormous debt as ever to my wife Ingaret Giffard,
for editing my MS.

Half Crown Cottage,
Aldeburgh, Suffolk

CHAPTER ONE

DEPARTURE

I MUST begin with the mood in which I took on the journey to Russia if that journey is properly to be understood. For years I had been in trouble with the image of Russia presented to us in the outside world. My own life has compelled me to travel much and the process has convinced me that one never really knows another country unless one knows it through the life of the individuals who compose it. The characters revealed to us in newspapers and books or smeared on to the crowded international canvas tend to be more and more over-simplified and over-drawn until the responses of the individual suddenly acquire the dimensions of caricature. Even more than these cartoon inaccuracies what alarmed me on my travels were the factors of impersonalization and dehumanization in the pictures countries painted for themselves of other nations, and years ago I began to cast around for correctives. I found the only effective one was holding on firmly in my imagination to such personal relationships as I had been able to form in foreign countries. I discovered that if I had but one clear portrait of an individual to which I could refer the collective abstractions that confronted me their exaggeration and inaccuracy were speedily exposed. Finally this scaling down of monstrous over-simplifications to their fallible, questing, and constituent human proportions came to appear to me as one of the most urgent tasks of our day. I could understand possibly that a nation might be tempted to bomb a country which is regarded as filled with dire monsters. But I firmly believed the temptation could be resisted the moment it saw the potential enemy as a people like itself, struggling each day to get to its office desk, factory bench or plough. Even in the war, when all life seemed abandoned to the power of the vast inhuman collective forces of the day, the rule had proved effective for me. Thus in the horror of a Japanese prison camp I discovered that by clinging to my memory of friendships formed in Japan years before I not only preserved my own spirit from the bitternesses of the moment but even evoked in the most brutal of our gaolers something individual and human which stood us all in good stead throughout those long inarticulate years of captivity.

In peacetime in the foreign countries to which I was unable to travel I found also a substitute for direct personal relationships in their art and literature. Literature particularly provided my imagination with specific glimpses into the common, questing flesh-and-blood reality of other countries, which put the generalizations purveyed to us into a human context and perspective. The more I travelled the more I realized how much one owed the artist and the writer. There was, for example, my own experience with France. I knew French literature before I knew France and consequently no matter how anti-French the popular waves of emotion or tone of the newspapers at any given time, I remained comparatively immune because, thanks to my reading, the French remained for me a people of a rich, diverse and endearingly paradoxical individuality. I was able to translate into the idiom of my own environment the statement of character personified in the immense range of literature from Villon to Daudet and as a result I possessed a feeling of kinship with the French which nothing could destroy. When I came to live in France later I was amazed at the number of doors already opened wide in this way for me to an understanding of the French.

Now my trouble with the Russian image was precisely that I could not discover a Russian individual in it. No matter what and how much I read or how closely I scrutinized my newspapers the Russians remained a vast, uniform, impersonal undifferentiated and forbiddingly ideological mass. Worse, the characters I met in contemporary Russian literature just would not take on any recognizable individual shape but seemed to insist on performing predetermined official roles wearing always the same fixed masks, like characters in an ancient Greek play. I felt this impediment so keenly and thought it so dangerous that I discussed it once with three Russians whom I met at a conference held in Switzerland for writers from behind the Iron Curtain. I think all of us from Western Europe were dismayed that we were never able to talk to one of these three alone. We had, of course, no sinister design on their corporate Russian self but the three Russian writers clung to one another so persistently that we were forced to conclude they

did so by design. The best I could do was to tell them that, thanks
to their pre-revolutionary literature, I knew the vanished Tsarist
Russia far better than I knew the U.S.S.R. I had had close relationships in my imagination with individual Russian characters who
invested the knowledge I had of the period with a warm, vivid and
living human reality. But I had had no such help in trying to
understand contemporary Russia. All the characters I met in
Soviet literature seemed oddly unreal, illustrating some special
ideological point. We could not understand them, I pleaded, as
we ourselves wished to be understood until we knew them as
individuals and could read of them as such.

The three Russians, however, protested that in their literature
they were represented in their entirety and that what obsessed
their deepest and most personal imaginations were indeed these
rhetorical slogans, these broad objectives and personifications of
the Soviet version of dialectical materialism.

Frankly I did not believe them. Instead I clung to my belief that
behind the approved masks, there was a human personality to be
discovered in Russia as rich and warm as any in the world. Yet
subsequently such contact as I had with Russia and the Russians
in the outside world was not encouraging.

There was, for example, the period in 1961 that I spent in
Berlin. There I failed utterly to perceive what might be behind the
Russian mask. I remembered East Berlin and the intangible but
none the less real cloak of unease that was thrown over me the
moment I crossed the line which divided it from the West. Even
the apartment houses in the reconstructed part of the sombre city,
built to the Soviet prescription, seemed to stand rigidly and appre-
hensively to attention, all dressed in the same severe graceless and
aggressive architectural uniform. I remarked in particular the
Russian war memorial. It was built on top of a vast grave into
which some eighty thousand Russian dead had been bulldozed.
Somehow it seemed enough to the Russians that their soldiers
were collective in death as they had been in life. In the West huge
organizations are maintained in all our armies to make certain
that after death the individual can be identified, given decent
burial in a separate grave and his sacrifice acknowledged with a
cross bearing his name, number, date of birth, time and manner
of death. But this Russian Memorial implied that these wide

differences between the Soviet world and our own were matters that involved not only life but death itself. Climbing up the tiers of steps to the top of the building the depression which this realization caused in me was increased by the wreaths piled high on the balustrades. It happened on that day to be the anniversary of the battle in which the eighty thousand men had been killed and the wreaths were new and their artificial flowers bright. I looked closely at the inscriptions. They too were all official and collective with dedications like: 'The workers of the shipbuilding yards of Rostock salute the glorious Soviet dead' or 'The collective farmers of Silesia pay everlasting homage, etc. etc.' I looked in vain for some wreath or posy of flowers saying no more than: 'Jack remembered with love from Jill' or 'Bill from his ever-loving Mum'. None the less my belief persisted that behind the opaque official front there was a man and his humanity to be discovered and honoured, and until this were done no real understanding between ourselves and the Russians would be possible. I thought, therefore, that I would make the people behind the mask the main object of my journey to Russia. Whether I was over-naïve in thinking I could do this under the circumstances existing in the Soviet Union today, the account of my journey will show.

My first step was to turn for advice to all my friends and acquaintances in London who knew the Soviet Union. The most experienced shook his head doubtfully when I told him I would need at least three months for my journey. 'I doubt if they'll give you a visa to stay in Russia for as long as that. They don't like visitors to spend more than a few weeks in the country. Moreover they don't like individual travellers but favour groups of tourists committed to one of their standard itineraries.' He then suggested that I should plan an itinerary for as short a stay as possible, put that up, and once in Moscow try to get an extension if necessary. 'If they like you,' he concluded, 'and are convinced of your good will you might get your visa extended.'

Another expert quarrelled immediately with this advice declaring emphatically, 'Once you've agreed to a date and a travel plan with the Russians they won't vary it by a yard or a second. Take my tip and ask for all you want now.'

So I pruned my plan like a tree in danger of being exhausted by bearing too much fruit and eventually went off with a considerable letter of recommendation to the Soviet Embassy in London.

I had never been to the Soviet Embassy before but it had always seemed to me somewhat incongruously housed in Kensington Palace Gardens, an area so expensive that Londoners know it as 'Millionaires' Row'. More curious still was the old-fashioned air in the reception rooms of the Embassy itself. Décor, furniture, plush, leather and lace reminded me more of a club than an advanced twentieth-century Embassy. I would not have been surprised to see an oil-painting of Mr Gladstone instead of portraits of the Soviet leaders on the panelled walls. However, in this eminently respectable atmosphere I was received over a period of weeks with an old-world courtesy by officials invariably wearing black suits of a conventional cut and speaking first-rate English. They always listened to my requests with patience but even at this early stage I received an inkling of the overwhelming centralization of the Soviet system. It soon became clear that, courteous and helpful as officials in London were, they could do little more than sympathetically refer my requests to Moscow.

This aspect of the Soviet way of life is so fundamental that it is as well to come to terms with it at the beginning. I had been determined to rid my mind of preconception in order to receive as fresh an impact of the human reality of Russia as possible. Yet here, right at the start, I found myself contrasting this portentous procedure with what happened to me when I last went to Italy. Then the whole matter had been settled for me in five minutes by a charming girl in her teens. But here, in the Soviet Embassy, I was not sure that they would take me in at all! I did not conform to the normal Soviet tourist rule. It was even suggested that since I was visiting the Soviet Union on behalf of an American magazine I should apply for facilities to the Russian Embassy in Washington! I explained several times to the Embassy that I was concerned not with Communism but with the ordinary people of Russia and their great land. But I got the impression that the purpose of my journey to which I attached so much importance did not really make sense to the officials who interviewed me. They were too polite to say so, however, and instead let their native good sense triumph over their official distaste of exceptions by begging me to go to their State travel organization, Intourist. They assured me there would be no difficulty over a visa once I had an approved Intourist itinerary in my possession. I went, therefore, with my original travel plan to Intourist in London. They at once authorized my own efficient travel agent to deal directly with their headquarters in Moscow. From there on I was struck by the speed and decision with which Moscow reacted. Moscow knew its own mind in these matters. Its 'No' remained 'no' however eloquently I reasoned against it. So I had to accept a travel plan which allowed me far less than half the time that I had asked for in my application for a visa.

The visa itself was another story. The maximum delay of ten days promised to me at the beginning stretched to twenty. Either a messenger or I myself importuned the Soviet Embassy four or five times a week. Each time we were politely asked to come back the next day and the visa would be complete. Once the mystery of the delay seemed explained when my passport was returned because there was said to be no 'proper' space in it for a Soviet visa. A young diplomat explained that the only empty space was on the back of the page which bore my last visa to the United States and where the imprint of the American eagle on the United States seal had come boldly through the page. Clearly its presence in the midst of a Soviet visa could not be contemplated, so I immediately obtained a new passport and handed it over for its virgin pages to be ravished by the Soviet seal-makers. I thought that now, surely, I should have it back, stamped, within ten days at most. But five more empty weeks went by. Then, just thirty-six hours before I was due to leave London Airport for Moscow, my visa arrived. It gave me not merely the eight weeks I had asked for but threw in another nine days for good measure, and I had no trouble later in getting my visa extended in Moscow for further weeks. The experts still insist that I was inordinately lucky. All the same I think there is something else to be discerned in all this. If one accepts with as good grace as possible all the conventional tourist formula which the Soviet Union offers then I believe one has far more chance of success than is commonly supposed. Also a great deal depends on the individual and I am certain I could not have done a quarter of the little I managed to do had I not been genuine in my proposition to the Russians that I sought only to learn something of the humanity of their people.

Usually I travel in the simplest manner possible but on this occasion the complexities of arrangements made for me on the best available advice made me feel rather ridiculous. My suitcase was packed with almost every conceivable variety of clothing from the lightest tropical bush-jacket to the warmest ski-ing underwear. There was one exception. I had discarded a dinner-jacket on being advised that it was scorned as the most *bourgeois* of symbols in the Soviet Union. My financial provisions too had been as laborious. Instead of just a single book of traveller's cheques from my bank I possessed also traveller's cheques issued by the Russian State bank, credit coupons on Intourist and a tactical selection of sterling and dollar denominations. I tried also to get some roubles before leaving but so great is the Soviet fear of black market dealings in its money that these are not legally obtainable in the outside world and can only be taken in and out of the country at peril. Breaches of currency regulations in Russia are punishable by death.

Never had I bought so many different kinds of tickets for a single journey, either. I fully intended travelling by trans-Siberian railway from Moscow to Vladivostok but all my appeals for the requisite permission had been turned down by cable after cable from Moscow merely repeating: 'No Intourist facilities Vladivostok'. My only hope of changing the official mind, I was assured, lay in applying for a ticket by rail and sea all the way to Tokyo. So in addition to the London-Moscow return ticket demanded by Intourist, and the vouchers covering the limited provisional itinerary, I was equipped with documents enabling me to come back to London via Japan, Sweden, Finland, India, Greece or Austria! I may be pardoned for repeatedly thinking with envy of the hero of one of my favourite travel books, *Round the World on a Wheel*. In the nineties of the last century he had decided to go round the globe on a bicycle. With no currency or visa restrictions the idea was no sooner thought of than done. One fine day this wheeled Drake in Norfolk jacket and knickerbockers just stuffed his pockets full of five-pound notes and mounted his bicycle for the nearest Channel port. By way of France he cycled without mishap across Western Europe into

Russia, through Siberia and, with the help of ocean ferries, on and around the world and back home again to his first good cup of tea in months!

I had been pressed, too, into carrying almost as many medicines as I would take on a major expedition into the wilds of Africa. A friend's chauffeur who had once driven some exceptionally privileged tourists around Russia in the brief period when this was allowed, remonstrated gravely with me on the fell incidence of 'tummies' in Russia, quoting Uzbek, Khazak, Tartar, Crimean, Ukrainian and other Left-wing varieties of tummy troubles and I might have been persuaded by his eloquence to add to my collection of drugs. I never had great cause to regret my decision not to do so.

On top of all this I had to take with me soap and all sorts of modest commodities of which the Soviet Market was reputed to be in short supply, and which, I was assured, would be far more welcome as tips than money. In the end, the impatience induced in me by so unaccustomed a fussiness in preparation was only appeased by the conviction that no contingency could arise on the journey for which I was not now fully prepared. Nevertheless after going through my list with great concern the wife of an old friend went to her storeroom, and as I left thrust a small parcel into my hands with the ominous words: 'You'll need this'. Back in my room at the hotel I found it consisted of several packets of the best *bourgeois* toilet paper.

I myself thought only one section of my preparations inadequate: I had very little reading matter on Russia with me. Anxious to get my own impressions of the Soviet Union I had thought it better to postpone reading until the end of my journey. All I had wanted to read beforehand were some first-rate histories of Russia before the Revolution. Even in primitive countries which have no written histories of their own, the life of a people never begins to make sense to me until I have uncovered the verbally transmitted story of their past legends and myths which, in my view, influence the patterns of behaviour just as a concealed magnet affects a field of iron filings scattered on the surface of a table above it. Nor was the importance of the Russian historical past diminished for me by the fact that Soviet Russia had apparently wilfully rejected it. History has its own metabolism. At its deepest level it is independent of the denials and manipulations to which nations seek, periodically, to subject it for temporary ends and I feared that without access to this submerged idiom I would be unable to interpret the meaning of the contemporary scene. So I went hopefully through the bookshops in London only to discover that Russian history, in the sense that I sought it, no longer appeared to be on offer. Histories of the Bolshevik Revolution, and the last Tsarist years, and still more histories of the post-revolutionary years filled vast shelves. But even comparatively recent historians like Pares and Maynard were unobtainable or out of print, as also was Richard Charque's short history of Russia which had appeared some time before like a chink of light in the black-out of the moment. So, grateful to the greed with which I have always read world history and putting my faith in the library of the British Embassy in Moscow, I had to set off with only my Russian grammar and dictionary, the Marquis de Custine's *Voyage en Russie* written some hundred and twenty years ago, the remarkable history of Georgia by an old friend of mine W. E. D. Allen, and a set of the Geographical Society's admirable maps of the Soviet Union.

It may have been merely a sign of how difficult it is these days to be objective about other countries when they are continually debated on radio and television, or it may have been a warning that despite my good resolutions to the contrary I had already taken up an attitude to the journey well in advance of my experience but at Heathrow it appeared to me that the Soviet Jet in which I was to fly to Moscow was keeping its crew very much to itself. Nor, I realized with amazement, were there any Soviet hostesses among the dozens of different nationalities which brightened our dull, pre-travel mob. We had to set off to find our aircraft by bus without any feminine guidance. The aircraft itself, too, took some finding. It was tucked away on its own at the far end of London Airport out of reach of casual contact with the English world around it. I liked the look of it even at a distance. It was cream coloured, with a little red painted on it. It had a nice clean line and a simplicity of proportion in design. I found myself giving it an immediate vote of confidence. Although it had only left Moscow that morning the aircraft was already turned about and hovering on the edge of the main runway like a bird with wings stretched and impatient for its homeward flight. But we met none of the crew until we stepped on board. At the head of the gangway three young women in neat outfits of Siberian blue received us with great formality. One wore a cap, one a silk kerchief tied peasant-wise round her head and the other had nothing at all on her minutely curled yellow hair. Yet the expression in the three pairs of eyes was the same: withdrawn and uncommitted. Their manner too was grave, detached and impersonal without any hint of a smile with which their colleagues among Western nations inevitably welcome the traveller on board. They showed us all to our seats in a businesslike manner, told me in English with hardly a trace of accent, how to fasten my safety belt, and then in what seemed to be a remarkably short space of time we were taxi-ing into take-off position on the runway. One of the young women presented me with a boiled sweet on a tray. Notices in Russian and English flashed on the screen in front of us and scarcely had I time to marvel how the Russian alphabet made these warning notices look oddly like quotations in Greek from Homer, before we left the earth easily and without a jerk. It was one of the most purposeful and streamlined departures which I had ever experienced.

So at last I set off from London Airport on a lovely morning in April. The honey light, the larkspur sky with a sail or two of cloud on the edge of the blue, the green bud bursting from the dark bark of the patient trees proclaimed with typical under-statement the defeat of a long winter and the tender re-beginning which is spring in England. Would it be the same in Russia when I landed there in a few hours' time?

I sat back to examine the aircraft and companions like someone studying the programme of a new opera before the rise of the first curtain. My seat was as comfortable as – the smile came to me unbidden – a dentist's chair, and I could lean back as far as suited my purpose. There was no one in front of me and I had a clear view into the alley leading to the cockpit. The furnishings were grey and chromium, austere and oddly clinical. But the smooth effortless way in which the jet climbed into the gentle blue over England reassuringly demonstrated that the engines and aerodynamics of the plane had been the main consideration. The luggage racks, too, were woefully inadequate and the reason for this evaded me until I started travelling on the internal air services of the Soviet Union. There the luggage racks were still smaller but adequate because their passengers carry pathetically little on their journeys. But I, in my first ignorance, thought it to be just an oversight in design.

I was still in the midst of speculation of this kind when our noon-day meal arrived, unannounced by menu, wine list or inquiry of any kind. The young hostess of the silk kerchief appeared suddenly at my side with a tray and informed me with great seriousness that I could have vodka, beer, wine or Russian champagne with my food.

I asked if I could have mineral water instead.

'Of course,' she said with a touch of asperity as if somewhat insulted by the doubt implied in my request, and promptly fetched me a whole bottle.

On my tray was a lavish portion of black caviare, smoked salmon of excellent quality, sardines, shrimps, tunny fish, ham, tongue, mixed salads, a chunk of butter and several kinds of bread including the wonderful Russian black bread with the harvest tang of the corn still in it. I imagined this to be the whole of my meal. But I was wrong. Unlike the luggage racks, food in the air in Russia is more than generous. A dish of hot red Bortsch followed, a huge fried steak with onions, cabbage and a mound of roast potatoes pursued the soup and, if my stamina had been equal to the occasion, I could have had some cheese, chocolate éclairs and fruit as well. Having already eaten more than usual I bowed myself out of the race over a cup of coffee.

I began now to take notice of my fellow passengers who, pressing on regardless, were wiping the sweat from their brows with paper napkins. There were only nine of them; seven, judging by their conversation in the bus at Heathrow, were East Germans and one, a shy, apprehensive African, and a plump, untidy man who by his looks could easily have been a confirmed beachcomber from any intellectual foreshore of the Western world. He earned my respect not only for a superb display of one-upmanship by coolly ordering a second éclair when even the perspiring East Germans had been forced to retire, but also by reading a large album of piano music throughout the journey as most people would read a thriller. I thought that the grave young woman who

was serving me would contrast my consumer performance un-
favourably with those of the others so when I thanked her I
apologized for my failure to eat on to the end, confessing, as I
pointed at a straining button, that I had already eaten more than
I normally did. Instantly she laughed with pleasure and the
sudden change from a formal almost melancholy expression into
laughter was unexpected and enchanting. I felt utterly reproved for
having momentarily suspected her of being incapable of fun and
I stress it here because it was my first encounter with what I
believe is one of the most typical characteristics of the Russians.
They are not a smiling people. With them the smile is generally
only a preliminary to laughter and this perhaps more than anything else gives them their reputation for melancholy. The nuances
of feeling for which the Western world uses the smile are either unknown to them or provided for in other ways. Indeed later I
gathered from my Russian friends that they find our frequent use
of the smile rather tiresome and meaningless and tending to
bring laughter into disrepute. But for laughter itself the Russians
have a great capacity and respect. I have enjoyed laughing with
them more than with any other group of people except my own
primitive countrymen in Africa. And because this young air
hostess was the first to show me the laugh behind the mask I
continue to remember her with gratitude.

Soon after we had a demonstration of gaiety of a different sort.
Our trays had hardly been cleared away when an officer appeared
in the alleyway. He was the first of his kind that I had ever seen
and I was struck at once by the looseness of the uniform on his
stocky frame. Even the slight draught from the ventilators
appeared enough to make his wide trousers and coat flap about
him. Male clothes in Russia, except on some of the city young,
seemed designed deliberately to flap. It may be that Soviet tailors
are still secretly obsessed with memories of an idealized peasants'
blouse and loose trousers that could be tucked into jack-boots
without impeding the movement of the knees, but whatever the
reason I have never seen so many flapping figures as in Russia –
except when I was young, among the Boers of my own people.
However, standing there apparently indifferent to his passengers,
the officer beckoned imperiously to his three hostesses. They
immediately went to him and all four vanished behind thick

grey curtains. Ten minutes later the three young women reappeared, laughing among themselves and obviously keen to
share the good news with us. My own hostess made straight for
me and said: 'You will be glad to know that it is now Yuri
Gagarin Day. The captain of the aircraft sent for us so that we
could all congratulate and thank one another on our achievement.'

Two things about her announcement impressed me. The first
showed how the whole crew had identified themselves with
Gagarin's achievement and I imagined that, in this, I was looking
into a microcosm of the Soviet world. It implied that their minds
might be conditioned first to depersonalize and then to collectivize Russian achievements as thoroughly as they had collectivized
industry. There certainly was no trace of any temptation to
personality-worship in my young air-hostess for when I con-
gratulated her, saying how much we all admired Gagarin and
what a charming as well as brave person he appeared to be, she
immediately became very serious.

'Oh yes, he is nice enough but in my view there is a danger of
people making too much of him,' she replied. 'After all he was
only a link in the chain and to my mind achieved less than Titov
and the others. Titov's was a far more serious contribution to
science than Gagarin's. And the ones after him were greater still.'

The second thing that impressed me was the way she assumed
that I would be as delighted as she was and that the occasion, like
the food, had to be shared equally with us. Yet there was something just a little forbidding in having one's participation so much
taken for granted. I had an uneasy feeling there could be the
makings of a *hubris* in this – a tendency not merely to collectivize
but also to universalize Russian experience and achievement,
automatically converting their relative into an absolute significance. However, I rebuked myself for making too much of too
little. I warned myself that I must not read between the lines
before I had read the lines. I had anticipated that this might be
the main inducement to error when persons brought up in our
comparatively frank way of life came into contact with closed
systems which display only selected aspects of themselves as I
had been told did the Soviet Union.

Meanwhile, it was amazing how on such a clear day the characters of the countries on the way to Moscow stood out on the

ground below, even at thirty thousand feet and at six hundred
miles per hour. Thus England appeared indefinable and unpredictable like the national spirit, absolute only in its commitment to its own processes of growth, but with many a twist and
turn in the landscape as it resolved its difficulties on earth. That
'the longest way round is the shortest way there' seemed implicit
in this pattern and under the mellow light of spring towns,
villages, farms, meadows, hedges and gardens seemed to grow
out of it like the finger-prints of a thousand and one seasons
which one reads in cross-cuts of the great redwood trees of
California. The Channel itself was little more than a flashing
stream, and then suddenly, after the pragmatic earth of Britain
was the Continent, clear-cut, articulate and doctrinaire. One
had just a glimpse of the Gallic lands to the south before Holland
absorbed the whole of the view, establishing itself in one's senses
as a major act of will and the deliberate product of an obstinate
determination to have its own way. After England it was astonishing how often the Dutch scene followed the shortest distances
between points, took short cuts, was managed, arranged and
abounded in precise geometric patterns wherever river and ocean
permitted them. Germany was only a glimmer of yellow sand on
the horizon, but Denmark was laid out neat, polished and orderly
like a soldier's equipment for inspection on a parade ground.
The pattern appeared dedicated to a conception wherein everything, even beauty, was put to definite use. Over Copenhagen the
day was blurred with afternoon smoke and one was dismayed
by the speed with which our own pace, together with the sun's,
had advanced the approach of night. The Baltic in that ash-blonde
light was a shallow shadow and only after Riga did one see again
a pattern of manufactured land under the levelling light. The
change was startling for the basic design of Europe was not
asserted except by outposts, themselves threatened by an immense
mass of featureless earth and forest advancing from the East.
Towns, villages and farms still repeated spasmodically in miniature the shapes of the lands to the west, and the sun would pick
on a set of walls, or a spire, only to reveal them illuminated and
immersed in the increasing solemnity and shapelessness of the
earth. Soon however even these fragments of the ancient pattern
melted into the older scene. One was abandoned utterly to a

level-topped vision of a strange flat earth stretching from horizon to horizon, its cover of forest and lengthening afternoon shadows rarely broken by any clearing or act of man, though often gleaming with the burnt-out silver of lakes, streams and marshes. It was extraordinary how empty and vast the earth now looked from such a height. I stared at it long trying in vain to encompass it in some single envelope of imagination. But for the first time I was excited by the feeling that I was on the verge of encountering an earth as abundant as in Africa. Yet there was one difference. When I discovered what it was it turned out to be a mere trifle, yet it affected me. There was no smoke rising up from this new earth below me. I remembered the smoke over the housetops of England and the smoke always rising from savannah, plain and forest in remotest Africa, and somehow this absence of smoke made a dismal impact on me. It was as well, perhaps, that I did not know then how characteristic this was of the Russian scene and how I would come to appreciate Homer's lines wherein Athena tells the gods of Odysseus's longing to see again 'the smoke leaping up over his native Ithaca'.

I landed on the international airport at Sheremetevo some twenty miles from Moscow just before sundown. The air was surprisingly warm, the light like olive oil laying a gloss on the slender pines and birches of the woods that still crowd in on the capital. The calm was immense and not a shiver of air stirred the frail branches. Beyond the trees rose neither mountains, hills, mounds nor even towers. On such level earth in so level an evening the sky achieved its fullness of space and height. And that, too, was very Russian. Great as the effect of this immense land is on the senses, that of the sky is always greater. After the bustle, the noise and the traffic of Heathrow, the stillness was astounding. All the time while I was in the modest and unpretentious reception building not a single aircraft arrived or left the airport. It felt oddly isolated and provincial as if I had arrived not at an entrance to one of the world's greatest capitals but in some remote country backwater. Our reception in the airport building, too, added to this impression. Gone was the formality which had seen us into the plane. Instead a rural casualness was characteristic of the persons who met us. I detected no sign of rigidity, arrogance or suspiciousness in my own reception. It is true there were still no

smiles and the customs and immigration officials, leaning casually
in their loose uniforms against their counters, looked almost indifferent. They stamped my declaration forms without reading
them and passed my bag without opening it. They took no interest in the books and papers I carried. I have seldom seen
officials fussing less. All the time a young Intourist girl stood
by me telling me what to do in admirable English, and when it was
done she summoned a car with a mere wave of the hand so that in
a remarkably short time I was on my way through the woods to
Moscow.

CHAPTER TWO

MOSCOW – THE CAPITAL

Moscow stands at the centre of the great Russian plain but just beyond the woods some wind of time had raised a gentle ground swell in the earth. Breasting the first slow wave of land, I saw the city itself in the last light of the sun. I do not know precisely what I had expected but I was disappointed. I suspect it was partly connected with a vague belief induced in so many persons of my generation that somehow the horrors of revolution, civil war, invasion, famine and all the many other cruel denials of life inflicted on the Russian people would be redeemed by a break-through into something truly new and original. And there was little to be seen in the city's skyline just then that was particularly beautiful, noble, visionary or original, except the light of an unusually pure evening upon it. That light was alchemical and it transformed Moscow into a city of gold, the tops of the spires and pinnacles drawing the rigid forms of the few skyscrapers after them into arrows of gold aimed at the arched and timeless blue. The gold, alas, declined as we came nearer into putty-coloured bricks and concrete slabs piled upon one another in huge square building blocks like cakes of yellow Sunlight soap heaped into shape. Though new these building blocks were not only unoriginal but depressingly like those I had seen in East Berlin. It was a sobering thought that despite all the miles separating Moscow and Berlin the architectural pattern could be the same. The closer we came to the city the smaller appeared the power of invention in the vast design. The skyscrapers themselves struck me as early Manhattan rather than Soviet in their inspiration. The great square apartment-blocks were inferior versions in the process of proliferation of grey functional cells and dissemination of concrete sclerosis that has abolished the reflexes of so many architects of the modern world. But where these processes in most countries are curbed by the intrusion of buildings from the past, and the stubborn insistence of masses of people to live in a design of their own, there was no such relief apparent in the scene in front of me.

One approach so resembled another that no matter how much we changed course I continually had the Alice-in-Wonderland feeling of emerging at the point from which I had just departed. Nor was there any indication that the future would be different. The city was in a fever of building. Scaffolding and builders' cranes protruded everywhere like clothes pegs hung on the city's skyline. But what was impressive was the scale and a certain dynamic implicit in the scene. It was rather awe-inspiring to see this city of over seven million people topping the slight swell of earth grandiosely spoken of as the Lenin Hills, and advancing over the passive plain to sweep wooden villages out of its way and take light concrete bounds over rivers, canals and streams. There was no straggling, no ribbon development which disfigures the approaches to so much of metropolitan England. It was an advance as disciplined as that of a Brigade of Guards, an all-out frontal attack of buildings in battledress and under unified command marching shoulder to shoulder in the broad ranks beloved by the Russian military against the defenceless land. In that sense alone the scene was new and dynamic and some sort of a counter to any feelings of disappointment aroused by the monotony and poverty of design. I was, indeed, compelled to ask myself how such a result could have been avoided in the Soviet scheme of things? Could any government of a people so long and notoriously ill-housed as the Russians have afforded to sacrifice the pace made possible by standard design and mass-production of buildings to the slower approach demanded for the art and grace of individual design? I was to be in and out of Moscow a great deal and every time I returned to it those things that had worried me in my first view of the city somehow seemed to be more understandable.

The driver of my car certainly shared none of my misgivings. He was downright proud of it all. Speaking good German he would repeatedly say as he pointed out some fresh developing prospect: 'There was a village there a year ago and look at it now!' Once he pointed out a grey apartment eminence rising like a rocket from the ground to remark laughingly: 'I went by here yesterday and since then they have added three storeys to it.' He paused before commenting proudly: 'We have increased our capacity for pre-fabricated buildings so much that we now build faster than the Americans.'

It was my first lesson in the profound complex of Russian self-esteem. From the production of pigs to hydrogen bombs not the western European countries but the United States of America are the provocative standard of comparison.

'But what happened to the people who lived in the demolished villages?' I asked.

He answered readily, 'Oh, they were given the first chance to have apartments in the new buildings.'

'But I understood from you that they were farmers. What becomes of their farming land and livelihood?'

'They are either given new work,' he replied unperturbed, 'or if they insist on wanting to farm they are sent to other collective farms. In any case the State takes care of them.'

Two things stood out for me in his ready response. He spoke of farming as if it were no different from other work and showed no obvious appreciation that it had deep and ancient roots in a particular earth of its own. The other was the subtle change of tone which came into his voice when he pronounced the words 'The State'. The words came out with awe and subsequently, almost without exception, I heard the same tone in every voice, young or old, that mentioned 'The State' to me on my long journey through the Soviet Union.

Now for all I had seen up to this moment Moscow might have been set down in a desert of history without a past and only this stiff pre-fabricated present straining to repeat itself in the future. But suddenly, beyond the river filled to the brim with sunset colours, there was a flicker of fire and shape of flame. It came from the red brick walls, turrets, spires and domes of the delicate sixteenth-century Novo-Devichy Monastery, a survivor of one of the earlier religious establishments which once earned Moscow the description of 'City of Forty times Forty churches'. The monastery blossomed among the concrete cubes like a rose and its impact on my imagination was considerable. It was as if I were witnessing in it a quiet assertion of faith in man's gentleness, patience and maturity so very different from the furious all-out investment in the collective will and mass energies of the directed world which surrounded it. We travelled on at an easy pace through the oddly silent and ordered streets between the tall buildings which line the new suburbs of Moscow. The streets

themselves were perhaps the most pleasing feature of the city.
They were unusually wide and made straightly for their objectives
in the grand Roman manner. Among them the ranks of buildings
were neither quite as uniform nor as crowded as they had appeared from a distance. There was plenty of room between one
block and another for both light and manoeuvre. In this respect
the design expressed something of the Russian's love of space and
distance around him. For a while here and there a few old wooden
houses like fragments of some stage silhouette of a pre-Revolution
play still beggared the portals of apartment houses, but they soon
vanished. So wide was the design that I never appreciated how
high the new buildings were until I came to go up in them. Although
it was obviously one of the busiest hours of the day the streets
seemed curiously empty. Cars, buses, trucks, all of a strikingly
uniform design flowed easily in two broad streams. The two
streams, wide as they were, still had room to leave a lane free in
the centre between them. My driver explained the lane was left
clear by decree for ambulances, fire engines and State vehicles.
Even so there were no traffic jams and the only times I was to see
any were on State occasions when whole areas were abruptly
sealed off without warning for ceremonial traffic only. The pavements too were wide and filled with people who seemed to be
plodding doggedly in colourless masses between their huge impersonal apartment blocks. Their pace struck me as that of a
country people trudging home from their fields at the end of a
long day, rather than the brisk step of persons released from
bondage in metropolitan offices. That was one curious aspect of
the first impression Moscow made on me. I had little feeling of
being in a world capital. There was no impression of self-
sufficiency, which is instantly evoked in the visitor by London,
Paris, Rome, Peking and even in Vienna despite the irrevocable
disappearance of the Empire which gave it birth. On the contrary
my feeling was that of being somewhere deep in the country in a
huge village that had suddenly grossly exceeded itself. I tended to
go on feeling this everywhere too, except in the squares and
streets around the Kremlin. There it would instantly vanish and I
would find that the glow of history which I had witnessed in the
silhouette of a solitary monastery was suddenly blown into a
leaping, vivid and strange barbaric flowering. This strange complex

of buildings, boxed-in and over-topped by a vast new world
of brash construction, was enough to give Moscow the heart of
living history without which a city no matter what its size can
never be great, and to make it a capital not just in the administrative and political sense but also in the imaginations and emotions
of men.

However, I had no chance just then to follow up the impression.
It was already nearly dark. I had barely had a glimpse of the incredible outline of the Moscow fortress and had just seen the
slender towers and spires of the churches huddled for shelter
within its walls hold their gilded domes lightly like soap bubbles
high in the last iridescence of the day, when we drew up outside
my hotel on the opposite side of the square facing them. Four
untidy little boys rushed up as I got out, three eager to swap coins
and stamps. the fourth begging for chewing gum as if it were the
status symbol of his age-group. But all four withdrew the moment
a Commissionaire in a splendid Metro-Goldwyn-Meyer uniform
came out to help me.

The hotel was the National, built at the beginning of the
century and from the outside it looked even older. It could easily
have been one of the establishments favoured by mid-Victorians
in the provincial watering places of Europe, when indoor sanitation and lifts were inventions almost as startling as sputniks.
We entered by swing doors, to my surprise ignored the reception
desk, staffed entirely by impressive-looking women in rather
dowdy clothes, and entered a long room labelled 'Service Bureau',
the office maintained by Intourist in this as in all other hotels to
which foreign tourists are sent. The staff there too was entirely
feminine but younger and smarter in appearance. Each girl sat
at a desk and telephone of her own, gravely and self-assuredly
dealing with an odd assortment of travellers, cashing their
cheques, ordering their cars, booking long-distance telephone
calls, getting tickets for concerts, theatre and ballet, and finding
them appropriate billets for their stay. Some of these travel-
stained gentry under the strain of prolonged jet propulsion
through time and the seasons were irritable and inclined to be
boorish. I heard one irate lady voyager command an undersized
husband to 'Call Kennedy!' if he did not get what he wanted.
Another strapping fellow, bursting with good health, promised to

let Congress know all about his reception. Others turned on all
the charm they knew as if inside they were composed of nothing
but milk and marzipan. One Oriental couple appeared to be
lavishly equipped with nylons as the means of continuing their
policies when all other means had failed. I hate to think what all
these serious young ladies must have thought of the world beyond
the Soviet frontiers if these were a normal sample of the peoples
who crossed them. But outwardly they appeared unaffected, kept
their heads and their emotions to themselves, quietly doing what
only they knew they could and had to do. And that, I must confess in fairness to the travellers there, took a very long time. An
hotel which took as long anywhere else would soon have been
out of business. For instance, the National is a smallish hotel yet
it took the grave young lady dealing with me three-quarters of an
hour to discover the number of my room. That was not due to any
lack of trying. She must have dialled thirty numbers in that time,
asked again and again in the same emotionless voice for 'Ad-
ministrator' and after a brief conversation rung off, to begin all
over again without trace of impatience or despair. Somehow I
was convinced that it would not help to interrupt or importune
her as some of my neighbours were doing. I sat silently by the
desk fascinated, watching her unvarying approach to the invisible
world at the other end of the line. I had a feeling that in this
trifling episode I was looking through a tiny glass into the character and state, if not the history, of a nation. I was certain that
nothing would stop this quiet young woman, nothing would
make her alter tone and pace until she had achieved her object.
Finally she handed me the number of my room and summoned a
porter to take me there, all without apology, comment, or, of
course, a smile. I must add however that in the following weeks
after I had a great deal to arrange through this particular young
lady, I learned much from her behaviour and above all, perhaps,
how wrong I would have been had I put down her apparently
mechanical and docile application to a lack of spirit and will of
her own. Within the entanglements of an unnecessarily complicated
system she was most efficient, with a spirit, self-esteem and surprising gaiety of her own. She told me one day how, unable to
endure any longer the tyranny of a narrow, boorish and unimaginative official in her world, she had persuaded some of her

colleagues to join with her in subscribing under his name to the leading Soviet Journal devoted to pig-breeding. Thereafter, this national pig-breeder's Gazette appeared on the official's desk each week on the day of publication until the point pierced home; he had a nervous breakdown, and left. That he had a nervous breakdown over so subtle an affliction seemed to me something to his credit.

My room on the third floor was vast. The ceiling seemed thrice as high as that of any hotel room I had ever known. I thought of course this was a peculiarity of the age to which the hotel belonged, but I was to find that this love of height is still deep in the Russian builder not only of skyscrapers and apartment houses but of coaches and trams as well. He will accept the need to economize on floor space and crowd his accommodation on the ground, but he insists on a sense of the sky for a ceiling, with the result that I have been in Russian apartments almost higher than they are either broad or long. What this love costs the Soviet Government in time, labour and money must be prodigious. A Western architect, for instance, would easily have built half as many storeys again in the same height and space as that occupied by the proud thirty-storey Ukraine Hotel in Moscow. Anyone who is inclined to think of the Soviet system as a product of pure reason obedient to objective laws of history and economics has only to look closely at Soviet buildings to be confounded and also, perhaps, to be oddly reassured.

As noticeable as was the size of my room so too was its old-fashioned atmosphere. There were curtains of Victorian lace over the glass of the high wide windows and massive curtains of plush hung on rings and rods on the walls at the side. There was plush with tassels and plush alternated with club leather on the chairs. Little knitted white doylies lay on the dressing-table and sideboard and a white muslin cloth with glass beads at the hems covered a jug of water. More heavy plush curtains concealed a room within a room in which stood a bed covered in white broderie-anglaise and a door gave on to a small bathroom, unventilated and of old-fashioned but adequate plumbing. Two massive oil-paintings, in heavy gilt frames, fulfilled the Victorian order of refinement in the room: in one a troika driven by someone looking remarkably like the poet Robert Browning on his way to beard Mr Barrett of Wimpole Street was ploughing gallantly through an immense flat snow-covered landscape; the other showed a placid afternoon scene, deep in the country with meadow, river and woods sparkling with sun and no hint of the great night to come. Both paintings were innocuous and picturesque enough to have come straight from the illustrations I used to see regularly as a child in 'The Sunday at Home', and both hung leaning at an angle well away from the wall as if to make certain that nothing of their implied message should be missed from below. I thought this too merely a by-product of the period of the hotel. Actually it was a rigid fashion in picture-hanging that applied from the Polish frontier to Kamchatka and Murmansk to Tashkent and Sochi, in all the hotels, sanatoriums, railway stations and restaurants, though not in museums. Somewhere, I suspect, at some Party Congress a directive about the precise angle of frame to wall had been issued.

What was modern in my room was the telephone on my desk, the official glossies in English, French and German on the table and the hotel rules and regulations in these three languages, as well as, of course, Russian and Chinese. Only a telephone directory was missing. I appealed in vain to the porter when he appeared with my bag. He seemed not to have heard of telephone directories and referred me to a massive lady sitting at a desk at the head of the stairs leading to the floor of my room. In time I was to know her and her kind well. There was always one of them on duty night and day on every floor of every hotel I ever visited. From their desks they would command maids, keys, linen, laundry, trays, messengers, etc. as absolutely as a Captain commands the life and movements of his ship. There appeared to be almost nothing they did not know and in my experience it was impossible to get on or off the floor of any hotel without their knowledge. Once late at night at Alma Ata I surprised one asleep on the couch beside her desk. I tiptoed by so as not to disturb her but looking back along the long corridor from the door of my room I saw her on her feet, wide awake and watching me intently. Had I had any secret life I wanted to lead I might have found them very trying. As I had none I thought them an extremely convenient institution. Also, remembering how once I had nearly been burnt to death at night in a fire spreading unobserved from an empty suite next to my room on the twelfth floor of an hotel in Los Angeles, I found them a great comfort, particularly when I was told that one of their special functions was O.C. fire precautions. Of all the ones I met the one on my floor in the Hotel National was the best, yet she too failed me about my telephone directory. I had no option but to go back below to the service bureau. There another young lady produced a small book hardly bigger than a pocket diary wherein apparently she had the addresses and numbers of the staffs of all the Embassies and foreign concerns in Moscow. A larger directory was not available and to this day it remains a mystery to me how the Russians themselves telephone to people whose addresses and numbers they do not possess beforehand. Once I had the number, however, telephoning was easy and the service good. Particularly was this true of the Russian international telephone service. I had for obvious reasons expected difficulties there but I found it easier to get through to my home in England than to the American and British Embassies. Moreover the line was so clear that I recognized the distinctive sound of my own telephone ringing in my drawing-room in London. I was impressed too with the quality of the English spoken by the Russian operators. From the time I had boarded the plane in London the standard of English of all the Russians whose function it was to know it had been so uniformly high that I had to accept this as the rule and not the exception. At first I believed it to be a tribute to the importance of English as a world language, but I was to find the same exacting command with Russians speaking French and German (both of which I knew well), and Chinese of which I had a smattering.

After my telephoning I went in to dinner. A place had been reserved for me at a table in a window looking over the square on to the Kremlin. A miniature Union Jack flew from a chromium mast planted in a heavy metal base in front of me. Now the British flag is one of the most difficult to make correctly and is very easily flown upside down. Half the Union Jacks one sees flown by the British themselves from the bonnets of their German cars abroad are upside down. In that position they are, by international code, signals of distress. But the miniature flag on my table was as correct as any flag flown over the parade ground of any Guards' regiment in Britain. All this may seem trifling but it impressed me at the time as a pointer to a meticulous regard for detail for which I was not prepared. The colours of almost all the nations of the world too were flying over the tables around me. This too I was to find a rite rigidly observed throughout the Soviet Union. I took it as an official gesture of welcome to foreign visitors until one day an experienced foreign correspondent tried to convince me that these flags were one of the favourite Soviet devices for concealing microphones to record the conversation of guileless travellers like myself. I never unscrewed one to find out whether he was right and it made no difference either to my appetite or conversation at table.

While I sat there by this pocket mast-head of the British world the hotel orchestra began to play loudly and energetically. It played the sort of dance music one hears all over the world and the noise it made overwhelmed all conversation. The real travellers in the room were either too tired or dazed with distance to respond but the Russians rose immediately from their tables. They took to the crowded floor in front of the orchestra rather like adolescents going to their first grown-up dance. However outworn both music and steps were to me, the Russians danced them obediently, even gratefully. The men danced still in their flapping grey and brown suits with solemn unsmiling faces, but the women, obviously dressed in their best, danced with zest. Their best was a short evening frock of rayon, primly cut, some lipstick and a lone ornament on wrist or hair. A factory girl in England would have rejected most of the costumes as too spartan for her Saturday night at the local Palais de danse but so colourless had been the appearance of most people that this occasion appeared almost festive. I sat there for half an hour before I could get a waitress to serve me. The delay was not her fault for I have seldom seen women working harder or more willingly. It was the fault, I am certain, of the system which I was to encounter everywhere that I went in the Soviet Union. When she did appear my waitress, a sturdy young woman dressed in a demure uniform of black, with a small white lace apron and lace cap, took my order in English and marched off with the step of an infantryman into the crowded kitchen approaches somewhere out of sight. She had hardly gone when a brawny Russian smelling of home-made soap and vodka seated himself opposite me. Coatless, his shirt sleeves rolled up and collar wide open at the neck, he seemed totally unconcerned that he was the only person dressed in that way in the room. Perfectly at ease he gave me a friendly inquiring look and addressed me in passable German. I was to be amazed how many of the ordinary people of Russia, probably as a result of the war, spoke some German. He told me he was a master locomotive-man from just outside Moscow and was up in the capital for Gagarin Day. Who and what was I? I told him. At once he shook my hand until it hurt and offered me a vodka. Before I could reply the National Hotel's equivalent of a *maître d'hôtel* appeared at his side and began speaking to him. I could not hear what was said but it made the locomotiveman very angry. He protested vigorously but the *maître d'hôtel* took him by the arm, gently eased him out of his chair and persisted talking and urging him thus until he allowed himself reluctantly to be led away. At the exit, however, he turned about abruptly. Superbly unselfconscious and in a voice which even the orchestra could not muffle, he shouted right across the crowded room at me: 'Give my greetings to all master locomotivemen in England!'

I called the *maître d'hôtel* and asked: 'Why did you do that? I was enjoying his company.'

'It's against the rules,' he answered primly and pointed to a placard at the far end of the table. It stated plainly: 'Reserved: Intourist.'

I had half expected him to say, of course, that the man was not properly dressed and to that extent had done him an injustice. One of the endearing things about the Russians is that they would scorn turning on a man just because he was not well dressed. Their own snobbery on the contrary still runs strongly the other way although it is beginning to change with the young. So clearly my locomotiveman's sin had been only that he had tried to break a rule and Soviet rules I gathered from the *maître d'hôtel*'s tone, were holy laws that knew no common exceptions. It made me begin to wonder why the official rule had to be so inflexible when the people eating and dancing around me looked so predisposed to conformity. It was the beginning of an awareness of a funda-mental paradox that nagged increasingly at my understanding all the time that I was in the Soviet Union.

I was still thinking of it when I drew the curtains in my room late that evening. Across the square the walls of the Kremlin glowed like the coals of a dying fire and the gold bubble domes emerged from their spires and towers bright as burning glass. Somehow the paradox seemed implicit and enshrined in these fantastic shapes. I looked at them again at four in the morning when a protracted noise outside drew me to the window. The square and the streets feeding it as far as I could see were being cleaned by numbers of women in black with black shawls around their heads. They were some of the millions of war widows in Russia and like figures of hooded fate they swept by these splendid walls that knew perhaps more about killing than any others in Russia.

I was up early on a lovely spring morning. Already a long queue was forming on the far side of the square and was my first glimpse of a sight I got to know well. I came and went in and out of Moscow many times and always the queue was there early and late in the day forming up patiently for admission to Lenin's tomb in the Red Square around the Kremlin Corner facing me. The rate of admission was slower than the growth of the queue for at nightfall it was always larger than at morning. Not knowing then what the purpose of the queue was I went outside to have a closer look at it. The hooded war widows had done their work well. The streets were immaculate and absolutely tidy. I did once, by accident, drop a slip of notepaper out of my pocket and let it fall in this very square. Immediately a determined young woman seized me by the arm, halted me and pointing at the paper said sternly: 'Comrade, that is not a cultured thing to do,' and she stood beside me like a policewoman until I had picked it up.

But the obedient queue shuffling along patiently ahead of me certainly was incapable of so elementary a breach of Moscow rule. I had not long joined the tail-end of it when a man in front turned round and asked: 'Tourist?' I said 'Yes' and at once he stepped aside and beckoned me forward. I hung back but he insisted and from there on I was voluntarily passed on quickly from one rank of the queue to the other. Whenever I hesitated people around me combined to urge me on in the friendliest possible manner and to make me feel not like an intruder but an honoured guest. I am certain no official exhortation or command could have brought this about. All sorts of terrible shortages over many years have made queueing for almost everything everywhere in the Soviet Union (except oddly enough on the underground railway), an even more sacred institution than it is in Britain. The Russians would have had no patience at all with anyone who had tried to jump his place in the queue. Yet it appeared a natural point of honour wherever I went for them to yield their places to the foreigner in their midst. By the time I arrived at the head of the queue I was inwardly appalled and humbled by the numbers of old and tired men and women who obviously had had a long and difficult journey behind as well as in front of them and yet had insisted on my taking precedence. In the process too I had a striking glimpse of the astonishing variety of races who made up the Soviet Union. Ninety per cent of the people, I suspect, were visitors to Moscow. I did not know Russian or the Soviet Union well enough to tell Russians, Byelo-Russians, Ukrainians, Lithuanians and Moldavians apart. All I could do was to see them as an inter-related group clearly distinguishable from the others. More than half this group seemed to belong to the same indeterminate types as the rest of us Europeans. With different clothes and haircuts, physically they could have been British, French, or Scandinavian. There were only a few round flattish faces with high cheek bones, skin scarred by frostbite, turned-up noses, pale complexions and pale blue eyes. Almost all the mature women were short and stocky as if raised to fetch and carry burdens up to the limits of their strength. But occasionally I saw young girls taller and slimmer as if better food, sport, automation and increased leisure were beginning to have their effect in producing a more elegant type. The men with their grey-blond faces varied from pale intellectuals with eyes of a deep burning blue to large, broad men with the frames of Japanese wrestlers, suet-pudding faces and smallish deep-set grey eyes. Most of the men were clean shaven though a few still had goatees and all types, as well as the Europeans, had one marked thing in common: a dedicated expression as if their eyes were focused not on the world without but on some invisible dimension within. This look, this state of mind, it seemed rather than any definite physical type, was the mark of the Soviet Slav.

How different, however, the impression of the non-Europeans in the queue! Georgians, Armenians, Uzbeks, Tartars, Turkomans, Azerbaijanians, Mongols and Buryats to name only a few of the minority races the Soviet have forcibly bound in their iron union, stood out distinctively from the Europeans by their build, mould of face, cast of eye and texture. About none of these was there any of the feeling of boundless impersonal nature that the Slavs gave out. An outward-bound temperament, vivid and individual, was near the surface of their spirit, glowing in the eye and imparting if not always *élan* and pride then at least a certain separateness to their personality.

This was all the more remarkable for, apart from the odd *tiubeteika*, the embroidered skull cap of Uzbekistan, everyone was dressed alike in mass-produced clothes. Toneless browns, greys and some black in badly cut suits of cheap materials were the favourite choice of the men. Grey hats a size too large with large brims pulled down on to their ears were their favourite head-gear. Boots and shoes were unpolished and often down at heel. Among the men all these signs of a disregard for their appearance were so general that I suspected it could be in part deliberate, a much deprived nation making a virtue out of necessity. Part of it too could be the result of some article of old-fashioned Soviet faith that made the kind of importance we attach to clothes a *bourgeois* heresy. Perhaps too it was concerned with notions of honour among the aristocracy of workers which the Soviet Union claims to be, a mass orchestration of inverted pride which made an aristocrat like Tolstoy and so many intellectuals of his day prefer a peasant's blouse and cap to a frock-coat and top-hat. The little colour there was came of course from the women's pink, yellow or blue kerchiefs and knitted woollen jumpers. That wild, swift, almost barbaric sense of colour I had first seen in the exiled Russian ballet between the wars, and now again in these Kremlin shapes towering over us, seemed to have vanished or been driven underground. There was not even a single woman's hat to be seen on this first morning, and the overall effect was that of a shapeless, anonymous mass of grey, brown and black, shuffling along steadily beside the Kremlin walls. I grew up among a spartan people who thought far more of what a man was than of what he wore. But I do believe that there is a connexion between people's state of mind and the way they dress. When a patient who has been critically ill begins again to take an interest in his appearance it is a sign of returning well-being, and not only individuals but nations, too, can be ill and convalescent. It is for this reason that, later, I attached much importance to the discovery that this sense of dress is changing rapidly among the young of both sexes.

When at last I turned the corner into the Red Square Lenin's tomb added to the growing sense of paradox in me. At first glance it seemed as complete and arbitrary a break with the past as does the Russian Revolution to those with only a surface knowledge of Russian character. Made mainly of red basalt so deep in colour as to be almost black, it might have been designed by an inferior and fanatical convert to early Cubism. There were no curves nor any angle other than right angles. Its shape was so rigid and uncompromising that it seemed to have by-passed both heart and imagination. It drove a chill through me as it established itself in my senses as a symbol of the will committed without reference to its human context to the execution of one single idea.

I passed through the uprights of the tomb between two young sentries with pale blue eyes, earnest, open faces and the best polished boots I was ever to see in the Soviet Union. I went down the stairs under a yellow artificial light. For the first time I caught a whiff of the smell of a Russian crowd which I was to encounter in all public places, waiting-rooms, planes, buses and trains in the Soviet Union, a sniff of a laundry basket on the weekly collection morning. I turned right into a square inner chamber and there, neon-lit, lay Lenin, Russia's one and only mummy. For a short while there had been two of them, for Stalin, likewise embalmed, was allowed to share a place by Lenin's side before he was extracted and buried in the earth like any ordinary mortal. In that light Lenin looked extraordinarily like a wax model of himself in Madame Tussauds in London. His sandy-coloured beard was trim and pointed and everything about him was neat and orderly. He looked like a typical early twentieth-century *petit-bourgeois*, the image most abhorred by his disciples. That this perishable being – the embalmers already have been called in once and the tomb closed while they dealt with an out-break of decay in the body – should have been enshrined as an imperishable symbol struck me as profoundly significant. The parallel that leapt to my mind was again the Pharaohs of Egypt. With them too, though with far greater imagination and validity, an effort had been made to make mortal flesh and blood immortal. The parallel implied for me something at the heart of the Soviet conception of life that was profoundly recessive. For all its twentieth-century trappings, its applied science, its protestations of being objective and rational, it is basically neither new nor modern but is a reversion to an exceedingly ancient and primitive state of spirit. Officially the State may have abolished God. No one to this day can become a member of the Soviet Communist Party unless he is an avowed and active atheist. Yet for all that other gods have moved in to occupy the vacant spaces left in the Soviet spirit and there before me lay the first god in the records of mythology to wear middle-class mufti. I confess it did not entirely surprise me. I have always believed that the pattern of what we call God is universal and constant in the human spirit. The most dynamic and creative energies in life are accessible only in terms of such a pattern. Men either serve it freely with all dedication of which hearts and minds are capable, or try in vain to reject it, since its energies are indestructible. But if this pattern be prevented from legitimate expression in life it will enter by some back door of the spirit and work its blind will illicitly on men. It seemed to me, standing there on the most hallowed ground of Soviet Russia, that something of this last sort may have happened to the Soviet spirit. I began to suspect that no real understanding of Russian behaviour would be possible unless one saw in it expressions of an archaic, religious and profoundly superstitious system. On the tail of my thought and as I was on my way out, I glanced back. A middle-aged man abreast of the glass case lowered his head and crossed himself. Some moments later a young girl and after her an old lady did likewise. All three were separated from one another by other persons in the queue and therefore presumably unrelated. But three of a kind seemed evidence enough of the complex and contradictory state in the spirit of a nation.

Around me the squares and streets were now full of people making for work with that odd unfocused look on their expressionless yet rustic features. The perpetual fear of not being in time which accelerates the pace of everyone in New York, London and Paris, was missing. It was revealing, too, how everyone pushed and elbowed aside old, young, or ailing without a word of apology and without apparently giving offence. The end, they seemed all to agree, justified the means. Yet how wrong I would have been had I taken this to presuppose a lack of consideration to the needs and feelings of others. I had just joined a small queue at the edge of the gardens under the Kremlin walls to buy a snack from a woman in a white smock in charge of a trolley loaded with ice-cream and caviare sandwiches thinking that this must be the only capital in the world where workmen can start their day with caviare sandwiches when a voice behind me asked: 'English?'

I said 'Yes'.

'Buy then,' he told me in deliberate English: 'the red and not the black caviare. It is of very much better taste and much cheaper.'

Touched by his obvious anxiety to help a stranger I did as he advised and instantly the belief that he had been helpful brought an expression of delight to his rough-hewn features.

Munching caviare before breakfast for the first time in my life I hastened back to my hotel, firmly putting behind me the temptation to look more closely at the Kremlin. I did so because I had no intention just then of staying longer in Moscow than I could help. Capitals, I believe, should be the end and not the beginning of a visitor's schedule. They should be reserved to gather together and sum up all the ravelled ends of one's experience as they do the life of their nations, otherwise they tend to turn all that follows into a kind of protracted anti-climax. So I spent the morning trying to complete my itinerary for a journey to the country with the young lady at Intourist who I discovered had been dealing with my affairs since the beginning.

She was as charming as she was firm in obeying the rules of her establishment. Any request out of her experience or the normal scope of Intourist was politely but inflexibly declined with the one phrase: 'Sorry, no Intourist, there.' Thus Vladivostok was immediately ruled out with a firmness which precluded any further discussion. A request to go by steamer from Baku across the Caspian to Krasnovodsk and from there by rail to Ashkhabad,

Bukhara, Samarkand, Tashkent, Alma Ata and on to Novosibirsk was also rejected. But a journey by air to all those places
(except Novosibirsk and Krasnovodsk) was proposed instead.
Norilsk, the exciting new town built within the Siberian antarctic
circle, a journey by steamer on the Lena River, a visit to the
Jewish autonomous region, and many other of my requests
appeared so uncalled-for that this most patient of young ladies
was at last moved to a typically Russian protest: 'But why are
you so interested in going to all these places for which Intourist
have not facilities when we can offer you more places to go to
than you can possibly visit in a whole year? If you insist, I
cannot help you. You had better ask the Foreign Office.'

For a moment I thought nostalgically of my last visit to Japan
(a country which all the Russians I met regarded as reactionary
and oppressive), and of how easily I had been able to wander all
over it as the impulse took me without restriction or supervision
of any kind. But how explain to people who have never been out
in the fresh air or had a window open, that the room they live in
is stuffy almost to the point of suffocation? I realized how futile
such an exercise would be. So I thought I would take the young
lady's hint, concentrate on what she could offer me and then turn
to other agencies like the Foreign Office for help. The moment we
started working in this more positive way the mood changed for
the better and she promised, during the month I would be away
from Moscow, to try and arrange two of the journeys she had
been inclined to reject at the start: a journey by train to Khabarovsk in the Far East; and a voyage down the Volga. I must add
too that I left her with the feeling that the many refusals were
not due to a desire to hide sinister matters from prying foreign
eyes. Many places are out of bounds because they have not got
proper accommodation for tourists and a natural desire to
present their country to foreigners in the best possible light is
understandable in a new, raw, awakening society like that of the
post-war Soviet Union. Of course suspicion of the outside world
and excessive security accounts for a great deal of inhibition and
the ban on rail journeys to Central Asia and places like Vladivostok is imposed by the Ministry of National Security. But I am
also sure from what I saw that as living accommodation im-
proves in Russia and as new hotels and roads are built, the areas

of absolute restriction will be found to be far smaller than any of us can imagine at present.

My business with Intourist done I went to pay my respects to the British and American Ambassadors. Back in London some of the people who knew Russia well had advised me strongly against this. Diplomacy in the Soviet mind, they had warned me, was merely a euphemism for spying. But much as I valued their experience I rejected their advice. I was convinced that my only chance of discovering what was natural to the Russian people lay in being natural myself and ignoring my friends and my country was not natural to me. So I set out happily for the embassies without misgiving of any kind. But it soon became clear to me that the guide produced by Intourist was not as happy as I was. When I first asked him to take me to the British Embassy I had a suspicion that he did not like the prospect at all. When we arrived at the embassy gates he refused to let the driver take our car through the gates and made him park it outside. Although I asked him to come in with me and wait in comfort inside the embassy he refused to leave the car. I had no option but to leave him there, and on return an hour later to find him still seated rather grimly in the same position in the car. When he asked 'Where to next?' and I answered: 'The American Embassy' his dismay was almost comic. There too, he andt he car stayed outside as before, only this time on my return he looked not only grim but pale and I was not altogether surprised when he came to me after lunch to say his wife and children had all fallen unexpectedly ill and he had to return home immediately. With that he introduced me to a young girl guide and hastened away. Though he was a nice man and one of the most widely travelled Russians I ever met I did not see him again and the episode left me with a sense of unease that I never lost completely all the time I was in Russia.

My plane for Central Asia where I had decided to begin my real journey was due to leave at midnight. My new young guide informed me that I had therefore ample time to go to the ballet, theatre, opera or circus. I chose the circus which I thought might bring me nearer to the ordinary people of Russia: and also I have loved circuses since childhood and had not seen one for many years. I never regretted the choice. I enjoyed myself so much that night at the Moscow Circus and learnt so much from it that wherever I went in the months to come I never missed a circus. In fact a pattern of circus, ballet, opera, theatre, cinema and Park of Rest and Culture imposed itself naturally on my leisure wherever I went. The experience gained in this manner was for me revealing. Through it I seemed to enter at once an extremely old and extremely contemporary world. I found the circuses even more significant than ballet, theatre or opera for the importance of the circus to the ordinary people themselves is evident. First the circus has a permanent home in all the major cities of the Soviet Union and in the blue-prints of the new towns springing up all over the country a circus building too is included. To a person like myself who knew circuses only in their itinerant forms of great bell tents and marquees piled in painted caravans drawn creakingly along country roads and lanes by the placid and wrinkled pachyderms of India and Burma, some of these buildings seemed almost too good to be true. At Rostov-on-Don, for instance, the circus building with its front of soaring Corinthian columns and classical gable all patiently reconstructed after the destruction of the town by Hitler's hordes, has really to be seen to be believed. Inside it has more glittering tiers than a Hollywood wedding cake. Tier upon dazzling tier rise to a vast domed top, and boxes each lined with rich red velvet and finished off in curved cream and gold balconies festooned in plaster of Paris flowers, fruit and figurines *à la troisième empire*, mount above them. The circus itself, the symbolism of tight-rope and flying trapeze, the pantomime of harlequin and clown, the dogs, horses and wild animals finding meaning in submission to the will and spirit of man, were all presented with a lavish abandon, a zest for danger and a reckless disregard of the norms of chance and safety that seemed to come straight out of antiquity. Over and over again I was to feel that I was witnessing the continuation of a tradition that had been founded by gladiators and tempered in the hungry arenas and implacable amphitheatres of Byzantium and Rome. The response of the toil-worn crowds in their shabby clothes added to that impression. Sealed off by their system for some generations from the outside world as was the ancient world by its ignorance, they would look, their faces naked with wonder, at the appearance in the ring of the lions, apes, leopards, hippopotamuses and pythons. So living a bond existed between spectators and performers that the latter seemed spurred to ever more exacting and dangerous demands on their nerve and skill. I saw a beautiful young Armenian girl after taking what seemed to me far more than legitimate liberties with a trapeze, so fired by the response of the crowd, that she went farther still. Her attendants produced an enormous black eagle which might have been the model of the bird one sees in Renaissance pictures feeding on the liver of Prometheus bound to his rock on Elbruz. Dark as one of Macbeth's midnight hags that giant bird was unhooded and placed on the top of two bars of a trapeze without being tied or secured to it in any way. It sat there swaying, balancing itself with its wings outstretched and its eyes green and hard as rhinestones with angry apprehension above a beak sharp as a Saracen's scimitar, staring through the limelight at the tiers of gaping human faces around and above it. Its talons were so long that they seemed to go twice round the bar of the trapeze and were great enough to have carried off many a lamb to its native cliff top in the mountains of Armenia. However this slender young girl seizing the lower bar of the trapeze in one hand then had herself hoisted about a hundred feet above the ring. There she began to swing high and fast from one side of the dome to the other. By this time all lights were out except a solitary spotlight kept directed on the eagle and the girl, see-sawing violently through what now looked like empty and unsupported space. The eagle's wings were stretched wider, trembling like a tuning fork. It looked as if at any moment it might fly off and attack the slight, sequined figure of the girl who was provoking it from below. From time to time in fact the two of them swung up and down so fast that it looked as if the eagle had her in its talons and was carrying her off into the night. But she herself seemed totally impervious to any sense of danger. At the climax she went through a terrifying series of turns and aerobatics on the trapeze until finally she was left hanging by the toes of one foot from the lowest bar, zooming like a swallow through space, her arms stretched out and smiling with a strange ecstatic expression on her young face. Meanwhile the eagle looked down on her, growing ever blacker, angrier and more frenzied as if he were the earthbound one and she had the freedom of gravity and wings. There before our eyes, so high up above the sawdust of the ring with not a net spread out below to break the impact should she fall, it all turned into a strange and moving kind of heraldry.

Then again the acts done with wild animals and horses were as astonishing. Here there was an identification of man and animal and a communication of the one with the other which I think we have lost in the West. With the horses in particular the skill and colour of Tartary and the Golden Horde were added to those of Byzantium and Rome. The horse became merely an extension of the will and spirit of man. There was it seemed nothing man could not do with a horse. In addition to all the wild, acrobatic and daring riding I saw the troops of Kazak, Cossack and Armenian horsemen attack one another on horseback with glittering foils and a savage skill and abandon that seemed only a sabre-edge away from the real thing. I saw them play a mounted lacrosse in the ring, only supreme skill preventing the players from being crushed or kicked to death among the plunging mounts and flying hooves. As for the wild animals, no two acts were ever alike. They always had something extra of imagination and risk to add which one had not seen anywhere else. Even I, who love horses, could not fail to respond. The acts with tigers especially were superb. I have always thought of the tiger as an Indian animal. In Central Asia and the Far East I was to meet him in no less a state of glory as native of the forests and mountain valleys of the Soviet Union. At Alma Ata where I saw the finest assembly of Siberian tigers looking as if they had stepped straight out of Blake's poem to 'burn bright in some forest of the night', I made friends with the man who caught and tamed them. It all began in a curious way. Startled I had woken one night thinking I had heard a lion purring in my room. I had switched on the light and come to the conclusion that out of African homesickness I had dreamt the sound. Coming back to my hotel for lunch the next day, however, I discovered the real explanation. A dense crowd had gathered in front of the hotel and everyone was looking up at a window next to my own on the first floor. From the window an enormous tiger was looking down benignly at the crowd and sitting on its back was a little girl with yellow curls aged no more than two. Beside the tiger stood her attractive young mother and her father, a tall man with deep blue eyes and a sad face. This is perhaps the clearest illustration I can give of the place the Soviet circuses have in the ordinary people's lives and imagination. From the man himself I learnt a great deal about circuses and everything he told me brought home the profound love the ordinary Russian has of the natural things of his native country. He himself had started life as a trainer of dogs. When I asked why he no longer trained them he said 'Because of the war'. Apparently when Hitler's armies seemed invincible, he had been made to train dogs to dash out snapping at the heels of tanks. Then when fully trained he would take them into the battle areas, strap contact mines on their backs and set them at armoured German vehicles.

'It was better than sacrificing our own men of course,' he explained, distressed at the memory, 'but it was treachery to me and ever since I felt I had lost the right to train dogs again.'

All these aspects of the circus represented for me the aboriginal stock, the Roman root, on which its 1963 content was grafted. This contemporary flowering came in a great measure from the clowns. Myself I have never seen clowning so good or so varied. One of the clowns' main functions was to involve the audience in whatever was happening. They had proxies in the audience, posted at strategic points in boxes and ringside seats where they became a target for the sallies of the clowns and the fellow-victims of their foolishness. 'He who gets slapped' did not become a pre-revolution Russian classic by accident. Something of this, of course, is traditional in all circuses, but what made the Russian circuses different was the large scale on which this was practised. It was done, my experience suggested, to produce a feeling of *being together*, for whatever else happens to him in life it is this emotion, I believe, which most Russians prize above all others. Bored with his palaces of culture, denied access to the best ballet, opera and theatre by a subtle system of privilege that the new technological, artistic, and power aristocracy in Russia has created for itself, the ordinary citizen comes to his circus as much to overcome a growing sense of separation as to be entertained, and through the clowns to express his protest against the pricks of an over-exacting system. Often workers from a single factory will buy up all the tickets for a circus performance and pour into it together. The feeling of at last all *being together* which they communicate on these occasions has an extraordinary, almost tangible power. I managed to step into just such an audience once in the great industrial town of Rostov-on-Don where the workers of a leather factory had taken over an entire circus. As the evening went by this feeling became so marked that it almost overwhelmed me and I felt in danger of losing my identity. There were moments when I ceased to feel a foreigner – and for all the friendliness I encountered I felt more of a foreigner in the Soviet Union than in any country I have ever been in, even Japan. In between the acts the workers in their shabby clothes proudly promenaded up and down the marble corridors of the circus building. On all floors in the shining entrance halls with granite floors and Greek pillars as well as in restaurants and cafeterias the factory hands played dance music. Everybody danced with everybody else and I myself saw nothing strange in waltzing round the floor with the unknown young woman who came up and asked me to dance. This sense of Russian 'togetherness' had gone far beyond words and only the dance in its unity of movement in music and body and sexes could express it. It was, I am certain, a significantly Russian evening, woven of the authentic stuff of the national Russian spirit, and it did for the community what I have seen the great tribal dances do for primitive communities in Africa. Something of all this was implicit in my experience at my first circus that night in Moscow and subsequently became so important a reference point that I have felt compelled to deal with it here at the beginning.

Another thing that emerged most clearly at Moscow was the contemporary point of the circus. One clown, for instance, would put a riddle to another.

'What,' he would ask portentously, 'is something which is very sharp and very rare in our country?'

The other without a word went out of the ring and returned holding up a grossly magnified razor blade for all to see!

The audience was helpless with laughter at this point and it took me some time before I learnt that for months it had become practically impossible to get razor blades in the Soviet Union. One provincial town even had sent a deputation to the relevant department in the Kremlin, complaining that unwanted beards were sprouting on old and young alike because safety razor blades were unprocurable. It was nearly three months after this evening at the circus before I myself was able to buy a safety razor blade in Moscow. A long series of Soviet atomic tests were being conducted at the time, new sputniks had just been despatched to outer space, yet the supply of razor blades had been overlooked! There in the circus the pattern of an entire system was held up under a microscope, the immense contradictions in the uneven economy of the country, the brilliant achievement in a few selected fields of development and the vast areas of comparative unconcern and neglect were reflected in the limpid mime of two clowns.

Then again there was the clown who wanted to buy his sweetheart some flowers. He went first of all to the State flower sellers. They had no flowers and they swept haughtily by the disconsolate clown taking care their skirts did not brush against him. He turned to private enterprise who had flowers but demanded an exorbitant price that he could not afford. He rejected them – only to find his girl would not have him without flowers. So he was forced to buy from private enterprise and the last view we had of him was walking out of the ring, arm round his sweetheart but without trousers – they had been part of the desperate bargain.

There was an even more telling example of the dilemma of the modern Soviet citizen. Some days later I read in a newspaper that a black market in the flowers of the mimosa had just been liquidated. A group of people on the warm Black Sea coast had taken to flying mimosa buds to the capital and other cities still in the grip of winter and they had made a fortune – until caught by the police.

'What will happen to them now?' I asked a Russian acquaintance.

'Oh, I expect the principals will be shot,' he told me calmly. 'Profiteering out of the needs of one's fellow men is a crime in the Soviet Union.' But, I added to myself, failure to meet them apparently is not.

Then in the circus there were all sorts of skits against bureaucracy. This was not surprising because the campaign against the bureaucrat and red tape has the official sanction of the Party and is all the rage in the Soviet Union. By sanctioning this campaign the rulers of Soviet Russia have tried to divest themselves of any responsibility for the bureaucratic defects of their system. Newspapers, comedians, clowns, private citizens can all rail as much as they like against bureaucracy provided they do not blame the Party or its leaders for it. The result is that in the fast growing volume of satire one encounters villains who are almost always anonymous unless they happen to be little men. One cannot imagine any Russian satirist, for instance, doing to Mr Khrushchev what the perpetrators of 'Beyond the Fringe' did so profitably and successfully to the Prime Minister of Britain to everybody's, including Mr Macmillan's, amusement. In the Moscow circus, therefore, the bureaucrat is just a pompous, cigar-smoking, over-nourished, hard-drinking man at a desk, a facsimile of the classic Soviet caricature of the capitalist. A timid citizen comes to apply for a post and is kept hanging about for no reason except that the bureaucrat wants to have several more swigs in secret at his bottle of vodka. When he condescends to see the common little man at last he fires questions at him like bullets from a machine-gun. Has he got his card of identification, photograph of himself, his wife, his children, parents and parents-in-law, all their marriage and birth certificates, references from previous places of employment, legal certificates of discharge, school certificates, certificate of national service and so on and on? At each request the little man slapped the relevant document on the desk while the bureaucrat got obviously more and more perturbed that he might in the end have no excuse for turning down the applicant. The final despairing question was: 'Have you got your mother-in-law's finger-prints?' When these too were triumphantly produced the bureaucrat pulled out a pistol from the desk and shot himself. So much did this simple pantomime reflect the private world of all that the audience long roared its delight.

All the while a man in a well-cut grey suit at my side had kindly explained to me the meaning of the clowning wherever he felt the point would be obscure for a foreigner. In the interval, he introduced me to his wife and daughter who was studying English at the University and he was altogether so kind that I asked them all to come back to my hotel with me for some refreshment. He looked as if he wanted to accept but then became embarrassed and declined politely. Unwisely perhaps I pressed him, pointing out how early it was still – circuses, ballet, theatre and concerts all begin at 6.30 in the evening. That made the whole family uncomfortable and the girl felt compelled in the end to explain, obviously disliking herself for what she was about to say. 'We would like to come but it would not be clever,' she said in a low voice, her face red. Realizing she had meant 'wise' and not 'clever', I walked back to my hotel, rather ashamed of having pushed her into such a predicament.

Early as it was, the streets were nearly empty. The windows of the buildings on the way already dark. People in Russia, even in the capital, go early to bed. There are no night-clubs, no prostitutes walking the streets and almost no policemen or 'militiamen' as the Russians called them. I saw instead of police a patrol of young people of both sexes with red bands round their arms who everywhere volunteer for the duty of keeping public order. They went by looking bored and unemployed. I was not surprised for no capital could have looked more law-abiding than Moscow did just then, as if it were inhabited not by men and women of the world but by the villagers that I suspect most Russians still are in their secret hearts.

CHAPTER THREE

CONVERSATION IN AN AEROPLANE

IT WAS another story at Vnukovo Airport. Unlike the international airport where I had arrived it was as active even at midnight as Etna in full eruption. The noise of planes arriving and taking off was incessant. The brilliantly lit departure halls, restaurants and side-bars were crowded with people. On benches, against the walls, and in the corners sprawled weary travellers. Many of them were elderly women in black, thick woollen scarves and knitted shawls around their shoulders. They lay propped against their bundles waiting with silent uncomplaining patience for a seat to turn up in the crowded planes. During all the time I was in the Soviet Union I only once travelled in a plane with a seat to spare and over and over again had to make my peace with the sight of scores of tired, shabby-looking people being turned back at the barriers for another long wait in the same noisy departure hall which I was impelled to the front by officials so that I could have first choice of the unoccupied places in the aircraft. There was something frightening too about this silent acceptance of their fate implicit in the expression and attitudes of these waiting figures. I longed for them to be irritable and bad tempered about what was happening to them. Some expression of disapproval I believed might have been healthier in the long run however convenient acceptance was in the short. I felt they should push, shove, importune, badger, the bland officialdom which condemned them to such unknowing waiting and inadequacies instead of just doing it vicariously through clowns in circuses. In that moment I became aware of another characteristic of the Russian people which had been nagging at my mind for recognition ever since my arrival and which subsequent experience confirmed. They have an overwhelming instinct to conform, a tendency to be incapable of doing openly what others are not doing and of challenging authority or the general decree on a specific issue. The comparison that came to me unbidden was with the primitive black crowds I had seen over many years waiting in just that fashion with just that look on railway stations and public offices in Africa. It was to recur to me again and again until finally I grasped its significance.

I myself did my waiting in comfort in a quiet room apart. It was astounding the difference a first-class ticket made in conditions of travelling. The privileges that money and power could buy seemed at first sight no less great than in our own world. But once in the large jet aircraft bound for Tashkent, all differences between one passenger, one class and another seemed to vanish. The competent young air-hostesses seated whoever had succeeded in boarding the aircraft first with admirable impartiality – first-class tourists excepted. One young Army Major who appeared towards the end thought the seat allocated to him not good enough. He stood arguing with a very young hostess in the centre of the gangway. She reasoned with him patiently and courteously for several minutes. He responded likewise but with unabated determination to have his way. I expected one or both of them at any moment to lose their temper and raise their even tones. Yet neither of them seemed even tempted into anger and that to me was not the least remarkable thing about the incident. The whole aircraft meanwhile had gone silent as it watched this protracted tussle of wills. The odds I would have thought, from what I had heard of the prestige of the army, were against the girl. She, however, seemed to draw on some secret source of strength. I suspected it was the mystique of public rule which I mentioned earlier on. As if airport regulations clothed her in shining armour she stood her ground until, convinced that the Major was impervious to reason she asked with the utmost composure and apparent irrelevance: 'How old are you, comrade Major?'

The Major fell like an inexperienced babe in the trap. 'Thirty-five,' he answered.

'Then why,' she asked quietly, 'do you behave as if you were just fifteen?'

At that the Major bowed his head in defeat and went to his proffered seat without even an overt sign of temper or resentment. Or was it altogether so creditable? Normally the question would not have occurred to me but I had seen so much phlegm and lack of emotion in behaviour in so short a time that I began to wonder if so even a temperament could be altogether true, or if true then might it not be too true to be good for the people concerned?

At my table in the aircraft was another soldier, an Armenian Colonel in the Soviet Army. There were also two Russians in civilian clothes with us. The Colonel was a soft-spoken, gentle little man with large melancholy black eyes. The melancholy was oddly impersonal too as if it came straight from the experience of his people who have been persecuted longer and more brutally by all sorts of conquerors than perhaps any other race in the world. All the Armenians I was to meet wore on their faces the sadness of history which strangles individual laughter at birth and leaves predominant in the personality only the dour determination which had enabled Armenians to endure against great odds of life and time. This Colonel was the first to speak to me. One of the Russians had just asked the hostess for a vodka and had been refused. The Colonel spoke up then to explain to me that no alcoholic drinks of any kind were allowed on the internal services of the Soviet Union and to ask if it were the same in my country? I said it certainly was not so either in Britain, Western Europe, or America. At that he changed the subject and asked if there were Armenians in Britain? I said 'Yes'.

One of the Russians immediately joined in to remark laughingly: 'Then I bet you they are all rich by now!'

The Colonel dismissed that with a sad little smile and wanted to know if I had heard of an Armenian who had become a famous actor in Britain some fifty years ago. I had not and tried to console him by telling him of the only notable Armenians of whom I knew, Saroyan, Michael Arlen, the Gulbenkian family and so on. It seemed to please him to know that somewhere in the world there were places wherein Armenians could make good. Then inevitably he talked about the threat of war. Why were the Americans such warmongers? I told him he was wrong: I knew the United States well and there was no more idealistic or peaceloving nation on earth. Then why, he persisted with Armenian obduracy, were they arming themselves, why the Nato bases, why nuclear bombs if they did not mean to attack the Soviet Union? Simply, I said, because like the rest of us they are not certain that the Soviet Union would not try to impose its policies by force on them and their allies. 'They really believe that?'

he exclaimed in amazement – repeated what I had said to the other Russians and all three began laughing at so preposterous a proposition.

But was it so preposterous, I asked, after what the Soviet had done since the war to East Germany, Poland, Czechoslovakia, Hungary, Baltic Republics, Roumania and Bulgaria, and had even tried to do in Korea?

But what had the Soviet done in these countries, the Colonel exclaimed with gentle astonishment, but to go in at the wish of the peoples concerned to protect them against Neo-Fascists and the new economic imperialism. And if the Americans really were such idealists why in their recent nuclear tests in the Pacific had they waited always until the winds were set to carry the radio-active fall-out over the hungry and defenceless millions of south-east Asia and southern China?

The bias of the statement made me angry, so I told him to his face: 'That you know, is not true.'

'But it has been stated so publicly in our newspapers!' he remonstrated.

'Your newspapers are lying,' I told him.

'How can you possibly know that?' he asked, taken aback by my uncompromising tone.

'This is how I know it,' I told him. 'I was in Canada when you started your nuclear tests again in the Arctic on a greater scale than any others before. The radio-active fall-out was carried by the winds over the North American continent and many people and newspapers then said that you had deliberately waited for the winds to do just that.'

'But that,' he said incredulously, 'was a lie!'

'How do you know it was a lie?' I asked.

'Because we would never do a thing like that.'

'Well,' I told him, 'just as you know it was a lie as far as you are concerned, so I know it is a lie about the Americans.'

I would not have been surprised if our brisk exchange of words had not turned him and the two Russians at our table somewhat against me. But on the contrary they seemed to have warmed to me for my plain speaking and the one who had asked for vodka turned to me saying rather apologetically: 'All the same I do not like Americans.'

Before I could answer his companion asked sharply: 'Do you know any?'

'No,' he answered, 'but I do not like what I read about them.'

'Well, you have no right to speak like that. You are very wrong,' the other Russian told him reprovingly: 'I have met a lot of them. They are very nice people and, what is more, they are *very like* us.'

'Oh, I know the people are all right,' the other one answered, 'it is really only their arms monopolists and their military that I do not like. They are the menace. But of course the ordinary people are good people like ordinary people everywhere.' He turned to me anxious to conciliate: 'You know, we say that the Americans produce everything in their country except birds' milk!'

They all three laughed at the saying, and it was all to me a revelation of the strange love-hate emotion that the Russians have about America. They admire and imitate it more than any other country in the world. At the same time they hate it and despise themselves for feeling compelled to admire and copy it.

Did I, they all three asked finally, think there would be a war?

No, I said, not if we tried to think about ourselves and life in a new way. I had been distressed by our conversation because of the assumption in their minds that all the danger to peace was the fault of a villain called America. That was the old discredited way of thinking which had produced wars in the past and inevitably induced people in Britain and America too into thinking all their troubles were the work of another monster called the Soviet Union. The new way of thinking which could prevent war would be if we were to become increasingly conscious of our own shortcomings rather than those of our neighbours. Could they too think of their own society like that? If so, the tensions between us would become less dangerous. I myself thought the greatest problem of our time was to find a means of resisting evil without ourselves becoming evil in the process. I quoted them one of my favourite proverbs 'that all men tend to become the thing they oppose'. As a result all over the world today we saw forms of social, national and international tyrannies being abolished merely to set new and other tyrannies in their places.

This seemed to strike a deep response in the Russian who had spoken up for the Americans for he remarked as much to himself as to me: 'I believe we have just escaped that kind of tyranny in the Soviet Union.' And I knew he was thinking of Russia under Stalin.

'What is wrong with co-existence then ?' asked the other Russian.

Nothing, if sincere, I answered. But something else too was necessary: the ordinary people of the world, who we all four had agreed only wanted peace, had a great responsibility. It was the ordinary people who had to prevent our leaders from going wrong by insisting that for no matter what reason, they never imposed their will by aggression on other countries. I was certain we could do this in Western Europe and America. Could they do the same in the Soviet Union?

The Colonel spoke for them all. Evading my question he mentioned again the European arms monopolies and economic aggression by imperialists which he seemed to find worse and less honest than military aggression, and having spoken his set piece the lateness of the hour overcame him and he fell asleep. The other Russian who had wanted vodka did the same. They both sank easily into their sleep with apparently no dividing line between waking and sleeping and one of my clearest impressions of the Russian people is their capacity for sleeping at all sorts of hours and in the oddest of places. It was as if centuries of experience of long severe winters had equipped them with a private system of hibernation. They also had something else that went with it. They could do without sleep and break out into long sustained bursts of activity and feats of endurance in a measure I have not seen in any other people except the primitive black people of Africa.

I, however, could not sleep. It seemed to be extraordinary to be plunged so soon into this kind of discussion before I knew even the physical layout of the land. I wondered if this was exceptional. However, I was to find that everywhere peace and the fear of war were an obsession in Russians of all walks of life. I had this kind of conversation many times with peasants, workers and artists alike, and always it ended for me in the question which the Armenian colonel had evaded: could the peoples of the Soviet Union impose the same disciplines on their leaders which we could? From the little I had seen of the people I was **not** encouraged to believe it could. It seemed to me that they were a great conforming people: that the deeper part of their history which had become the national state of mind as well as their present system made it impossible in the short term to impose their will on their leaders. One of the most depressing aspects of Russian history is the total absence of the peaceful processes of evolution. Instead of an orderly routine of change one encounters repeatedly violence, assassination, massacre and terror. Instead of an individual challenge of authority there are inducements to mob action and rioting, so that the doctrine of the inevitability of revolution as the only instrument of historical change which is propounded by Marxist-Leninists seems to be more a subjective effort at Russian self-justification than the objective assessment of history that it claims to be. But, I wondered, could not this all be changing now? Such a possibility would make every day gained in the avoidance of war of incalculable value. And was not the response of the one Russian to my remarks about evil and tyranny a symptom of a groping towards such a change?

I looked up and found that he alone of our companions was awake and watching me, as if wanting to talk. I had been looking out of my window down at the earth and had noticed how often the lights of great cities appeared strung around some dark patch of land like necklaces of Arabian jewels. It was amazing even in the dark how the sheer size of the country got through to one. So I told this to the Russian. He warmed to my remark at once and began talking to me about the land of the Soviet Union. He talked unusually well. Russians, I found, were at their best when travelling. Physically and mentally they are people still on a journey and so journeys release them from complex reserves and fears of all kinds and set them talking naturally and openly. He was no exception and moreover he knew the Soviet Union well. He was, I discovered, a distinguished and widely travelled person. I wish I could say who he was and what he did but I am afraid to do so for his sake. He loved his country deeply and was an ardent protagonist of its way of life. Yet to quote him in person still does not seem to me safe for I came away from the Soviet Union feeling strongly that all sorts of opinions which looked innocent enough to me might get the people who hold them into serious trouble. What is permissible in opinion appeared to be a matter of Soviet metaphysics that I could never hope to understand. Moreover it was a system of metaphysics built not on principles of rock but on shifting sands. What was permissible today could easily be lethal tomorrow; the orthodoxy of today the heresy of tomorrow. This started as a feeling but it became so strong that after nearly three months I was convinced I must not write of anyone I met in an identifiable fashion. Perhaps I have exaggerated my fears but because of this the people I met will remain anonymous.

This Russian now told me that it was right to begin with a feeling of the immensity of the land. I must build on that as perhaps the greatest single fact necessary for understanding his people and his native country. But he feared that it would take time before a stranger could realize how immense the land was. He wished he could convey all that immensity to me not just as a physical fact but also as the emotion that was in him and all his countrymen. To begin with, did I realize that the Soviet Union was more than two and a half times greater than the continental United States? That it was only a third smaller than Africa, three times the size of Australia and bigger than South America. In the West its territory began at the Polish Frontier near Kaliningrad in a long yellow spit of sand running out from the Southern Baltic shore into a shallow grey sea and stretched in one unbroken mass eastwards for more than 6,000 miles to Cape Dezhnev on the Chukhotsky Peninsula. Indeed that was not the end yet for one would have to go out into the Bering Strait to Ratmanov Island to find there on the frontiers of America's newest State the easternmost extremity of Soviet territory.

'I have spoken there,' he said his pale grey eyes twinkling, 'with Soviet and American Eskimoes and could not tell the difference between them. Nor could they!'

So wide apart are the two extremities of land that it is day in one when it is still night in the other. He himself had once flown in a fast jet aircraft from Baikal to Moscow, made four landings on the way and each time as they landed the sun had set and each time they took to the air the sun had risen again. The southernmost point of the Soviet Union was near Kushka on the borders of Afghanistan, only about 800 miles from the Tropics. The northernmost point was well inside the Arctic Circle at Cape

Chelyuskin in Siberia, a bare 800 miles from the Pole. These two ends were more than three thousand miles apart and though the actual time differences now were not so great as between west and east, the seasonal ones were greater. In an hour or two for instance we would be flying over south Turkmenia where spring comes in January. There the winter was short and could hardly be called winter at all. But in the north at Cape Chelyuskin even in midsummer the winds still piled up giant hummocks of ice on the shore. Already in Turkmenia, ploughing and sowing would be done and the spring nearly over, but in Uzbekistan where we would land in a few hours we would find the earth aglow with purple heliotrope, scarlet poppies and wild red tulips. Yet the appletrees around Moscow would not blossom until late in May and in the far north of Siberia the tundra rivers would not be free of ice until the end of June. There by August the ice and frost would start their march to the south. In the extreme south the bamboo shot up at the rate of a yard a day. On the northern Siberian shore it took the straggling larches a century to grow the thickness of a man's middle finger. In the south they would already be harvesting the grain while in Kamchatka the snow was still falling. That, measured in the seasons was the physical frame of the Soviet Union. But inside this had to be fitted the massive and endless diversity of detail. To start with there were the rivers. He started with them, he said, because he believed the history of Russians as a conscious and separate people, began with the rivers. It was the rivers that first gave them, to use a French expression, a *raison d'être*, a meaning in the emerging world and a way of communicating with one another, the civilizations and the commerce of antiquity. And surely no land on earth was ever blessed with such rivers! Even to this day the length of navigable rivers in the Soviet Union exceeded the mileage of their extensive railway system. Their great rivers flowed north, west, east and south. Some of the greatest never even reached the sea so vast was the land, and like the Volga flowed 2,300 miles from its source in the middle of the Great Russian plain, and finished in the land-locked Caspian in the far south; or else like the Amu-Darya and Syr-Darya, two of the greatest rivers of Central Asia, just fed the enclosed Aral Sea. Above all I must not forget the Siberian rivers, which were perhaps the greatest such as the Yenesei which

was over 2,700 miles long. The rivers of European Russia, he
would say, flowed out of history into the present. The rivers of
Siberia and the Far East flowed out of the present into the future
of his land. Then there were the seas, inner and outer. Did I
realize that the Soviet Union was a great sea power; that its coastline was twice the length of its land frontiers? Three of the world's
four oceans lapped Soviet earth in twelve seas, each one different.
Thus the Black Sea did not freeze in winter but the Kara Sea was
dotted with ice-floes even in summer. In the Baltic the difference
between high and low tide is only a few inches, but in the Penz-
hina inlet of the sea of Okhotsk it is thirty-four feet. As for the
lakes they varied from the world's largest, the Caspian, to the
deepest, Lake Baikal, which Chekov had described as unique.
There were great mountain ranges from the Pamirs rising fiercely
to their crowning summit in the 24,390-foot Mount Stalin* to the
ancient and gentle Urals whose highest point, Narodnaya attains
a mere 5,800 ft. There were valleys where life had to breathe deep
and fast to survive at an average level of over three miles above
the sea. And there was the decline of all this tossed and tormented
earth into the great plains to the west, east and north of the
Ukraine for thousands of miles, plains where he had sat on his
horse amid grass so high that the yellow tassels brushed his lips
and which, when they were autumn-bare, were just filled with
sky and space. He spoke of these plains with a warmth that not
even the rivers had been able to raise in him. Clearly the core of
his spirit like that of his people too was a wide, wide plain.

Then east of the plains, he continued, came the plateaux and
hills of Siberia, and then the earth became inflamed again until in
Kamchatka it erupted in the world's highest volcano, that spitfire
called Klyuchevskaya Sopka. But oh! the distances, he stressed,
the worlds between its fires and the cold Pamirs where the largest
glacier in the world, the Fedchenko, inched its way through time
into the abysmal valleys below. In one world there were ever-
green palms, the lotus flower of Egypt, roses, hump-backed oxen,
camels and pink flamingoes, while in the other were dwarf-
birches, violets amid snowdrifts, wolves and Titian hair and the

* Soviet geographers divide the sea into four oceans, not five or three as
we do, and Mount Stalin inevitably has been renamed and is now the Peak
of Communism.

arctic owl. Then again north of the plains, the desert and the fertile steppes were the forests, the greatest forest area on earth, so dense that on a dull day at noon he had had to use a lamp to find his way through them. In the south hard against the mountains lay the extreme desert of sand burnt bare by the sun: in the north lay the tundra stripped naked by frost and long winds and white with the dust blown from the brittle ice which lies on the permanently frozen earth. Two kinds of a desert, in fact each with its own challenge to the people of his land. There were too the great strange, forbidding islands. In the north, Franz Josef Land, Novaya Zemlya, the New Siberian islands and Wrangel Island, were all of frozen inhospitable earth with black cliffs and white bergs, and hardly a tree. But now through permanent occupation and scientific research they were found to have remarkable mineral uses. His people, he said, possessed a greater capacity for meeting the challenges of winter, solitude and physical hardship, than any other people. For instance he knew a man who had lived for more than a generation in a cave in the Bear Islands and done research of the greatest value. What is more he had grown into one of the wisest and gayest of men. To hear him talk of his long winters alone in his cave was to listen to a Buddhist speaking on the ecstasies of silence and contemplation, above all to hear him speak of spring was to experience the process of life as it must have been at the first beginnings. This man's first intimation of spring came from a large white bird and when his calendar told him the time was near he would look out daily for this bird. Then came the moment of magic when he first saw it! All around him was night but suddenly, so high in the sky that it caught the rays of the sun below the horizon, there was this bird of flame to announce the spring ... the original fire-bird! From these islands which, thanks to their new ice-breakers, they could keep open for three months a year, one could go down through the Bering Strait to the other islands, Ratmanova, the Commander Islands, the Kurillics and Sakhalin. Here thanks to a warm pacific current and the volcanic earth, life was somewhat easier and more abundant. In the Kurillics and Kamchatka alone there were more than 200 volcanoes of which at least sixty were active. The bird and sea life there was incredible. White whales rolled, huffed and puffed in the waves there, blowing fountains of pearl into the air. He had even seen islands so packed with birds, seals and walruses that one could not walk on them. From a distance their silhouette looked like some strange design of Bavarian baroque carved in amber. All this far-flung and diverse land had its singular human contact of just on 220 million people of 185 different racial groups. Nearly 160 million of these were Ukrainians and greater Russians, 8 million Byelo or White Russians, 6 million Uzbeks, 5 million Tartars, 4 million Khazaks, 3 million Azerbaijanians, 3 million Armenians, 3 million Georgians, $2\frac{1}{2}$ million Jews, $2\frac{1}{2}$ million Lithuanians, $2\frac{1}{4}$ million Moldavians, nearly 2 million Volga Germans, 1 million Turkoman, 1 million Kirghiz, $1\frac{1}{2}$ million Chuwash, and innumerable smaller minorities like the Bashkir, the Buryats of Siberia, the Yakuts, the Golds and Chukchi hunters of the Far East, the Nentsi of the Tundra down to even two villages of Russian Negroes in the Caucusus. These groups were organized into a hundred separate nationalities and concentrated into the fifteen republics that constituted the Soviet Union of today!

There then, he drew breath, were some of the relevant facts but how convey the emotion? He would have to be a poet, painter, dancer and musician in order to do so. He would only suggest I should listen to Russian music with an alert ear for he believed that one characteristic which distinguished it from the music of other countries was that it had within it just such an immensity of scale. Russian music had a permanent background, as in Rembrandt's paintings, of great space and vast silences. It expressed the immensities; the song of the first bird at dawn, the vast stillness of the night, the howl of a pack of wolves on the rim of the great Siberian plains, and their emptiness and isolation, the sound of a hunter's horn in the vast woods and forests of Russia, the wings of the wild swans beating the air over a Siberian river with the ice beginning to form along the edge, the wind stirring before the rain in the horse-high grass on the Steppes, the voice of boatman calling to boatman, the unending quest – but always it was sound coming from afar and going farther still. Today there were other sounds and new rhythms to be added; the hum of hydro-electric turbines, factory sirens and the exhausts of tractors break silences of woods and plains. But the bigness of the land was still underneath and dominant over all. In between one note and another the same great silence and space claimed them all. It might be melancholy, but it was a noble sadness. The same was true of Russian painting. Apart from the saints in their jewelled and discredited ikons it was only the landscape that really inflamed their painters' vision. This was true also of poetry. The land was its deepest source of inspiration. He recited Voloshin in fast, impeccable French and left me time only to note:

> '*Mais toi, tu ne rêvais depuis ta tendre enfance*
> *Que de vastes fôrets, d'hermitages rustiques*
> *Que de Courses sans but, sans route en gré des Steppes.*'

He quoted in not so good English from Lermontov's *My Country*:*

> 'Ask me not why but love I must
> Her field's cold silences,
> Her sombre forests swaying in a gust
> Her rivers at the flood like seas.'

So on right down to the young for whom the contemporary Yevtushenko spoke when he wrote of the exiles in Siberia:†

> 'They crumbled its soil in their fingers,
> Questioned, understood, possessed,
> Felt it as earth and tied by blood to them,
> Drank its water and let their children drink.'

And what of the novels? I asked.

The typical Russian novel too was long like a Siberian river finding its way to the sea, he replied. Surely the novelists of no other country had tales so long and winding to tell? Of course he knew the exceptions but the Russian genius more than any other flourished most when it was free to move on and expand in its native land. That, for instance, he would say, was one marked difference between the French and the Russian spirit. The Russian spirit thrived on expansion; the French tended to live by contraction. The French were to the point and epigrammatic. But the Russians were always in difficulties with the immensity of what they felt compelled to express. Always, whatever the medium, above and beyond it was the greatness of their native earth, their

* From Babette Deutsch's translation.
† From the translation by R. Milner-Gulland and P. Levi, Penguin, 1962.

great mother. It gave them all their '*shiroky*', their 'wide-open spacious' nature, the quality they loved above all in human beings. Scratch a Russian in office, factory or school, and you would find at heart a wanderer and a kind of sailor. Yes, that was it! They were all land-sailors filled to the brim with the ocean reality of their country as any old salt with that of the sea. Look at their history too. The dominant factor there was the greatness of their land. Invaded as no other country, perhaps, in the history of the world, with no initial barrier of sea or mountain to protect them they survived because the bigness of the land defeated the invaders. As the great Pushkin had said: 'Russia had the loftiest of destinies. Her boundaries drained the strength of all her invaders.' My friend added: 'Not only from external invaders, but from all the tyrants, and despots who oppressed and made slaves of the people and invaded them from within.' Always, he went on, there was room for escape, even against their own native oppressors, places like the great forests of the north, the marshes and marches of the Don, and increasingly Siberia, which ironically was both a region of exile and a home of freedom and independence for the Russian spirit. That was what gave Russian history its unique quality. The history of other countries might be told in terms of Headmen and Chiefs, Kings and Queens, States and Parliaments. Indeed that old-fashioned way of telling history has been attempted in Russia too. But basically it was the history of a people committed to an act of supreme faith in the land and its greatness. Not rulers or administrators but the prolific, lower strata of ordinary common people and the land determined their history. However unchronicled and unrecorded the people, thanks to this supreme act of faith with their native earth, they not only maintained their identity but over and over again swallowed their conquerors. They settled and tilled their earth and when denied that right in one place moved on to another, in the process doing something greater than conquering the earth. This is the history that counted in Russia and would count tomorrow. All other history, however dramatic and spectacular, was ephemeral and irrelevant.

But surely, I asked, there must have been some good in their rulers? However, he dismissed them all with scorn: Catherine the Great was just 'a German whore'; and Alexander who defeated

Napoleon 'a *poseur*' of the worst kind. Did I realize Alexander would spend as much as two hours in front of a mirror dressing himself and practising his gestures before an Imperial reception? How could such a flunkey be called a man? Ivan the Terrible did some slight good in pushing back the Tartars and bringing about greater unity among the people, but he was superstitious and mad. Peter the Great was the only real man among them and he was a man of the people.

Did the young people, I asked, feel about their history as he did? Even more so, he replied. They believed that the people and the land made Russia what it was, and would make it too in the future, whatever the appearances to the contrary might be.

At this point one of the notices was flashing a warning that we were about to land. So I said good-bye to my friend at Tashkent. He thanked me for the chance I had given him of talking so intimately, so '*po dusham*' ('soul to soul') with a foreigner, a way of speaking I was to find that was most important to Russians. I said that I had to thank him for he had done all the work, and I had merely listened '*dusha-dushe*'. He laughed at that, shook my hand again, bowed slightly with his hand on his heart and left. I thought that was the last I would see of him, as I was leaving within the hour for Alma Ata, but I was wrong.

CHAPTER FOUR

TASHKENT

I BEGAN then my meeting with this land of which he had spoken so eloquently high-up in the air between Tashkent and Alma Ata. My brief acquaintance with the flat, formless northern approaches at sundown (already an age away in mind though only a day or two in time), seemed hardly worth the reckoning compared with the vision the dawn brought up to my window. Away to the south-east the sky was without cloud or haze and flamingo-pink with cold. The earth was still in the dark but the mountains of Kirghizia and Tadzhikistan were already visible, royal with height and solemn with snow, flying the colours of the dawn like battle flags from their crests. No matter where I looked there were other ranges behind them breaking in wave upon wave out of the sea of darkness like the white horses of a great storm pounding towards the shore. So impressive were they that it was difficult to realize that they were still only foothills in the greatest complex of mountains in the world, which from Karakoram and Pamir to Tien' Shan and Muztagh Ata, are part of the same storm, the same terrible vortex in the heart of the earth which reaches its climax in the Himalayas. Here some hundred years ago in the search for natural barriers against invasion the Russian Empire had come to stand fast until today Russia looks down on the ancient peoples of Asia from the battlements of a great classical citadel. For an hour or more, flying at six hundred knots, the mountains not only kept pace with us but produced more of their kind. To the west and north-west, however, as the sun found the earth, the land fell away quickly into low hills and far away produced a shimmer and a blur which belonged to the dry, flat plain, which there began its two-pronged drive westward towards Europe and north-eastward into Siberia and so for more than 2,000 miles swept on towards the Arctic Ocean without a hillock to impede it. This contrast, this opposition between two irreconcilable principles of earth, reached its most dramatic expression at Alma Ata, for there in front of us the Tien'Shans or 'Mountains of Heaven' rose sheerly out of the low land of Khazakstan like a wall with watch towers of 15,000 and 17,000 feet high under permanent snow. Behind us lay the diminishing valleys and the edge of the great brown plains where long patches of earth were under the plough and the Soviet virgin lands began. This immense theatrical backdrop of mountains on the orderly agricultural scene remains most vividly in my mind.

'The mountains are more than twenty miles away but don't they feel near?' remarked the young Russian who met me at the airport of Alma Ata. He was from the city of Gorkiy and new in Central Asia.

'Don't you like the mountains?' I asked.

He hesitated, decided to be frank and said: 'It's not that. Only I don't like being hemmed in. There's no prostor there.' I asked what he meant by 'prostor'. He indicated at length that it meant all sorts of feelings that came from having unlimited space around one.

Between the airport and the city the road was dense with traffic, most of it heavy trucks. I counted seventy trucks before I saw one private car.

'Why is the road so crowded?' I asked seeing no destination for the traffic except the silent mountains.

'This is the main road to China. The Frontier's only about 150 miles away.' He seemed surprised that I had not known but I had not thought of Central Asia as having outward-bound main roads. Yet not only China I was to find, but Mongolia, Afghanistan, Iran and Turkey are well served by similar roads. The ancient silk-route and its tributaries today are highly mechanized.

For all its nearness to China and its location in the heart of Central Asia, the city of Alma Ata itself in appearance was essentially Russian. Starting life as the garrison town of Vierney its population as recently as 1933 was just over 50,000, almost all of it Russian. Khazaks and Kirghiz, nomad herdsmen and horsemen, moved with their flocks according to the seasons living in their felt tents and their *yurtas* and scorning the towns much as they had done in the days of Genghis Khan. But the wife of a distinguished Russian writer who was born in Alma Ata told me she could remember neither Khazak nor Kirghiz living in the town in her childhood. Stalin's planners and economists had taken it in hand. Today it is a city of half a million people, with two-thirds of them still Russian. This kind of expansion meant that inevitably on the outskirts there were those stiff regimental apartment blocks that I had seen in East Berlin and the outskirts of Moscow and was now to see in every town and city from Central Asia to the suburbs of Leningrad and from the Baltic Sea to the Pacific Ocean. So when I was told it was impossible to be shown a new apartment here the girl who guided me consoled me with the remark: 'You'll have plenty of time to see new apartments in other cities later on.'

'But they will not be the same,' I protested.

'Don't worry,' she urged me gravely, 'they are all the same wherever you go in the Soviet Union.'

Taken aback, I exclaimed: 'But don't you find it depressing to have the same apartments for everyone everywhere?'

She bristled at that and reproved me: 'Why should I want anything any different from any of my fellow citizens? What is good for one is good for all. We are all equal in the Soviet Union.'

It was my first elementary lesson, delivered there against that back-drop of mountains not two of which were alike. What we accept and value as expressions of individual taste can easily be suspect in the Soviet Union as forms of dangerous self-indulgence, *bourgeois* deviationism and lack of solidarity. It was to be a perpetual source of astonishment to me on this journey how refreshed and comforted one was when one perceived any variation in the uniform Soviet pattern. The stunning effect of such uniformity has to be experienced to be believed and I myself could well understand the reaction of a young Swedish architect who broke short his travels after only ten days in the Soviet Union because he could endure 'the horror of such uniformity' no longer.

But in the older part of the city the garrison pattern remains with much to soothe and divert the eye. The streets are broad, meet at right angles with military correctness and are lined with elms and poplars. What is more, everywhere there are gardens and orchards. Apple, cherry and apricot trees already were swollen with sap and about to bud, and water tumbled in busy irrigation furrows and in the stone-covered *arkys*. In the centre of the city were the public buildings, brash and new, all built on the Soviet office-of-works idea of classical design, Greek columns, gables, apexes and so on with just a dash of oriental ornamentation and arching thrown in, the mass-produced building that has become a status symbol and one which every self-respecting Soviet town insists on having, despite the official campaign against them. Almost daily I read of party resolutions and exhortations in the newspapers against the passion of local governments for Greek columns, and ominous warnings against their extravagance, but even the newest of the towns seemed unable to resist these architectural badges of respectability and self-importance.

'You see,' the young Russian who met me told me proudly, 'we Russians had to come here because the local people were very backward. They needed education, science, engineers, doctors and 'zoo-technicians'* [a word that always makes me smile] and they could not provide them themselves. So they asked us to come and educate them and help them to a new way of life.'

Accustomed as I was from history to the euphemisms of Empire this one seemed to me even more glib than most. He might have been one of Cecil Rhodes' or Lord Milner's young men justifying another conquest in Africa in the nineteenth century. Again I was reminded how dangerously old-fashioned if not archaic is much of Russian thinking. The lace and the plush are not only in their hotels and houses but in the windows of their spirits. I am certain this young Russian believed every syllable of this discredited Imperialist patter.

The same theme was repeated to me by others I met, particularly at a meeting I had with three writers. (It was extraordinary how all my official contacts were invariably *à trois*.) They represented the three main racial groups of Khazakstan: one, the Khazak, had a fine Mongolian face and head; the Kirghiz some nobility of Turkish and Afghan origin in his features; the third was a Russian, tall with shrewd, blue eyes. They received me in their publishing house and at ten in the morning offered me a bottle of their local champagne and a plate of delicious apples. The fruit they said was the best in the world, hence the name of their city which was the Khazak for 'Father of Apples'. It was a rule with them never to drink in their working hours but they would

* It meant experts in animal husbandry.

waive it in my honour. Khazakstan was, they said, after the Russian Federation, geographically the largest Republic in the Union. In fact their republic was bigger than Western Europe and its progress enormous. The population was racing for the ten-million mark. Animal husbandry was still immensely important but industrialization had overtaken and surpassed it. The discovery of the vast Karaganda and Ekibasutz coal-fields, iron ore in Turgai, polymetals in the Altai, oil at Emben, phosphates from Kara Tau and hydro-electric power from the mountain streams had transformed them into a highly industrialized modern state and abolished the old easy-going nomadic ways for ever. Farming, animal husbandry, all was collectivized and mechanized. Nor was there any illiteracy to speak of, as proof of which they showed me their catalogues of millions of copies of books published in the Russian, Khazak and Kirghiz languages. They were, they said, now a fully independent people voluntarily joined to the Soviet Union and free to secede at any moment if they wished to. But how could they want to after all Russia had done for them?

I said that after what had happened in Hungary I thought this right to secession must be illusory. (It was interesting the unease produced always and everywhere by the mention of Hungary, sometimes expressed in indignant rejections, and at others apologetically.) Now apologetically they said that Russia had intervened only because requested to do so by the people of Hungary.

Illusory as the right to secede which the Soviet Constitution confers on the members of the Union may appear, it would be a great mistake to conclude therefore that the powers of the republics are altogether negligible. There is undoubtedly, in the restricted totalitarian sense, the development of a commonwealth idea, a concept of dominion status in existence in the Soviet Union. That this is so, curiously enough, is largely the work of Stalin. It may well be that when the final history is written this may be regarded as one of Stalin's greatest achievements. A Georgian and therefore a member of a vanquished but proud minority, he seems always to have had some regard for the feelings of the conquered, a sense of the importance of allowing some form of self-expression to the various racial groups in the Union. One of Lenin's first and rare sympathetic references to Stalin years before the revolution was praise for his grasp of the 'colonial' problem. The time was to come when he would describe Stalin as 'a cook of dishes too spicy for my taste' but he never seems to have wavered in his belief that Stalin was the man to deal with the minorities, and the present constitution is proof of how ably and indeed (in its totalitarian concept) how liberally he did so.

But as we talked nothing could disguise the fact that I was talking to two colonials in the presence of one of their conquerors and colonizers. We are so obsessed with the European image of Empire as a world of overseas and far-flung possessions that we are apt not to recognize the existence of Empire in countries like China and Russia, who have annexed and retained immense neighbouring lands as colonies as ruthlessly and completely as Britain, France or Spain ever did. So now the lively and passionate interest that the two natives of the area took in the cause of colonial emancipation in Africa could easily be a sign of some deeply rejected sense of their own nationality. But how could one tell for certain? If there were people conscious of such feelings they would not or could not express them in print. Even Lenin when he was compelled to compromise after the revolution and restore some measure of private enterprise and reward in the Soviet Union, never compromised with education, newspapers and propaganda. These remained firmly in the ruthless hands of the State. Expression of private opinions in these matters, open criticism of official ideology, is non-existent and considered the worst of crimes. All three of them vehemently rejected any suggestion that they were part of an Empire. They insisted that they were a free and voluntary association of peoples and I had to leave it at that. I asked instead if the virgin lands had been a success.

An outstanding success, they all three said. The stories I had heard of riots in some of the new towns, they declared, were just exaggerated accounts of hooliganism. To be 'uncultured' (*nekulturny*), or to be a hooligan was one of the direst social crimes a Soviet citizen could commit. Comedians on the stage, clowns in the circuses, newspapers and their correspondents were continually making war on the hooligan. A new phrase had been coined to express this disapproval and people were told to 'stop hooliganating' (*dovolno huliganit*). These hooligans, they said, were mostly young delinquents, the '*stilyagi*' who had rushed to the virgin lands in the hope of escaping from the consequences of their irresponsible behaviour in the West and making some easy money. But they had long since been weeded out or disciplined and more than 120 million acres of virgin lands were now under proper cultivation in properly organized State farms. Yet if all was well why were the newspapers full of stories of mismanagement and corruption in the virgin lands, of chairmen of farms and Party being sacked for errors, and particularly in Khazakstan of complaints of neglect and sabotage of tractors and other farm machinery? Already it seemed I had no escape between the devil of accepting the rosy picture full of plausible statistics of proliferating prosperity presented to me by people like these, and the deep blue sea of completely rejecting it all and falling into a state of permanent suspicion. Yet some common-sense assessment between the two extremes must be possible.

And yet in the days that followed as I moved in and about the country around Alma Ata, another and more positive impression grew in me. There was no mistaking a sense of purpose, of direction and of belief in the future of life. People were trying to build where there had been no building before. It was not building to my taste but was it not better than no building at all? And ultimately did it not have a power of increase? The collective farms that I saw may have been isolated show pieces but they set an example where there had been none before. There was the shining proof of irrigation canals and conducted streams vanishing into the shimmer and dust of the hot-dry plains. On the journey to Lake Issyk from the snow-covered summits of the Tien'Shans the waters from the heights were coiled like metal tape on the brown earth or flashed like spangles against the shivering poplars. I could understand the young Gorkiy Russian's pride in them all.

Below the line of beautiful Tien'Shan firs the herdsmen were moving their great flocks from one sheltered slope and meadow to another. The whole country seemed on the move, cattle above and sheep below. Down among the foothills on the edge of the plains the air was already bitter with the smell of wormwood and ringing with shrill cicada music. On the plains themselves the tractors threw up a chocolate dust behind their ploughs and at noon the bare wooden State Farm centres, austere and insufficient like encampments built in a military emergency, were almost empty because most of their people were out working the land. Many a herdsman rode by with a karakul hat on his head. Deeper in the hills some even wore the white and black felt hats and quilts of Kirghizia as they stood guard over their flocks. But most of them wore the cloth caps and pale-blue slickers straight from the nearest clothing factory. The horses alone still evoked the memory of Genghis Khan. They had slim ankles, sturdy barrels, shaggy necks and proud heads that lifted easily. They might have been modelled on the horses dug out of some Manchu tomb. Their step was quick and electric and made an exciting sound as precise as any percussion instrument on the earth. Their riders rode them as if they had been born to them, reared on their milk and nourished on their blood just like the ancient Tartar hordes. But the roads, bad as they were considering the century, were full of other traffic, mostly those sturdy dusty dark green trucks of Russia, all alike and loaded to the brim, lurching and bumping along endlessly into the blue, apparently impervious to the stresses and strains of such going and such distances. Among the mountains were ski-ing slopes, Olympic-size skating rinks and above all an observatory manned by scientists as dedicated as any in the world. To me they appeared utterly detached from the sort of considerations over which the growing city below them gossiped furtively, and completely interested in the evolution in outer space of the beautiful nebula of Andromeda which was the observatory's particular speciality. In the city itself universities and schools bursting their seams with sallow students and tidy, well-behaved, clean children, were often working three shifts a day to deal with the numbers. Somewhere in all that a private, vivid, purely Khazak or Kirghiz dream of the future might still be hidden. I would not be surprised if it were not so. But I would be surprised it it were not a diminishing one. The hand of the provincialism which is destined perhaps to replace the ardours of nationalisms everywhere in the emerging world seemed already heavy on this great land tucked up against the great mountains in that far-off heart of Asia.

'Next time you come,' the writers exhorted me when I said

good-bye: 'Come and stay some weeks. We'll take you every-where and even do some hunting and fishing as well.'

It was, I took it, at the best their way of saying they had en-joyed meeting me. For the rest it was a polite insincerity. They knew as I knew that the day when it would be permissible for them to show people like me around freely might be inevitable, but that the day was not yet.

From Khazakstan I flew south to go deeper into Central Asia. On our left the ranges of mountains stayed with us though slowly losing height and some of their snow. On our right the valleys petered out, the water-courses vanished, the grass slopes and the great patches of newly ploughed earth disappeared and the land became flatter, drier and hotter. A friendly Russian sitting next to me looked at the plains and the mountains, shook his head and remarked: 'The mountains do not harmonize with the plains!' I did not contradict him though for me the two were the point counter-point until we came down to the earth of Uzbekistan at its capital Tashkent.

Seeing it from the air in daylight for the first time Tashkent was like a bigger version of Alma Ata: with a population of over a million it is twice its size. It too first saw life as a garrison town and its firm expanding impulses were Russian and imperial too. Its outskirts also were marred with the inevitable office-of-works apartment blocks. But once on the ground the imprint of Manchu and Mongol seemed fainter; Indian and Persian, Pathan, Afghan, Turkoman and even Tibetan nearer. Above all the influence of waste-land and desert and the uncompromising state of mind and spirit that went with them was strong in the air. One knew at once that here one moved into a more complex land not just of the nomad, but also of man prepared to stand fast and be architect of his own life and fortune. Proof of that was in the ancient Uzbek quarter of the city, diminishing but still there; in the existence of the ancient religious colleges like the Medresses of Barak-Khan and Kukeldess. Above all it was in the unevasive eye of the people. I saw more persons in national dress here than almost anywhere else in the Soviet Union. Even the man who rejected the full traditional white robe which is cut low to expose the wearer's sunburnt chest and wore instead a cotton shirt and worsted jacket, would still cling to the national skullcap, the *tiubiteika,* embroidered in black and white patterns, as if to indicate that whatever the function and appearance of the body, the head inside still was purely Uzbek. Some of the older men went further still and wore the turban. The women on the other hand had discarded the *paranja* or *chachvan,* the thick black, horse-hair veil which used to cover the whole of their faces. Even the *khalat,* the bright dress of lovely yellow and red stripes, was vanishing fast. But many of the younger girls though they might manicure and paint their nails and lips still wore their black hair in many shining plaits. Yet it would be a mistake to suggest that Tashkent wore only Uzbek colours. For here mixing freely with Uzbek come Kara-Kalpaks from across the desert, as well as the natives of Kirghizia and Tadzhikistan and many another Asian region beyond the Soviet frontiers. They turn the markets in the native city and shops of Tashkent into gay, colourful and animated places quite unlike the staid, pompous, unsmiling official centre of the new town. Among them, the Kirghiz seemed to cling even more to their traditional state of mind than do the Uzbeks. The Russians have given them industries too, taught them to grow sugar-beet, cotton and other crops on irrigation along the edges of the desert. But all of them in heart and many of them in practice, are nomads still. Deep in their mountains, they move with their flocks in the winter from one rich sheltered meadow to another, in summer high up on the mountain slopes dressed in their quilted gowns, leather boots with skin overshoes and white felt hats with black brims. Their *yurtas,* felt tents spread on wooden lattice frames, are easily transported on horses or camels. Where they are pitched for days at a time in some rich valley they achieve an ancient splendour with carpets spread on the grass inside, blankets and colourful cushions piled against the sides, guns, knives, scabbards, bridles and skin bags full of *koumiss,* the mares' milk they love, suspended from the walls. This nomadic way of life too the Russians say is now collectivized. When I asked how, they said that mobile radios, creameries, schools, dispensaries, co-operative shops, film projectors, our old friends the 'zoo-technicians' are allocated to each nomad group and accompany them everywhere on their seasonal round among those profound mountains. But there is nothing collectivized or tame about the look in the eye that they bring to bear on Tashkent.

Then again come the Tadzhiks from deeper still among the mountains, one of the oldest races in Central Asia who do the best they can by cultivating their stony soil. The highest culti-vated fields in the Soviet Union line those deep valleys, the soil to rejuvenate them often being carried in baskets from the valleys below. But in the Ferghana, the Hissar, and the Vashk valleys and the flat arid lands the population is at its densest growing some of the best cotton in the Soviet Union. For them as for the Kirghiz, Tashkent seems their own natural capital. The fact is that when the Russians combined into a single unit the three Uzbek states of what used to be Turkestan and made Tashkent its capital, they set it on the way to becoming the dynamic centre of the whole of Central Asia. One feels this immediately on arrival. One knows at once that one is at a crossroads of geo-graphy, history and the spirit. For instance, I was in and out of the airport six times and on each occasion I met someone whom I knew or who knew me; an ex-Australian soldier who had served under me in the war; a woman who had seen me conduct a tele-vision series in Britain; a West African envoy whom I had known as a student in London; a South African coloured boy from the Cape of Good Hope; a Japanese friend from Tokyo and an Indian official who had worked with me in Java in 1946. In the modern quarter of the city where the pillars of the buildings of state are given a self-conscious archness the evidence of crossing and re-crossing of races, purposes, personalities and minds is greater and of course more complex. There is no doubt who controls and re-directs all this traffic: the master-hands and minds are Russian. Of all the many towns and cities I visited in the Soviet Union I thought Tashkent one of the most decisive. Here the grand design of the Soviet Union seems more obvious and to bite deeper into life than anything I had yet seen. For instance life is more in-dustrialized; the canals are longer, broader and their gleaming sword-thrusts pierce deeper into the vitals of desert and distance. The glass of fashion is the Ferghana Canal already lined with mature trembling Lombardy poplars, for so rich is the soil when watered that a tree will grow up in five years. The canal is broad as a river. Conceived and made by Russians, it leads the waters of ice and snow across the dry plains to feed what has become one of the most fertile regions on earth, the Valley which gives it its

name. On the way everywhere minor canals draw off water for
fields of alfalfa and paddies of rice, showing green behind little
brown walls of mud. There the water is protected against evaporation by great mulberry trees charged with the green of China and
thick with broad leaves that still make a sound like ancient silk
in the breeze. There are orchards too of apricot and peaches and
melons blown to bursting strewing the ground and, of course,
there are the vineyards, the vines bent double with the weight of
grapes which taste of Muscat and press into wine worthy of
Omar Khayyám. There are roads petering out into the far-off
desert haze but at that point even the karagash-trees with their
globes of dark green leaves fall out of line and refuse to accompany
them. But above all there is cotton. More than three-fifths of all
Soviet cotton is grown in this part of the world. Year by year new
irrigation channels add to the amount of cotton grown and the
desert is forced to yield more and more. Even the remote 'Hungry
Steppe', the Golodnaya, is now a great cotton centre. Cotton has
never been my favourite plant and is always a tricky crop. In this
part of the world I thought it could be more tricky and a friend of
mine, one of the greatest cotton experts in the world, who had
seen the cotton growing here had been even more dubious than I.
I certainly could not share the ingratiating sentiment of a well-
known French fellow-traveller who called the green patches of
cotton grown in this far outpost of Islam, 'the prayer carpets of
the new world'.

One of its greatest defects and possibly a source of great future
tragedy, is the Soviet State's failure to accord agriculture a place
in its own right instead of relegating it to a subordinate role in an
all-out process of industrialization. But meanwhile the cotton
factories of Uzbekistan, in particular the great plant of Tashkent
which produces 300 million yards of cotton a year and is filled
with girls and women of many races, confidently produce garishly
printed goods for the rest of the country. I thought these plants
impressive and the arrangements for the welfare of their workers,
the clubs, the clinics, the Palaces of Culture, the apartments and
all that figures in the National Marxist-Leninist stereotype of
these things, seemed good enough. But I cannot say honestly that
I found conditions Utopian or even as good as our own. On the
contrary I believe no girl from Lancashire would have tolerated

working for as long as I saw the women working in Tashkent. Two years ago in Japan at Osaka I saw a new mill which outstripped this plant and provided better working conditions. There was something satanic, too, about these mills fuming, spinning and humming away with insect industry and obsession in the heart of Asia. But apart from the mills, apart from the factories producing plant for more mills far and wide, apart from the inevitable tractor installations where the canals end beyond the green of the cotton and where the great dry steppe gives over to the desert, there was another, older world less resilient to change. There I found men in Astrakhan hats sitting in the shadow cast by their horses, watching their herds of *karakul*, the black-nosed sheep which figured in the Old Testament story of the bargain the fugitive Jacob drove with his uncle Laban. From there onwards to the land of the Kara-Kalpaks and the shores of the Aral Sea, wherever the oasis of cotton ended abruptly in the arid brown earth, life would re-emerge in this Old Testament pattern.

Important, however, as all these aspects of life made Tashkent, significant as is its role as capital of a country of ten million diverse people, I thought the extra-territorial function at which I have hinted was perhaps greater. Its natural function as a meeting-point of many cultures and minds is a new point of departure for the peoples of Central Asia. I expect it was realization of this that made the Komintern choose it as the location of one of their main schools of world revolution before the war. Immediately after the war in the upheaval in Indonesia I met a famous Javanese rebel who had been trained in Tashkent and had lived there from 1926 until 1946 when he was secretly sent back to his native country. He told me of the colony of persons like himself from all over the world who were in Tashkent training and waiting for their moment and the call of history. I did not try to find out but I suspect that such a school no longer exists. It would be too crude and double-edged an instrument for the people who run the Soviet Union today. But Tashkent has become one of the most important centres for legitimately spreading Soviet influence by providing free education and technical training for certain selected young from all over the world. Not even in Moscow did I meet so many young foreigners studying anything from astronomy, meteorology, civil engineering, and medicine to painting, music and ballet. Among them the number of students from Asia was naturally the biggest, and the numbers from Western Europe very small. This was so, a foreign newspaperman assured me, because it was part of a deliberate plan to make Tashkent an exclusive centre for re-educating the so-called under-developed world but all I know is that I myself met numbers of students from the West in Kharkov, Kiev, Moscow and Leningrad but none in Tashkent.

The students, specialists and technicians from the outside world training in Tashkent seemed to me very lonely people. Those who spoke English welcomed me like a brother. They were not the least interested in my political views. What mattered was that I was someone they could speak to in a language other than Russian. Some of them soon got to know my habits and when I turned up at the vast Intourist hotel where I was staying I would invariably find one or two of them eagerly awaiting me. I came to look forward to these occasions myself for I too was beginning to experience some of that loneliness caused by the unqualified assumption in the official life around me that Soviet values were absolutes. This means that there is no real give and take possible in the world of the imagination, and ultimately there is no greater loneliness than such a breakdown in natural communication between human beings. The students all felt this instinctively and it made not only a bond between them and me but also between them and the Uzbeks. They went to the Russians for their teaching but turned for their comfort and pleasure to the Uzbeks and other natives.

One night at the first curtain I walked out of a performance of the local ballet. It really was too much. Based on the life of Strauss the super-refined sentimental evocation of Habsburg Vienna, the golden-syrup rendering of Strauss's music, the costumes and décor as real as illustrations in a book of nursery fairy tales, finished me. I went out feeling as if I had been fed on pink marshmallows and white candy floss. The walk along the wide streets generously lined with trees, by somnolent white houses with orchards growing behind them, and the astringent air of early spring coming down from the thawing snow on the mountains soon brought me back to my senses. By now I had been reading also several examples of the literature produced under organized supervision in Central Asia and other autonomous regions, and I was beginning to be aware of some of the artistic limitations in the Soviet concept of self-determination for its subject races. National history was allowed to be written in a harmless Walter Scott manner but contemporary life was portrayed according to the prescribed Soviet pattern and in it I had as yet found no expression of a national self or character. The national ballet I had seen was folksy to an alarming degree and the prudery of local Palaces of Culture where girl dancers had long pink slips tied by elastic round their ankles so that their legs should not show when they twirled their skirts around, I could hardly take as a sign of emancipation. There is a limit also to the gusto with which human beings can go on dancing approved bits of their history to a bored audience of fellow-workers. The implication seemed to be that art, past, present and future belonged to the Soviet. Yet what was the Soviet doing about art for the masses? The pernicious anaemia of it all contrasted strangely with the vigour of the conception one met in schools, colleges, irrigation and industry.

So I came back to my hotel to find three students, two Afghan and a Bolivian, at my usual table. Soon we were joined by two Indians and a West African who placed the biggest tin of black caviare I have ever seen on my table, invited us to dip in and set us the example by doing so with a soup spoon. At a rough estimate such a tin of caviare would have cost me £70 in London! The South American who had been in Tashkent eighteen months spoke first. He said he had always been against class and race distinctions, against poverty and the exploitation of one human being by another. He thought that Russia had sincerely tried to do away with all these things and brought great progress to Central Asia. Certainly his post-graduate teaching in Tashkent could not have been improved upon anywhere in the world. All the same he was deeply worried. Without grave reservations he would not like to see what he saw around him extended to his own country. They would have to find their own way in South America but could he get his professors and fellow-students to see that? He shrugged his shoulders and said the effort was considered heretical. But what made this Russian rigidity all the stranger was that the Russians seemed unaware of how it had failed with the natives of Central Asia.

Had it, I asked?

Here they all tried to talk at once. . . . They said I should go, as they did, regularly to the tea- and coffee-houses of the land and listen to what the people said. . . . Many people were not at all grateful for what the Russians had done for them. They recognized the economic and other benefits brought to them by the Soviet system but, the South American stressed, their hearts were not engaged and they felt conspicuously apart from it all. The West African added, tending to see all the problems of life in terms of injured self-esteem, that their pride had been hurt. Were not the Central Asians the descendants of the Golden Horde who had for centuries vanquished the Russians and now had been vanquished in turn?

Then did they dream actively of regaining their independence? I asked.

They shook their heads and all agreed that the natives of Central Asia felt powerless and accepted their present condition as permanent. That made them fatalistic but not happy nor self-creative.

They spoke of criticism of the system, I said, but apart from its utterance in tea-house gossip how did it reveal itself?

One Afghan, an engineer, said the whole thing was just a general disassociation from and indifference to Soviet notions of progress. For instance, I must have read about the sabotage of tractors and other agricultural equipment in Khazakstan and Uzbekistan. He was certain it was not sabotage but just that the native people did not care to bother about these things. One Indian said a lot of the criticism came out in jokes and funny stories. It was then that I heard, for the first time, of Radio Armianski, the wireless station to which is attributed all sorts of satirical comment on the system of the Soviet Union. The station exists, of course, only as a figment in popular imagination, but its function is so compelling and active that while I was in Russia the Government appointed a commission to investigate the phenomenon and to recommend means for dealing with it. They were all amazed that I had not heard of it and gave me many examples.

For instance it was said that a geologist wrote to Radio Armianski and asked if it could help him to get a truck from the state to take him on an urgent technical expedition. After six weeks without reply he protested to the station and got this apology: 'Sorry we have been unable to answer before because we have not yet stopped laughing since we got your request.'

Then there was the official campaign against the passion of Local Authorities to house themselves in great neo-classical edifices with frontages of imposing columns. Khrushchev himself had railed against these columns as over-expensive embellishments. Hence, according to Radio Armianski, a Russian architect on a visit to Athens when shown the Acropolis and asked what he thought of it, patted the marble columns with his hand and said: 'My dear chap, mere embellishments, and a waste of money.'

The Afghan engineer added an illustration of his own. He told us that at his institute an expert attached to the radio station in Yerevan, the capital of Armenia, had appeared one day to lecture to them. When he announced that he was from the radio station in Armenia the class laughed so much that it was many minutes before he could begin to speak. It all sounded harmless enough that evening in Tashkent but I was to remember it vividly some weeks later in Moscow when I read of the expulsion of an American newspaper correspondent because he had made a collection of typical Radio Armianski stories and cabled them out to his newspaper.

I asked how serious local dissatisfaction and longing for greater independence really was?

One of the Indians said quickly that in his view it would all decline quickly and vanish as a national manifestation. Human nature being what it is it would merely lose its local character and merge into larger more universal dissatisfactions and resistances that one day would transform life in the Soviet Union. He said this for many reasons but for one all-important one. The State had never let go its grip on education, art, and propaganda and in recent years it had started something in education which he thought absolutely decisive for the future. He was referring to the introduction of boarding schools in the Soviet Union. Did I realize, he asked, that there were already more than 2,000 boarding

schools in the Soviet Union? That meant that from a kindergarten level to the stage where they passed out years later for
higher education, more than 600,000 children were already away
from their homes and the influence of their parents and receiving exactly the sort of education that the State wanted them
to have. By 1965 the system would have expanded so much that
two and a half million children would be educated in boarding
schools. More, the Soviet Prime Minister had said that the State
would not be satisfied until ninety per cent of all children in the
country were at boarding schools. At present there was some
criticism of these schools on the grounds that only the children of
the privileged were being accepted and that this, combined with
the shortages of places in technical colleges and universities, was
creating a new *élite* in Soviet society, a new aristocracy of
specialists, the economically, politically and socially powerful.
But from what he had seen of the Soviet capacity for doing things
quickly in a big way grounds for such criticism would quickly go.
The poorest in the land could afford these schools for the parents
paid at most ten per cent of the school fees and sometimes
nothing at all. It was very interesting to him that when the Ambassador of his country had asked the Soviet Prime Minister
recently if he would not find such a system too expensive, Mr
Khrushchev had snapped back: 'It will be cheaper than having a
lot of juvenile delinquents on our hands. It is necessary for our
people to be able to work in factories and the fields with their
minds untroubled by the thought of their young running wild in
the streets.' So this innovation, the Indian student concluded,
killed two birds with one stone. It made certain that the young
grew up with the right Soviet ideas: and it also made it possible
for both parents to work in a Society where already the labour
shortage was acute. He would advise me to go over a boarding
school in Tashkent if I wanted to know the answer to my
questions.

I did just that and spent a whole morning at the largest boarding school in Tashkent. There were about eight hundred children
of all races there: Russian, Uzbek, Khazak, Karakalpak,
Kirghiz, Tadzhik and so on. Yet because they were all treated and
dressed alike one had to look closely into their clean attentive
little faces before one could perceive the racial differences

between them. They were all in the same spruce spotless uniforms, the little boys in a sort of young Commissar's get-up, the little girls in white blouses and dark brown pinafores. The boys all had their hair close-cropped; the young girls had theirs parted in the middle but braided into a single plait behind. Most of the children I saw of both sexes wore round their necks the red kerchief which is the badge of the Young Pioneers Organization. Those who did not were too young. This organization is the Soviet equivalent of a Boy Scout, Temperance and Sunday School movement combined, in which the growing child is taught in ways agreeable to him like hiking, camping and organized games, how to practise the basic elements of Soviet ethics. For instance, on becoming young pioneers they take an oath 'to love the Soviet Union, to live, to study and to fight according to the teachings of Lenin and the Communist Party'. In other words through this organization they get their first practical grounding in the commandments of the National religion. Out of it they graduate naturally into the Communist Youth Organization, the powerful Komsomol, and those who do not lag by the way go on into the Party itself. At the moment there are close on forty million Young Pioneers, twenty million Young Communists and about ten million Party members. Through it too in his hours of leisure the child is impressed with the all-out importance of conforming. It was significant how constantly the Victorian parallel came to my mind on this journey. Just as the Victorian child was taught that goodness lay in setting one's house, one's school, one's team before oneself, and from this going on to serving one's nation, one's Queen and one's God, so now the conception confronting me for the first time in that school in Tashkent seemed much the same, with one all-important difference that they had nothing beyond Lenin and the State to serve.

Indeed Lenin was God and the Party his one and only Church. I had no doubt that what I saw made sense only when interpreted in terms of religion; just as I had no doubt that I had never seen a better behaved bunch of children. There were certainly no obvious non-conformists there.

All these eight hundred children were taught to look after themselves as much as possible, to make their own beds, help in kitchens and gardens, lay and serve in turns at table. They made a good job of it all under spartan living conditions and were kept so occupied that they could have had no time for either introspection or discontent. In the classes they were keen and most attentive, their relationship with their teachers easy and free, in spite of discipline which appeared to me old-fashioned if not severe. The main reason for that, I suspect, was that all the teachers (like almost everyone I met on this journey) truly loved children. Also education and the people who could dispense it, were valued as highly as in any nation of the world. Both the learners and the teacher had no doubt that they were involved in an operation of great social importance and meaning. Judging by what I saw at Tashkent and elsewhere that terrible phenomenon, the teacher who only teaches because he has not been good enough for anything else, does not exist. What doubts one had arose only on account of what was taught and its ultimate purpose. Nor could one doubt but that their teaching was thorough.

I had not been there long when the teachers of English took me to their classes. I spoke to the pupils and they answered me in remarkably good English. I do not think any people attach so much importance to pronunciation and phonetics as do the Russians. A profoundly musical people, in their teaching they give the sound as much importance as the idiom. Even here in Central Asia this school was equipped with a library of recordings of English voices, and a studio where teachers and children can record their own speech, play them back to themselves and compare them with the original versions. They insisted on my reading something from the textbooks into their tape-recorder. I was reading happily from a page marked Lesson 21 when the content of what I was reading began to trouble me. It got more and more extraordinary until I turned the page and saw at the bottom that the extract was from *Uncle Tom's Cabin*. They asked me to continue with the next lesson. The same bewilderment came over me when I turned the page and saw it was from Charles Dickens. If I protested that the *conditions* described in both extracts were a hundred years out of date no one, I was certain, would believe me.

So instead I said to the headmaster: 'I am glad your children read our English and American classics. I only hope you do not teach them to speak as the people do in these books?'

He looked somewhat puzzled and asked why not?

'Because,' I told him, 'if they do people will laugh at them. It's such old-fashioned language. We stopped talking and living like that more than a hundred years ago.'

I think the thrust went home.

Finally there was a slight incident before I left which seemed to me significant of life in the Soviet Union in general and its education in particular.

'Incidentally,' I asked the teachers who assembled to see me off, 'what do you do about teaching your left-handed children?'

They looked dumbfounded until one of the Russians said brusquely: 'We have no left-handed children here or anywhere else.'

The attitude implicit in this dismissal of what is a universal educational problem drove home the point that the Indian had made about boarding school education the night before. Neither a left-handed child nor a left-handed spirit nor a left-handed nationalism had place in the future for which this education was a preparation.

During this period I had met a native of Uzbekistan who like many of his countrymen had a great feeling for literature and poetry. Somehow I had mentioned Omar Khayyám to him. Immediately that had roused an interest which grew to an extraordinary excitement when I told him of the FitzGerald translation which had made Omar Khayyám into an English classic. His delight really knew no bounds when I told him of a cockney bus-conductor in London whom one day I heard reciting Omar Khayyám to a pretty passenger as she stepped on board:

> 'Here with a Loaf of Bread beneath the Bough,
> A Flask of Wine, a Book of Verse – and Thou
> Beside me singing in the Wilderness –
> O Wilderness is Paradise enow.'

He had asked if he could bring some friends to meet me and just after my visit to the school three of them were there to meet me mainly to hear more about Omar Khayyám and the English. I recited all the stanzas I could remember. They took it all in. Only a deep feeling of what they, their race, their culture and their past were denied in the present could have given them such pride and joy in these English translations and recognition of worth they implied.

Of all the stanzas the one which really seemed to come home to them was:

> 'The Worldly Hope men set their Hearts upon
> Turns Ashes – or it prospers; and anon,
> Like Snow upon the Desert's dusty Face
> Lighting a little Hour or two – is gone.'

Their eyes as I recited this turned to look first at the shimmer of snow on the purple mountains then to the glitter of the quicksilver day over the far-off desert. Whatever their dreams or hopes the expression on their faces just then betrayed the conviction that they had as little place in what lay ahead of them as that snow on the face of the encroaching desert. The silence between us was like a heavy shadow until one of them sighed and said: 'I wish I could go to your country and meet that bus conductor.'

Then they all three laughed as men do in order to rid themselves of the embarrassment of emotions they know to be in vain.

'I'll send you all translations of Omar Khayyám from England,' I said to them.

The promise of so small a service had no right to exact such gratitude and I can only hope that the books reached them for, since sending them off months ago, I have had no acknowledgement nor word from any of the three.

CHAPTER FIVE

SAMARKAND AND BUKHARA

ON the way to Samarkand and Bukhara the sun became hotter, the dry steppe merged quickly into the desert proper, and the earth became sand which stretched west and northwards as far as one could see. Yet to the east and south the purple mountains stood firm flaunting a feather of snow in our faces. Mile after mile flashed by and I would expect them by the second to vanish or decline but always above the yellow haze they hung in the window of my plane as still as a Japanese print on a paper wall. As we swung round from Samarkand westward towards Bukhara still they conformed and increased again in stature until they reached another climax in the mountains of Armenia and Georgia. Only when one has travelled with them thus does one realize the prodigious extent to which Imperialist Russia, by conquest, made a frontier for itself out of one of the greatest natural barriers on earth. But what excited my eyes and imagination even more than the imperious mountains were the desert and the narrow chain of fertile oases that connected the few passes through them with routes to the Caspian and other worlds beyond. There lay the great silk-route, one of the bloodiest thoroughfares of all times, which began in China, or Marco Polo's Cathay, and linked up here with other trails to Persia and the Middle East, Byzantium and the Levant, and the countries of Europe; the land, as its ancient name implies, 'where the sun went down', hence the '*Abendland*' of Spengler. That name alone is enough to establish the unrecorded course of our several histories. Hemmed in between mountains and desert, around some miracle of water in arid sand, grew up dense settlements which thrived on the traffic of history and provided points of arrival, consolidation and departure for some of the greatest forces of invasion and counter-invasion the world has ever seen. Until the Russians, after centuries of suffering under invasions, themselves turned the tide on them, the invaders generally came from the East. But long before the Russians, the Greeks, Romans and Persians marched and counter-marched before these mountain ramparts and lofty gateways to the Far East. Here are rivers that were known under other names to Herodotus such as the Jazartes, or the Syr Dar-ya and the greater Oxus or Amu-dar-ya. Samarkand itself is reputed to be the Maracanda founded by Alexander the Great. Yet before this articulate record begins there is evidence that here there was a far greater coming and going of men and cultures of the ancient worlds than we can imagine. One of the greatest fallacies of our way of telling history is the unconscious assumption that communications on any significant scale in the world are a European development started in the fifteenth century. But the urge to know the unknown, to learn what is not yet learnt, to submit the old and the outworn to rejuvenation by the new and the untried, to trade and to travel and at the worst to convert and to conquer, is built into the spirit of man and was present and active at our beginning. Anyone who doubts this should look at the relevant evidence as I have done; as for instance the remarkable collection of gold ornaments now housed in the Hermitage in Leningrad which Russian archaeologists have excavated out of the earth, sands, clays and gravels of the Soviet Union from Siberia and Central Asia to the Black Sea and the Ukraine. This gold, fresh as if just extracted from the mint, shows not merely Greek and Roman influence but also the subtle impact of Babylon, Chaldaea, Assyria and even the first dynasty of Egypt. No ruin, sculpture or painting has ever moved me more than this gold straight out of the spirit of man when the world was young.

So far back does this traffic and travel reach that there are signs that even the climate has completely altered since it first began. We know, for instance, that the great Central Asian forest once reached the outskirts of Teheran and may even have stared at its own reflection in the Caspian Sea. We know too, that the desert has encroached since then, the Caspian level itself sunk, and here even to this day a wind stronger than the average will blow the sands apart and reveal the ruins of some great unrecorded city. These sands which derive their names from their colour like the Kizil Kum or red sands, and the greatest of them all the Kara Kum or black sands, cover another world almost as effectively as the sea covers the lost City of Atlantis. Here, too, even in recorded time, they have encroached to stifle life. For instance, you can look down on the Murghbab River, stabbing the brown with a fork of unexpected green before it vanishes into the sand, and peer into the enigmatic haze which lies over the ruins of one of the oldest cities in the world, Merou Shahou Jehan or Merv the Queen of the World. And just as they turned the tide of human invasion here too the Russians have gallantly made it one of their foremost tasks to stop this thousand-year-old encroachment of the desert. The canals, the irrigation furrows, the long wide belts of trees to break the force of corroding winds and give healing shelter to redeeming earth which they are cutting, ploughing and planting, is a truly stupendous task and achievement. All this gives hope and a new point to the future, yet the past still lies heavily on the face of the land and in the spirit of the native-born peoples. They have trafficked for so long in the stuff of history that neither the present nor indeed the future can remove a certain paralysis with which the brilliant memory of their past obsesses them.

How brilliant this memory is is nowhere more manifest than in Samarkand or Bukhara. Here there is still more of the old than the new. Once the Russians have made up their minds that a place has historical worth there is nothing they will not do to preserve it and no limit to the love – there is no other word for it – with which they will do it. Science and education (and in their view history shares both categories) evolve qualities of enthusiasm and dedication among all sorts and conditions of Russians. Once convinced that they have no revival of nationalisms in this part of the world to fear, they have set about with a powerful will to preserve all that is best in old Samarkand and Bukhara. Their restorers have even set craftsmen working in the cloisters and cells of many mosques using the same methods as their prototypes of the Golden Horde to produce tiles of the exact shade to replace the broken and missing ones. Had they not done so there is no doubt these cities of sun-baked brick would have crumbled fast. As a result enough remains of the old Samarkand to explain why the world that gave it birth so excited Elizabethan England that Marlowe could write 'Tamberlaine the Great' and why Flecker could become so ecstatic about it in his 'Golden Road.'

I myself first saw Samarkand from a rise across a wilderness of crumbling ruins and great graveyards which lie between it and the airport. Suddenly we caught a glimpse of painted minarets trembling in the blue astringent light and the great Madonna blue domes of mosques and tombs shouldering the full weight of the sky among bright green trees and gardens. Beyond the gardens and the glittering domes still were those watchful mountains and their evocative snow. Marx called religion 'the opium of the people', and religion was so obviously the main impulse that raised those sparkling minarets, domes and arches that they made me think of lines in a ballad written by William Plomer, a friend of mine:

> The hypodermic steeple,
> Ever-ready to inject
> The opium of the people.

But the irreverent association soon perished in deeper contemplation of these solemn shapes of a vanished world. I found myself thinking instead of the thrill I had on catching my first glimpse of Damascus after crossing the desert from Syria. The light, the orchards and many of the trees were the same but deeper still was the sense of coming into contact with one of the most astonishing cultures in history, the world of the one and only Allah and his prophet Mohammed. Behind all this was an even older awareness with its roots in the world of Scheherazade, Darius and Xerxes the Great; the first great westward expansion of Eastern peoples which may have been ended in its migratory sense but is still going on in the mind and spirit of Central Asian men. Samarkand was the far northern gateway to it all. But when I thought of the other points of contact I had made with it, Granada in Spain, Fez in North Africa, Khartoum in the valley of the Nile, the Sunda lands of Java, Karachi and the Persian Gulf, then the scale and vigour of the vision which animated that world completely over-awed me.

But if this is the general impact of the old Samarkand on one's imagination, it has its own specific impact. It speaks to one of Tamerlane or Timur the Lame and his grandson Ulug Beg, the great astronomer. One of my greatest defects as a traveller is that I am not sufficiently moved by ruins and ancient monuments. I find the buildings of the past seen out of context with the age and civilization which produced them strangely unreal, as if they do not conform but even tend to contradict the things which gave them being and life in imagination. But these cities of the Golden Horde are exceptions largely, I think, because their original impulses are not yet exhausted. Whether the mosques were merely preserved for historical interest or not, everywhere I found people in national dress worshipping openly in some, or furtively in others. I think the building that moved me most was the Gur Emir, the blue-domed tomb of Tamerlane himself and the plain tombstone of jade from China which marks where the great conqueror now lies in his small coffin. Even the names of the buildings have the authentic ring of history like the Hazreti, Shakh Zindeh or shrine of the Living King; Tilla Kari, the Mosque of Gold and the Shir Dar, the lion-bearer.

Yet the memory of Samarkand which stays with me most clearly was more humble. Coming back to the city from the country on my last evening we passed some unusual elms and I stopped to look at them. They were, my guide told me, perhaps a thousand years old, older certainly than Genghis Khan. It was very still and the mountains away towards Persia were purple, white and pink in the declining light. A flock of fat-tailed sheep (the same kind of fat-tailed sheep that my ancestors saw a Hottentot keeping when they landed at the Cape of Good Hope 311 years ago and 9,000 miles away) tended by some Tadzhik children moved slowly home in the distance leaving a trail of yellow translucent dust in the air. Then from the city came quite clearly the call to prayer from mosque and minaret. I had not expected any calls at all and it made no difference that some of the calls came over loud-speakers. That this could still be uttered alone was important. Then beyond the trees an old man had appeared on a donkey, dismounted, spread a prayer mat on the ground, and kneeling down face towards Mecca he began to pray. No one who has not travelled in a country without gods in the natural sense can know how moving such a scene can be.

My companions however were oddly embarrassed by the sight. 'Some of the old people,' one of them said, 'are still very superstitious but we'll soon change all that.' And he laughed.

His laugh drove all feeling of reverence out of the evening and after it the night gathering fast over the painted and domed city seemed all the darker.

Bukhara had something of Samarkand in reverse. It was dedicated to the memory of Tamerlane and Ulug Beg in general and the kingdom of Allah on earth in particular. Once it was the holiest city in Central Asia. Elsewhere, so the proverb ran, light came down from Heaven but in Bukhara it went up like a moon to the sky. Marco Polo called it *'une cité moult noble et grant'*; an Elizabethan adventurer, Anthony Jenkinson, called it a 'greate cite' and wrote of its 'high walles and divers gates and many houses, temples and monuments of stone sumptuously built and gilt'. At one time it possessed over a hundred religious colleges and close on four hundred mosques. No wonder that for all its cruel and bloody past it was called Bukhara-es-Sherif or Bukhara the noble, and the gossip about it in the markets of Aleppo, Istanbul, Venice and Casablanca had a powerful effect on the imagination of Europe. It drew the adventurers of all races towards it as it did Marco Polo. Not many of them arrived, and nearer to our own time as the traffic of silk, spice, jewels and slaves which passed through it became ever more threatened, the more dangerous things became for the travellers, whether they came openly as ambassadors or disguised as Dervishes. There is, for instance, the terrible story in 1843 of the lost and murdered English Colonel Charles Stoddart and the Irish Captain Arthur Conolly (still remembered in local legend as Khan Ali). Stoddart had made a bad start with the Emir of Bukhara by going against centuries of custom and riding his horse into the presence of the ruler. He then made it worse by refusing to kow-tow to the Emir and hitting out furiously at the officials who tried to force him to his knees. As a result he and Conolly were kept in a dark cell for many months but sometimes put in a pit (which I saw), where the Emir kept reptiles and scorpions especially bred to torment his prisoners. They were executed in the end because they refused to save themselves by becoming Moslems.* Then there was Giovanni Orlandi of Parma who was battered to death because he could not prevent the Emir of Bukhara's watch from stopping. These and similar tales penetrate the sealed and cloistered reality of the fantastic city like infra-red rays warning of a fog. They should be

* Fitzroy Maclean: *A Person From England.*

read by all who want to see in the round, not only Samarkand and Bukhara but also other cities on this tributary of the great silk route such as Khiva, which has just been opened to tourists. Seen in terms of the price paid in human suffering their splendour and glory lose some of their lustre and the fundamental paradox of life increases. One is farther off than ever from understanding how men can pursue beauty so ardently in its physical forms and yet deny it so completely in spirit and behaviour.

A bare generation ago Bukhara was perhaps the least changed of all cities of Uzbekistan. It was still contained within its white walls and towers which, were it not for the mountains and their snow on the horizon, might have been set in south Arabia. But the walls now have been pulled down (to let the air into the place, the Russians say) except for some crumbling ramparts flanking a tranquil little stream outside the town. At what used to be one of the richest market places in the world, pitched in the shadow of the great Tower of Death, today one buys ice-cream instead of slaves; watches, and mass-produced trinkets and fizzy drinks instead of opals, diamonds, gold, lapis lazuli, and turquoise jewellery. Few of the four hundred mosques remain and most have vanished without even leaving a trace. Others have changed their functions; one, for instance, now being a popular billiard saloon, another a palace of culture. Only one of the religious schools is still open, another has been turned into an hotel, and yet another into a records office. A park of rest and culture, public gardens and a sports stadium have been built in their midst. The Liabi-Khans, the beautiful tree-shaded pool, in which the three hundred wives of one Emir used to perform their evening ablutions, is an unofficial swimming pool for street urchins.

Yet enough of the past remains, the Kok Gumbaz or Blue Domed Mosque, for instance, and the vast Mir Arab in the centre of the city still stand and have their dedicated following. Moreover everywhere there are walls of red and yellow bricks covered with algebraic arabesques like maps of the profound and intricate Moslem spirit itself. The Zindan or prison, the death-pit wherein the Emirs kept snakes and scorpions to torment the men they threw in them, the Tower of Death from which the condemned were hurled, the mausoleum of Ismael Samani built by the founder of the Samanid dynasty in the ninth century, the Ark or the great fortress of Bukhara and even the modest shrine of Chasma Ayub or Job's spring, all remain. As I looked at the blue domes, the towers, the shrines, the bleached gold and red walls in the distance and the desert behind me and contemplated these names, the extraordinary Pentateuchal coming and going of men and creeds that went into the making of the history of this world was uppermost in my mind: in particular the manner in which Jew and Moslem happily contributed to one another's well-being until the recent creation of the State of Israel. Beside me at the time was a local man who proudly called himself not Uzbek or Russian but a 'Bukhara Jew'. The moment we met he announced this fact to me quite naturally and later added that the Jews of Bukhara and Baghdad were the oldest Jewish communities in the world. It was strange to think that here, cruel as the past had been, it had been kinder to Jews than had the Russians or the Germans. This man certainly talked to me of the past of Bukhara as if it were his own.

All the time I saw signs of how intently the Russians were urging the locals by example and exhortation to modernize their ways. My hotel was filled with only two classes of people: tourists, and Russian engineers and technicians. I like to get up early to enjoy the cool of the day and were this not an old habit of mine I would have been forced to it for like most hotels in the Soviet Union the rooms had no curtains either broad or thick enough to draw against the day. At one moment it would be dark and the next a wild and imperious dawn would appear like a summons of fate in one's windows. I would get up quickly, shave, bath and hurry down, meeting all sorts and conditions of men in striped pyjamas on the stairs with kettles in their hands fetching boiling water for tea out of the giant electric samovar of the hotel – everywhere, except in the trains, samovars have been automized and electrified in the Soviet Union. Outside, the benches against the hotel would be crowded with Russians waiting for transport to take them to their work. The transport invariably would be one of those standard dark-green Russian trucks covered with dust and crowded with sleepy local labour. I expect most of the workmen would have called themselves Uzbek but their features seemed to possess something of every race that has ever lived from the Persian Gulf to the Urals, and from Everest to the

Golden Horn. They would tear off in their trucks in a great hurry
and leave the fine dust hanging like haloes around the bright
green trees. Not once did I see a private car among them: even
the most imposing among the Russian technicians in the hotel
seemed grateful for any place he could find for himself on the
crowded trucks. They seemed simple, kindly, likeable and friendly
men, rather lonely and doing their work well if only because they
had no option. They had the same sort of fatalistic look about
them as have my poorer Afrikaner countrymen who are condemned to make a living as foremen in charge of gangs of African
labour in the Union or Rhodesias, making roads and building
dams far away from hamlets and cities for people who they believe neither want nor need them. Only I would say the Russians
were far better educated than their counterparts in any other
country in the world. One morning, for instance, one of them
making a place for me on the crowded bench, looked at
me and said with a marked tone of interrogation, 'You, Jack
London?'

Taking it to mean that he wanted to know if I had read Jack
London, I answered, 'Yes, me Jack London.'

His face lit up like a torch, and he seized my hand in a grip
that hurt and asked: 'You Galsworthy?'

'Yes, me Galsworthy,' I answered.

'You *Forsythe Saga*?'

'Yes, me *Forsythe Saga*,' I told him just as his truck arrived.

For a moment it looked as if he was going to make the truck
wait so that he could continue a literary interrogation that was
giving him great joy. But one glance at the crowded vehicle convinced him that he had to conform. He swung himself on board,
but once in position, his arms round two locals for support, he
looked at me and shouted in a voice worthy of Chaliapin:
'Galsworthy a very good boy!'

With that battle cry for his sense of culture, he vanished down
the road carrying whatever he had of Jack London and Galsworthy (the writer *par excellence* of British people of property
and their decline) into the heat and burden of another day of
building regulation blocks among the blue and yellow minarets
of a vanished world.

At Ashkhabad, the Capital of Turkmenia, a region the size of

Spain and of nearly two million people, the mountains of the Persian frontier were a bare twelve miles away and the desert seemed to press right up against their base. The low white houses of the town built in wide green avenues running at right angles to one another repeated the pattern of the Central Asian towns of the Russian garrison origin. But the people had now changed subtly and the emphasis of character and race shifted markedly westward. There was more evidence of temperament, something of Spain and Spanish Morocco, and I walked into my hotel to find a waitress and a waiter shouting at one another because one of them had laid a table badly. The relief, after so much averted and hidden spirit not to mention Russian conformity and phlegm, was immense. Some of this immediacy and vividness too was still reflected in the people's clothes and their arts and crafts. It seemed no accident that red was the favourite colour of the people. I saw a lot of men in dark-red gowns and great black fur hats, their women in flaming dresses of deep red too and silver ornaments flashing against their olive skins and dark-black hair. Even the younger ones who wore modern clothes did so with a clear sense of style and taste that I had not seen before. Then the background of their beloved carpets was invariably red and I do not believe I have ever seen so many beautiful shades. Every little oasis – and life in Turkmenia is either oases or nomadic life – had its own shade of red for its carpets. Neither in Samarkand, Bukhara nor in any town in Persia, the locals claimed, did they make carpets as fine as in Turkmenia. They took me to the local factory to prove their point. In the sense that there was nothing contemporary in the patterns which a hundred or more local girls wove in this factory, the visit was disappointing. But to the extent that it showed me that what was best in traditional carpet making was preserved and reproduced there, it was most impressive. Yet even in so traditional an industry there was for me an alarming sign of the least desirable of Soviet ways on the natural spirit of the people. My guides took me proudly to see a girl who was a heroine of Soviet Labour, an honour which is to the new Soviet working man what the Victoria Cross and Congressional medal of honour are to British and American serving men. This girl, it was said, produced more than double the number of carpets of any other girl in the factory. Now all the girls I had seen up to this moment were working steadily and easily at their weaving, occasionally pausing to talk to one another and not afraid to satisfy their curiosity about my visit by thoroughly looking us all over. But this heroine of labour did not pause once to look up or listen to us. I spoke to her and she did not seem to hear. Head bowed over her work, fingers passing threads of different colours through the frame in front of her as fast as they could, her eyes moving in the hypnotic way of spectators at a tennis match from one end of her pattern to the other, she seemed living not in the present nor in the past but far back in some insect moment of life where such awareness and energy as the unit possesses are all invested in the perpetual reproduction of the same old nest. Admirable as this might appear to a white ant to me it seemed a frightening denial of life in so comely a young girl.

Dismayed, I asked: 'Does she do this all day?'

'Oh yes, from the time she comes in until she leaves,' the manageress remarked with pride as she took me away to show me in their store of carpets all the range of patterns from the smooth carpet beloved of isolated desert communities like the peoples of the Pedinsky Oasis and the settlement of Kerky, and the delicate designs from the luminous oasis of green and gold in the dark Kara-Kum which is called Mary.

'Could I buy one of these carpets and send it by post to London?' I asked, so attracted was I by a Mary-red design, which seemed to have come straight out of a desert sunset.

At that she went into protracted and anxious consultation with everyone in sight. On my journey I was amazed continually how quickly persons in authority would go into committee with subordinates when an unfamiliar problem confronted them. I mention it here because the phenomenon in my experience was so widespread that I believe it appears at all levels of the system from the lowest to the highest, not excluding the services. I think it is this which mainly distinguishes Russian totalitarianism from that of the Fascist dictators, even from that of Stalin. Contemporary Russian totalitarianism is not naturally dictatorial. Somewhere deeply ingrained in the people there is an imperious pattern and belief in consultation which the totalitarian cannot ignore. All this became clearer as my journey progressed but here in the carpet factory at Ashkhabad I was at first inclined to interpret it as a sign of panic, so I intervened by appealing to their pride. I said everywhere in the world where I had travelled I had bought things to send home by post, could I not do so here?

They seemed confused and countered that it might be easier if I bought the carpet and carried it with me. They added that they had never sent a carpet off like this before, only through the appropriate State selling organization.

I suggested that as they had told me they were all pioneers of a new way of life could they not make that carpet a pioneer of a new way of trade? I was certain that once it became possible to sell carpets in this way hundreds of other visitors would follow my example and buy from them.

The phrase 'pioneer' struck a chord among them and immediately it was plain they were going to do their utmost. Three of them took me to the local bank to cash a traveller's cheque to pay for the carpet. Ashkhabad has not long been open to tourists and was far away from the routes favoured by visitors. I had been warned about the difficulties of cashing traveller's cheques in Russia. Yet here it was a quick and painless process. We went back to the factory to find the carpet packed. The whole factory, except the heroine of labour, rose to their feet to wish me a gay 'good-bye' and 'come again'. Another deputation took me off to see the authorities and three hours later to deposit the carpet at the post office. It arrived in London before my postcard announcing its despatch. Even the Swiss post office which is, in my opinion, the best in the world could not have been swifter.

Back at my hotel I found I was the only tourist there though it was full of the familiar Russian technicians. There were many Turkomans too, gathered for some convention and all night long they seemed to be wandering in bright Ali-Baba dress up and down the stairs with kettles big enough to make forty teas. The talk among them all I gathered was of irrigation and cotton. The vast Central Asian irrigation scheme of which I have spoken was everywhere extending and multiplying its shining dependencies in the dark desert. Cotton, which perhaps seemed to the expert to be a mistake in the colder Tashkent earth, here in Ashkhabad, said to be the hottest place in the Soviet Union, appeared far more appropriate and rewarding. Animal husbandry (the Karakul in particular), the vineyards and the production of melons always stood the farmers in good stead in this arid earth. They told me, for instance, of oases where they grew vines eight feet high in deep trenches and the melon harvests ran into hundreds per acre. What a pity I was just too soon, one remarked, to taste their special grape, the Kishmish, small but sweetest of all, and their best melon so fragrant and full of savour that they called it Guluyabi – 'Rose oil'. All this mattered greatly to them, but in the future cotton would matter more. Where before only camels had walked, already barges and motorboats were sailing across the desert in canals filled with water from the Amur-Darya, the Oxus of Greeks and Persians five hundred miles away. There was no doubt that they showed more excitement about these events than any peoples I had met before. In this, too, I read some slight confirmation of my impression that the spirit of the man had moved nearer the classical west.

The next day I was driven deep into the desert to see the latest extension of the great 500-mile Kara-Kum canal. The land was so even that we were upon the cutting before we saw it. As yet no water flowed in it – that event was celebrated two months later – but the people knew what they were going to do with the water when it came. Some of it, they said laughingly, would go for pleasure and they pointed out a place where they were going to build a lido for the water-deprived people of Ashkhabad.

What about seepage and evaporation? I asked, looking at that thirsty, scorched land with no vegetation except isolated tufts of coarse grass and twisted tamarisk trees that threw no shade.

Nearly a third of the water would be lost that way, they said shrugging their shoulders, but even so the cotton they would grow would make it worth it for it would be the best in the Soviet Union.

Would they grow it individually, collectively or on State farms? I asked.

The word 'individual' struck them with horror. Did I not know, they asked with indignant rhetoric, that no one worked individually in the Soviet Union, no one that is except cobblers and dressmakers and then only provided they worked alone and employed no one else? No, the cotton would be grown either collectively or on State plantations.

As they told me this we heard the sound, distinct and clear on the quivering desert air, of camel-bells. We all turned towards it and saw coming through a gap between two high sand-dunes whose wind-rippled surfaces were shining like shot artificial silk, a long string of dark-brown camels, swinging from side to side as if for ever cradle-borne in their long, patient strides towards the far-off city. I could not think of those archaic highly individualistic animals as collective or State-owned and was about to ask the logical question when they, no doubt instinctively anticipating what was coming, exclaimed: 'Oh, do look at our collective camels!'

CHAPTER SIX

BAKU AND TBILISI

FROM the air above Ashkhabad the sands of the desert seemed to go darker still. To the north I could see no end to it and the canal quickly contracted from the gleaming vital sword-thrust it had appeared on the ground to a pinprick in one's memory. A melancholy settled in me and I had to remind myself of a wise saying from my own past to the effect that 'sadness is rarely in the landscape but in oneself'. I wondered how much it had to do with the fact that I had just been reading the history of this country and still fresh in my memory were descriptions of the desperate plight of thousands of men, women and children who fled in vain across this desert a bare eighty years ago and were massacred by the Cossacks of the Russian General Skobelev, the conqueror of the last of the Turkomans.

Like most British people I have an instinctive and totally irrational love of deserts but here, for once, I was relieved to see the greater and lesser Balkan hills come out of the plain and beyond them the glint of the waters of the world's greatest lake, the Caspian Sea. As we approached Krasnovodsk, an important-looking Armenian beside me pointed out the busy port and railway terminus on the eastern shore and a lesser glint of water on the northern horizon, apparently detached from the greater. That was the strangest of all Caspian sub-waters, I was told, the Kara-Bogaz-Gol or Black-mouthed gulf. Once not long ago the water of the Caspian used to flow through the narrow entrance which links the two, replacing the vast losses due to evaporation by the sun on this desert-locked lake. But the waters of the Caspian itself have been falling rapidly and today the shallow Kara-Bogaz-Gol has to be fed by water pumped into it from special reservoirs. It was a pity I could not see it, my companion told me. It resembled a moon-sea in a moonscape more than any scene on earth. The water was so heavy with salt that it lay in a sultry glow, inert. Then when the heavier winds blew it discharged crystals which the storms piled in great white heaps gleaming on the sombre shore like bones in an open grave. These crystals, of course, were collected and like everything else in the Soviet Union put to practical uses. A vast new industry in fact was founded on them.

But what, I asked, if this steep fall in the Caspian level continued? Was there no danger in that?

His dour dark features came as near to the light of a smile as Armenian history allowed and he answered that Russian geologists had evidence to show that the fall was cyclical and would in time be followed by a rise. Yet even if it were not, a plan already existed to deal with the problem. Did I know that not far from the source of the Volga which was the Caspian's greatest source of supply, rose other great rivers whose waters flowed northwards and added only to the quantities of superfluous ice in the Arctic? They were going to turn these rivers round, force them back into the catchment areas and tributaries of the Volga, and so make them to flow into the Caspian. I was not to doubt but that the Caspian would be restored in due course to its highest levels. Its great fish and bird life would be multiplied to their ancient prodigality, the moisture content of the desert air raised, and the rainfall itself increased. As he spoke of these rivers and what Soviet man would do with them he got in his eye what I came to call the 'river-look'. All the Russians I met had it, so predisposed were they to be river-conscious. It could be so intent on some faces, particularly those of the hydro-electricians and river experts, that it was just a little bit mad. Their voices too changed as do the voices of the Swiss when they talk about their mountains, the English about the sea, or South Africans about their veld. Both look and voice became more intense when he told me, as an example of what they could do, how they had solved the falling water problem in Sevan, the great lake of his native Armenia. This lake had been tapped and its waters released into a remarkable river, the Razdan, which fell some three thousand feet in seventy miles. As a result so many power-stations had been built on its banks that Armenia produced more electricity per head of its two million people than any country in Europe. But in their eagerness to carry out Lenin's decree 'to electrify' the engineers overreached themselves and woke up one morning to find that the level of Sevan was sinking fast. However, they soon put that right by diverting new water into the lake! There now

appeared an 'electrification' look on the Armenian's face. There
is a profound electricity mystique in the Russian soul. They believe it to be a miracle that will transform not only man's physical
being but also ensure his spiritual transformation and ultimate
salvation from evil. Accordingly I found myself thinking of a
charming story told by Vera Inber, famous as the woman poet
of Leningrad's gallant fight against Hitler. In this story she tells
of a visit paid by his grandchildren to a cultured Greek of the
old school in Odessa, a city of great cultural traditions.

'And what is your little brother's name?' the old gentleman
asked his young granddaughter when she arrived.

'Rem,' she replied.

'Ah! short for Remus,' he replied, thinking of Uncle Remus.

'Nothing of the sort,' the terrible new world child replied. 'It
stands for Revolution, Electrification and Metallurgy.'

But the new generation have long since turned their backs on
this fashion which bestowed on a child in the first red flush of
revolution any name that could evoke the new industrial and
mechanical dream. Now they draw once again exclusively on the
old traditional Russian names. But the belief in science and technology runs as deep as ever and is all the more formidable because what it has lost in prestige it has gained in intelligence.
At the same time the look on the Armenian's face and the story
of Sevan explained a memory that had stayed vividly with me.
Some time before, flying low in an unpressurized plane along the
Turkish frontier, I had had a glimpse in the twilight of his native
country Armenia. It was a fascinating sight more like an illustration out of a book of legends than a vision of contemporary
reality. The valleys were deep, long, winding and filled with the
brown tide of evening. Flanking them were peak upon peak of
mountains steep as a back-cloth for melodrama, and many an
uplifted head was wearing a citadel like a tiara gleaming in the
twilight. The land looked old and full enough of history to confirm its claim to be the land of Ur-artu, one of the oldest states in
the world which existed more than three thousand years ago.
Then, as I watched, suddenly the night had come down like a
curtain on the show. I was prepared to find the performance over
but not so, for instantly as far as I could see the darkness of
Armenia began to flash with electric light. I had just come all the

way from Tokyo and nowhere else had I seen such a display of electric lights. What was even more remarkable was that the lights ended abruptly at the frontier. In fact the electric lights were the frontier, for on the Persian and Turkish sides as far as I could see the whole land to the south was in darkness.

I told my Armenian companion this and he took it as a compliment. Like all the members of minority races of the Soviet Union he was hungry for a recognition of the special character of his own people which clearly life, as he knew it, did not give. He showed his gratitude for it now by pouring out all the information he had of the world over which we were flying. He spoke of the great fishing industry in the Caspian with its centres at Astrakhan and Baku, of mullet, sturgeon for food as well as caviare, bream, pike, skate and another species of migratory fish which spawn in the rivers and then return to the lake. Seal-fishing, he said to my astonishment, too, was an important occupation in the northern Caspian where they were caught on the ice in winter. Yes, despite the glare and the heat around us here in the southern Caspian it could be bitterly cold in the north. That part, particularly the Volga delta, was his favourite country outside Armenia. The steppes around in early summer would be covered with flowering grasses, lit by large purple-red peonies, yellow loco-weed, wild sweet-peas and white and lavender lilac. In summer you would hardly be able to hear yourself speak for the quicksilver sounds made by skylarks or the deep buzzing of the bees flying through the warm golden air, which was so heavy with scent that they seemed to move slowly fighting their way not through air so much as a rendering of their own unwaxed honey. At every delta, fork and rivermouth mile upon mile of tasselled reeds would be straining and trembling like the chords of harps with the song of wild-fowl. Here, alas! he made a gesture of distaste at the shore below, there was only this black desert for ever trying to push the blue, life-giving waters back.

We were over the Caspian by now and he pointed at the shipping converging on Krasnovodsk to show that the sea more than ever retained its ancient function as a vital waterway, today carrying not furs and pelts in exchange for silk, spice and jewels, but oil from the South in return for manufactured goods from the North. Indeed the traffic up the Volga, from Krasnovodsk to the interior, was greater than the traffic down river. After this impressive converging of sea-borne traffic the green-blue surface of the sea went blue and then almost black. Oh, my friend said, the Caspian was as full of contradictions and whims as a woman! Calm one moment as now, stormy the next with waves so high that even professional sailors were sick! First shallow and full of light, then profound and dark as now. Just where we were now, he said, half-way between two shores (both, at thirty thousand feet, nearly out of sight), the sea was more than three thousand feet deep. Soon, however, the shallows came and with them a new excitement. We saw the latest extensions of the oldest oil-field in Europe with their frontiers extending right into the sea. From the land, in a glare so great that it obscured the day, the giant derricks strode like pylons carrying power far out into the waters. My companion talked of this drilling for oil in the sea as a purely Soviet invention and something that could not happen elsewhere in the world. It was remarkable how even so educated a man seemed to be without comparative standards of a world kind. His one unfailing comparison, as with everybody else I met, was with conditions in Imperial Russia before the revolution. The fact that this method of comparison left out of account the progress that might have been made even if the Revolution had not taken place, never seemed to come to his mind. I was provoked once or twice to draw attention to the great progress made in science and social welfare in non-Communist countries without revolution. That was always dismissed as something achieved by exploitation of the 'masses'. But he was a sensitive, almost poetic observer of nature and I felt genuinely sad to part from him at Baku.

There both the land and the oil-fields looked their age. The earth for miles seemed bare, wrinkled and worn-out with time. The pumps on wells, already more than eighty years old, drew up oil from great depths, their pistons moving with the slow trance-like motion of things near the end of their days. Not even in Texas have I seen so many derricks crowded in so small a space.

Then suddenly nearer the city the earth seemed to revive. It was covered with yellow flowers, grass appeared on the dunes, trees full of light and colour came into view and the guide who had met me told me that every year more and more of the sterile earth along the Azerbaijanian shores of the Caspian, the territory of which Baku was the capital, was being redeemed. Like all the Azerbaijanians I met he was intensely proud of Baku. This was something I had not encountered yet on my journey. I had come across many other forms of pride, such as pride in the greatness of the Soviet Union and its technical achievements, but this intense metropolitan consciousness was new to me. It suggested there was a move in the spirit of man away from the Central Asian attitude and towards the West. It was significant in this regard that one of the first things this man wanted to know from me was whether Baku, as everyone in the city believed, closely resembled Naples? He took me as soon as he could therefore to an appropriate height to deliver judgement. We looked over the wide curving bay, its blue waters, busy harbour, neat well laid-out streets and broad esplanade. Alas! there was nothing Neapolitan about it that I could perceive but as I did not want to disappoint him I broke the news to him as gently as I could adding that the scene did have something of the Mediterranean about it. Later this impression became more specific and I told myself it was a continuation of something Phoenician or Carthaginian at the early classical end of the Mediterranean Sea. Indeed it was remarkable how much of a sea atmosphere lay around the shores of so land-locked a water.

My first evening there was on a Sunday and the esplanade was crowded with sailors in neat dark-blue uniforms strolling about with girls on their arms. The parks of rest and culture had more sailors in them, taking on the locals either at chess or a kind of Azerbaijanian chequers. They sat playing on the public benches, the boards on their knees and the public clustering around to comment expertly on every move. The rails of the benches themselves were painted in several different colours. The locals were touchingly proud of these as another sign of their progressiveness. Their Mayor, they said, had ordered his officials to see that there was variety of colour in Office-of-Works paintings. Too much uniformity was bad for people. I was to find that all the Mayors all over the Soviet Union had told the same thing to their appropriate officials as an all-Party decree had just been issued against uniformity in such matters. The result was that all benches all over the vast Soviet State merely became uniformly different! Whatever the colour of their benches, however, there was in the people of Baku something of the gaiety and light-heartedness which one associates with every sailor ashore. I spent an evening at the Palace of Culture of the Union of Sea-men where the girls appeared in the ballet dances buttoned up modestly to the chin with their skirts tied by elastic to their ankles as in Central Asia. Their mouths pursed, they went through one demure folk movement after the other. It was too much for the audience who no doubt had seen the same show countless times before. Soon a natural wit made a comment aloud which sent the hall shaking with laughter. A male singer who looked like Chaplin in his 'Gold Rush' days gallantly follow-ed on with a Caspian flamenco and was ironically cheered into silence.

If I had shut my eyes I could have believed myself among an audience in Marseilles or Port Vendres. It was all fresh revelation of a phenomenon that has never ceased to astonish me and one which our highly rationalized conceptions of history do not suffi-ciently take into account: the existence despite what we call history of a special Mediterranean world. The beginnings of this world are as remote as they are mysterious, its tenacity un-believable, and its present-day validity even greater than many of us realize. Although it has no institutions to perpetuate it and its inheritance has been divided and parcelled out between many nations and cultures, deep down in the spirit of all those who have possessed themselves of a share the ancient fragments re-discover their aboriginal affinities and from the Pillars of Hercules to the Hellespont, Constantinople, the plains of Troy, Mount Cassius, the Levant, Alexandria and Tangier, the fragments re-unite to create a unified temperament and attitude to life. The result is that whether he calls himself Greek, Turk, Levantine, Arab, Tunisian, Spanish, Provençal, Italian or Dalmatian, there is in existence in our midst someone who makes sense only when conceived of as Mediterranean man. Consciously and in every demonstrable way this south-west shore of the Caspian was part of the Soviet Union but there was no doubt in my mind that by instinct and intuition its loyalties were slanted the Mediterranean way. I met repeatedly a largeness of gesture and personality that made me think of the land of Marius far more than anything

Russian or Asian. The essence of the man of this world, as I knew him, was his absolute commitment to his belief in beauty of gesture. Morality was not a sense of Puritan or Old Testament rules but an extension of a sense of beauty, inner aesthetics becoming outer behaviour. Rags and tatters did not bother him. Only the figure he cut in his own spirit was important; he could only be poor if that figure were ugly or mean. In fact royalty was implicit in the man and just as I had learnt in Mediterranean Spain not to admire too emphatically anything in the homes of my Spanish friends because often they would immediately give it me, so I had to learn here to be careful even in asking the way for not only would many people insist on going to great trouble to take me to my destination themselves but possibly put me in the appropriate street-car and try to pay my fare for me! This happened once coming back late at night from the Palace of Culture when a begrimed workman half asleep with fatigue in a tram roused himself to take me back to my hotel at his own expense.

Finally there was this 'city-consciousness' of the people. Mediterranean man is pledged in his deepest self to a city with access somewhere to the sea. Not the countries so much as the power and glory of the cities of his world still bewilder and amaze our imaginations. Crete, Troy, Carthage, Athens, Rome, Constantinople, Alexandria, Venice or Marseilles stand firm in the centre and splendour of the earliest Mediterranean dawn. Baku in a modest way preserved something of this tradition. And to add to this sense of the past the waiters at my hotel now addressed me in French. I would sit there in a window looking over the broad bay and watching with envy the fat Caspian steamers sail out for Astrakhan, Balykshi, Krasnovodsk and other parts of Russia to which I was denied access, and have long discussions with the *maître d'hôtel* about French literature, Flaubert was his favourite author and *Salambo* not *Madame Bovary* his favourite novel. The historical novels about the ancient Mediterranean world were his preference he told me with animation and many a colourful gesture. The tide of individual temperament for which I had listened in vain on this long journey was now active and audible in him and others. There was a sea within as well as one without: and this was not a bad preparation for Georgia.

In terms of human history Armenia and Georgia are old yet in geological time they are young. The fantastic piles of mountains that dominate the scene in both countries are not worn down by ice-ages and the long winds of time as are the gentle Urals of Russia, but are freshly arrogant with youth, their lines as clear-cut and definite as that of any chain in the precise though smaller ranges of Japan. I got to know these mountains well from the floor of their deep long winding valleys for I went up them as far as the roads would allow and always the scale was immense. Only from the air did one see them as a college of apprentices to the master Himalayas, soaring out of the earth not yet fully qualified, but ambitious and aspiring. The summits of Elbruz and Kazbek alone are awe-inspiring enough and at first glance explain the intense personification they have demanded in Mediterranean myth and legend. Prometheus was bound in chains of the imagination to the former: and the valleys that both mountains shelter have been protected by dragons and selected as keepers of the Golden Fleece. Human time is so much more brief than geological time that the first impact of this dramatic land on our imaginations inevitably had to be mythological. Indeed the first link between pagan myth and Christian tradition is the identification of it as the Old Testament land of Japhet. But however brief the human contact with this land much of its lofty drama seems already prescribed in the heart of the man.

My first impression of the crowded airport lounges, both V.I.P. and public, at Tbilisi, the capital of Georgia (as the 1,500-year-old city of Tiflis is now called) was that the men in it were taller than any I had yet met and the women too were taller and straighter. Both sexes appeared refreshingly unselfconscious and looked one straight and boldly in the eye. The voices of the men were as deep as their valleys and as animated as their rivers and they talked, laughed and joked incessantly making such a din that even the noise of aircraft starting up on the busy runway outside was sub-dued. The tide of temperament of which I have spoken here moved in the sound of authentic high seas swelling and making urgently for the shore.

'Oh, these Georgians!' the Russian who was with me ex-claimed with the sort of reluctant affection with which the British serviceman in India used to speak of the Pathans on the north-west frontier: 'They are so impetuous! You know we always like to have them as guards on our railway bridges and other important public installations. They will call "Halt" only once to people approaching. If the people do not stop immediately then they'll shoot them down at once. But as for us Russians, if we are put on the job it takes us a year of warnings before we shoot!'

I had been in Georgia only a moment yet I understood him, partly because I was not wholly unprepared for the idea. During the war on my long march into Abyssinia to outflank the Italian lines, one of the officers who accompanied me, W. E. D. Allen, had told me a great deal about Georgia. He has written perhaps the best English work on the history of people and Georgia. He had spoken of them as the people nearest to the Irish in temperament and had used a phrase that came back to me now: 'the aesthetic irresponsibility of the Georgians'. One night while the lions were roaring round our camp I also remember Allen saying that the Georgians and the Irish were the only people who ever fully realized the positive creative uses of irresponsibility. They refused to take their conquest and conquerors seriously. They would fight their invaders savagely not for any principle but out of sheer love of life. Yet once forced to yield, in contrast to their dour and dogmatic neighbours the Armenians who merely got themselves repeatedly massacred for their love and stubbornness of principle, the Georgians behaved as if nothing really important had happened to them. They remained their laughing, gay, unchanging and unchanged selves not stopping for a moment to confer dignity on their conquerors by treating the conquest seriously. Logically, out of this attitude, as with the Irish, grew a certain disdain of forethought and prudence and although many an alien creed and system came and went the Georgian and his quicksilver temperament remained.

I stress this at some length here because it not only shows how much nearer I had drawn to the Mediterranean world of our origins but because, henceforth, I was to find that all the minority peoples who have been bound to Russia either as an integral part of the Soviet Union, or as satellites, had evolved techniques of their own for denying their conquerors. What seemed to me most important was that within the limits of their own temperament and national character all these peoples, Bulgars, Roumanians, Czechs, Hungarians, Poles, Latvians, Moldavians, Esthonians and even the Ukrainians of little Russia, have in all the years of invasion and persecution acquired techniques for preventing conquest and political domination from penetrating their own spirit or, as it were, reaching their individual souls. Some of those techniques differ widely. The Polish reaction, for instance, unlike the Georgian, comes from an almost unbelievable sense of national and moral responsibility and a daily routine of personal courage applied to a degree unequalled in the history of Europe. But the awareness of the existence of these profound mechanisms among all peoples for protecting their quintessential self seems to me indispensible for any long-term assessment of the future of Communism and Western man. Neither British nor Americans any longer can remember what it means to be invaded and conquered so long ago is it since the experience. Consequently they are in danger of underating what they have and the value of what they are. Coming from a conquered race myself I was alarmed during the war lest in defeat the British might no longer know how to deal in their spirit with conquest and so be unable to find their way back to being their true selves. Today I think I did Britain an injustice. But I am certain the fact still needs stressing to both British and Americans because of an inborn imperviousness that both nations have to the qualities of these subjugated peoples and to the value of their contribution to life. Perhaps the most telling illustration of this was an encounter that I had one night back in Tashkent with a member of an important Roumanian delegation housed in my hotel. He had dined and wined well and finding I spoke French stayed with me until, as in all hotels all over the Soviet Union, promptly at midnight the lights were extinguished. Then he made his point with characteristic national indiscretion: 'Ah, *mon cher*, this Russian affair with my country is but an incident, a trifle in our history! It will make no difference in the end. We've been through such things many times before and emerged ourselves again. Mark my words we'll do so one day again – and perhaps, sooner than you all expect.'

Beside him, above all beside the Georgians, the exiled Russians looked a melancholy, dour and colourless bunch. I could not help

feeling profoundly sorry for them and I was to feel this with increasing intensity. Yet I never felt sorry for the Georgians. There
was a certain envy implicit in the Russian regard for their minorities. Hearing them talk of Bucharest and Prague, I was to realize
that they might even be jealous of them however much their
Marxist conscious selves reassured them of their superiority.
Perhaps part of them longed too to be individualistic in the
Roumanian, Georgian or Bohemian way. One of our greatest
fallacies is to assume that power influences only the powerless.
Actually powerlessness has not only its own secret defences but
also its own subterranean accesses into the hearts of the powerful. It is two-way traffic of the most subtle kind. All the change
that is being wrought by the Russians on the great varieties of
peoples and cultures on which they have imposed their iron will
implies that the Russians themselves inevitably must change even
as Imperial Rome was changed by its conquests. I never realized
this more clearly than I did on this journey. There are ways of
losing that can be conquest: there are ways of gaining that are
loss. The only conquest that is ever valid is conquest by living
example. As Shakespeare says in the *Rape of Lucrece*, any other
form of it is bound merely to 'Prove bankrupt in their poor-
rich gain.'

Meanwhile I enjoyed myself hugely in Tbilisi and the country
round about. There the Mediterranean mood of which I had a
whiff in Baku was all-pervasive. In the evenings the people of the
capital would come out on the pavements and walk up and down to
enjoy the spring air talking, arguing, teasing and occasionally
quarrelling with one another, then darting into the nearest café for
a glass of reconciliation. Their reflexes, unlike the Russian, were
entirely unconditioned. They appeared unpredictable but in their
personal relationships they were never neutral. They had too this
sense of inner royalty (actually, I was told, many of them claimed
to be princes: one census a generation ago put their proportion as
high as one in seven). Almost all had style and wore their clothes
with an individual elegance which overcame the mass-productive
patterns. I saw many young people of both sexes who dressed just
as their age groups did in Chelsea. No matter how policed the
State, fashion and style were paraded in Tbilisi and this consciousness of dress and style goes back a long way. Du Bois de Mont-

périeux states that in 1839 he counted in Tbilisi 126 tailors, 104 bootmakers, forty barbers, four master goldsmiths, five clockmakers, sixteen painters and eighteen Balalaika players!

Finally for me the Mediterranean element was agreeably plain in the building of the city itself. Although modernized the houses with their tiled roofs, terraces and balconies remained Georgian. Strung along both banks of the deep Kura River they formed a city not squat and square but elegant, individually motivated and varied. Moreover for the first time here were churches with spires and bells. Ever since the third century Georgia has been Christian and the battles it has fought for Christianity are as tenacious and heroic as any in history. In fact not only in the capital but out in the countryside, either in superb fragments or restored as historical monuments by the indefatigable Soviet department of archaeology churches, monasteries and Christian fortresses still cover river and ford and hillock. All bear marks of the tides of violence and invasion which constantly submerge them. These marks are plainer still in the shattering impact on the peoples who were caught in them and who still inhabit the high land. Though the main population here is Georgian, hidden in deep valleys or on mountain meadows are remnants of fierce tribes like the Chechen, Ingushi and Kabardinian. Only twelve years ago the Ingushi were still reported to be skirmishing with the Russians and they still go their ancient chivalrous way in the mountain recesses, dressed in doublets covered with embroidered crosses, puffed sleeves with silver buttons, woollen stockings, leather sandals and dark hair cut in monks' fringes. Up there there are also two villages of Caucasian negroes and a single village belonging to a tribe called Ginukh, who though only 200 strong, maintains a separate identity. Some of these fragments of once powerful races made the mistake of sympathizing with the Germans in the last war in the hope of regaining their independence. They were made to pay dearly for their error by Stalin (or Joseph Djugashvili) himself a Georgian and once a student of orthodox Georgian theology and still so much the 'local boy who has made good' that there were violent riots in Tbilisi and other towns when the Party started denouncing him and undoing his handiwork. However, Stalin banished the guilty peoples to Central Asia and Siberia and only now are broken remnants of them beginning to reappear among their native mountains. The one thing in common between all these gallant survivors of history seems to be a profound code of personal honour. The Abkhazians, who after the Georgians are the largest racial group of this region, have a special word for it. They call it '*alamys*' and the concept is still so real to them that while I was in Georgia I found stories still being written about it and one of the foremost national writers, Mikhail Lakerbai, has written several. Lakerbai tells, for instance, a true story of a young girl who found that she was going incurably blind. Feeling unable to be nothing but a burden to her family she put on trousers and threw herself under a train. When the body was being laid out by the women of her family they found that beneath the trousers she had put on her whitest and finest underclothing.

'But why?' Lakerbai asked the man who told him.

'Alamys,' was the answer. 'Alamys. She thought that in running over her the train would leave her naked. So to avoid that she put on trousers. You see, alamys is stronger than death.'

For me nothing is more moving in men and their societies than their obedience to the demand of honour and to the realization that life without honour loses its meaning. I longed therefore to go deeper into the mountains and see more of these gallant peoples. Alas! I was told it was impossible. The excuses varied from declarations that the roads were still blocked by snow and avalanches, to protestations that there were no hotels, inns or other accommodation. So the best I could do was to go some eighty miles by car along the great Georgian military highway into the mountains. The beauty and variety of the scene were great. As the sea moves us by its sameness so did the desert behind me by the constant reiteration of its single truth which was like a solitary phrase of illumination repeated endlessly in Buddhist prayer. But these mountains and valleys moved me by their infinite variety. In the valleys themselves already it was spring; wheat, barley, oats were sprouting green, their blades precise and erect in the dark earth. Peach, apple, cherry, apricot and plum were in flower and against the giant mountains the blossom looked poignantly delicate and tender, clinging like smoking rainbow vapour to the trees. Cattle, fine-drawn by winter, grazed up to their ankles in new grass, and from time to time we met flocks of sheep feeling their way towards the mountains to follow closely the retreat of snow from the rich, high summer pastures. Some of their shepherds wore Caucasian tunics down to their knees, daggers at their belts, silver clasped cartridge cases on their chests, soft high-boots and bashlyks or capes flung back like a challenge over their shoulders. Many were exceedingly tall and watching them stride towards a distant flock of sheep, a long stave like a spear in hand and a high hat like a helmet on their heads, they reminded me of one of Daumier's studies of the elongated knights of La Mancha.

Sometimes I would get out of the cab to examine a church or ruins, and always I was amazed at the richness of the past that remained in them and the deep imprint of Byzantine mosaic and frescoes left on the crumbling walls. A ford that Roman legions used to cross was pointed out to me, and also a road followed by Pompey the Great.

At Mtzkhet, which was the capital of Georgia until the fifth century, sheep were grazing in the precincts of the Cathedral, which was built on the site of a miraculous tree said to have gushed oil when struck by St Nina. The Cathedral, despite the sheep, was still in use and people still gather on Sundays to worship around the tombs of the ancient kings of Georgia. This fact, combined with what I had seen of the character of the peoples, contrasted sharply with the impression received at Gori forty miles on. We stopped at Gori because I was anxious to see the museum which had been made of Stalin's birthplace. Though this museum became one of the most sacred shrines in Russia and Stalin in physical terms was more powerful than any Georgian monarch, already it was out of grace and favour. In Stalin's day indeed the attraction of the museum and his cobbler father's house and workshop was so great that an enormous hotel was built in the vicinity to cope with the numbers of devout Communist pilgrims and tourists who visited it. Now the portentous hotel was empty, dank and gloomy. The museum and Stalin's home were both shut, it was said, for repairs. There in his birthplace in the land where fierce and stubborn loyalties might have been active to preserve his memory it seemed the last fatal indignity, and proof of how brittle authority can be even in so powerful a system as that of the Soviet Union.

I had four people with me, a dashing Georgian chauffeur who drove the car as if it were a Roman chariot going into action, a sensitive young Russian student of English, and two spirited young Georgian women both apparently experts on local history, and since the hotel restaurant in Gori was closed I asked if we could not find some simple café in a village somewhere in the mountains where we could eat?

All four of them laughed heartily at my question because it appeared that there were no such things as cafés in the villages nearby and even if there were what kind of people did I think their villagers were that they could fall so low as to allow a visitor to eat in a café? No, they would take me to a collective farm in the hills where we would be more than welcome. Then they were all four suddenly grave and the Russian student spoke for them. Before we went would I mind if they asked something of me? Please, when we got to the collective farm, would I break my habit and not decline to drink with the people there?

I replied that much as I loved wine, ever since my years of famine in a Japanese prison it had disagreed with me. Besides, I added, their own leaders disapproved of drinking. I quoted Mr Khrushchev who had just delivered a picturesque tirade against drinks of all kinds.

They all looked most depressed until I quoted Mr Khrushchev. Then they combined to dismiss his opinion with disdainful sniggers and assured me no Georgian would understand a guest not drinking with him and would be deeply offended and hurt. In fact they would not dare take me to the village they had in mind unless I promised to drink.

'Very well then,' I said, 'I will drink.'

At this the girls clapped their hands with delight and the driver, his eyes eager, swung the car from the military highway and made for the mountains as fast as possible.

'They will probably offer you a cow's horn full of wine,' the young Russian said reminding me of a South African explaining a Zulu custom to a visitor from abroad. 'If you can drink that down in one draught you will achieve great honour and our day will be made! And do not worry, I have a good head. I'll see you home!'

I was spared the Georgian horn-of-plenty. Indeed for some hours it looked as if we would be lucky if we got anything at all to eat or drink while we waited in vain for the chairman of the collective farm to join us in the committee room of his village. From the windows of the room I had a good view over the valley and the huge collective estate. It consisted of almost every form of farming, arable, livestock, fruit and vineyards. Poised high on the slopes of the foothills of the Caucasus the village at the centre of the estate was an attractive cluster of rust-red roofed houses. Most of these were built over huge cellars, had steps of stone or wood leading to a cased-in veranda on the second floor, and were surrounded by orchards, pig-sties, fowl-runs and gardens. Water ran briskly along furrows on either side of the main street and when I leaned out of the window this added a glassy tinkle to the sound of bees lost in the rainbow spray of blossom over the orchards and the songs of larks rounding the blue sky to drop, as George Meredith wrote, their 'silver chain of sound'. Occasionally, the bleat of a sheep or mooing of a cow threw a note of deep concern into the heart of the busy sound. Large white geese and fat ducks waddled about the street like aldermen or lay in puddles with an oddly proprietorial air, while from far above a head of snow looked down over the bar of silver where the foothills ran out into the blue. The snow looked oddly alive, as if it were the head of a large white bear warily watching the stealthy upward climb of the green. From time to time a horseman in Circassian habit would come clattering down from the heights on a pony with a long mane and tail that seemed to touch the ground. The pony seemed to be two sizes too small for the rider yet it travelled the ground with a quick step and a spirit that seemed to be in the sinews and breath of the land itself.

I had just about given up hope when at last the chairman arrived. He, too, was a big man but obviously Russian. He was dressed like all State and collective farm dignitaries in regulation blue knee-breeches, with black leather jack-boots, and a blue tunic tied with a belt round the middle. He threw a faded blue cap on a chair, sat down at the head of a table with a plush cloth on it, threw off a sigh as big as himself and apologized handsomely for the delay. Like all heads of farms that I had met and was to meet, he looked tired and exceedingly worried. Yet his physical stamina was undiminished by the cares of his function, for he took me round his complex and extraordinarily mixed farm (I am tempted to say mixed-up farm) with great speed. When that was done he conducted us to a house in the village which belonged to one of his farmers. On the way we passed the single room that served as a farm school. It was full of children who looked not as if they were taking instruction but listening to a fairy tale. This enchantment with education of people, children, teachers and leaders everywhere runs like a thread of gold through my impressions of the Soviet Union. We passed the farm shop filled with so spartan a stock that it made the lowly native trading-stores of Africa glow like palaces in my memory.

I am certain the farmer's household had been given no notice of our coming for when the farmer's wife and daughter, who were washing their linen, saw us walk into the yard they were genuinely startled. They immediately sent a young man who was pitching manure to run into the fields for the father, and themselves conducted us up the steps into their house. We went through the closed-in veranda, where in the corners stood two brass bedsteads covered with spotless white knitted covers and the metal gleaming like burnished gold, on into the small living-room where some hard chairs were set round a table. Here two more brass bedsteads were ranged against the walls and through a doorway leading into the only other room I saw two more beds. On the walls were two portraits set in red plush within wooden frames of two sons killed in action in the last war. Between the beds was a smaller table with a combined radio and gramophone upon it. Both doorways and windows had white lace curtains over them. I knew of no farm labourer's cottage in Britain as small and as austere as this farmhouse, but also I know of none more princely in its atmosphere.

The moment my Russian companion saw the radiogram he went to it, examining the records, and without asking our hosts' permission selected one and began playing it. Wherever I went in the Soviet Union this was done without exception, so drawing my attention to one of the great status symbols of the Soviet citizen and proof of progressive well-being. In the same way and for the same reason on the few occasions that we came across refrigerators they were opened and looked into ostentatiously by my guides. Refrigerators indeed were in a class all their own and I was touched to see how even in Moscow itself in the most modern hotels they were proudly displayed in a position of honour in the dining-rooms where no one could fail to notice them. But there was another aspect of the incident which seemed to me to be more significant. It seemed to be part of the deep collective instinct in the Russian character, an instinct which existed long before Marxist ideology was thought of and which is a part of their sense of belonging to one another. When I saw this young Russian turning on the gramophone and our hostess and her daughter responding delightedly it reminded me of the Stone Age people I know in Africa. Once when short of food I had offered to divide up what little we had amongst the community. However, these people had looked at me and said: 'Do so if you wish but why bother? If one has everybody has; if one eats everybody eats.' And the deeper I went into Russia the more pronounced this trait became. Here on this Georgian collective farm the reaction of our hosts could still be explained as part of the boundless hospitality and abundance of Georgian character. But all Russians, by nature, are not in any way less hospitable.

In the absence of our host the chairman took command of the table. We had hardly sat down when half a dozen glass beakers full of rose-pink wine just drawn from the cellar below us were placed on the table. Platters of black bread, smoked garlic sausages, cheese, crushed walnuts wrapped in a flour and honey paste, thirty hard-boiled eggs, and bowls of curds and whey quickly followed one another. Outside the sound of a chopper at work on wood in the yard and the continuous noise in the kitchen indicated that the mountain of food and wine on the table was merely the *hors d'oeuvres*. Empty as my stomach was it contracted with some alarm at these indications of what was to be expected of it. Not so my hosts and companions. Relish of the feast ahead had brought colour to the cheeks of the women and the eyes of the men were bright with the fever of their hospitality. When the daughter of the house appeared breathless with some spotless but thread-worn hand-towels and a cake of hard blue soap, they seized on them eagerly. Back again, we went into the yard. Propped against a fence stood a cracked basin. Warm water was poured into it and I was forced to be the first to wash in it. We had hardly got into the living-room when the farmer himself arrived, breathless. He was a small man, one of the few small men I saw in Georgia. He had lost an eye in the war, been wounded seven times and clearly still suffered physically if not mentally from what he had endured. He was dressed in the cheapest of working cottons and yet after the first meeting I noticed neither his appearance nor scars and disfigurements so illuminated did he appear to be by the dignity of the courage with which life had invested him.

The moment he was seated the chairman rose to his feet. Towering over us all, his arms waving like the flails of a windmill to stress his words, he began the toasting. The first toast was to the peace of the world. He emptied a tumbler full of wine in one long gulp, so did the others. I had one modest gulp which left my glass seven-eighths full.

'*Do dna*! *Do dna*! To the bottom! To the bottom!' they all shouted at me.

'Look you, Tovarich,' the chairman said. 'Could there be a more important toast than the peace of the world? Well then: *do dna*!'

Do dna it was. I seized eagerly some bread and cheese anxious to lay a solid foundation to the elemental swilling that was inevitably to be my lot but I had not taken a bite before the chairman was on his feet again. This time he drank to the friendship between the British and Soviet peoples: It was always 'peoples' in the Russian mind. Not once did I hear a toast of friendship between Britain and the Soviet Union or America and Russia. I tried a modest swallow but again the chairman asked with unanswerable rhetoric if friendship between our peoples were not important? Well, if so then, *do dna*. Again I had to drink up all the wine in my glass. This was followed by toasts to friendship with the 'peoples' of the United States, the State and collective farmers of both Britain and America, all proposed in such quick succession that I could not have explained, even if I had wanted to, that as far as my country was concerned we were drinking to a farmer who did not exist. We then drank to my wife. Seeing that I had only sipped at my glass I was asked if I did not love her? I '*do-dna*-ed' it all over again. I was trapped and all I could do to reinsure myself against the future was to eat as much and as fast as I could. Yet I hated giving up without a last effort. So I got up and proposed the health of our host and family thinking I could surely command the volume of liquid I swallowed in a toast of my own. Not a bit of it. I was promptly told that two thousand years of tradition compelled a proposer of a toast to establish its sincerity by draining his glass. Then I gave up and prepared to relax and enjoy it. The change in my attitude was at once obvious to the rest of the table and when, without prompting, I drained my glass at the next toast the young women present clapped their hands, the men roared applause and our hostess appeared in the doorway to smile the first smile I had seen since I left London. From that moment the pressure of toasts grew slightly less and I found a certain calm and sobriety in the midst of the fierce storm of hospitality rather as a ship does when it has given up trying to sail against the gale and turned to run before it.

I was helped in this by the fact that at this moment the chairman chose to make a speech about his collective farm. He spoke, characteristically, not about his farm in the present but in the future. He was brimful of what the farm was going to achieve in the years ahead and the plans within the wider Soviet plans that he had for it. He concluded by saying that of all his farmer-workers our host was one of the best. In fact our host had no less than 246 out of a possible 365 labour days on the collective farm to his credit. He therefore thanked him on behalf of all the people of the Soviet Union for his example. Stooping down he drew the battle-scarred little man to him and kissed him full on the lips before we drained another glass.

What did our host do with the time that he did not give to the collective farm? I asked the chairman, anxious to keep him talking rather than toasting and drinking.

That was simple, he replied, he devoted his time to his own private holding and stock. Though our host made a good living out of the money he received from the collective farm those profits were divided between all workers according to the number of days worked. But our host could also increase his income greatly by selling his own produce.

'Where does he sell it?' I asked.

'Have you not been to the open market in Tbilisi?' he exclaimed, surprised.

'Yes,' I told him. 'I spent an afternoon there and was much impressed by the lively bargaining that went on between producers and consumers!'

'Who got the best of it?' he asked, his shrewd eyes creased at the corners ready for a laugh.

'The producers, I think,' I answered.

He roared with laughter, slapped me affectionately on the shoulder and remarked: 'No one can ever get the better of these chaps, I do not mind who it is. Not even . . .' He broke off suddenly as if he feared he was about to be indiscreet and turned to our host exclaiming: 'That's so, isn't it? No one knows better how to drive a bargain than you!'

Meanwhile more and more food appeared on the table, deep bowls of mutton and potato soup, fried chicken, delicious young cucumbers cut unpeeled in slices covered with sour-cream, and the fiery Georgian dish, Shaslyk, wood-spiced grilled cubes of mutton on skewers which, with that young wine fresh and innocent as the spring air outside, tasted succulent. Yet good as it all was I noticed that my Russian companion enjoyed nothing so much as the bread, and watching him I realized that all Russians seemed to eat bread as if the very eating of it gives them a kind of reassurance. Bread has always been the main Russian food and rarely have the Russians been able to be certain that there would be enough of it. The history of the frequent famines in Russia makes the grimmest of reading. There have been several under the Soviet régime; the war years were all lean years; and even after the war for years few Russians had enough to eat. The young Russian whom I was watching had told me moving stories of how he himself had had little to eat as a child and how he was taught that it was sinful to leave as much as a crumb on his plate, and how his mother had kept him alive only by setting out every morning at dawn to collect potatoes or potato peelings and other scraps from the farms, returning only at sunset to keep him alive with such meagre gleanings.

Talking of this had given him a personal emotion. Putting his hand on his heart he had exclaimed: 'I do not know how it is in your country but it is for these reasons that we Russians so love and respect our parents. When, as I have done, you have seen your father fighting for his country and your mother labouring and sacrificing herself to feed you you are just filled with love and gratitude.'

Every bite of the black bread baked out of corn grown in the war-weary black soil of Russia was a defeat of the terrible history within him and a reassurance against the uncertain future. And what applied to him in this regard applied, I think, to all Russians I met. They all ate far more bread than was necessary; and produced also a greater variety of breads than any people I have ever known. I saw shops in the great cities where in order to cope with this craving they sold more than a hundred kinds of bread of every texture, from white to nigger-brown and midnight black, from snowy puffs of twist-bread to poppyseed rolls and grey Minsk pistolets. But nothing ever equalled the black bread that was meal and reassurance enough in itself. No matter how tempting, varied and abundant the dish on the table, the hands of the Russians present would all first reach for bread. I never got used to the sight and it never failed to move me because the whole terrible past of the land seemed to me to preside over the act. Indeed despite the wine and the Georgian laughter, the sight of this young man's hand repeatedly reaching for the bread like that of a somnambulist feeling for support of the wall of some long winding corridor of time made a deep impression on me and I told myself that I should always remember it.

I was plucked out of this line of thought by the Georgian girl next to me suddenly asking as if it were a matter of urgent and universal importance: 'Are there many bed-bugs in England?'

'No,' I answered disconcerted.

'Are there perhaps a few?' she insisted, her dark Georgian eyes large and shapely like those of a Byzantine Madonna, now bright with curiosity.

'There may be but I have never seen any,' I replied, thinking bed-bugs must be a problem in her and other Soviet lives.

'Why is that?'

'Perhaps because the English are a fairly hygienic people,' I said.

'More hygienic than us?'

At this, assailed by all the experiences I had had of wayside sanitation in the provinces and not least of all the appalling arrangements on the collective farm, I did not see how I was going to answer her truthfully without giving offence.

I was saved by the other girl tugging at my arm and saying appealingly: 'Please, the Comrade Chairman has asked you twice to drink to the strengthening of the bonds between all the agronomists of Britain and the Soviet Union.'

For once I was delighted to comply but my glass was hardly on the table when the Georgian girl was at it again, saying: 'I do not understand about bed-bugs and hygiene, please . . .'

Once more I was saved by her companion's intervention. The Comrade Chairman had just proposed a toast to the strengthening of bonds between the 'zoo-technicians' of Britain and the Soviet Union.

I rose to confirm this in such a rush of anxiety to escape from my female questioner that to my horror I heard myself saying distinctly: 'I drink to the bed-bug technicians of Britain and the Soviet Union.'

Luckily no one noticed the slip! I sat down and warned by the look in my interlocutor's flashing eyes I decided to take over the questioning in order to defend myself.

'Are you married?' I asked.

At once she shook her head and became very sad.

'Then you must be engaged?' I insisted.

Again she shook her head and became sadder still. Her voice dropped to a whisper. It was all her fault, she said. She did not like the attitude of men to women in Georgia. She did not want to have her marriage arranged for her. Her voice dropped lower. . . . Did I think a man from England could ever want to marry her?

I said I was certain England was full of young men who would be happy and proud to marry her if they had the choice.

Well then, she beseeched me, could I get someone from England to marry her? She was really very unhappy in her life in her native country. It was a man's not a woman's country.

It didn't seem to be my lucky day. However, I said lightly: 'You will have to give me some idea of the kind of man you have in mind. Then I can pass the news around on my return.'

She brightened. 'First of all,' she said, 'he must be tall.'

I nodded. It made sense that the image of man in a Georgian woman's heart would need to be tall.

'Secondly,' she went on confidently, 'he must be someone rather like Fidel Castro.'

Whatever one may think and feel about Castro I would hardly have picked on him as a symbol of sex-appeal so, amazed, I asked her why?

She replied at once. 'He is tall. He is a fighter. He is against injustice. He is energetic and gets things done.'

I could have reasoned with her over her dubious example but the Comrade Chairman had just proffered a toast of 'all the farm-workers of Britain, America, the Soviet Union and indeed all the world'. Hard on that he asked if I would join him in a toast to a great English writer? He asked it with a sudden diffidence that was most striking in so big and assertive a personality, a rather touching revelation of the awe that culture evoked in him and his people. Would we, he now pleaded, his rough-hewn face suddenly young with shyness, would we all please drink to Jack London?

It is the last toast of any significance that stays in my memory. Not long after, with honour satisfied or so my Russian companion assured me, we were once again in our car outside the house with the chairman, our host and family and a collection of curious neighbours waving and calling: 'Please come again, come again soon.'

The car seemed to shoot off from dead stop into instant flight like an arrow from a bow. I had a vision of white ducks and geese fleeing before us like eiderdown on a gale. We drove straight into a sunset that turned the sky into a flaming Byzantine Cathedral and it says a great deal for the wine capacity of Georgians that our chauffeur, despite the speed, was able to drive us back without accident. It says even more for the honesty of the wines of Georgia that my step on arrival was steady. But remembering that in Russia the Russians dispensed the same uninhibited hospitality not only with wine but also with vodka, I resolved never to do anything of the same sort again. And I think in the light of what does happen sometimes to foreigners who drink too much in the Soviet Union, this was a wise decision.

CHAPTER SEVEN

DELEGATION COUNTRY

A DAY or two later I came to the other Georgia, the Georgia beyond the mountains which stretches along the Black Sea coast. Coming down through the pass and the broad valley in which the airport of Adler lies it was difficult to relate the one with the other. Away to the north the mountains were purple and the snow yellow with distance like a travel-stained polar bear. But here running down to the sea they shook themselves free of snow and of all association with Himalayas and Alps. The air became moist and mild and a mixture of subtropical and temperate vegetation between the sharp slopes and the sea became as bewildering as it was fecund and tall. Pines, oaks, birches, elms, box-trees, ilexes and cedars, their trunks hidden behind giant ferns, their branches hung with fat creepers and their heads in the clouds, fought one another for position on the mountain sides. Large aeroplanes passed continually overhead and appeared to be landing at the rate of one every five minutes. Helicopters filled with passengers too important and too impatient to travel by road roared between the airport and the Black Sea resort. The roads themselves were crowded with the familiar green trucks but now for the first time private cars appeared in noticeable numbers. The feeling of history entrusted to the land behind one vanished from the world of man. This world was new and all the more brash because of the contrasting impression made by the Black Sea and its steep coastline. Near the flat steaming sea, the earth, with vineyards and flowering trees hanging on to the crowded slopes, palms on the waterfront, lilies in pools and cypresses standing above them, expressed the dreams of other and vanished men. Those cypresses, their tips flickering like candle-flames in a draught, were at the centre of this irresistible evocation of the past. Cypresses have always gleamed in my imagination like light at the end of a long tunnel perhaps because they may have been the first tree chosen by men to accompany them on their long and enigmatic journey through time. The scent of cypresses after rain is a smell translated and made aromatic in a way that not even the frankincense, myrrh and arboussiers of the antique world can excel. No matter where they grow, in Southern Africa, on the hills behind Golgotha, in Greece or Etruria, cypresses bring with them a sense of dedication out of the earth. For this reason I suspect the Italian primitives loved to insert them in the background of their portrayals of annunciation, birth, crucifixion and resurrection, if thereby they could bear witness in reverence to revelation. Even D. H. Lawrence and van Gogh, both modern artists with a heightened perception of man not as an egotistical fragment isolated by the contemporary *hubris* of rationalism but linked and interdependent in awareness with all living and existing things, have recognized the claims of the cypress on their senses. I myself had thought that no cypresses could equal the two growing by the entrance to my own home on the highlands of Africa, the male sixty and the female fifty feet high and both throwing long, swaying flame-shadows on the blood-red earth. But now, along the Black Sea coast, I saw hundreds of miles of cypresses that were much taller than my two childhood friends and fired with such passion that they made tallow of the earth. And since spring was pouring in, all around them grew white and purple lilac and mimosa, each bud a tiny explosion marked by a puff of yellow smoke until whole slopes appeared invested by the advance infantry of summer. Then there were flowering eucalyptuses, white and gold acacias and occasionally a magnolia tree, its moon-colour laid on as thick and smooth as the finest Chinese lacquer and its leaves fat with green. Finally, with a particularly haunting blaze of its own, a ghost bright enough to walk by day, there grew the Judas tree. The cypress and the Judas tree, visually poles apart, were yet joined by the invisible axis of a spinning sphere of meaning. I watched them growing side by side from Gagri to Sochi, and so on to Yalta, and I marvelled at the precision with which myth, legend and art had used them both. One seemed born to dedication whereas the other appeared ready-made for deception; a flower of evil with a fatal sea-siren beauty of its own. This strip of Black Sea earth was so busy growing things that at moments, away from the noise of trucks and aeroplanes, I thought I could hear the vegetable traffic hiss like a furnace at my ears. But perhaps the most dramatic sight of all were the deep, gaunt gorges, trees peering over the rim and basins filled with blazing water from the snows and glaciers of the mountains. They would widen at the mouth allowing the vineyards to come down from the hills and to lie broadly between sparkling olives and mauve fig trees. Here one could not fail to think of the Mediterranean and the Romans, Tartars, Turks and Russians who had fought one another for centuries for the land and its passes which linked both east and west. Though the new Russia seemed to have claimed it all for good the Mediterranean in some strange way was still in possession. Whenever I looked at the dark sea I found myself thinking of the black ships of Greece. Whenever I looked at the land and saw one slow curve after another drawing a thin line of silver surf between the fuming dark water and the high mountains hovering ash-blue behind the veiled sea vapour, I thought of the Scythian hordes of Herodotus and other vivid pagan tribes some of whom had fought on the plains of Troy. The further west I went the stronger this impression became until in the Crimea I found the vanished Greek colonies who joined nature in shape as well as mind. The Black Sea is a kind of Siamese twin to the Mediterranean and is still so remembered through the place names that not even Stalin was tempted to change them. For instance, Yalta is derived from the Greek for 'beach'; Alupka from the Greek for 'fox-holes'; and Livadia from that for 'meadow'.

The Russians themselves have been so impressed by all this extraordinary richness of their vegetable kingdom on the Black Sea that at Sochi they have a fully qualified agronomist as head of their tourist bureau. I believe this appointment and the official attitude which occasions it to be unique. I cannot imagine any other government or travel organization going to the trouble and expense of detailing a qualified scientist to instruct tourists in the facts of the botanical life of their land.

It was for me another indication of how genuine and profound is the Russian respect for knowledge. The only sad thing about the Sochi arrangement being that I suspect it was wasted on tourists. The ones I met had other priorities in their mind and though few could have failed to enjoy the lavish and beautiful vegetation of the coast they were not interested in a technical breakdown of their impressions. The Russians who were aware of this found it, I suspect, a symptom of the levity and irresponsibility of the *bourgeois* world, but happily the majority of them never noticed it. After three generations of the new order they themselves were so conditioned that they could never pass by an opportunity for fresh knowledge. For instance guides and interpreters, whenever I used an expression that they had not heard before, would immediately whip out their notebooks making me repeat and explain it while they wrote it down. So most Russians that I met seemed to be not only gourmets but gluttons for knowledge and any idea that a human being might need a rest from the pursuit of learning would have seemed like treason and the blend of escapism and idle curiosity displayed by the average tourist to these shores must have been utterly inconceivable to them. Happily for me a regard for the vegetable cover of the earth, particularly grasses and trees, has always been a hobby of mine and I counted my meeting with the Sochi agronomist to be a stroke of great good luck. Together we gave the coast line from Sochi to Gagri and back an exciting inspection. When we had finished with the natural cover we examined the cultivated one. There almost every sub-tropical and temperate plant seemed capable of growth and an impressive effort was in progress to take advantage of the early summer and turn it all into an advanced market-garden for the rest of the cold-bound Soviet Union.

Part of the effort was collective; part of it organized in huge units of State farms. I cannot tell how productive and rewarding these market-gardens were in relation to the labour and lavish equipment used on them. I only know that one day when it was pouring with rain and we were driving at the usual reckless pace along the coast, all three Russians with me suddenly burst out laughing.

'What is the joke?' I asked.

They pointed at some huge State-farm vegetable plots laid out neatly in the rigid geometrical patterns so beloved by the faithful Marxist-Leninist. Through the dense rain we saw one water-sprayer after the other fully turned on and methodically adding their pre-ordained quota of liquid to the rainfall!

'Just like a State farm,' the chauffeur commented with scorn. 'It is their day for watering these plots so come what may they'll water them!'

'Perhaps they just forgot to turn the water off,' another Russian seriously tried to excuse the scene.

'Forgot!' the chauffeur insisted, still laughing derisively: 'Forgot that they'd remembered to turn it on too, perhaps.'

The incident connected instantly with something I had just been reading in Ilya Ehrenburg's latest memoirs. There he has a moving description of the fate of Nikolai Ivanov, at the outbreak of the last war Soviet Chargé d'Affaires in Paris, who had reported to Moscow French inquiries about the possible purchase of arms from Russia during the German advance into France. Arrested on his return to Moscow in December 1940 Ivanov received a five-year sentence in September 1941 (three months after the German invasion of Russia) for *'anti-German activities'*.

'This is difficult to imagine,' Ehrenburg commented. 'With the Germans driving fast towards Moscow and the papers writing daily about "Fascist dogs", some official in State Security was calmly dealing with a file opened at the time of the Nazi-Soviet pact. He had put a number on the file, set it aside, and forgotten its irrelevance.'

What I saw now in the landscape seemed a warning that it was still in the nature of the Soviet System to be perilously prone to forgetfulnesses of these kinds.

On another occasion the agronomist took me to an experimental citrus station on the sunny hillside above Sochi. I forgot the precise nature of the main experimental work of the station except that it was designed, like so much of the applied research that I saw in the Soviet Union, to finding a short-cut through complex processes of growth in order to speed up production. For me the occasion, apart from the beauty of the place and the devotion given to it, was memorable because it gave me another illustration of the compulsion the Russians have to universalize their aims and experience. The sense of a special mission to redeem life and save the world which marks so much of Russian literature (and at one moment drove the early Muscovite church fathers to think of their unready capital as a third Rome, the sole guardian of the one and only true dogma of Salvation) is potentially present if not active in most Russians today. They are a nation of missionaries and even this botanical station above Sochi felt the need for conversion. Accordingly the men in charge of it had proclaimed one of their largest experimental plants, 'the tree of universal friendship'. All visitors of distinction were invited to make a graft of citrus upon one of its branches. The head of the station, an elderly scientist with beautiful manners and an obvious love of his work, would himself show visitors how the grafting should be done. When it was over he noted their addresses and his staff thereafter kept them posted annually about the progress of the experimental hybrid they had inflicted on this tree. He had several albums full of photographs of visitors taken in the act of grafting, and two volumes of the 'bag' of visitors and their comments collected in this manner over the years. I called these last 'game-books' because they reminded me of those morocco-bound pages kept in English country houses for record-ing the time, place, participation and numbers of birds shot on each estate. The grafting done, each visitor was presented with a minute knife as badge of his membership of the order of this tree. It had something of the symbolism of a religious rite about it as if implying that life everywhere else would increase by being grafted on its great Russian shoot. Turning through the books of record I was struck by the numbers of well-known men and women from all over the world who featured in them. In fact the one tree had already run out of grafting space and a second near-by had to be employed. I have been in botanical gardens, her-bariums and experimental stations all over the world but this was something new and something, I thought, that could only happen in Russia.

When we were not exploring the land I had great difficulty in resisting pressures to take me to see more and more sanatoria. The Black Sea coast is a great vineyard and market-garden coun-try but it is also a great sanatorium country. The name sanatorium is misleading to us. The Russians use it to describe not only hospitals and convalescent homes but also the greater number of recreation and rest homes. For miles around the popular resorts the immense sanatorium buildings stand shoulder to shoulder and the time is rapidly approaching when the coast line from Batumi to Odessa will present an unbroken front of concrete colonnades just as the Mediterranean Coast line from Malaga to the heel of Italy will be transformed into one unbroken chain of hotels, apartment blocks and petrol stations. The warm climate, of course, makes it a natural playground for people condemned to live year after year through the full round of harsh seasons in the great interior. The State and the workers' unions have all realized this and given the building of accommodation and the provision of amusement facilities on the Black Sea coast almost as high a priority as that of heavy industry. What they have done already in this way is most impressive. As a result about four million people spend their annual leave in the Black Sea region: and still the feverish work goes on. Sochi alone provides accommodation for close on a million visitors a year. Yet quite apart from the obvious natural attractions of the region I believe that another more subtle element is mixed up with it.

The Black Sea coast was once the playground of the aristocracy and the privileged classes of Tsarist Russia. Some of the villas and the palaces they built for themselves to occupy, perhaps for only a few weeks a year, still stand. Cheek to cheek with the mass-produced buildings of the new régime stand also a few crumbling Genoese, Turkish or Venetian residences. They all have a curious unreality about them because their inspiration is so obviously imitative and un-Russian (except that it still *is* a Russian instinct to copy the Wes). Built by craftsmen out of materials brought from the area tha was being copied, there are vast houses among them like huge Swiss chalets or the hunting lodges of minor German princelings. There are pallid stereotypes of formal eighteenth-century architecture such as the palace of the last of the Tsars at Livadia. But perhaps the most astonishing building of all is the palace just beyond Yalta built by Prince Vorontsov, an early nineteenth-century governor of the newly conquered area who was the person most responsible for starting the Riviera fashion on the Black Sea. The son of a Russian ambassador in London, he spent much of his youth in Britain and was deeply influenced by it. To this day his impact on architecture in Odessa, which was his provincial capital, is still visible in some splendid façades that might have been lifted straight out of Regency London. But the palace he built just outside Yalta with the labour and craftsmen from his own serfs – he is said to have had thirty thousand of them – is a dream fulfilment of all the buildings that ever impressed his imagination. In the heart of it is a lavish Russian orchestration of a stately home of England, but the exterior is a bewildering mixture of the Taj Mahal, Welbeck and the Albert Memorial, and thrown in for good Victorian measure, some Landseer-like lions staring out to sea. Even at this distance and so far out of their time context, these buildings that remain make one uncomfortable so it is not difficult to imagine what the masses of contemporary Russians felt about them. There is in all of us a mechanism that one might call the 'revenge of history'; a vendetta which, if we are not careful, we conduct against these aspects of the past that we believe to have injured us and which we imagine cannot be repaid until we in turn have done to life what it has done to us. To all Russians one of the attractions of the Black Sea development, I think, is because it is a way of getting even with their appalling past. Early in the Revolution Lenin issued a decree turning over to the people the Palaces and luxury resorts of the Black Sea and no one is allowed to forget the fact because the decree is carved in letters of marble and gold on the pedestals of Lenin's Black Sea statues. The Tsar's palace itself was turned into a sanatorium and the ordinary people who inhabit it seem to this day to glow in the fact. But perhaps the best way of understanding what all this means to people who have gone through Revolution and Civil War is to turn to literature and read stories like Malyshkin's *Train to the South.* But the importance of the Black Sea sanatoria in applied Soviet ideology is stamped on the buildings. They are as clearly franked in this vengeful communication with the past as any letter passed by censor in time of war.

When the agronomist took me into my first sanatorium in the fiery Matsetsa Gorge outside Sochi, he waved his hand at it proudly and exclaimed: 'A veritable temple of health, don't you think?'

I was so surprised at his choice of words that I instinctively parodied his tone.

'Indubitably,' I replied.

'Indubitably? Indubitably?' he repeated instantly, whipping out his notebook. 'Indubitably? What is that?'

'Without a doubt,' I answered.

'Ah, without a doubt,' he remarked, and wrote it all down.

But I had been interested in the phrase he had used for it was a true one. The Soviet State may build no churches but it does build many kinds of 'temples'. Factories, railway stations, Party and administrative buildings, offices of Economics and State planning organizations, and other institutions of the system right down to the glorified Trade Union and State pensions and boarding houses on the Black Sea coast, have all suffered an inflation of form in no way concerned with their functions but derived purely from the unemployed religious energies of a people who are naturally deeply religious and yet denied any legitimate religious expression. And the agronomists' 'temple' was just the right word for all the Greek columns, Roman colonnades, classical marble arcades and other manifestations. No doubt now that Mr Khrushchev and the Party have launched a campaign against this form of architecture these buildings will disappear. Indeed there are already signs of the new trend visible in the latest buildings rising on the hillsides. But my first Sochi institution, like so many others, was unashamedly and extravagantly pagan.

When I walked through the great portals into an immense marble hall, with exalted ceiling and massive gleaming red granite pillars, I may well have been induced to reverence had not the smell of the high Matsetsa waters stopped me. These waters are so charged with minerals that after a time they burn the skin and have to be administered for human ailments under expert supervision. The claims made for them vary from curing sterility in women to arresting baldness in men and if nastiness is a measure of the quality of a medicine the smell in this sanatorium should be proof of its excellence. No temple I have ever known has smelt so much like a lavatory, and the miners, factory-workers and petty officials who filled every cubicle and room of the establishment must have been truly devout to breathe in the sulphurated air as they did. But the neighbouring residences were full of sun, fresh air and a wide open view of the sea, 'temples' with interiors like copies of the palaces of the condemned and vanished aristocracy. All of them had large theatres wherein the visitors were expected to produce their own plays, ballet and other cultural entertainments. I thought the people I saw rehearsing looked rather mournful, as if bowed down by a system that would not leave them alone but was forever prodding them on to other prescribed activities.

The beach really was the only place where they could find them-

selves in a state of inactivity and oblivion and this, I think, together with their long harsh winter accounted for their utter
abandonment to the sun. It is true that the State wireless
pursued them even there, the din of the radio resounding in that
lovely setting. And there was more talk than music on the air. The
dreary official exhortation, elucidation and indoctrination, is
exceedingly high in all Soviet broadcasting. But wrapped in the
sunlight as in a honey-coloured blanket of Iberian wool I
believe the people lying on those beaches shoulder to shoulder for
hundreds of miles did not even hear it. Exhorted from the cradle
to the grave I believe them to be adept at hearing without hearing,
otherwise they could not have lain there inertly for so long. In
other nations and other places, the sea revives the instinct in
people to romp and play. Here it seemed to induce only an overwhelming desire to forget; not to speak, not to move, to do
nothing but to love and be loved by the sun as if thereby something would grow within them where nothing had been allowed
to grow before. I found the sight very touching as if all these
people were lying there not as whole people but more like
convalescents after some terrible sickness.

Another small incident interested me while I was visiting the
sanatoria.

I asked if they had any single rooms.

The question seemed utterly incomprehensible to the officials
who reported, amazed, But why should we have single rooms?'
and they looked at me as if the mere desire for such a room would
be perverse or unnatural.

They had rooms for two but the majority were comfortable
dormitories. Yet it would be wrong to assume from this that
Russians have no instinct for being alone. One day when a young
acquaintance and I were talking about the beauty of the coast he
suddenly remarked, 'It's lovely yet I would not like to come here
for my honeymoon.'

'Why not?' I asked.

'Too many people here. You are never alone.'

'Where would you go then?'

'Take a room in some small village deep in the country near a
river where we could go rowing by ourselves and close by woods
in which we could walk alone.'

He spoke then I think for all Russians. Much as the sun and the sea have come to draw them the pull of the village and the countryside is older and stronger.

Faultless as the knowledge of my agronomist appeared to be on his own subject it was either not so good outside it or he did not feel so free to tell me some of the other things I wanted to know. For instance, motoring in and out of Sochi as we did for some days he never failed to draw my attention to any monument or building of importance. But there was one exception. In one of the squares stood the only statue of Stalin that I was to see during the whole of my long journey. We passed it at least twice and often four times a day. The moment we came abreast of it the agronomist would look the other way and silence would fall upon our conversation.

One day I could bear it no longer and said: 'Ah, I see there is a statue of Stalin. Could we stop and have a look at it?'

'I am afraid we have no time,' he explained, embarrassed. 'If we stop now we shall be late for our appointment at the television studios.'

I tried a second time and again there was a plausible excuse. Then I tried to talk to him and my other acquaintances about Stalin. I remarked that I had been told that Stalin liked coming to Sochi: where then had he stayed on these occasions? They said they did not realize that he had ever visited Sochi and had no idea where he had stayed. Allowing for some ignorance there was also in all the Russians that I met a conscious determination not to be curious and not to know too much in case the knowledge might prove dangerous. So much was this true that I soon dropped asking similar questions because I saw that it made me suspect. I did venture once to explain to the Russians that I came to know best how different all this was in Britain and America. All visitors to Washington wanted to know where the President lived. All visitors to London wanted to know where our Queen, the Prime Minister and other prominent people lived and there was neither secrecy nor lack of popular curiosity about such things. I repeatedly read in the newspapers that Mr Khrushchev was resting in Sochi so I asked where I could see his residence? Why could he not tell me where Mr Khrushchev lived?

'I honestly don't know or I would show you,' he told me. 'All

I do know is that he lives like any citizen somewhere among us. *How*, not *where* he lives, is the important thing.'

Seeing how unwelcome this and kindred questions were to my companion, there and then I surrendered.

Finally, besides being great holiday country the Black Sea coast was also great 'delegation' country. I had already met some odd delegations in Tashkent, Alma Ata and Baku but now, from Sochi onwards, the land was teeming with them. I would find all the best places in the hotels reserved under the appropriate flags for visiting delegations. The official Soviet mind works naturally in numbers: single units are anathema to it. It rarely if ever invites just one person to visit Russia, more generally it is a group. The scale on which these invitations of carefully selected and vetted groups are issued is tremendous and unique. Travelling on my own I was a conspicuous oddity, usually regarded with incomprehension and sometimes with suspicion. I did not mind that, nor did I mind the small dining-room table that was usually my lot, squeezed in at the far end of the room between a huge refrigerator erected like a monument of progress against the wall and a gleaming stainless steel all-electric samovar. There I could sit in peace watching the delegations and occasionally overhearing a revealing word or two of the conversation. What is more I found myself travelling with the same delegations for days at a time and, without speaking to them, got to know their characters rather well. The Roumanians were the only delegations who really seemed to me to be enjoying themselves. Untroubled by conscience of any kind they could be as light-hearted and sparkling as the Georgian champagne so liberally poured into their glasses. The Czechs were perhaps the most serious, gravely pragmatic and determined to extract the most out of the situation. The Bulgarians were tremendously obstinate and determined, filled with the lugubrious disillusion of regular customers of the Soviet establishment. Significantly I saw no Polish delegations. In all the time I was there I met only one Pole. That was in the centre of Siberia and he was on a lone mission like myself. But I met several East German delegations and I regret to say that they had an extremely unpleasant effect on me. They appeared thoroughly ashamed of themselves, as if knowing what they were doing was wrong but did not have the courage to desist. They never looked either me or one another in the eye and ate in a way no human beings should be allowed to eat.

For a time one German delegation, a small party of Americans, and I, found ourselves repeatedly in the same hotels. The looks the Germans gave the unsuspecting Americans were filled with an animosity I could not understand. This I could not resist mentioning to the cultivated Russian woman who was in charge of the American party and whom I had got to know rather well.

'It is perfectly true. They hate these Americans,' she told me. 'I wonder if you can guess why?'

'Because of the war?'

'Oh, no, nothing real like that,' she laughed. 'It is simply because the Americans always leave some food uneaten on their plates. The East Germans leave nothing on their plates and not even a crumb on the table. They think it wicked of the Americans and a sign of how spoilt and wasteful they are.'

'They must hate easily then,' I remarked.

At that she gave me a sharp look and asked with some tartness, 'But don't you realize that the Germans are a very dangerous people? Won't you, the French and Americans ever learn your lessons?'

Then one evening at Sochi an East German tourist-ship steamed into the neat little harbour and my hotel instantly was full of East Germans dining ashore and they and the delegation merged as one. I was amazed how quickly the atmosphere of Black Sea and of Russia vanished from the foyers, lounges and dining-rooms. The place became part of East Prussia and the dance-floor full of swaggering, overbearing dancers insisting on German music and German dances. I have travelled extensively in West Germany since the war and I believe that the German people, particularly the youth of West Germany, will never again allow their country to be obsessed in the Hitler way. But the behaviour of the East Germans that night was like that of the tourists I had encountered just before the war pouring out of Goebbels' '*Kraft durch Freude* (Strength through Joy)' ships to take possession of whole towns in the Mediterranean, the Madeiras and the Canaries.

Any idea that I might have been alone in my impression was quickly dispelled by the Russian dining with me. Normally he and I sat for long talking over our coffee but on this occasion we had hardly finished when he asked: 'Would you mind if we left now? I would rather like some fresh air.'

'No,' I said, getting up at once and, since it was so unusual for him to make the first move, I asked: 'I hope you are not feeling unwell?'

'No,' he said. 'It is just that I cannot bear the sight of that German officer dancing with that Russian girl that way. Please let's go.'

But the delegations that really disturbed me most were those of mixed international and professional communists and fellow-travellers brought together from all over the world. It was extraordinary how, though they came from different races and cultures, they all managed to have the same look. There was no joy in any of them. They ate and drank sparingly and hardly ever spoke to one another. Words, one felt, were reserved for tracts and lampoons; speech for conferences. They would sit tight-lipped not seeing the lovely earth glowing at the windows but only the scene of some implacable memory within. Once in Odessa I sat near a table with an Australian, Indian, Iraqi, West African, Ceylonese, Dane, Japanese and Frenchman, each delegate with his national flag placed in front of him. Before long the physical differences were eliminated by the expression on their faces of a single mood. This occurred so often that I realized as never before that what loosely we call 'Communism' is a state of mind long before it emerges into the world as dialectical materialism. Moreover it is a state of mind which obsesses people who have never even heard of Marx, Engels or Lenin and it can obsess many people who are fanatically opposed to the political communism of either Russia or China. As the French say, 'All men tend to become the thing they oppose.' Until we have all recognized this state of mind and its causes we shall never know properly how to deal with its secondary manifestations in our own societies or in international politics. It is the existence of this state of mind in the world which makes Russia dangerous, not Russia herself. What Russia is does not imperil us. But what does imperil us is what the world through the predispositions induced by this state of mind imagines Russia to be. This fantasy can go so deep that it makes irrelevant all the contradictions, paradoxes, inconsistencies and bewildering changes of fronts which mark the individual behaviour of those who profess Communism as well as the inconsistencies of its ideological application in society. All these can be freely exposed. Man can lie and deceive quite openly as the expediency of the moment demands because deeply there is the one predominant purpose of a highly charged and polarized mind which remains unchanged. For this reason Communism as a social or political philosophy makes no sense to me. But conceived as abnormal psychology it is full of a sombre meaning. The quintessence of it is perhaps that the original love of life, of justice and of man which gave birth to Communism has long since been cast out and forgotten. In their stead is left only the shadow of the vanished substance of these creative urges and abstractions of hatred and the spirit of revenge reign in their place. This hatred is so great that it makes man not only incapable of ever experiencing the reality of love but also of recognizing it when offered to him. In the world around him this man is forever condemned to see only food for the hate which impels him from within and this sets him apart from normal men and certainly from the majority of the Russians. The Russians are not, I am convinced, a people naturally pre-disposed to hatred. They are a people of great feeling; indeed they have so much feeling that they are repeatedly caught out by it. Communism among them has definite roots in their own history but has little to do with the state of mind of which I am speaking though they have had and still have leaders who are afflicted by it. Moreover in so far as they themselves have been motivated by historical hatred and revenge, in the three generations since the revolution they have had both the time and endured the suffering which is necessary to get these negations out of their system. They have had their proper revenge on history and there are signs that they are at heart sick and weary of what is left of hatred in their society. In fact the urge to re-appraise induced by their experience, together with a certain innocence conferred on them by their terrible history, gives them some immunity against the negations of the ideology that the State professes to practise. But the professional Communists and fellow-travellers that I observed in these delegations had neither the excuses nor the in-built immunities of the Russians. They did not see even Russians or the Soviet Union as they really are. They had no real affection for it nor respect for its achievements and values. They were there merely in the cause of their own inner hatred and they valued the Soviet Union purely as an additional instrument for the spirit of revenge to which their lives were pledged, revenge against the society of their origin which had wounded or was still wounding them.

It was most revealing how objective discussion was impossible with these people. In this too they were unlike the Russians whom, as I got to know them better, I found to be remarkably open and ready for discussion. I tried on several occasions to talk to some of the British and French delegates but in the end I gave it up because I met nothing but the same bigoted and angled responses from them all. Words had lost their ordinary meanings and were made to serve any purpose that suited their underlying state of mind. They propagated with the greatest cynicism the most transparent half-truths and falsehoods. For instance, I heard a British Communist who had just had an honorary degree at a Russian University conferred on him tell a group that if such a degree had been offered to him by Oxford or Cambridge, Harvard, Yale, Princeton, the Sorbonne or Heidelberg, he would have scorned it because these were not free universities. They were, he said, merely organs of reaction dedicated to the mental isolation and enslavement of the working classes of the world. Universities in Russia were the only free higher educational institutions in the world. I am certain he knew that he was lying but that was not important because, as one of his party said to me when I discussed it with him afterwards, 'The truth of the historical process we serve is infinite. No lie can diminish it but on the contrary it has a place where in the end all is made pure.'

This impression was all the more unpalatable for me because I was now dependent for news from the outside world on the newspapers and magazines produced by men of this kind. The only foreign newspapers on sale in the Soviet Union are Communist papers, chiefly the East German and Italian papers, the French *L'Humanité* and English *Daily Worker*. These are available at all the airports, railway stations and news-stalls everywhere in the Soviet Union from Central Asia right across Siberia to the Pacific Ocean. The piles of unsold back numbers I saw on my journey convinced me that the State must lose heavily on the arrange-

ment but perhaps it regards it as one of the easier ways of sub-
sidizing Communist ventures beyond its frontiers. From any of
these newspapers it was impossible to recognize the world I had
left behind me. There was no humanity in *L'Humanité* – not that
that would have worried its editors because, like most Communists, they have an archaic belief in the magic of words. This
perhaps accounts in part for their belief in the importance of the
lie. They believe in the power of words to alter the nature of
reality rather as the ancient Cornishman believed in the spells and
curses of Merlin. This is part of a mechanism of retrogression, a
throw-back into old and discredited patterns of the spirit. I am
certain the founders of *L'Humanité* thought that title was enough
to make its concern humanitarian and its nature human. Yet the
France of *L'Humanité* (as I read daily) was an abstraction of
hatred, a country full of unpunished assassins, corrupt judges,
greedy heartless exploiters of labour, hypocritical priests and
Fascist dictators. The intemperate character of its reporting, the
distortion and invention was of a Grand Guignol kind. Then the
Daily Worker on its pages had mostly reports of strikes either
planned or in being, of workers being sacked or about to be
sacked, and nothing from book-reviews to political comment and
musical criticism, that did not serve its grand design of social
revenge. The obsessional preoccupation made them both boring
and rather frightening. Read in a wider international context it
could have presented itself to me as a harmless democratic way of
letting off steam. But here completely alone in Russia and cut off
for weeks from all contact with the western world, I felt that I saw
its true character for the first time. It has always seemed to me
extraordinary that, in law, the counterfeiting of money should be
a serious crime incurring heavy penalties (in Russia counterfeiters
are shot) but that fabricating, inventing and falsifying news should
go unpunished. I have been told authoritatively, for instance, that
some newspapers during the war in Korea carried reports 'from
our own correspondent at the front' when there were no correspondents there at all. The news received from agencies and copied
from other newspapers were merely changed round to conform to
particular ideological fronts in the campaign. Yet no one in any
country can be called to account for this because there is no law
under which they can be charged.

What amazed me most after all this was how comparatively well balanced the Russians were about the outside world. I could only conclude that like all artificially isolated or imprisoned peoples they had an instinctive system of ascertaining what was true in their daily news and propaganda diet. Every thought, every articulation of meaning from painting to music, carries within it evidence of its correspondence to the truth by the impact it makes on our senses and imagination. This was forcibly brought home to me in over three years of captivity in a Japanese prisoner-of-war camp. Denied all official news except Japanese propaganda sheets we all quickly evolved a technique for sorting out the true from the false. On this journey I found myself quickly resorting to the same technique and I believe the Russians as a whole react in the same way, otherwise they could not fail to be grave casualties of the daily doses of poison administered to them telling them of the forces of evil which are reported to be marshalling against them. They are helped in this, I am certain, by rumours of a contradictory kind which their own travellers in the outside world carry back across their frontiers; by books and flashes of news overheard on the radio; by their own natural disbelief in the infallibility of rulers daily demonstrated to them. Even so the distorted picture that they have of the Western world and its intentions, and particularly of America, is alarming enough. The only really heated discussions I ever had with Russians were about the United States. Though I disagreed with them equally over their view of Britain and Africa the Russians did not really mind that disagreement, largely due to the fact that Britain was relatively unimportant in their thinking. But America always provided the standard of comparison. This was made clear to me one day by a bank clerk whom I met on the beach where I had gone to escape the attentions of a persistent Indian member of a fellow-travelling delegation. The Russian himself came from one of those vast new industrial towns which have been built in Siberia since the war: Kemerovo. He told me that a deputation of their coal miners had just returned from Britain.

When I asked what they had thought of the country he replied: 'They thought your methods of mining out of date compared with ours, but I did not really question them very much. You see, what really interests us Russians is the comparison with America.

Until we have surpassed the Americans we shall not consider ourselves even to have begun. Is it true that the cafeterias in America
are so wonderful?'

Yet he and his countrymen would be inclined to accept what I
said about Britain out of their natural respect for the feelings of a
guest. For example a woman I met at Yalta, a music-teacher, at
the end of a long discussion, remarked kindly: 'Why do you not
come to live under Communism with us? I am certain you will
be happier here. I feel so sorry for you going back to so much
trouble in Britain. . .'

It was my first intimation of how the foreign papers, together
with the official Soviet news system, had penetrated even the inborn defences of the Russians against distortion of the truth.

Taken aback, I asked: 'What trouble do you mean? Is there
any special trouble?'

Feeling she had made a gaffe the woman blushed while her
friends immediately rushed in to change the conversation.

'Of course not, of course not!' they all asserted, anxious to
change the subject.

But about America they had no such reservations. Their attitude in that regard was ambivalent to a remarkable degree.
They admired America more than any other country in the
world and at the same time they envied, disliked and feared it.
No one I met ever made a secret of the national determination
to surpass America's industrial and material achievements. The
achievement of the greatest industrial output in the world seemed
to be a matter of profound personal and national self-respect
in the Soviet Union. So much emotion was roused by discussion
of these matters that I would often find myself suddenly in deep
waters. An experience I had at Yalta served to illustrate clearly
for me the unexpected lack of direct simplicity in the Russian
attitude to the United States.

CHAPTER EIGHT

MY YOUNG FRIENDS IN YALTA

I STAYED at Yalta for five days not only because I liked it best of all the Black Sea resorts but because after so much constant travelling in planes, trains and motor-cars I wanted the kind of rest I could find only in physical exercise. I thought I would get it by climbing the grey hills towering over Yalta, hills that might easily have been the Alpes Maritimes in France or Italy. I started preparing for this climb by wandering round Yalta on foot and I discovered with delight that for all the building imposed upon it by the Soviet Office of Works its inner shape was essentially conditioned by its past. It has what Sochi lacked, a core and a population that was independent of the great tides of distinguished visitors, tourists and bemused and bewildered workers from the interior which ebbed and flowed through it with the seasons. What made Sochi memorable for me was its noble sunlight and magnanimous earth. But Yalta was a real little Mediterranean town with a character and a temperament of its own. I could understand why Pushkin, Nekrasov, Tolstoy, the painter Aivazovsky, and Chekhov so undying in his dying there, loved Yalta. After a morning spent on foot I joined the inert crowds lying in the warm afternoon sun on the shelving beaches and there I soon made friends with a group of the most pleasant young people I had yet met. I had been lying on my back for some time, had turned on my side and opened my eyes to see two girls and two young men watching me intently. Then from the other side of me I heard someone asking in English if I was English? Obviously surprised, I said inaccurately that I was and turned to face my questioner.

His accent was so good, his clothes so un-Russian, a Paisley kerchief tied so expertly round his throat and his open pleasant face so European that I took him to be Dutch or Scandinavian. But he turned out to be a young Russian engineer from Siberia.

'Be careful of him,' I was warned by the other four who were students at Yalta seminaries and had now come crowding round us. 'He is a "pirate".'

' "Pirate"?' I asked, studying their merry, shining faces.

'They mean,' said the young man speaking for himself, 'that I have not come here as most people do on a ticket from my Union to accommodation reserved for me at a sanatorium. I'm taking a chance. I pay for my own accommodation instead of having sixty per cent paid for me by my Union.'

'Can you do that?'

'Of course,' he replied. 'In all resorts there is a bureau run by the State where they keep a list of spare accommodation. All it means is that you may not get in.'

'What would you do then?' I asked.

'I would find someone to put me up. This is Russia after all. We don't mind crowding in to help one another,' he told me.

'Or he could cheat, like this pirate here,' the others exclaimed pointing out another young woman who had joined us.

She was beautiful and wore a bikini as nonchalantly as any young French film celebrity on the sands of Saint Tropez. She, they explained, had been in a sanatorium for three weeks and enjoyed it so much that she had persuaded her parents to send her money for another three weeks on her own. But she was from Leningrad – they stressed the fact as if it were the explanation of her behaviour – and did not like the 'pirate' accommodation offered her! She wanted to go to an hotel! But all the hotels claimed they were full. Undismayed she went to a friend of her parents, quite a well-known film director, and he accompanied her to an hotel, informed the manager that she was there for an important film test (Yalta has a famous studio which made among others the remarkable film version of Chekhov's story *The Lady with a Dog*) and said the tests would take at least three weeks. The manager, impressed by the film man's reputation, suddenly discovered that he had room for just one more.

The girls clapped their hands and the young men laughed with delight at the story. Clearly, as I was to find repeatedly, the young in Russia, as the young everywhere else, take great joy in seeing the Establishment outwitted.

'Imagine a man being such a fool as to believe such a story,' the engineer concluded. 'But you'd be surprised how stupid authority makes some people!'

The conversation then turned to me. They wanted to know everything about me. They wanted to know too about the life of young people in Britain and the relation between the sexes of their own age. Behind all this questioning there was great hunger for knowledge of the world outside that was most revealing, the hunger of people who instinctively feel themselves to be kept behind bars. I could not fail to recognize the hunger because once I had been behind bars myself. When Yevtushenko wrote the poem about his shame because he had not been to Rome and the other great cities and countries of the western world he spoke for millions of Russians. So I told them all I could. Towards the end one of the young women said that she wondered how a human being could sound as happy as I did. She declared that I sounded quite the happiest man she had ever met. I could not help wondering what she would have said had she seen me in what I would have called a truly happy state.

The young men were interested in more matter-of-fact things. They fingered my tie, said that until recently only exceptional people wore ties in Russia, said they liked it and asked how much it cost? I told them. They asked the price of my coat, flannel trousers and brogues, and were amazed because the cheapest ready-made clothes available to them would cost anything from twice to five times as much. I suggested that it might be because the official value of the rouble bore no relation to its purchasing power so that comparing costs in our respective countries in terms of official currencies would give a false result.

The engineer said that he had been told that the real value of the rouble was 10·50 roubles to the £1 as opposed to the official rate of 2·50. Was that so? I did not know the answer. I was certain that the official rate of exchange was unreal and punitive enough to be part of the cold war. I knew too that the purchasing power of the rouble varied according to the commodity. The foreign students at Tashkent had already told me that they estimated it as 8·50 roubles to the £1 for bread, 4 for meat, and 6·50 for clothes, but that for travel by either rail or plane it might well be 15 roubles to the £1. They told me too they were convinced that the official rouble was fixed with a wary eye on the dollar. For prestige reasons it just had to be worth more than the dollar so the Soviet pegged it at ten cents higher and, officially, ninety Russian cents (or kopecks) were equivalent to a hundred American cents. I did not say this to my new acquaintances on the beach but did ask them what they thought of the rouble-dollar exchange? By now a small crowd had surrounded me and it was still growing. A newcomer, a far older man who turned out to be a schoolmaster on leave, answered me. The rouble, he said, was the future currency of the world. He digressed suddenly to ask me if I had seen the American exhibition in Moscow some years ago? I shook my head and he launched into an attack on the exhibition. It was obscene, he said, an organized lie, an abuse of Russian good nature and hospitality, an attempt at sabotage! It was extraordinary how this exhibition could still rankle years afterwards among all sorts of conditions and men in Russia. Somehow it had penetrated Russian defences at their weakest, showing up the appalling inferiority of the Russian standard of living in material things and the terrible lack of consumer goods. Such material things are not dead matter in Soviet ideology but part of the laws in the creed of social redemption, so it is perhaps not surprising that the comparisons implied by the American exhibition should have proved so odious to the Russians. But this afternoon was my first experience of it and I was not prepared. Then after the exhibition the schoolmaster launched into a tirade against conditions in America: for instance the lack of a National Health Service. Did I realize that the Soviet Union had free medical services? I had already been impressed by the fact and told him I had been amazed by the speed and willingness with which the best doctors along the coast were summoned to administer to the sick, including foreigners. I then added, quickly, 'We have the same service in Britain, you know.'

He brushed that aside as of no consequence. American social inadequacies were what interested him. From medicine he went on to decry the American lack of security for workers, the warmongering reactionaries, dollar imperialism, the arms-monopolists, colour-prejudice and all the rest. I answered back as best I could but I soon saw that merely countering his facts made no impression either on him or my young acquaintances. They scorned any reply in their own statistical coin. So I began to answer them in terms of feeling and at once seemed to get through to them even, in measure, to the older man.

Had he ever been to America? I asked.

As always the fact that he had to confess that he had never left his country disarmed him.

Well then, go to America, I urged him. I have been there. Of course there are many imperfections – but no one criticized them more than did the Americans. Frankly they were far more self-critical than the people of the Soviet Union.

'We have nothing to be critical about in Russia,' the older man countered – and immediately lost some of the support he had evoked in the young.

That was not the point, I said. The point was that if he went to America he would realize how one-sided his view was and be surprised at how much he would come to like the country.

Did I like it? he asked.

I loved it, I told him. Several of my greatest friends were Americans.

What did I like about them so particularly, he asked rather unpleasantly. Their power or their enmity to Russia?

I told him that I liked them because they were a generous people who did not pretend that they knew all the answers to life. They were a searching, questing, self-critical people seeking for themselves and the world a better way of life. Americans, I added, were certainly not the enemies of Russia but were very fearful of how Russia might use her own great power in the world.

He laughed uproariously at the idea that anyone could be fearful of Russia. Yet the fact that I, whom I think they all had come to like a little, declared openly that I loved America was immediately respected by him and the others.

They acknowledged my point obliquely by at once exclaiming: 'Ah, the American people, we are certain they are all right! The people everywhere are good. It is just unfortunate that the Americans are exploited by their systems.'

Their reaction made a deep impression on me and thereafter I never neglected to talk to my acquaintances, not out of my knowledge but out of my feeling. And as my journey progressed I realized that this realm of feeling was the truly important world to most Russians. It accounted in part for the extraordinary lack of concern they show for the detail of the socialized outer objective world. And in part it accounted for the ruthless determination which Russian rulers from Peter the Great to Stalin have been forced to use in order to get their people to take notice of the material facts of life. Indeed the present system in Russia can never be fully understood unless one realizes that it is also an attempt at compensation for a people whose instinctive, national characteristic is feeling.

That evening, just as the sun was setting, I came down from the hills and the woods in which I had been watching a lovely herd of deer. The sunset hours are charged with mythology for me and the sun going down over the Black Sea coast, the steep line of that old Greek Euxine, were Homeric. Rounding a bend I caught up with the group from the beach strolling towards the town and talking with great animation among themselves. On seeing me they immediately broke their ranks and insisted on my walking in the middle with them. They had just been discussing modern music, jazz, rock-'n'-roll and all the rest. They wanted to know what we thought in Britain of a score or more of singers and con- temporary composers, mostly American, of whom I had never heard. Their knowledge of even the very latest popular Western music astounded me and whenever I had to confess ignorance of some pop song-writer or singer they could scarcely believe it and would try to prod my memory by singing snatches of the songs in English to me, always ending up with the same remark: 'Now surely you recognize that one?'

I was so amazed by their knowledge, since I knew there was hardly a foreign record of juke-box music on sale in Russia, that I asked the engineer how they managed to know all these tunes.

'Oh, we get it all from our tape-recorders,' he answered.

'But where do your recorders get the music from?'

'From the "Voice of America", of course,' he said, paused, and added: 'It's the favourite music of most young people today.'

'But what about your own music?'

'Oh, we have our own jazz too but personally I prefer American and English, though the French are doing some fine syncopated stuff too.'

'How do you know that?' I asked.

'From the B.B.C. and the Swiss national broadcasting stations,' he replied.

'But what about your own traditional and folk music?'

He made a slight face and told me that traditional music was all right in its place at feast days and official celebrations but that he and his generation had had enough of it.

'I could murder the fellow who wrote that song about the Ukrainian looking at the towel his mother had given him,' he added. 'It's really terrible stuff! Not contemporary!'

One of the girls who was studying music in Yalta agreed with him. Bach, not Tchaikovsky or any other Russian, was her favourite composer too and she saw no conflict in her classical and contemporary tastes.

The particular song mentioned by the engineer had pursued me all round the Soviet Union and I heard it at least once if not thrice a day. It used every folk-music cliché in the Russian repertoire. The theme was of someone far from home looking at the long embroidered towel made for him by his mother which is the badge of manhood and adult honour in the traditional dress of the Ukraine. It was a good example of the sort of music the Party thought good for uplifting the people.

Another young man who was interested in the theatre was disappointed that I had not seen Osborne's *Look Back In Anger*. I feared that my theatrical and musical ignorance suggested to them all that the young in Britain and America must be having the same sort of trouble with their elders as they had. They too, I gathered, were by way of being 'angry young men'. Osborne's play, the young man told me, had been a most revealing piece for him and its performance in Russia had taught him at least one important thing. Would I like to know what that was?

He drew me apart behind a rock at the side of our path and said he would show me. 'Please watch carefully,' he exhorted.

He thereupon undid all his fly buttons, promptly did them up again and exclaimed: 'There! You see?'

'But see what?' I asked.

Disappointed, he begged me to watch more carefully and did the same thing more deliberately all over again.

Again I had to shake my head. He repeated the action for a third time before he gave me up, explaining: 'The hero in the play in one scene turns to the audience and also unbuttons his fly. Until I saw him doing it I never realized I buttoned mine up the wrong way. I always used to button them up from the top to the bottom. But he did it from the bottom up to the top and, of course, it's much easier that way. I shall always be grateful to the play for teaching me that.'

I had not expected under a system which is so much a vast – sometimes brutal – Pavlov experiment on men and women to find such openness of mind, such an unconditioned young nature, such an innocent and artless spirit. Many people to whom I have told the story since have laughed heartily over it. But I was not tempted to laugh. I was oddly moved by the incident. It seemed to me to increase my awareness of our own responsibility to the future in an almost terrifying manner. It convinced me how much the example we set matters even down to the smallest detail. If we fail in that we fail not only ourselves and our own young but also the young in Russia. The example we set, our capacity to practise what we preach, to live out in the routine of life the fine things we think, are our only true ways of winning the clash between ourselves and 'Communism'. I could elaborate but the parable of the fly buttons speaks clearly enough.

This openness of mind in the young seemed to me to extend to the past as well. One of the many things for which I am grateful is that these young people showed me how free they were of the emotions provoked by the Revolution. Unlike their elders they were under no emotional obligations to it. They had never known any other system so they took the revolution for granted and saw no reason why they should 'keep up its appearances' for it. In that regard they were utterly different from the generation of the schoolmaster who had joined us on the beach.

I had just been reading a great deal of Russian literature about the Revolution and I could see few traces in these young people of the state of mind which obsessed the men who brought it about and fought the Civil War. Nikolai Ostrovsky's *How the Steel was Tempered*, for instance, I had found a terrible book on a terrible subject, redeemed only by the doomed writer's – he died young as a result of wounds, living only long enough to finish his book – courage and capacity for enduring without hope or charity in his heart and faith only in the blind endurance which has brought the Russians out of their abominable past to where they stand today. I had also tried in vain to make my peace with the poet Mayakowsky who so obviously was carrying a cross of great gifts together with hatred, anger, violence and the failure to find meaning in either his own or his nation's suffering. His claim to be in love with the future – all Russians have a great deal of the same thing in them to this day – did not convince me. Loving the future can be a way of hating the present. True love is love of the difficult and unlovable, both here and now. There are two main sources of corruption in life: the corruption caused by power and the corruption caused by suffering. We all recognize and condemn the corruption caused by power, but we tend to excuse the corruption caused by suffering which is so clearly condemned by the full implication of the New Testament admonition to 'turn the other cheek'. The whole meaning of life seems to dwell in the evolution of a man proof against these two corruptions. Genius, however great, cannot feed indefinitely on negations. Perhaps it is because Mayakowsky knew this that he committed suicide. Besides Ostrovsky and Mayakowsky I have read many other writers and had developed a certain capacity for detecting the mood of the Revolution in the people I met. The older ones clearly seemed both to hate their history and feel ashamed of it, which made it difficult for them to understand our interest in their past, even in their old buildings. They were far more concerned in showing one the brashest of their ugly new towns than any historical monument. Even the tourists photographing ancient monuments were suspected of conducting some propaganda war against Russia by trying to show how backward she still was! But the young people that I met were clear of all that. They belonged to an age-group from which, so a young writer assured me later, Chekhov's oriental, as well as Oblomov and Dostoievsky, 'man' had vanished.

And had Dostoievsky's 'grand inquisitor' vanished too? I asked.

But they had scorned to reply. In so far as they still had any deep emotions about history they were mainly directed against their personal past. I had various hints that they all had decided views and feeling about Stalin but were unprepared to discuss them with a foreigner out of loyalty and a natural desire to present their country in the best possible light. Perhaps, too, out of a lingering fear of their security police? As an example of this the young theatre enthusiast now told me of a new Russian play he had just seen called *Friends and the Years*, which had moved him very much because it showed, first, how the State and the people had moved apart over the years, how relations between them had deteriorated dangerously, and then, at the last moment, how the two had come together again.

'But have relations between the people and the State really been so bad?' I asked him.

'Very, very bad,' he told me.

'In what way?'

At once he had second thoughts, looked embarrassed and then said evasively: 'I have the scripts in my luggage. I'll bring it to the beach tomorrow and then we can go through it together.'

But I was not to see him or the script of the play because he never again joined our group.

Towards the end of our walk just before we reached the town the young engineer put his hand on my arm and called out to his companions, 'Listen! Please, listen!'

We stopped and listened. The Black Sea was bound with a broad band of deep red to the darkening sky. The grey tops of the hills behind us rising above the woods were purple, and in the black woods themselves as in the valleys flooded with night, the nightingales had started to sing with clear outward-bound voices. We listened and then, as we walked on, I found myself telling them of the attraction of the nightingale for our own poets. They insisted on me giving them an example. So impressed had I been by their attachment to their own contemporary age that I rejected Keats and recited slowly and deliberately from *Sweeney among the Nightingales*:

> 'The host with someone indistinct
> Converses at the door apart,
> The nightingales are singing near
> The Convent of the Sacred Heart,
> And sang – within the bloody wood
> When Agamemnon cried aloud,
> And let their liquid siftings fall
> To stain the stiff dishonoured shroud.'

'Ah, T. S. Eliot,' remarked the young woman studying chemistry.

I could not imagine her counterpart in Britain or America recognizing a quotation from a poem by Pasternak or any Russian poet. Even recognition of T. S. Eliot would have been unusual.

'You amaze me,' I told her. 'I thought you all disliked Eliot's poetry. After all your literary director, Fadeyev, used to say that "if hyaenas could use typewriters, they would write poetry like Eliot".'

They roared with laughter at that and the young man who had told me of *Friends and the Years* exclaimed: 'Thank God, those days have gone for good!'

It was the first time, too, that I had heard anyone invoke the name of God.

That evening back in my hotel there were no nightingales singing! Instead there was the inevitable Ukrainian 'Towel Song' repeatedly encored.

At dinner the local guide who was dining with me asked suddenly, 'Do you see that man at the table over there? Who and what do you think he is?'

I thought that he was just carrying on with a game that I had got him to play with me since we met a few days previously, namely, trying to guess from their appearance the nationality and occupation of our fellow diners. This man, tall and dark in the way that Swedes sometimes are, had an odd fellow-traveller look about him.

'A Swedish journalist?' I suggested.

To my astonishment my response seemed to irritate my companion.

'No! He is not Swedish. He is Russian, I tell you he is Russian!' he reiterated with evident distaste.

'Well, a Russian journalist then?' I guessed again.

He looked at me as if he could not believe my stupidity.

'Well, what is he then?' I asked.

'I cannot tell you,' he answered. 'I can only tell you that he is an unpleasant, hateful and nasty creature. Don't ever try to speak to him.'

'But how do you know this? Have you spoken to him then?'

'Yes, I have spoken to him,' he answered grimly, still angry over the memory of their meeting.

I knew then that it was no longer a game. I felt that he was trying to warn me in some way. For the first time now on my journey I felt uneasy. When later in Moscow some foreign correspondents told me that the Soviet had representatives of the State Security Police permanently stationed in their big hotels involuntarily I remembered this man. Also, something happened on the following days that, in retrospect, seemed to support my belated suspicions.

The next day again I met this group of young people and had a chance of talking at length to the young engineer. He was in some way different to the others and walked among them with the ease and confidence of a leader. By the time I had finished my talk with him I had learnt that his father was a general in the Soviet Army, and his mother the sister of someone high up in the service of the State. Unlike him they did not come much to the Black Sea any more. They preferred the forty-miles stretch of sand at Riga Bay on the Baltic and regularly took a villa there in the summer. Of course, the climate there was uncertain and not as good as on the Black Sea but it had lovely sand and shallow water, he told me, though he himself preferred a more reliable sun and deeper water.

If the climate at Riga was so much more unreliable, I asked, why did people go there at all?

At that he smiled charmingly and remarked that there was not room for everyone to come to the Black Sea. Besides – he hesitated before saying it slowly and deliberately – to go to Riga was the 'snobbish' thing to do. This was the first time anyone had openly given the growing social phenomenon a name in my presence.

I complimented him on his English and asked how he came to know it so well?

He told me that in his profession, apart from technical subjects, everyone had to qualify in one Western European language, either French, German or English. Most of them chose English and he assured me that already close on five million people spoke English as a second language in the Soviet Union. He also gave me a new insight into the thoroughness with which Russians teach foreign languages. He told me that now in the major cities of the Soviet Union they had schools wherein pupils from the kindergarten upwards were taught everything, including Russian, through the medium of the foreign language their parents had chosen for them. It was to me a remarkable illustration of how utterly objective the profoundly subjective Russians can be in pursuit of knowledge, ignoring the cost in money, time, emotion or pride, to gain the purpose they have set for themselves.

He then asked me what I earned? I told him and at the same time tried to explain what income tax in Britain did to our earnings and death duties to our savings. That horrified him. In Russia income tax was at the very most thirteen per cent of income. Death duties did not exist. Having never known any other system he was quite unaware of what it cost them in other ways. For instance, since the State controlled all agencies of supply and distribution whenever it wanted more money it raised it not by increasing taxes but by lowering the prices paid to producers or by increasing prices in the State-owned shops, or doing both simultaneously.

My young friend added that he thought our way of levelling out incomes by taxes and death duties could not be effective because the differences between poor and rich were so great.

Before I could reply in terms of our Welfare State another young man commented that our way clearly couldn't work so well, otherwise we could not have as many millionaires as we did. How many in fact did we have? he asked.

I could not answer specifically – I have never been interested in millionaires as such – so I could only say 'far fewer today than before the war'.

Then did I know how many there were in America? The country was as stuffed with millionaires as Kiev chicken cutlet with butter, the young man thought, and he laughed aloud.

Again I could not answer.

All the time the young engineer had been listening to us with an amused, faintly cynical look in the eye and he intervened now to say: 'But I can tell you how many millionaires there are in the Soviet Union. We have over five hundred of them!'

The remark fell like a bomb among his friends and they looked horrified and unbelieving.

'I can prove it to you from State documents if you like.' The engineer, amused by their consternation, stuck to his point, adding 'After all, when we have created our "state of abundance" at the end of the twenty-year plan we shall all be millionaires. So why worry?'

This 'state of abundance' which was their great prerequisite for Communism always cropped up in conversation. People young and old believed in its inevitability so much that while I was in Russia Mr Khrushchev publicly rebuked the people for it, warning them that the 'state of abundance' would never come unless they all worked harder and paid more attention to the present. But the young, far better off materially than young people had ever been in their country, were beginning to wonder what they were going to do about life itself when they had achieved their 'state of abundance'. They were beginning to suspect that there was some deeper meaning to life that had escaped the attention of their elders and for which they were not being prepared.

All the same there was a tremendous gap between the income of the engineer and that of the Russian 'millionaire', which was far greater than that between their counterparts in Britain where the millionaire pays tax up to 19s 6d and more in the pound. Though I did not press the comparison my friend earned £600 a year (reckoned at the official rate of exchange of 2·50 roubles to the £1) which is less than a qualified engineer does in Britain. On that £600 however the Russian explained that he did quite well, could even afford to be a bit of a 'pirate'. His rent was only five per cent of his income – it was never higher than seven per cent anywhere – and soon too he was convinced all rents would be abolished in Russia and all transport and accommodation free. It was useless to dispute with them their use of the word 'free', useless to stress again that nothing in life is 'free' but has to be earned and paid for as he and his kind paid with their labour and their time and their imagination. Useless, too, to confess to my belief that the more indirect the method of payment the more wasteful and costly the system. Their system already is far more approximate than ours whatever else one may find in its favour. Daily I was appalled by the amount of unproductive paperwork it exacted. I had the impression that their proportion of accountants and book-keepers, of checks and counter-checks, of inspector-accountants and of inspectors of inspector-accountants, must be by far the highest of any country in the world. The amount of documentation demanded by the simplest things seemed to me appalling. Also how much simpler and cheaper if tourists like myself had been allowed to pay directly with money for hotel and other services. Instead I was issued with one set of coupons for hotel accommodation, another for food, another for car chauffeur and guide, another for air, train and sea travel. All these coupons had to be collected, checked and somewhere converted into their financial equivalents. My guides too travelled on coupons and the discussions and arguments that went on everywhere were endless. The interpretations of value were not alike in any two places and the contradictions and variations funnelled into the central accountancy depot must have taken a nightmare of resolving. For instance, I could never eat enough food to cover the amount allowed for on my coupons. The waiters were not allowed to give me the difference in money between the food I had eaten and the amount I had paid for the coupon and they were always most concerned about this for they clearly felt I was being cheated if I did not eat up to the full price of the coupon. So they would offer me chocolates or wine to cover the difference. Since I wanted neither they were distressed until someone hit on the device of paying me back in small jars of caviare. Thereafter I took my change everywhere in caviare and was able to present a jar to each of my friends on my return to England. But the inefficiency and waste of such ways could not be communicated to the average person because he had no other standard of comparison. And, to be honest, I did not try very hard to bring the point home to them. I was there to learn and not to convert. I was happy enough to drop this kind of conversation with my young people and talk of other things.

What impressed me most about them, perhaps, was that we all seemed to laugh at the same things. For instance, they insisted on taking me to a waterside café and ordered coffee and wine and chocolates. The wine they told me was a Crimean Madeira. I thereupon told them about the song from *At the Drop of a Hat* – 'Have some madeira, my dear!' Their knowledge of English was good enough for them to see the point at once and I thought they would never stop laughing. Thereafter, they insisted on my going through all I remembered of the revue, and as they still wanted more I had to draw on *Beyond the Fringe*. My supply ran out before their appetites.

Singing snatches of 'Have some madeira, my dear,' and still giggling over it, they walked back with me towards my hotel. Since they had refused to allow me to pay anything towards our refreshment I asked them all in to have tea with me. To my dismay the invitation first startled and then embarrassed them.

Then suddenly the engineer, his direct open nature hating the fact that he could not respond as his instincts prompted him, said loudly: 'Yes, why not? After all, why not?'

The others remained silent, looking straight in front of them. It was obvious that my invitation was a problem and I felt sorry I had given it, so much did it spoil the atmosphere among us.

After a silence the engineer spoke again to say: 'It might be difficult for us all to come. Perhaps it would be better if we all met and gathered on the promenade again. We would like to take you for another walk.'

Relieved, I fell in readily enough with his proposal. 'Good. What time?'

'About six this evening,' he replied.

As we were talking we had reached the entrance to my hotel. Waiting by it stood the man who had angered my Yalta guide so much at dinner the night before. He did not appear to be aware of us and I do not know if his presence there was sheer coincidence. All I do know is that I walked up and down the waterfront for two hours that evening but I saw no sign of the young people. I looked for them everywhere in vain for two more days knowing that the majority of them lived in Yalta and that the two 'pirates', the Leningrad girl and the engineer, were there in residence for another fortnight. But I had to leave Yalta without ever seeing any of them again. And I cannot believe that they would have avoided me out of their own free choice. So, unhappily, the feeling that I had broken through some sort of barrier with these charming young people abandoned me and I seemed back in the moment where I had started.

I must stress however that this was the only incident of its kind that occurred during my journey and I never worried unduly about this sort of thing. There may have been concealed microphones in my rooms, as the Moscow correspondents assured me there always were, but I did not try to find out since I had nothing to hide. I may have been shadowed but I believe I was not. Nor, I am sure, were my bags ever searched in my absence. Yet numbers of letters addressed to me 'c/o the British Embassy' and a few of mine to the British Ambassador and Minister in Moscow never arrived. On the other hand several long telegrams of mine from Central Asia and Siberia got through to the Embassy with exemplary dispatch. But of this man dining near us in a Black Sea hotel and awaiting my arrival outside my hotel I am not at all sure. I still feel uneasy when I think of him and particularly when I think of my Russian companion's outraged reaction to him.

CHAPTER NINE

JOURNEY BY SEA

BEFORE I left the coast for good I flew to Odessa to sample a voyage in a Russian ship on the Black Sea. My interpreter had volunteered to accompany me since the ship was calling at Yalta on the way to Batumi, and he was disappointed because we did not stay long at Odessa. This Ukrainian city has a great hold on Russian imagination, due not merely to the significant role it played as a seed-bed of the Revolution but to the fact that it has been for thousands of years a firm point of contact between a savage interior and the civilizations of the outer world. It has, despite its turbulent and changing history, an unchanging tradition of enlightenment and predisposition to free-thinking and culture. To this day Soviet artists frequent it and speak of it with affection. One has only to read the work of contemporary writers like Paustovsky and Vera Inber to discover the warm esteem in which it is held. Some of Russia's greatest musicians and singers received their training there both before and after the Revolution. The vast opera house (an imitation of its Viennese prototype) is still one of the first sights proudly pointed out to the visitor. In Odessa one is more aware of the wide world beyond the Soviet Union than in any other city. This sense is heightened by the fact that the young Duc de Richelieu, a refugee from the Revolution in France, whom Alexander sent to it as governor not long after Catherine the Great had conquered it, had stamped upon it the ineffable character of a French aristocrat of taste. Count Langeron who followed him walked closely in his tracks and was succeeded by Prince Vorontsov, who added a marked influence of Regency England. Though Odessa was almost destroyed by the Germans after an heroic defence in the last war the Soviet State restored it with meticulous loyalty to its original pattern. It did this not only out of respect for its past but also because Stalin had his own strong feelings about Odessa. Legend has it that he started his revolutionary career as a bank-robber in the city robbing money to pay for the board and lodging of Lenin and his fellow conspirators in second-class English boarding-houses and Swiss *pensions*. But paradoxically the Greek colony of Odessa, one of the oldest and most important of all on the Black Sea littoral, appears to have vanished at Stalin's behest. The Crimean Tartars too, one of the oldest and most vigorous branches of the race that overran Russia for centuries, were rounded up on a charge of having collaborated with Hitler's armies and deported somewhere into the vast Soviet hinterland. Since then the Soviet Government have rescinded the order of exile for these and other minorities and plans have been made, it is said, for their rehabilitation.

From such a place I could obviously have learned a great deal and passed many days agreeably enough. But it was not metropolitan facts, information and impressions that I was after. My main interests always had been the people and I longed for more contact with them. My hotel on the waterfront was so crowded with delegations of the more unprepossessing kind that I despaired of meeting any Russians in it, and my experience of the past few weeks therefore suggested that it was best for my purpose to seek them out in the country or to travel with them. After doing the round of Odessa with the help of a woman guide who spoke fluent French, seeing sanatorium upon sanatorium and the new Odessa surrounding and overtopping the old in exactly the same barrack-room style, I found myself increasingly impatient to get aboard and into my ship. Yet I was there long enough to enjoy the devious interior of the old city, to enjoy the evening air with the thousands of men and women crowding pavements and streets for the same purpose after work, and to stand on the famous Potemkin steps, looking down on the neat harbour crowded with ships of all nations beyond which was anchored the Soviet Antarctic whaling fleet. Somewhere I was sure all this coming and going between a closed and an open world must be having repercussions in the minds and spirits of the people who crowded the city. But I never got near enough to any single person's mind to detect signs of it.

The people we spoke to were always helpful, kind and hospitable – someone in a café seeing I was a stranger paid for my coffee before I could stop him and disappeared through the door before I could thank him. But there never was any chance of prolonging such brief contacts as I had. However, the Union of Soviet writers did inform writers in various places of my coming and for my brief meetings with them, particularly those in Siberia, I shall always be deeply grateful. They would turn up at all sorts of bleak aerodromes to meet me and to see me off and to arrange journeys and visits to the countryside for me. I could not imagine writers anywhere in the world, even in the hospitable friendly Japan, turning out so willingly to meet and help a writer from another world. It certainly has never occurred to me to do so. But unfortunately, according to the young woman who took me around, the writers in Odessa either had not been told of my coming or were not available. I tried to make friends with her but, understandably enough, I was just another tourist. The only time she appeared to see me as something more was when I used a French idiom she did not know. Then out came her notebook and a request for elucidation. In the course of one such exchange she confessed to a passion for light French music. My knowledge of popular French music was definitely pre-war yet my tuneless rendering of '*J'attendrais le jour et la nuit*' and '*Plaisir d'amour ne dure qu'un instant, Chagrin d'amour dure toute la vie*' moved her close to tears.

Because of its heroic and protracted battles against the Germans, Odessa had a great many dead. Even after it had fallen soldiers, civilians, men, women and children hidden in the labyrinthine tunnels, mines and slopes cut deep into the limestone foundations on which the city stands, carried on a clandestine war of ambush, sabotage and night-sorties against the Nazi garrisons. So like all the main cities of Western Russia it had lit a Flame of Remembrance in the cube of an anonymous monument of stone to the fallen. All these flames everywhere were referred to so consistently as the Eternal Flame that the two words had fused and become one. The Russians seemed to me to be peculiarly addicted to this welding of adjective and noun into a single unit. It was always Heroic-Soviet-Labour; Our-Collective-farmers; etc. Satellite countries were always The-Free-Peoples-Democracies and our democracies were always War-Mongering-Imperialisms. I repeatedly thought of the American General Gunther who once when addressing a meeting of peers in London told them to their delight that he had reached the age of sixteen before he realized that the 'goddam-British' were two words! I felt that the real thaw in Russia of which the intellectual west was speaking so much would come only when these nouns and their adjectives fell apart. However, with all this in mind we arrived at the Memorial.

Brisk and competent the young woman said: 'Please come now to look at our Eternal-Flame-of-Memory.'

Unfortunately the Eternal-Flame was out.

The young woman however, not the least taken aback, merely said without the glimmer of a smile: 'I am sorry the Eternal-Flame is not burning today,' and turned her back on the monument!

The only person with whom I seemed to have real human contact in Odessa was a boot-black. Just before embarking I walked with my guide round the city trying to find a boot-black willing to polish my shoes. Boot-black after boot-black turned me down. One said he was tired, another claimed that his working day was over, another had run out of the right polish, and yet another begged to be excused because he did not have the right brushes for foreign shoes like mine. I thought them the most independent body of men I had yet met in the Soviet Union but my companion had another view.

'The trouble is,' she told me, 'that it doesn't matter how many shoes they shine a day they get paid by the State just the same!'

I should, of course, have known that even boot-blacks would be State-employed. No matter how wasteful the system of accounting needed to control these small enterprises, the fact that everything was run by the State had been hammered into me. Only a few days before at Yalta I had been rebuked in the friendliest manner by my Russian companions. I had watched at work a solitary individual who cut profiles with scissors out of paper for visitors at forty kopecks a time. One lone man at such individual work, I had been convinced, could not be State-employed. But he was and I was duly lectured on the vanity of ever expecting any exceptions to the rule save those I have mentioned earlier.

When at last we found a willing boot-black, he turned out to be a man who had lost both his legs in the war. He was only the second war-mutilated person I had seen – my Georgian host had been the first. When one considered that twenty million dead is the official figure of Russian war casualties the number of mutilated survivors must run into many millions too. Yet one sees so few of them that there are rumours among foreigners that they are rounded up and kept out of normal sight. This Odessa boot-black, however, had his pitch on the corner at two of the main Odessa streets. I do not believe he would have taken me on had he not been told that I had just come from England. Then it turned out that he had an only daughter who was taking English as her main subject at Moscow University. That established, I became one of his family. He took far longer than necessary over my shoes, asking me all sorts of questions and ending up by telling me they all had had enough of war in Russia and only wanted peace for all the world, and asking if I thought the Americans would start an atomic war? His life after all was a wreck – but what of his daughter? Tears came into his eyes as he asked not only of me but also of a crowd which had collected to listen to our conversation what was the use of having children and sending them to university when it could all be destroyed in a second?

I told him of our mutual longing for peace and added that the ordinary people in my world feared his country in the same way that he feared us. This last thought was utterly foreign to him and he brushed it from his mind as vigorously as the dust from my shoes.

When he had finished he asked eagerly: 'Could boot-blacks in England or America have done your shoes as well?'

'They certainly could not have done better,' I answered.

To my amazement the little crowd of onlookers round us broke into applause. Clearly they were not only hungry for news of the outside world but also needed some sign of recognition from it of what they too had accomplished.

'My greetings,' the boot-black called out after me, 'to all the boot-blacks of England and America!'

We embarked just before sunset and long before sailing time in a twenty-thousand-ton liner. I was disappointed it was not Russian built. The '*auf*' and '*zu*' on the taps in my bath suggested that it was part of German war reparations to Russia but the

crew, at least, half of it women, were all Russian. From the boat-
deck I watched the passengers coming on board. I was the only
foreigner in the ship. An officer stood on the quay at the bottom
of the gangway collecting tickets. The crowd of passengers driven
by the anxiety most people feel when faced with a new experience
pushed and jostled one another a great deal and the officer himself was often elbowed out of position and importuned and
shouted at from all sides but he never appeared irritated or
moved even to exhort the crowd to order. The people in the
crowd too never lost their tempers with one another though I saw
women with babies in their arms roughly pushed aside by burly
men and parcels and suitcases in the crush squeezed out of
people's arms to fall to the ground. My companion told me of
some French people to whom he had acted as guide, who were so
irritated by the persistent jostling from a crowd that they lost
their tempers and started to lash out angrily at everyone in their
vicinity. The Russians were horrified at such lack of travelling
manners presumably because it was personal retaliation and not
the collective, impersonal pressure they were all applying to get
through a bottle-neck. Yet I thought even so phlegmatic an
officer as the one at the gangway would lose his temper with
some of his passengers. I saw seven persons sent running back
to their hotels for their tickets. Then two slightly tipsy men tried
persistently to cheat him. One of them had left his ticket at home
too, only this time this passenger was determined not to go back
for his ticket. On the word of an honest Soviet workman, he said,
he had paid for his passage and that, as far as he was concerned,
was more than enough. When the officer refused to let him on
board he pretended to acquiesce. His companion with the ticket
started up the gangway and when certain that the officer was not
looking, leant over the side, and dropped his own ticket back on
to the quayside. His friend picked it up and again presented himself at the gangway. This time he was allowed through. Winking
at the passengers lining the rails of the ship above him he got to
the top of the gangway but there unfortunately waited another
officer who had seen the whole performance and who turned him
back. Thereafter the two men, undismayed, tried more elaborate
strategies. They even changed places, coats and hats with the
light-hearted connivance of other passengers, who suddenly

seemed to enjoy joining in a scheme aimed at outwitting authority. To their credit the two officers took it all in the same spirit and when finally the ship moved off and the man was left disconsolate on the quay one of the officers threw him a lemon and that too raised a good laugh.

I encountered the same casual forgetfulness all over Russia. At all the railway stations, airports and harbours, large notices and broadcast reminders begged travellers to make certain they had their tickets with them. It was for me another example of this instinctive neglect by the Russians of the world of physical objects. They seemed to assume that the feeling and the wish to travel was passport enough: and sometimes this neglect could have quite serious consequences.

About ten minutes before sailing a fat young mother had appeared, baby in one arm and a tower of parcels in the other. She too was found to be without a ticket. Tears left the presiding officer unmoved, and though the crowd on the quay joined in trying to make him change his mind he would not budge. The woman must go back for her ticket. That clear she acted at once, stopped crying, pushed her baby into the arms of a bystander and started running towards the distant heights of Odessa gleaming in the sunset. When she vanished our eyes went to and fro between the clock and her little bundle of possessions abandoned at the side of the gangway, though the officer himself seemed afraid to look at it. When the officer on the quay, after one final glance at the harbour gates, came slowly on board we all believed that we would sail away without the woman. The gangway was being slowly raised and the ship had just cast off at the bows when we saw the young woman come running towards us, screaming and waving her tickets at the ship. She stood opposite us still screaming and holding up her child.

There was no doubt now what the crowd on shore and the passengers in the ship felt about it all. They hated the ship for putting its schedule before the interest of the mother and the child. The bright air of evening between ship and shore was black with hatred and I was amazed at the power of it. The Captain on the bridge felt it too. But the big ship, alas, was already too firmly under way to make return possible and we swept by the end of the quay with a good thirty fathoms between it and the ship. At that the hatred of the ship lay even heavier on the air though not a sound came from the crowd on the shore. It just stood there silently, hating. I have often encountered this kind of silent communication of purpose in animals. I have never encountered it to such a degree in any crowd of people and I believe that at that moment I was witnessing a demonstration of one of the most significant elements of the character of the Russian people, their magnetic and indivisible unity in moments of crisis. On the face of it mother and child seemed defeated. Yet still the crowd refused to give up. Suddenly orders were shouted from the bridge through a megaphone to one of the accompanying tugs.

'Ah!' said my companion with a great sigh of relief. 'The Captain has ordered the tug to go back for the woman and child.'

When they were both safely on board at last the passengers did not cheer as I am certain a British crowd would have done. They just stood there silently watching to make certain that all was well and then without a gesture or sound broke up.

'You know,' my Russian companion exclaimed as he threw himself down yawning on a bench, 'I feel utterly exhausted – after all that.'

One of the best accounts of a *voyage-de-luxe* occurs in a story called *The Gentleman from San Francisco*, written in the ample pre-war days by Ivan Bunin, the exiled Russian writer of short stories, who won the Nobel Prize for literature just before his death between the world wars. The ship in which I travelled now reminded me of the class in which Bunin's Gentleman from San Francisco travelled and the reminder was not without its ironies. I had just been reading in my history books of the reaction of the young idealists of Bolshevism when Lenin, attempting to get over the terrible crises of the early twenties, compromised with some of the *bourgeois* practices. Many of these idealists when they heard that Lenin had thrown open the private peasant markets and started the trains running again for money, committed suicide. They would have committed suicide all over again, I believe, could they have seen their countrymen travelling in this ship. There were four different classes in the ship. The Captain in his cabin, over coffee and a box of delicious Russian chocolates, emphasized to me that though there were four classes in his ship there were no 'class' distinctions. It did not matter who a man was provided he had the money.

'As far as I am concerned,' he remarked, 'it is a simple matter of money. As they pay me so they travel.'

And the answer to these differences created by money is that they are purely temporary because at the end of the Twenty Year Plan 'the state of abundance' will eliminate them.

After all, I was asked by the other guests present, did we not have these classes in our ships too?

Actually, as I told them, I had never travelled before in a ship with four classes. All ships I knew today had only two classes and the tendency was to build more and more one-class passenger ships.

That amazed them all.

I myself believe that life on earth will never know real peace until men everywhere share wealth and opportunity fairly between them. Prosperous societies must level out the differences between themselves and the hungry millions who invest the greatest portion of our earth. I believe this to be the greatest issue of our time. It has us all by the throat, and should have us by the heart as well. Unease grips me in South Africa when I help myself to a fourth course from a tray held out to me by a black waiter at the dinner-table in some European home, or when an inflated American car driven by a prosperous farmer dashes by some African pedestrian in rags and tatters plodding along patiently mile after mile across the vast, empty landscape in search of work at a bare subsistence pittance. It assails me too because I know how inadequately I have met the claims of this problem in my own life. The same unease assailed me now in this ship. I should have thought that the avoidance of this ostentation of differences as symbolized by this four-classed ship was elementary. What my Russian fellow-passengers thought about it I do not know. They could hardly have been aware of it. Pacing up and down the deck before dinner I saw old ladies with black shawls round their heads looking for a sheltered place for themselves and their bundles on the boards against the iron bulwarks. I saw them looking out of patient, peering eyes through the windows at the stewards in white, starched jackets laying the tables in the first-class dining-saloon, candlelit, sparkling cut glass for white and red wine as well as water, ornate silver cutlery and peaked napkins spotless as Arctic snow by each place. Yet I was wrong if I imagined that the old ladies would be resentful about it. The vision merely brought a look of joyful interest to their faces as they pointed out each detail with delighted surprise and discussed it all with animation and interest. Perhaps had they shaken their fists I would have found it less frightening. Later I saw them lying on the hard deck, heads propped against their bundles, sleeping more peacefully than I was to sleep in my deluxe cabin that night. Just beyond them through the glass weather-screen which sheltered us I could see the fore-deck crammed with private motor-cars of Russians about to tour the Black Sea coast for their vacation. I remembered Fitzroy Maclean's account of a Black Sea cruise – it might well have been in this very ship – telling how, as the passengers were nearing Odessa, the loudspeakers suddenly called: 'Olga Ivanova, we are calling Olga Ivanova. This is to inform Olga Ivanova that her car and maid are waiting on the quay for her.'

The sea at night can be a mirror of strange uncomfortable magic whereby one is forced to face the reflection of one's own neglected self. The Black Sea under the starlight that night for me was just such an antique mirror. But in the morning I could detect no trouble in the passengers for the glaring contradictions of the night and I concluded that the days when Russians committed suicide about such things were over.

So we sailed down the coast with the lovely land always well in view. All morning long the loudspeakers kept up a commentary on the scene and read us appropriate lessons of history and economics. The passengers looked either indifferent or withdrawn as if all they cared about was the warmth of the sun on their faces. Indeed their capacity for withdrawal was great. At one moment all their senses were participating in the visible world; the next they would vanish immediately into their secret selves. The only people I have known who can perform this rapid change so easily have been certain primitive people in Africa. I myself have never sailed with so quiet, inert and well-behaved a bunch of passengers as in this ship. They did not stir out of themselves until we cast anchor off Sevastopol.

We lay there for a full hour staring at the distant harbour, the bare green hills overlooking it, and the far grey battleships inside all wrapped in sunlight like flies in amber while some submarine chasers described figures of eight in the flat blue water immediately around us. Considering the haste with which we had cast off at Odessa such a long wait seemed inconsequent but at last two small vessels came out to meet us: one, a smart naval pinnace, all spit and polish, brass and spotless yellow soap-stoned decks; the other a slow old ferry crammed with people, mostly beshawled women and their bundles. The pinnace was the first to reach us, reversed engines smartly five fathoms abreast on our starboard, and hailed our ship. It announced briskly that it was there to take off two generals. The bridge asked it to stand by and ten minutes later gave back its answer. The generals were not ready to disembark yet. They were at a game of chess in their cabin and would let the pinnace know when the game was finished. . . . The Russians lining the rail near me exchanged glances but no one smiled or laughed, either because chess is so serious a game in Russia that one could not walk out on it, or because this behaviour was what they took for granted in men of power. But when, forty-five minutes later, the generals announced that they were ready the pinnace was no longer ready for them. The crowded ferry, in trying to move itself against the gangway to disembark its passengers, had got its propeller entangled in our ship's mooring ropes and been brought to an awkward stop. Its plight was due certainly to no expert seamanship either on the part of the ferry or of our ship which had trailed its mooring ropes too low and loosely in the water. The crew of the ferry with their grappling hooks tried hard to get the propellers unwound, while the pinnace every now and then made piercing noises of protest because it could not get near to our ship. All efforts failed and then there occurred one of those national manifestations that I have mentioned before. Instinctively the officers and crew went into committee over the problem and the mechanics popped up out of the engine-room unsummoned by anything except instinct. There was no confusion or panic about the meeting and though I was aware how appalled a British or French naval officer would have been by the argumentative proceedings it seemed to me a natural and wise pooling of the best

experiences and ideas available in the circumstances. It was
also something which I was accustomed to see in the despised
African peoples and which I had learned to value and respect. I
have seen many a European led to disaster by rejecting this
instinctive committee-machinery in his African workers and
servants. Both they and the Russians tend to act collectively in
the face of any challenge and an officer or headman would never
lose face for consulting with his troops or villagers. A charming
illustration of this Russian trait occurs in *The Stovemakers*, one
of the few prose pieces by the Russian poet Alexander Tvardovsky, in which he describes how a Major commanding a military
district works quite naturally with its schoolmaster under the
leadership of a rough, peppery though expert old peasant. The
scene off Sevastopol might well have been a setting for another
story by Tvardovsky. After some minutes of discussion the officer
in command suddenly stripped, was firmly roped round his
middle, and then dived overboard. For about ten minutes he
dived and worked at the ropes round the propeller. Whenever he
came up for air he reported progress to a deck-hand who had
naturally taken over command and was directing him with a
grappling hook. When the officer failed his quartermaster stripped
and dived overboard, while another deck-hand rubbed the officer
down with a towel with lively concern and thoroughness. The
quartermaster, too, failed. Then two more of the crew dived overboard. They failed, too, to disentangle the propeller. Meanwhile
the generals, now wanting to get on shore, had appeared on deck.
They were both large and very fat men and clearly accustomed to
having their way. Yet from beginning to end of this amazing
episode they showed no signs of irritation. Finally it was our
own captain who decided calmly but implacably to put and end
to the problem by cutting the mooring rope which tied the ferry's
propeller to the ship. It solved his problem but not the ferry's.
When at last all its passengers had been taken off awkwardly
across the ferry's nose, hauled by hand hard up against the gangway, and when the generals had disappeared in their pinnace into
the harbour without a backward glance or wave of farewell, we
cast off and left the shabby old ferry drifting helplessly on the
waters. From time to time I saw some newcomer diving overboard. I watched until we were too far away to distinguish the

human figures on the decks and we left the ferry there as still as
the Ancient Mariner's 'painted ship upon a painted ocean'.

We were back at Yalta at sundown and ashore before dark.
Outside our hotel a woman boot-black was just closing for the
day. We could not persuade her to clean our shoes.

'What time will you open in the morning?' we asked her.

'I cannot say yet,' she answered loftily. 'Sometimes I open at
nine, sometimes ten, sometimes eleven and sometimes not until
the afternoon. So how can I tell you now?'

Before we could answer one of the passers-by, who as usual on
the coast had collected when they recognize strangers in their
midst, remarked tartly: 'In fact you carry on just like a
supreme Minister of State!'

That raised a good laugh but the woman, protected by the imperviousness of her craft, was not a bit disconcerted. She swept
out of sight like Queen Victoria, regal and unamused.

My guide laughed heartily. 'And you thought the boot-blacks
of Odessa independent!' he commented.

CHAPTER TEN

COSSACK COUNTRY

THE next day, coming through the pass over the saddle of the great Bear Mountain beyond Yalta on the way to the airport at Simferopol, I experienced my first Russian wind. It was blowing steadily from the north and came unimpeded all the way from the Arctic. The day, so warm here on the coast, suddenly turned cold and made me understand that it could be cold enough at Odessa to freeze the sea, and also how helpless and exposed lay the great plains of the Ukraine as well as those of central Russia to the savage, long-maned winds which drove across them. It was a wind which had an intensely personal effect as if one's emotions were as exposed to it as the land over which it blew. It brought an element into being which fundamentally had nothing to do with the land wherein one was travelling since the clear sun and the blue sky obviously was still dreaming of growth and warmth. But no wonder the hills looked so bare, the grass short as if cut by a scythe, and the vineyards and orchards well tucked-up against the slopes into the lee of broad valleys for shelter. And this was not the *only* wind. There was another that matched it in reverse and came charging like the cavalry of the Golden Horde itself through the Georgian passes and round their mountain flanks over the undefended Volga Steppes, to carry the power of the desert into the heart of the Ukraine and across to the foot-hills of the Carpathians. One wind kills with ice and snow; the other destroys with fire and dust. I never experienced the latter but I read with awe Paustovsky's description of one such wind which blew for a fortnight in his childhood near far-away Kiev.

'It came,' he writes, 'laden with sand, whirling and whistling, and sending flurries of birds' feathers and chips of wood flying through the air. A heavy haze obscured everything. The sun had grown shaggy suddenly and red as Mars. Broom-trees swayed and crackled. A heatwave scorched my back. My shirt seemed to be smouldering. Dust crunched between my teeth and pricked my eyes. By the first evening the sand-drifts were deep against the wattle fences; by morning green leaves were so dry that they turned to powder at the touch of a hand and trees stood as bare and black as in autumn. Women's wailing filled the cottages while men sat glumly in the shelter of walls, prodding the soil with sticks saying: "It's turning hard as rock. The grip of death is on the land, that's what it is, and we have nowhere else to go." "Yes," replied his father, "the desert is spreading to the Ukraine".'

I mention these winds not only because they are so savage a feature of the Russian climate and must have some subtle influence on the character of the people – they blow, for instance, right through Russian music – but also because they are a natural challenge which brings out the best in Soviet Russia. In its mass attacks on 'natural problems' Soviet Russia is at its most impressive. The child Paustovsky had asked his parents why a Chinese wall could not be built to stop this devastating invasion of wind from the deserts of Central Asia, and was told it was impossible. Today the impossible is being performed.

I flew twice low over the plains between the Black Sea, the Caspian, and the interior, and I was profoundly impressed by the vast belt of trees that the Russians have planted to break up the winds and shelter the cultivated earth. Over the Kuban, which experienced the devastation of desert wind most since it was closer to their source of origin, the patterns of drained marshland, green with cultivation, protected by belts of trees and cut by canals, stand out as sharply as a drawing on a designer's board. The change after Central Asia is great for the whole earth around oasis and canal is cultivated and busily pushing up green. As one goes deeper west and north the pattern gets denser and the cultivation more intense until the whole earth flattens out into a teeming seemingly unending world of corn, cattle and men, and as one progresses west evidence of even greater Soviet preoccupations multiplies. In the midst of orchards, plantations and immense sweeps of corn, great factory chimneys appear smoking fast and full like battleships steaming into action. Krasnodar, Armavir, Novorossisk and Tuapse stained with smoke the bluest of days which was all the more striking because Russia is essentially a smokeless land. But where there is smoke it is industrial and not domestic. All along the marches of this old Cossack world cities like these have outgrown their retarded agricultural selves and today are centres of engineering, industry and commerce.

Rostov-on-Don is perhaps most representative of how Soviet Russia has transformed the Cossack world. I came to it that day with lively excitement. It was to be not only my first experience of a modern Soviet city but also my first meeting with a great Russian river. The river did not disappoint me. With the Volga and the Dniepr it was to make a threesome which no others surpass. The great Siberian and Far Eastern rivers were wonderful streams, great living acts of God and nature, but they lacked the long association with man and the power to evoke history which these other three possess. The Volga, of course, was the waterway which led to Central Asia and the Caspian terminals of the Silk Route. The Don and the wide Dniepr with its greyblue Slavonic eye, were the river-ways to the world of Greece and, when Greece had crumbled, the passageway to the one remaining centre of Roman civilization in Byzantium. When I saw the Don first, I remembered my Russian companion in the aircraft on the way to Tashkent and what he said about the rivers of Russia being the beginning of a uniquely Russian way of life.

How far back that beginning lies in time no one knows for certain. No historian will do more than admit a probability that the Indo-European family to which the Slavs belong were here before the transition from a stone to a metal age. On record the first positive references to Russians occur in the colourful gossip of Herodotus in the fifth century, when first they appear not as warriors but as river traders. From then on these rivers were full of historical movement. Boats from the Baltic for instance would make their way up the Western Dvina to Smolensk, or up the Neva, across Lake Ladoga, up the Volkhov and by means of tributaries and porterage reach the Dniepr at Smolensk, sail down on it to the Black Sea and so on to the Golden Horn. This was the invasion route of the Baltic Goths in the second century before Christ. Others used the Don and the Volga according to their specific intent. For instance, the Arab writer Hordab saw Russian traders in Baghdad in the early ninth century. They had, he said, come by way of the Volga. All three rivers, Volga, Dniepr and Don, rose comparatively near one another in the same bleak, northern watershed. Moscow and Novgorod-the-Great both owed their importance and rivalry to the fact that they were natural terminals for the river-roads to and from the north and south. The silks, carpets, jewels and spices, the slaves and their colourful panders that light the fairs at Novgorod in the dark hours of the northern European beginnings, and all the traffic which comes down through history to us like a lantern procession out of a Japanese All Souls' night, were all carried on those rivers.

Every day from my hotel in Rostov I would walk down the banks of the river harbour and watch the big ships from Volgograd (as Stalingrad is now called), the Sea of Azov, and from Moscow itself, hastening up and down it. I would look in on the broad, luxurious passenger ships that sailed along its hundreds of inland miles; they were as comfortable as any cross-channel steamer plying between Britain and France and I would have gladly sailed out to sea in them. One of those I was told could take me to Moscow in four to five days and even to the Baltic and Murmansk. I promptly said I wished to go but was told firmly that was impossible. There were no facilities for passengers like me. I could only watch with envy the Russian peasants, Cossacks of the Don, no longer in embroidered blouses and jack-boots but in linen hats pulled down about their ears and cheap flapping, mass-produced clothes, minor officials, commercial and industrial messengers with little more luggage than a briefcase, embark and sail away on the closed and now mysterious river.

'Really to know this land you should see a Cossack village,' someone told me.

'Well, take me!' I said.

But again that was not allowed.

'Let us at least then go to a collective farm?' I pleaded.

Not even that was possible, I was told, because the Chairman, Secretaries and officials of State and Collective farms were all away at a conference discussing the arrangements necessary for one of the two great feast days (Prazdniki) of the Soviet year: May Day. I have never known such people for conferences as these collective and State farmers. They seemed to be conferring for one reason or another all the time I was in Russia.

'That doesn't matter,' I protested. 'I just want to look, not speak. Surely someone must be at home to milk the cows, let out the chickens and feed the pigs?'

But they remained obdurate. I was driven at speed through one village on the outskirts of Rostov on the edge of the plain to the north lying blue, silent and provocative in the sun of spring. I had time only to notice one thing. The inhabitants, farmers I guessed, were decorating it busily for May Day which meant bedecking every available space of prominence with red. Outside the collective farm office an official in a blue cap, blue serge suit and black leggings was loudly haranguing a group of men and women. He annoyed our chauffeur for he snorted with scorn and exclaimed indignantly: 'Look at him, the bureaucrat! He can't leave well alone! Fancy him telling people what to do when they've forgotten more May Days than he's ever known!'

For the first time I had no option but to get my knowledge of the life on the land here from books. My history told me what I wanted to know of the Cossack past. The origin of the name, I gathered, originally meant 'piece-workers' and indicated not a race but a vocation. They were military colonists planted along the Russian frontier against the Tartars. There their life was an extraordinary mixture of soldiery, farming and trading. They developed wonderful military resourcefulness and from boyhood to the grave were never parted from their arms and horses. When these southern frontiers became too tame for them they found an even greater outlet for their energies and fierce independent character in Siberia where, as at home on rivers as on horses, they pioneered the way to the Pacific. But how people with such a past fitted into the Soviet system and lived today was another matter. I turned hopefully to the books of one of the most celebrated of modern Soviet writers, Mikhail Sholokhov. Best known outside Russia for his novel on the Civil Wars, *And Quiet Flows the Don*, his writing is all about this part of the Soviet Union. He himself lives in Venshenskaya Stanitsa on the Don, a place so small that it is hard to find on the map, and neither success nor all the cultural inducements of the capital have persuaded him to leave his village. So I started reading *Virgin Soil Upturned*, as it dealt with a period nearer our own time than the Civil War. Yet as I read I experienced growing disappointment. In his awareness there seemed to me little comparison, little sense of the importance of specific human relationships as opposed to ideological ones, little appreciation of the importance of honour and self-respect in human beings. What he does describe brilliantly is a cruel world of violence and of brutal and insensitive people. One of his central characters, admittedly the villain, locks his own mother in her room in his house to starve to death because he is afraid she might betray the secret of a conspiracy in which he is engaged. His whole family night and day for four days can hear her begging for food and mercy, her sobs and voice growing fainter until silenced for ever and yet not a member of the household stirs to prevent her death. His heroes, of course, are Party Secretaries, collective farm officials and other instruments of the ideological will. They ambush and shoot down without trial or question a person they suspect of treason. Their deed itself is never questioned or submitted to any test of objective law or other impartial men. The only time these puppets of a slanted and sharply sided talent are deeply moved is when one of the collective farmers sees the light and applies for membership of the party. Somehow I could not accept that this world was all there was to Russia. I could not square Sholokhov's account with what I saw in people's eyes and faces even though that seemed intangible proof to put up against his solid talent and claims to an inborn knowledge of his subject. I could not believe that what he wrote was the last word on Soviet man and not something subtly slanted to serve or appease authority. So I put down this particular novel as if it too had refused me an entry into the life of the land as, physically, I had been denied entry to it by river and village.

Then strangely enough Sholokhov, himself, turned up in Rostov. I came down to breakfast one morning to find everyone discussing excitedly a rumour that he was staying in our hotel. The rumour caused as much excitement as would, I imagine, a rumour in an American hotel that Elizabeth Taylor had arrived in the night, or Princess Margaret in a country inn in England. All morning people would ask one another: 'Is it true?' or 'Have you seen him yet?' for the people of the Soviet Union spontaneously respond to the official policy of heaping honours and rewards on the intellectuals and artists who have served it well and added to its reputation in the world. I believe more main streets are named after writers and artists and more statues erected in their honour in the Soviet Union than in any other country. It has long since out-distanced the French who displayed a similar zeal in recognizing the part writers had played in undermining their Establishment. The Russian people themselves are great readers, too. They read in lifts, buses, parks, and I have even had chauffeurs who kept a book open beside them so that they could go on reading the moment the car stopped. Yet knowing this I was not prepared for such excitement among so calm and stolid-looking a public. We came across the writer himself at the airport. Thinking we had the V.I.P. lounge to ourselves I was playing the piano – only in Russia I imagine would a piano be regarded as an essential piece of airport equipment – when Sholokhov walked in followed by a posse of important officials from the city and airport. He was a smallish man, dressed in a suit of faded blue with a wide hat sitting on his ears. When he took it off he showed a fine high forehead, wide eyes both melancholy and shrewd at the same time. He was rather gnome-like, restless and full of energy. Certainly he was high on the list of the new Soviet aristocracy for he was escorted with great ceremony to the small feeder-line plane which was to take him off to his village. He took the ceremony abstractly and his wave of farewell to the officials on the tarmac could hardly have been more perfunctory. It was all due, I was told, to his dislike of fuss. The officials stood there waving until his plane vanished into the blue.

'He is a very wise man,' one of my companions told me. 'He will not go to Moscow on any account.'

I thought I could guess what he meant.

I got to know Rostov rather well during my stay there. The people of the city were extremely proud of the fact that they had not only completely rebuilt it after its destruction by the Germans in the war but also greatly added to it. It was typical in that regard of all the cities I was to see in the areas which had taken the worst hammering of the war. Even Volgograd had been entirely rebuilt and enlarged so effectively that the authorities have had to preserve one shattered building as a monument of what the city had endured in the war. Similarly Rostov's industries were all restored, flourishing and growing without any evidence of war damage.

The biggest farm-machinery works in the Soviet Union is located in Rostov. It produces the most intricate types of machines from grain combines, self-propelled mowers and maize harvesters. A sister works turns out electric-powered and self-propelled grain combines which seem to do their work with the quiet and effortless efficiency of sewing-machines. There are also boiler factories for power stations, electric locomotives, machine tools and so on and on. Nevertheless the remarkable thing is how free of smoke is this city of a million people on the edge of the Steppes. The inhabitants, of course, are very conscious of their industrial worth. The national mystique regarding the machine leaves no doubt in their minds as to the importance of what they are doing. Their pride is so intense that it annoyed an acquaintance from Moscow who whispered in my ear once: 'It's too much! These people talk as if they are the finest city in the Soviet Union!'

This acute industrial consciousness of the citizens of Rostov has made them build an astounding building. They have built an enormous theatre in the shape of an agricultural tractor. It towers over the principal square and really looks as if at any moment it might start to growl and the whole crouched concrete shape move forward to crush the shrinking buildings in front of it. The inhabitants all thought it a truly beautiful building. They pointed out how gloriously the architect had built an open-air Greek theatre into the driving saddle of the tractor. Against the crisp spring sky in an outline clearly demarcated, could I see the dip of the saddle? What more wonderful, they asked, than that art should be in the saddle of their great new industrial heaven on earth? I recognized that this was a matter of profound faith to these people and it is not only useless but wrong to argue with people about their faith. So I said nothing but this all left a deep impression in me of how elementary and over-simplified the Soviet view of life can be. And again how deep is the Russian capacity for projecting an inner vision on outer reality. It was another instance of how the inner feeling can completely dominate the physical expression.

Equally none of these people could understand my love of the old Armenian quarter of Rostov. When the town was founded as a customs post called Termenik in 1749, the Armenians, with their long nose for business, were already established there because

Termenik commanded important trading routes from the interior to the Black Sea, Sea of Azov and Mediterranean. They built themselves attractive little white-walled houses surrounded by trees and orchards and lived an industrious and individual life. For some reason the Germans were kinder to this end of Rostov than the rest (Engels Street, the main thoroughfare, four miles long, was razed to the ground) and left it almost intact. It was impossible to make my companions understand what a relief to the eye and mind were these individual buildings after the barrack blocks of the city. I honestly believe the Russians never see their buildings visually. In them they see only their good intent and the progress they embody compared to their abominable past. But in comparison to their new building our British ribbon development and the tape-worm proliferation of villas along the roads of England acquires an eccentric and rugged individualism.

Rostov too is proud of its children's railway. Since what is true of this railway is true of the whole of the Soviet Union and typical of the place of the child in the wider official plan it is worth looking at closely. Russian children, of course, have hobbies but they have them collectively. Hobbies are organized for Soviet children on a group basis by the State, through schools, unions, pioneer movements, and other collective organisms. There are, for instance stamp-collecting, model aeroplane, natural history, archaeological, camping and scores of other hobby clubs. What happens to a child who wants to pursue some lone interest peculiar to himself I do not know. I doubt if he would even as yet have room enough in the overcrowded apartments of the nation for the privacy that such an interest needs. And even if he had the privacy I doubt if he would be allowed to use it. Deviationism in the prevailing ideology would need to be stifled at birth. Anything conceived in isolation is still profoundly suspect. Besides the Russian state believes enormously in public criticism of people (though of course for councils of state, Party and higher officialdom it is another matter) so as a people they seem strangely unaware of how destructive to the emerging values of a child perpetual regimentation can be. I was to be reminded of this here at the children's railway in Rostov. There were more than three miles of track laid out in a park complete with lines, signalling systems, stations and workshops. On it travelled miniature passenger and goods trains carrying children and their parcels. From the selling of tickets to the driving of locomotives it was operated entirely by children, though supervised, of course, under the appropriate adult authority, and I am certain it gave the Rostov children an enormous amount of fun as well as useful training in the exercise of responsibility.

I asked if there were any conditions for joining the railway hobbies club?

None, I was told, all children can participate except, of course, if they did not behave and work well at school.

I do not know what happens to the child who does not fit in and conform to expectations in Russia. I suspect it may bear less thinking about than it does in our own world. But for those who conform Rostov has many crowded schools and some of the largest boarding schools in the land. One interested me particularly. It used to be a large military academy but now has been turned into an up-to-date boarding school which gives first place to children whose parents were either lost or mutilated in the war.

I have already mentioned the strange absence of smoke and how my eyes would look in vain night and morning for smoke to come tumbling down among the village and farmhouse tops. It was an absence that made the cold scene look colder still. But now in Rostov I realized that I was also missing the sound of bells. I saw churches but always their belfries were silent. I had long since had to accept the fact that I was travelling through a country that had rejected religion in the normal sense of the word. This had not been easy and it was the first time it had ever happened to me. Wherever I have travelled in Africa or the Far East the people had their own gods and one was surrounded by the atmosphere which can come only from the acknowledgement by a whole people of an overriding religious need. This is an atmosphere that does not depend on the existence of churches, or temples, and I have been deeply aware of it in the bush and deserts of Africa. But in measure it does depend on certain sounds and their archaic association in the spirit of man: a bell in Christian countries, a gong in the East, or a drum in Africa. But in the Soviet Union this atmosphere and its equivalent sounds are absent. For all the official lip-service to tolerance, the imagination, mind and will of a whole nation have been deliberately hardened against religion. Officially religion is allowed but in practice it is actively abhorred. Party exhortations and newspaper editorials are regularly urging the Soviet faithful to be more energetic in the task of converting people to atheism so that there is not only the absence of a religious atmosphere but also a highly organized and determined hostility towards anything that might recreate it. This really amounts to religion in reverse. I found it rather an unnerving experience which became less palatable as the journey progressed. I am not much of a church-going person myself but I began to long most intensely for these bells to ring out again. I think we have all become so aware of the negative aspects of organized religion that it is only by going into a world without it that we can realize again how much we owe to it and depend upon it.

I wanted to see several churches in Rostov but the young woman who showed me round could not understand my interest in them. She would or could not take me into them. She could not tell me their histories nor even their names and finally, irritated by my questions about a church on a mound dominating the river port and still not repaired after its war damage, she exclaimed: 'Why ask me these things? I am not interested in such places and never go inside them.'

CHAPTER ELEVEN

MAY DAY

I CAUGHT my first real glimpse of '*chernozem*', the famous black earth of Russia, on the way from Rostov to Kharkov. I have never seen more profoundly exciting earth, even its blackness was not the colour of negation but of the mystery of the great power of growth and rejuvenation with which it is charged. I would think that after the rivers of Russia this belt of black soil, which is hundreds of miles broad and runs from the east in Siberia to the west in Russia for more than three thousand miles, finally curving like a billhook southward into the Ukraine and down towards Odessa and Kuban, comes next to the rivers in historical importance. On it the Soviet Union still depends mainly for its daily bread. Along it once came the Tartar hordes feeding on the blood and milk of their ponies who in turn fed on the grass which grew twelve feet tall in the short summer season. Then back along it again went the Russians, sowing corn on the way, as they made for the Pacific. After the rivers this great black Steppe is the other broad road of history. It is remarkable how old this earth looks as if it were the original natural soil from which all other soils have been drawn. Geologists say it is a land of sawdust of the millenniums of ice-ages that cut down the original Urals to their present size and then left the fragments to rot in the suns and winds which followed them. They say it is older by far than the event of man, and somehow the colour and texture of it make one believe this.

On the day that I saw the black earth for the first time the sky was packed with storm-clouds. The lack of lustre and light should have made the earth darker but oddly enough it had a sheen upon it as the glint of ravens' wings, and where a shower of rain had left moisture it had a positive midnight brilliance. Against it a muster of river-gulls looked like a fall of snow. Bricks piled in a field for building blazed like coals of fire. Our first red chimney of the

Donbas* country caught in a ray of sun was as clearly reflected as an image in a mirror and lay on the surface of the earth like a length of burning metal on a blacksmith's anvil. The first of the corn breaking through was a bright astringent green. At first I expected that this unity of plain and width of sky was too much to expect even of a notoriously spendthrift nature. I thought that some hillock would be summoned to discipline the prodigal scene and to call such an immensity of flatness and space to order. But always beyond the next horizon there would be more. The horizon itself was a perfect circle as if it were nothing but the expanding circumference of a ripple started by a pebble in a dark pond wherein we were condemned forever to be at the centre. The impression the plain created was so deep that in time one became over-convinced by it and accepted it as an absolute. So much so that when one morning nearly two months later after a long and diverse journey that brought me to Siberia where I really did see the black earth end, I could hardly believe it. It was as if some enduring giant whom one had believed to be immortal suddenly had died: and it gave me quite a shock. That I who was a stranger to this earth could feel its end in such a personal manner gave me some inkling of what it must mean to Russians.

At the same time as the plain unfolded so the great pattern imposed by man upon it was revealed. I saw the new world of the mines and industries of the Don Basin. It is a most impressive spectacle of smoking chimneys, pit-heads, hills of slag and coal, factories and mills standing shoulder to shoulder for hundreds of miles, and ankle-deep in the fields of corn. In comparison the Ruhr, the Black Country of Britain, the reeking North of France seem miniature. And when I was to find similar worlds of industry extending all over the Soviet Union right across Siberia to the edge of the Pacific Ocean I had no doubt that in the end the Russians would get what they wanted and make themselves the greatest single industrial power on earth. That they should want this so much at the expense of so much else might be profoundly disquieting to a person like myself who has other priorities. But that they could achieve their desire I never doubted after my first glimpse of the Don basin. From there onwards the two Russias

* The Basin of the River Don, so rich in coal deposits that it was well developed before World War One.

lay side by side; industry and the plains. For all their propinquity how far apart they still were from one another became a question of vital concern to me.

This then was the one vision of all the hundreds of miles from Rostov to Kharkov where I arrived late one evening in pouring rain. Dark as it was it was light enough to see another war-ravaged city – the Germans occupied it for two years – totally restored and greatly increased. A city of about a million people, it presented the standard prescription for the Soviet design of living: a first-class university, several technical colleges, many schools, several theatres, much industry and so on. However, I was to discover there was one difference. It had a somewhat more independent approach and tended to put the things of the mind before industry. My first view of the Service Bureau in my hotel appeared to set the tone. I was apparently the only foreigner in the hotel partly because it was too early in the year for tourists and partly because it was the eve of the great May Day feast when people are supposed to have done their travelling and to be firmly in position. Already some days before at Rostov I had been warned that travelling for the next week would be difficult if not uncertain. It was not surprising, therefore, that I found the staff of the Bureau not at work and all engaged in serious pursuits of their own. One I discovered was translating from English a technical paper on metallurgy; another was studying French; another writing a philological treatise for a doctorate at the university; and a fourth absorbed in a manual of physics. When I told them my name they leapt to their feet to help me and told me they were expecting me and indeed had done some planning on my behalf. They had obtained a place for me on the stand for distinguished visitors at the May Day Parade. Would I like to use it?

'Can a duck swim!' I answered.

'Can a duck swim?' they repeated after me, puzzled.

I explained the expression while out came their notebooks. Laughing, one young man added: 'You may have to swim like a duck to the parade if this rain goes on! We are sad that you should see our Kharkov like this.'

I have from time to time had unusual hunches about the weather. I asked them: 'Would you like it to be fine tomorrow?'

'Of course,' they replied, 'who would not?' But what could anyone do about it?

But something could be done about it, I suggested lightly. In Africa the weather was capricious and often lethal, so every tribe had a person whose profession it was to make or unmake rain according to their need. I knew a very celebrated witch-doctor whose particular speciality was weather control. Would they like me to send him a message and ask him to ensure that the sun shone the next day?

I had said all this jokingly and expected only a laugh. But they entered into my suggestion at once as into a completely new game. . . . How would I get in touch with my witch-doctor? Even if he were on the telephone there was no time now for a long-distance call.

I tapped my forehead. 'My dear Watsons, I have my own methods!'

'Ah, Sherlock Holmes!' one of them, a girl, exclaimed with delight. 'Sherlock Holmes in person!'

I turned to her. 'Are you too going to the parade?'

'Yes, I am taking part in it,' she answered in French. 'After all one must show solidarity.'

'Then depend on it,' I said, 'the sun will shine!'

From then on they might have invented the game and carried it on with a touching mixture of flippancy and seriousness. Thereafter whenever we met they would ask, with an eagerness that amazed me: 'Have you been in touch? What was the witch-doctor's answer?' or something equivalent. All this made me realize another thing about Soviet Russia: how barren the Soviet mind and scene is of fantasy of any kind. Suddenly I felt sad that I had not brought Carroll, Edward Lear and the others with me for them to read. Those are the medicines too that the traveller in the Soviet Union needs to kill proliferation of the insect within himself. I longed now not only for fantasy of thought but the live human fantasies which one still encounters daily in the eccentrics of Britain. I realized again the natural wisdom of this deep instinctive respect and love that the English have for genuine eccentricity. And I realized how starved these young people themselves were for some fantasy in their own lives. It is difficult at this distance to explain how much pleasure their reaction to my fooling gave me and how important and hopeful an omen it appeared to be.

But next day it was far from fine when we got up early to walk the mile or so to the parade ground. The parade was not until ten yet during breakfast at 7 a.m. it was still raining.

'What about your witch-doctor now?' my companions teased me.

'There's plenty of time yet,' I told him.

'Oh, don't worry!' he laughed. 'I believe completely in your witch-doctor!'

Early as it was the streets were full of people. It was clear that if solidarity was the purpose of the exercise we were going to experience it with a vengeance. All the grey walls of the great grey dripping buildings along the grey wet streets were covered with red bunting and streamers and banners bearing slogans in white and gold. Many Russians that I met loved to tell me how all foreigners commented with pleasure on the absence of advertisements in their cities and landscapes and I had accepted it unthinkingly as true. But now suddenly I saw through it. In Russia there is only one advertisement: the State. The State advertises itself, its service, and products ceaselessly on the air and on the walls of buildings and station hoardings. From the moment one passes through the Berlin Wall and right on to the Pacific Ocean one is condemned to absorb the slogans and contents of the posters of the greatest advertising monopoly on earth. Never was I more aware of it than on this wet May Day morning.

Also as we came nearer to the square a kind of claustrophobia assailed me. I became uneasy and felt more and more as if I was walking into a trap. Part of it was due to physical causes. We were compelled like all pedestrians to follow one route to the parade ground. On the corner of every street security police, militiamen and soldiers stopped us and checked through our passports and permits before we were allowed to move on. Then repeatedly we met lines of militiamen coming down the street almost shoulder to shoulder to halt pedestrians at unexpected intervals and scrutinize identity cards and other papers all over again. Up to then everywhere on my journey I had been favourably impressed by the small numbers of police or militiamen I had seen about in the Soviet Union. I realized now that I had been naïve in assuming that their total numbers must be relatively small. Suddenly they were out in battalions and looking back down the broad street I could at one time see five rows of police going like combs through the pedestrians following us. When I looked to the front another rank was advancing upon us. Every side street was blocked by dark green military trucks backed on to the pavement and right into the buildings with no space between one vehicle and another. Each barricade was manned by soldiers too. European arrangements for the control of millions appeared unbelievably amateurish and casual in comparison with this. Perhaps this was part explanation of my claustrophobia. Each control point or rank of militiamen passed I felt to be another prison door closed behind me. But it was due also to the atmosphere I picked up from the crowd. The singleness of mood of the thousands plodding with us through the grey morning seemed to me stifling and threatening. Generally among an English crowd there is some individual who instinctively debunks the crowd values by doing or saying something to start a laugh. It was the absence of this kind of mechanism and the unseeing expression of just one unquestioned feeling on all faces as much as the elaborate barriers, barricades and check-points that accounted for the lack of ease in my mood. I found myself thinking in a new way, seeing us all sealed in like sardines in a tin with only one foreign fish in the catch ... and that was me. And there could be no escape. I am not given to anxiety-fantasies and I did not look for this sort of reaction. Then it came to me that perhaps my unease was related to the profound and complex suspiciousness inherent in authority in the Soviet State which forces itself to take such elaborate precautions for so innocent a day and so brings its own congenital mistrusts into what purports to be a day of joy and universal brotherhood to the ordinary Soviet man. Then something that helped to lighten my spirit did happen. It suddenly stopped raining and a beam of sun caught a scarlet banner high on a barrack-block and held it like a searchlight in focus until the gold of the hammer and sickle in the centre glowed bright. The clouds were parting fast and the blue sky coming through calmly and evenly.

'Your witch-doctor has been as good as his word!'

My Russian companion was delighted and put his hand approvingly on my shoulder.

By the time we arrived at the parade ground in the Dzershinsky Square the tops of all the buildings were steaming in the sun. The day, no one could doubt, was going to be very hot. Dzershinsky Square is, perhaps, the largest city square in the world. It certainly is the largest in the Soviet Union. The stand built for the spectators on the north side in the vast expanse dominated by huge official buildings looked hopelessly inadequate until my companion explained that it was purposely small. The whole idea of May Day was that everyone should participate in the processions and demonstrate their solidarity. The essence of it all was not watching but participating. He gave me a brief sermon on how the Soviet Union believed in action not inaction. The stand was quite big enough to accommodate the leaders of the people, delegations and visitors like myself. But most of the people on the move in the streets were on their way to their marshalling points all over the city.

So we took up our positions between the official box reserved for members of the Praesidium and high city officials, and a Chinese military delegation. Beyond the Chinese stood a large Cuban delegation under an outsize national flag, and all around and in between were older people and children too young to parade. The consideration with which the little children were treated was remarkable. Mothers would just thrust them into the arms of strangers in front of them and the children would be passed on quickly and carefully by willing hands to be given the best seats of all on the ground on the edge of the square. Men and women were all dressed unpretentiously and alike. There were not even any Ukrainian folk-dresses. Much later I was to see a few young people in the procession in their national costumes but at that moment the crowd was predominantly grey, brown and black. What positive colour there was came from the red of flags and decorations on the grey buildings.

This accounted for a completely unintentional piece of rudeness on my part. I was looking at a woman on the stand near me when my companion said: 'I am afraid you're making that lady uncomfortable.'

Indeed she had turned her back on us and was blushing.

'I'm terribly sorry,' I whispered. 'I didn't mean to be rude. But don't you see – she's wearing a hat.'

It was the first hat I had seen on a woman's head since my arrival in the country. It was also the only hat on the stand.

The other variation in tone came from the Chinese military delegation which, rumours had it, were studying the great battles fought in the Ukraine against the Germans on the actual terrain. They stood there composed and remote, looking most distinguished with their long military capes almost falling to their boots. Their uniforms were immaculate, fastidiously designed and cared for. In that they were unlike the Russian military who somehow always looked somewhat crumpled and uncared for. Even if one had known nothing about China or its history one could not have failed to conclude that they were representatives of a most remarkable people. Also the crowd-fixation of which I have spoken seemed absent in them. They did not merge as the crowds in the streets had done. Each man seemed to be an individual Chinese.

We were so early that we were in time to see the Army units arrive to form up for the parade opposite us. They came through a grey gap in the far end of the square in the green-brown khaki of the Soviet Forces. They marched in ranks of twenty, each man tightly shoulder to shoulder and each following on the heels of the other. One can judge something of a nation's character from the way its soldiers form up and march and one thing was very evident here: the marching men were dedicated to expressing the 'togetherness' to which the Russians are so profoundly attached. So successful were they that one seemed to see not fifty thousand men marching into the square but one. The crowd responded to the appearance of the soldiers and the emotion between it and them was silent only because it ran deep. Now for the first time I heard a word used which has great meaning and power in Russia. Someone near me speaking of the soldiers, breathed with deep satisfaction the word '*nash*' (that is 'ours').

So the soldiers marched, formation after formation, into the square which was still in the shadows although the pompous concrete tops were now wet with sunlight and the air below sparkling from the glint of bayonets. It was a formidable sight and it aroused again in me the feeling of being trapped in a dungeon of the past. As soon as the armed thousands were in position, officers and cadets from the great Kharkov Military Academy marched in to join them. They were dressed differently, in tunics of khaki but with blue breeches underneath, and the hands of every cadet and officer were covered in white jersey gloves. After the ferocious glint of bayonets their impression was most incongruous. In this impressive military scene those gloves were as white and prim as those of a Victorian governess. Once in position the inspecting General appeared in a jeep. At first we could not see the jeep, only the top of a huge man taking the salute at thirty miles per hour as he was transported, apparently magically, between the massive ranks, rather like a puppet in Moscow's famous puppet show flying airborne on invisible strings up and down a crowded stage. He was followed in due course by the General-in-Command. Wherever the General stopped to call out a formal greeting to a particular formation they would answer him with a unified shout of 'Ra! Ra! Ra!' which sounded more like a musical than a military response. When the General had gone to take up his position still stiff and upright in his jeep, opposite the State Box, the most remarkable demonstration of all occurred. The senior officers started a low wailing sound swelling from far down in their throats and quickly gathering volume. As it died away again in one group a neighbouring formation took it up and so passed the call down from rank to rank right to the far end of the square where it became little more than the sound of a gust of wind. Then it was passed back again all the way right down to the senior ranks who had begun it. It was beautifully done and made the hair on the back of my neck tingle. It was as if history were transformed into sound linking up those living thousands with their remote beginnings. I wondered if the Slav soul had evolved this call not only to keep a man in touch with the great rivers, woods and plains of Russia but also with his fellow men as they cross the wasteland of Time? The only sound comparable to it was when I heard the Japanese troops singing to keep contact with each other as they hunted us along the jungle footpaths of the Sunda lands of Java. Here in Kharkov too there was something of Asia in the sound.

The parade started after a short address delivered punctually at ten o'clock; a stereotype tribute to the army, workers, peace-loving Soviet system, a call to workers of the world to unite, and a warning, of course, against the Imperialist and Capitalist Neo-Fascists, Revolutionists, warmongers and so on. The crowd seemed to be apathetic until the brass bands struck up, thousands of troops swung into action, bayonets glittering and the march-past began. I expected the spectators on the stands to cheer when the first formation came past but it remained oddly silent. A professional May-Day cheer-leader had taken possession of the loudspeaker and for three hours exhorted the spectators to cheer or applaud but the response stayed indifferent. What communication there was between spectators and soldiery remained silent and this mute, unutterable participation in one single feeling was to me far more fearsome than any cheering could have been. And the march-past itself was not the least alarming aspect. Rank after rank passed, twenty deep, with fixed bayonets and the men were so close that the bayonets behind protruded across the shoulders in front, their points just below the cheek bones of the marching men. They marched in a markedly unseeing, ritualistic way, rather as if they were sleep-walking. This impression got exaggerated emphasis from the goose-step into which they broke as they came level with the spectators' stand. It is perhaps the oldest step evolved for the male animal to shake the earth and make his enemies tremble. The bulls of various species do something of the kind in field, bush and jungle before they charge an adversary, and I know tribes in Africa who still practice it and indeed do it better and more elegantly than any Europeans since it is still natural to them. But in this differentiated age it seems a degrading and humiliating step for civilized men. On a day supposedly devoted to peace and universal brotherhood it certainly revolted me more than the German goose-step or its Japanese equivalent, the Hocho-Tori, did in war. Then after the soldiers came the athletes. The priorities were informative in this parade and showed how seriously the Russians have taken to sport. There were endless platoons of sportsmen and women looking physically overstrained, somewhat malnourished and very pale. After the athletes came the Union of Workers to be followed by groups and family parties who joined in obediently to demonstrate solidarity. The three main streets of the city spilled into the square and all three were overflowing with citizens on the march so that the parade ground had to be reorganized to take their immense numbers. Those who came first were headed by what I took to be a large white dove of peace in plaster of Paris. I saw this ghostly white apparition emerge, pecking with a jerky motion like a clockwork pigeon, and it was not until it came nearer that I discovered that it was not a bird but a model of Lenin in plaster frock-coat, collar, tie and pointed beard, bouncing on wheels over the uneven surfaces!

After the statue came banners, all in red. My Russian friends kept on telling me that red, in Russia, is not only a colour but also a word meaning 'beautiful'. It lost its beauty for me that morning. Hour after hour just as there was only one mind, one emotion, and one idea on parade now also there was only one colour. It is true the red was occasionally relieved with the gold of a hammer or sickle. I longed passionately for a shade of a different colour. There are after all seven different colours in the rainbow. All are beautiful and all have a vivid meaning in mind and eye. I kept on thinking how differently the Italians, even Italian communists, would have ordered the occasion. But the banners, flags and bunting waved and brandished over all were all red for the spirit of the State and society demands this terrible conformity of everything in life, even in colour. I repeat it was terrifying and it thoroughly terrified me. The feeling of my isolation became momentarily almost overpowering: for I stood alone as the only Western European in a gathering of hundreds of thousands. Then in the purple shadows cast by the red banners of a vivid sun appeared something new to distract and relieve me: photographs carried on poles. Some of the photographs were of the Communist great, Marx and Engels (Marx looking oddly like Alfred Lord Tennyson about to recite the Charge of the Heavy Brigade at Balaclava). But there were far more portraits of Lenin, several of Mr Khrushchev and some of Mikoyan and a few members of the Soviet Praesidium. But there were none at all of Stalin. Yet these portraits of the living Soviet great were fascinating because they looked as if they all had just been taken off the walls of some private residence. They were like family portraits suddenly exposed to indecent public view and emphasized a feeling that had been growing in me. The Russians – and I mean only the peoples of the Ukraine and greater Russia – are still more of a vast family than a nation. That complex, conscious concept of a particular culture and civilization in action which is, in the classical sense, what one means by 'a nation' is still in the making in Russia, and the social reality is still more an unconscious, immensely extended, and instinctive state of kinship best described by the word 'family'. Accordingly there was a touch of patriarchal ancestor-worship about the parade. This crowd was carrying its portraits as its forefathers for centuries had carried ikons in their religious processions with Lenin as something of the traditional father-figure of the Russian world. Then at last after the portraits came the citizens, arm in arm, carrying sprigs of plastic flowers and bunches of anaemically-coloured balloons. Although the red flags still flew far and wide over the square and processions there was relief for the eyes even in this slight variation of colour. Suddenly a bunch of balloons broke free and soared high over the buildings, were caught in a breeze and flew gaily off out into the blue. They got the biggest cheer of the day, the cry of spectators as well as marchers breaking out joyfully at this unrehearsed and irregular event.

Not until one o'clock did the parade come to an end. By that time my Russian friend said some 700,000 marchers had passed through the square. Judging by the crush on the way back to the hotel I do not think he could have been far wrong. We got through the police, security and military checks only with difficulty. Returning by back ways I was astonished at how elaborate was the system of barricades and control. But the crowd, now suddenly in a demonstrative humour, took the frustrations well. Several men had produced bottles of spirit and decided to get drunk. Some were already bemused on public benches or in the public gardens, but one huge citizen gave a magnificent uninhibited display. In the voice of Chaliapin he berated a group of soldiers who would not let him through and told them that they were neither 'cultured' nor 'democratic'. For the rest the abuse was in Ukrainian Russian.

'You know,' my Russian friend told me, 'the Ukrainians have a peculiar dialect. When that fellow on the loudspeaker in the square was calling on "all the workers of the world to unite" his accent was so peculiar that it sounded exactly as if he was calling on "all the tramps in the world to jump in a hole". . . . It was all I could do not to laugh!'

He looked at me and we both burst out laughing as if we had just been released from some terrific strain.

Then he gave me another knowing glance and exclaimed: 'That witch-doctor of yours is good. His sun has turned you into a good Communist. Your face is as red as our flag and mine is on fire too!'

We both laughed again. And yet the experience, even at this distance in my memory, is not a laughing matter. It is one of the ugliest things I have ever experienced in peace time, a reversion to a pattern of life which surely is discredited enough in all our histories. I remember I arrived back at the hotel late and utterly exhausted. It was not physical exhaustion. Three hours on my feet in a hot sun would not normally tire me. But I felt assaulted, oddly sore in mind and most uneasy. I lay on my bed and opened a copy of *Lorna Doone*, a book I had not thought I could ever read again but had bought in Rostov as it was the only English book available. I did not move until I had read it through from cover to cover. I believe I have never read any book with so sharp a sense of pleasure and the reading of it brought me a most extravagant feeling of reassurance after the state of mind to which the day behind me bore witness. There seemed to be the stern stuff of reality at the core of this lush romance. It pointed a way. As we use our imaginations so we all inevitably become. And how different this imagining from the kind I had just witnessed. I say this not as literary appreciation but solely because it seems to illustrate a point in the day's experience. I had to go to Russia to discover *Lorna Doone* which held in it a certain realism beside which the parade that I had just witnessed became oddly unreal. I would say that trying to make the unreal real and the real unreal is one of the most marked and dangerous characteristics of our sharply angled days.

Anyway by the time I had finished reading my fatigue had gone and I felt refreshed and ready for a new day. But from that moment on I saw to it that I was never again without some reading in English. Wherever I went I made first for a bookshop and re-read some of Jane Austen, Meredith, Dickens, Thackeray, Mark Twain and Shakespeare all over again. Such reading made my journey easier and enabled me to take a more balanced view of my experiences. But as the weeks went on the feeling I had had worried me greatly because it set me apart from all the many kind and lovable people I met. They would ask me, 'Where did you spend your May Day? We hope you had a good time?' I falsely replied that I had enjoyed it, trying hard to see some parallel with our own great feast days and public holidays. But ultimately the parallel, for all the superficial resemblances, is not valid.

However, to return to Kharkov. That night I telephoned to my home in London and despite the lateness of the hour the remarkable long-distance telephone system of the Soviet State had survived the orgiastic onslaughts of May Day. It put me through in a few minutes but when the call was over the exchange would not allow me to pay. After all, they said, it is a long way from Kharkov to London and a very expensive business! Such a responsibility, the exchange clearly implied, was one too great for an individual and could be borne legitimately only by the State. Therefore on no account would they allow me to pay for my call. This was an instance of Russian State employees deciding for themselves how the State would want them to behave and cutting through the formidable red tape. For beneath this wilful and determined one-ness of which I have spoken Russia, too, is a crazy mixed-up nation.

I have described the day behind me as 'ugly' and I think this needs some elaboration. One of the paradoxes that gave me much trouble on my journey was the contrast between the delicacy, tenderness and sensitivity that I was aware of in conversation with the Russians I came to know best; and the total absence of these qualities in the world they were making for themselves. They seem indifferent to the appearance of things and are able to see in objects only the reflection of what they long for in themselves. In a way they are all natural Don Quixotes with the power to convert every mill on the international skyline into a tyrannical capitalist giant, apartment-blocks into castles in Spain, and Party bosses into saints. Only in music, it seems, is their taste infallible. But when it comes to the claims of visual realities they are incapable of meeting them. They are, on the whole, without a visual sense. The Japanese have one so highly developed that the appearance and presentation of objects, their shapes and colours, are matters of profound private and public importance. For them it is not enough to feel a thing is beautiful. Everything

must be made to look beautiful as well. Even the luncheon trays
sold by the poorest coolies on the railway stations and thrown
away immediately after eating, are things of beauty. This faculty
seems to me one of the most neglected in the Russian make-up.
There are great and compelling reasons for it, of course. All
nations go through periods when necessity compels them to
sacrifice all faculties to one all-important task. We only have to
remember how in two world wars we suspended our own private
and particular vision and devoted all to the winning of battles.
Something of this sort undoubtedly has happened to Russia.
Between world wars they have been engaged in a private war of
their own against backwardness, poverty and ignorance as well
as against the consequences of a Revolution which also created
many problems for them. For example at the time of the Revolution seventy-five per cent of the people in Russia were illiterate,
eighty-five per cent in Siberia and almost one hundred per cent
in Russian Asia. This was a problem to be overcome and today
it is hard to find illiterates anywhere in the Soviet Union. The
aim of compensating quickly for centuries of neglect has obsessed
their imaginations to the exclusion of almost all else. Anything
else is pushed into the background. This, of course, does not
explain how their remarkable feeling for music has survived. But
all nations have certain inborn preferences and capacities that
nothing can change just as they also have certain congenital
incapacities, and with the Russians this would appear to be a
complete lack of visual values. This incapacity was increased by
the national priorities provoked in the war so that now this
neglect occurs even in the fields of activity which have the highest
national priorities. No doors or windows ever seem to fit in the
new apartment-blocks, surfaces are not properly finished off, and
though the frame and foundations of Moscow University, itself a
shining pinnacle of glass, yellow stone and steel, are I am certain,
beyond suspicion yet the surfaces, floors and stairs are badly worn.
Again, although I never doubted a Russian aircraft's engine yet
the fittings and furnishings are always indifferent. The result all
in all is that outwardly life in Russia is ugly to a degree that might
prove unendurable were it not for the immense compensations in
the character of the people I got to know.

Here in Kharkov, after the parade, I reached a new awareness

of this ugliness. All Soviet towns have parks of Rest and Culture.
I had been to many and now here in Kharkov I realized that it was
useless to expect them to change in character. They could vary
only in size. The layout was always the same: and the statues were
always the same. There would sometimes be one of Gorky,
always in the same thoughtful pose, and always at least one of
Lenin. I came to hate not the man but these statues and portraits
of him. Every town and village had one; every railway station
had at least one if not two; every official building had either a
full length statue, a bust or both, and above every desk of importance was placed an oil-painting of Lenin in collar and tie. I
was to visit one small station in Siberia where a statue of a skier
was flanked by statues of Lenin, the only difference being that the
first faced the world nonchalantly, hand in pocket, while the
others with shoulders squared, clenched fists and raised arms
pointed a naked finger to the empty Steppe.

This matter of trying to spot variations in the statues of Lenin
became an obsession with me as if my own balance of mind de-
pended on the discovery of significant differences in portrayal.
They were, alas! few and relatively insignificant. Always the
kindly face with its shrewd eyes and look of far purpose, was
unvaried despite the positioning of hands or body. It was an
unanimated constant like the face of Britain's queen on our own
postage stamps. Yet nowhere was there evidence that Lenin
significantly had stirred the emotions of either painters or
sculptors, or that he had passed through any individual imagination or personal awareness to communicate the feeling of discovery which is the hallmark of a work of art. As a subject he
appeared to be taken very much for granted. Even so fanatical a
Communist as André Wurmser was compelled to pen mild
protest against the statues of Lenin in his pamphlet 'The Open
Heart', a title incidentally which in the way of the fellow-traveller
I have described, merely meant he had a closed heart to France. I
myself one day was so bothered by this insect proliferation of
the same Lenin image that I was trapped into exclaiming to a
Russian companion: 'You do have an awful lot of statues of
Lenin about the place!'

Instantly he snapped back at me: 'And why not? Aren't your
towns full of images and pictures of Christ?'

I had only to think of the dynamic, infinitely varied role that Christ has played in the imagination of western art to realize how wide the comparison was of the mark. However, I dropped the subject at once. But the important point was, to me, that this cultured and educated Russian had seen an identical similarity between the meaning of Christ, for us, and the meaning of Lenin to him.

But apart from this ghost presence of Lenin the other statues were no better. I had to get used to seeing at the airport entrances the statue of a man holding up a little boy who in turn holds up a dove with outstretched wings. The Department of Culture sees nothing uncultured in having the same vapid statue cast innumerable times and scattered all over the Soviet Union. Exactly the same thing is done to the Office of Works' idea of nymphs, fawns and gazelles all of which have as little character as the illustrations of my childhood heroes and heroines in the Girls' and Boys' Own Annuals. Weeks of this visual diet made me resolve never again to rant at our own excesses in sculpture and portraiture. And then on top of conformity was prudishness. All the time I was in Russia I saw only one contemporary statue in the nude and that was of a little naked boy sitting next to a little girl (discreetly clad in marble bloomers) on the edge of a pool in a park. In all statues, even when the woman is about to enter water, she is portrayed as wearing plaster bikinis, marble brassières and slips or some other kind of Soviet '*ceinture de chastité*'. No Victorian cover-up of sex was ever more complete. It was not a 'black-out' but an official 'white-out' blurring the whole field of sexual passion in the imagination. A great French artist once spoke in praise of the ideal female form as that of '*la femme faite pour être mère*'. There was little in these statues to suggest the figure made for motherhood: and even less to convince one that any of the male models had been made '*pour être père*'. Of course all this is part of the State idiom in these things. Immediately after the Revolution all over Russia there was a period of extreme licence and excess in sexual behaviour, legalized abortions, abandoned babies, neglect of children, and contempt for marriage as a *bourgeois* enslavement. But the reaction against it since has been widespread and profound. Officially the Party are both Puritan and Spartan in all these matters. Even the popular image of the Founder has been made to conform. For example, in that still popular Soviet play *Kremlin Chimes*, with civil war, revolution, a hostile world, ignorance and famine all about him Papa Lenin is made to say to the young sailor-hero when he learns that he is in love: 'The old-fashioned ways in these things whatever other people say are the best.' Anyway if I ever expected that something of the sense of adventure, of daring experimentation and imaginative reappraisal of society which the Soviet system purports to be would be reflected in their plastic arts my hours in the park of Rest and Culture in Kharkov saw them routed. I knew that henceforth I would enjoy only the air, the quiet, the trees and grass of these beneficial places (the State Radio always permitting).

Not the least of many paradoxes is that a system which purports to revere culture so profoundly, should in effect be so contemptuous of art as to suppose that it can be bureaucratically directed. In the Soviet Union the position of the artist and his own attitude to his role in life appear to be far from heroic. Or perhaps this is due not to contempt but to fear. The debt of new Russia to the artists, writers and intellectuals of the old Russia who faced firing squads and were imprisoned for their belief in freedom of art and thought is so great that its rulers must know something of the transforming power of art. Free art, free thought and free expression therefore appear to them as highly dangerous and as offensive *morally* as free love was to the Victorians. The painters and sculptors of the Soviet Union are artists in chains but it would be wrong to blame this entirely on the rulers. Their enslavement could not be so complete were it not for this strange indifference in the Russians for the visual world; and their instinct to coagulate and conform.

CHAPTER TWELVE

KIEV

AFTER such parks of Rest and Culture, how wonderful it always was to get into the real country again. There was nothing restricted about the great plain of black earth between Kharkov and Kiev. Smoothly and effortlessly it moved away as one advanced towards its rim, a flawless ripple in space and time. One's senses that had become so narrowed and directed in the city could now expand again. There was an unfailing therapy in the view of the Russian plains and our arrival at Kiev itself was no anti-climax. Destroyed in the war, rebuilt and expanded since in standard patterns, it yet wears its conformity with a difference. This is due largely to its original conception and to its history and situation, for it stands at the meeting of the two great roads of Russian history: the river and the black earth roads. 'Kiev,' Bernard Pares wrote, 'was a great and generous attempt to do the impossible. Along a single thin road running almost on the frontier of Europe with a nascent civilization, a hopeless political organization which had little in it but the fine spirit that prompted it, it tried to keep at bay the unceasing and successive waves of population which economic necessity drove out of Asia's storehouse of peoples along that other great road of the black soil into Europe. It is in the right angle of these two roads, black soil and water, that lie the meaning and pathos of early Russian history: and they bisect each other at Kiev which was at once the capital and frontier fortress of Russia.'

Something of this generosity, heroism and nobility has survived conquest and destruction. Even today nothing about the city is small or mean. The streets are wide and so generous that many of them have lanes of lime, poplar, chestnut, locust trees and gardens down the middle. The skyscrapers do not crowd the pavements but stand well back to give space, fresh air and quiet. Much has been preserved of what was good in the past. The same golden bubble domes I had left behind in Moscow again soared in the air among the modern apartment tops looking strangely detached from their towers and floating like balloons in reverse up into the blue. The great cathedral of St Sophia, each wall, ceiling and pillar a vivid and crowded Byzantine mural or mosaic, has been superbly restored by the Soviet. The crowds visiting it were so dense that I had the greatest difficulty getting in and around the church. Unlike my guide at Rostov who professed ignorance and indifference to the churches of the town the young girl who showed me around seemed to know all there was to know about this and other important churches. The explanation was simple. Public interest in the Cathedral of St Sophia was perfectly respectable because it had been declared an historical monument. One could safely enter because one went in not for religion but for history and art. Proof of this was in the difference in attendance between it and the other active churches which have not been proclaimed national monuments. There are no crowds there, only a few women worshipping inside and some old ladies outside as spectacularly beggared as any of Victor Hugo's in the *Hunchback of Notre Dame*.

'They make me sick,' a Russian friend told me, 'that's what the churches do to people. Those women have no need to beg for the State takes care of all. It's just greed. And I bet you all the time the priests are eating caviare and drinking wine all day from the kopecks collected by these filthy women!'

Fortunately there are also other churches preserved by the State. The Pecherskaya Monastery with its eleventh-century mosaics, although partially destroyed by the Germans, has the gate-tower church, the wonderful bell-tower and a surprising number of other buildings and walls coloured like the pages torn from a Nestorian hymnal, still intact. The Andreyev church built by Rastrelli and Michurin adds something of the Renaissance to the prevailing Constantinople theme. They all combine to give Kiev an atmosphere which few Soviet towns possess, for it is extraordinary that no matter where one goes in the world no town is visually complete unless it possesses either temples or churches. One has only to visit the vast new towns built in Siberia, which has no past, to be aware of this. The absence of churches and temples makes the buildings and houses look like chickens without a hen. Kiev is fortunate too in preserving intact the lovely Palace built for Catherine the Great by Rastrelli and also some romantic statuary from the past. But most fortunate of all is the

fact that Kiev possesses a hill with a view of its own. For some
strange geological reason the west banks of Russian rivers tend
to be much higher than the eastern ones. At Kiev the difference is
so marked that the bank achieves the proportion of a sizeable hill.
From there one has a remarkable view over the black Steppe and
above all over the Dniepr. If I had thought the Don impressive
the recollection was instantly excelled by my first glimpse of the
Dniepr. So wide and swollen with water that it is almost shapeless, it swims over the flawless horizon in what looks like a succession of lakes and is indeed a river worthy of so great a plain.
It looks unbridgeable but has already been well and truly bridged
and is about to be bridged again and again. Taking advantage of
the opportunities for reconstruction that German destruction
gave it the State has largely separated industrial Kiev from the
rest and transported it across the river and now is expanding it
night and day. Again this is the sort of thing which the Soviet
State does with imagination and increasing skill and confidence.
Wherever I looked beyond the river new buildings and factories
were springing up beside what was already a compact town of tall
chimney stacks, high mills and power stations. The feeling of long
pent-up and unused energies released and flowing in the wide bed
of a concerted plan was as tangible as the view of the massive
river making for the sea. Again there was little smoke in the air
for enormous beds of natural gas have been discovered everywhere below this ancient black soil of Russia. So to oil, black
coal and 'white coal' (as the Russians term the electrical energy
produced by damming their rivers), now there had to be added
an almost unlimited supply of natural gas. I was to find that even
Riga on the Baltic hundreds of miles north cooked and warmed
itself on gas from the Ukraine. Only fools would ignore the formidable implications of such a vision. The Soviet Union is at the
merest beginning of its industrial development. Yet even that
slight beginning is vast enough to overawe one with its size. The
smallest glimpse of the untapped natural resources of the Soviet
world already harnessed to the task of industrializing Russia is
something before which one's imagination boggles. What will
happen to the land in the process, and to the quality and texture
of human society, what will be the price to be paid in the values
and meaning of life is another matter. But when I saw the Donbas

I was certain that the greatest single industrial nation on earth was in the making before my eyes.

Meanwhile behind me there was the city and its history to explore. I have said that there was something noble about it and it is this quality that distinguishes it for me, from the other great cities of the Soviet Union. However much Russians love Moscow there is nothing particularly noble about it, nor about Novgorod the Great or even Leningrad. In their history Moscow and Novgorod were too often prepared to compromise for trade, money and power. For generations Moscow even collected tribute money for the Tartar despots from fellow-Russians and one of the princes who consolidated its power was called Ivan Moneybags. But Kiev, before it was subdued and overrun, had committed itself deeply to other values of life, and brought enough rough chivalry and sense of honour alive in Little Russians for an afterglow of it still to illumine the mind of the people and character of the country. Largely for this reason the Soviet conception of dominion states, which I first discussed in Alma Ata and Tashkent, takes on a meaning here which does not apply to the rest of the Soviet Empire. The 42,000,000 people of the Ukraine speak and write their own Slav tongue and they have a distinct and confident self-respect. Their own music and art does not make them afraid to match themselves in these things against the Greater Russians. The performances of the State Ballet of the Ukraine that I saw in Kiev were as good (my Russian companions generously said better) as anything I saw in Moscow or Leningrad. The size of the population, and its sense of cohesion and self-respect forces the Soviet to give the Ukrainians a consideration that they would not spare for others. The Ukraine even conducts in a larger measure than the rest its own Foreign Relations.* There are large colonies of Ukrainians in the outside world even on the prairies of Canada, with whom it has ties of immediate kinship. I encountered many parties of American Ukrainians discreetly visiting relations. I found, too, Ukrainians openly receiving and reading newspapers printed in America in Ukrainian Russian. This is a privilege not allowed, as far as I know, to any other community; indeed elsewhere it is a punish-

* There are three Soviet representatives at U.N.O.: (1) U.S.S.R., (2) Byelo-Russia, (3) Ukraine.

able offence. But in the forefront of the minds of the highly intelligent rulers of Russia must be the realization of how near they
came during the war to losing the Ukraine or at least creating a
desperate fifth column in their midst. I myself have seen the
documentary films of the rapturous welcome given to the advancing German Army there and the long columns of prisoners
who surrendered in hundreds of thousands without any serious
attempt to escape. For this, of course, there were two main causes:
the first historic and not unconnected with the self-respect and
individuality of which I have spoken: the second was due to
Stalin and his ruthless imposition of collectivization on the
Ukrainian farmers. No explanation of the history and psychology
of peoples has ever seemed less adequate to me than the climatic
and environmental one. Finns, Ukrainians, the Greater Russians
all have similar environments yet they all three differ because they
bring with them from the past different conceptions of the value
and meaning of life. The difference between the Russians and
Ukrainians is summed-up by something Tikhomirov wrote in
1888. The Greater Russian, he said, cannot imagine life outside
his society, to betray his peasant or village commune is for him
the unpardonable sin, to go against it is wrong. The Ukrainian
on the other hand says: 'What belongs to all belongs to the
devil.' The Greater Russian deduces his idea of his rights from
the idea of public welfare whereas the Ukrainian takes as his
starting point the exigencies of his individual rights. No wonder
Stalin's attempt to impose collective farming was so desperately
resisted in the Ukraine and for me the way Sholokhov glosses
over the terrible cruelty with which the resistance was crushed is
one of the blots on his manuscript. Some idea of the way the
Soviet went about it and the consequences of their methods have
long been international property since Maurice Hindus first
wrote *Red Bread* (itself a deliberate understatement as I happen
to know from a friend of mine, a woman artist, who travelled
with him). Stalin himself lifted a corner of the tragic curtain one
night to Churchill in Moscow during the war.

'Tell me,' Churchill had asked, 'have the stresses of this war
been as bad to you personally as carrying through the policy of
the Collective Farms?'

'Oh no!' Stalin answered, 'that was a terrible struggle. It was fearful. It lasted four years. But it was absolutely necessary for Russia if we were to avoid periodic famines.'

He continued his description until Churchill 'sustained a strong impression of millions of men and women having been blotted out or displaced for ever'. Though Stalin has gone the tragic picture has not yet been completed. Every day adds some terrifying detail to it. For instance the now famous *One Day in the life of Ivan Denisovich* by Alexander Solzhenitzyn, the novel based on the writer's own experience in a Siberian concentration camp, was followed immediately by a far more powerful work called *People are not Angels* by a veteran writer Ivan Stadnyuk, who is concerned in particular with the collectivization so brutally inflicted on the Ukraine and in general with the police terror, political opportunism and cowardice of Stalin's colleagues together with their indifference to the fate of the peasant everywhere in the Soviet Union.

I have no intention nor indeed any qualifications for writing a detailed history of these things. Yet some such awareness is necessary for the traveller whose interest goes deeper than mere enjoyment of the physical scene. There was always a strange persistent ghost following me around in Russia, the ghost of such memories: and no one I met would allow the natural thoughts about these things to come alive in conversation between us but always strangled them immediately at birth. Even in my own misguided country one cannot arrive without people immediately telling one about the latest injustices committed by the State against my black countrymen, and, given time, even going back to the horrors of the British concentration camps in the Anglo-Boer War at the beginning of the century. Discussion of these things is open, serious, concerned and constant. How different in Russia! Far worse things have happened and are still happening in the Soviet Union. But no one talks to strangers about them. Nor I suspect do they talk about them indiscriminately among themselves or even dare to admit them. Conversation tends to be a protracted euphemism in Russia but at last people are beginning to write openly though it would have been more in keeping with the heroic tradition of the writer in Russia if this had happened earlier rather than later. This ghost at my side in the Soviet Union was never so insistent as in the Ukraine and it evoked a melancholy like the blue of evening to preside over my memory of the country scene.

Once away from the thrust and bustle of those purposeful Ukrainian cities I would drive out over the great black plain and be startled to find how densely peopled it still was after such a past, though perhaps the peasants and their women working the earth appeared to me more solemn than peasants usually are. We would pass through village after village of tidy houses with white walls, blue woodwork and grey roofs finding them empty by day except, of course, for the inevitable school full of children who amazed one by their vivid starling voices and eager responses, and then just beyond the last wall there was the dark earth ploughed, sown, raked and ready for the rains of spring, as neat and circumspect as a bed just made for a honeymoon couple. I could not help remembering Thomas Hardy's words, 'Yet this will go onward the same, though dynasties pass.' But I was convinced that the account between Hardy's 'this' and the powerful prevailing dynasty was not yet closed, and that the great reckoning between them and the fast-growing industrial might of the land was still to come.

Often industry was working right along the parapets of what remained of the trenches of the vast battlefields of the Ukraine. Some of the bloodiest struggles of the war had swayed back and forth across these plains. One day I asked my guide if I could see a military cemetery for I imagined that, after such slaughter, there must be many. At once she took me back to the Eternal-Flame in the centre of a granite, stereotyped war-memorial. I shook my head and explained what it was that I wanted to see, but she became somewhat confused and said she thought there must be similar cemeteries in the Soviet Union though she had never seen one. She added that this monument was for all the dead and surely it did not matter to the dead whether they were individually or collectively buried! Once dead surely nothing mattered to the dead.

I did not try to explain. Perhaps it does not matter to the dead how they are disposed of. But I believe that their treatment of the dead is a matter of great practical import to the living. An important part of the way we live depends on our attitude to death and the dead. Indeed I think that the temptation to go to war could be more readily resisted in those peoples who break down the results of mass slaughter into its individual detail than in those who bulldoze the corpses into one vast impersonal grave. Communal graves do not haunt and warn the imagination so much as the vast reminders of single, known, and loved persons. The unknown warrior is impressive as a symbol; but the ghosts that pursue us are personal. Perhaps life in the Soviet Union could not be so impersonal and collective in the living if it were not also so impersonal and collective about the dead. A famous French general once told me that he thought the English uncivilized. I asked him why? His first reason was what he called 'their indecent haste to bury their dead'. I often wondered what he would have said of Soviet Russia.

Naturally on these battlefields I asked my companions about the war – which is always referred to as 'The Great Patriotic War'. In measure I could understand that. I think the new Soviet Russia came of age during the last war. For them it was a terrible initiation ceremony into the contemporary world and they naturally put its profound national consequences first. At the same time it is extraordinary how little the ordinary people know about the war elsewhere and about the part that France, Britain and America played in it. I read articles by military 'experts' who all gave the impression that Russia, save for some gallant Czech, Roumanian and Yugoslav Communist partisans, fought and won the war alone. We were scarcely mentioned. It is striking how a society which is continually exhorting the objective force and inevitability of history can show no concern whatsoever for the need of an objective presentation and interpretation of that history.

At first I thought my companions would be interested in my own experiences of the war. Even in so-called enemy countries like Japan and Germany I have felt a certain identification with people who have shared the same experiences. But in Russia the fighting men themselves seemed to me more forgotten in their collective burial mounds than any other war dead. So the lack of interest, which was sometimes a lack of belief and a sharp suspicion of capitalist propaganda talk, made me desist. One of the most destructive characteristics of the emerging societies of the contemporary world is their deliberate conscious falsification and invention of histories to suit immediate political purpose. No man is free to commit himself to an honest future until he has first been honest about the past. Only the truth can make men free of their own history. But the same perverse conviction which causes the Soviet leaders to regard lying as a legitimate instrument of policy inevitably demands convenient falsification of popular histories.

At one of the trenches I was shown the dug-out wherein Mr Khrushchev had had his headquarters. Again this problem of the lie as an instrument of policy raised an oblique head. In my travels I had heard a great deal about the heroic role that the Soviet Prime Minister, attached to the Military High Command, had played over this whole front. I had had described to me Mr Khrushchev's desperate attempts to get Stalin to allow a change of plan for a vital defensive battle. Mr Khrushchev had repeatedly telephoned the Kremlin to this end but he could not get past Malenkov, who at first said Stalin was not there and finally stated falsely that he had consulted Stalin, who had insisted that the pre-arranged plan should stand. The result was a major defeat and great loss of Russian lives.

Here in the trenches all this was freshly brought to mind and I could not help asking my companions why it had taken so long for the Party to expose the faults of Stalin and his closest advisers. Finally, did they not find it strange that Khrushchev could deliver a glowing oration at Stalin's funeral and help to carry him reverently to a place beside Lenin and then wait some years before denouncing him at the Party Congress?

I was instantly told that it was not strange at all. Mr Khrushchev had been quite right. He had proved himself a true leader. The nation was not ready for the immediate truth and would have been thrown into dangerous confusion by such an exposure. After all, did not we do the same things?

For instance? I asked.

Well, one of my companions asked what about the devaluation of the pound some years ago? He seemed to remember that only a few days before Britain devalued the pound the Chancellor of the Exchequer (Sir Stafford Cripps whom they all remembered for his good will to the Soviet Union), had formally denied to the world that he was contemplating devaluation although the decision to devalue had obviously been taken long since.

He undoubtedly scored a point and the incident taught me how well-briefed and informed about the outside world are Russians who have to deal officially with foreigners: a point that could be well remembered by all of us.

I withdrew from the battlefields to Kiev. The city was still re-covering from its May Day celebrations. Wherever I went I met people who expressed regret that they could not ask me to their homes but the truth was, they explained, they were all cleaning up after their celebrations and their homes were not yet fit to receive guests. Then I met a well-known Ukrainian writer who cheerfully asserted that he was a bachelor and that one of the privileges of that state was that he had been entertained during the celebrations and had not been forced to entertain. Would I like to spend a night with him at his home? I accepted, fully expecting his home to be an apartment in the city, but to my delight I found he really possessed two homes: a small apartment in the city and a villa in the country. He spent half the week in the city and half in the country, and it was his country home which he would like me to visit. Accordingly he asked me to join him at the office of his Union early in the evening.

He was busy speaking on the long-distance telephone when I arrived. He told me he was organizing a conference for young writers at which they could discuss and criticize one another's work and methods and they themselves be criticized and advised by experienced established writers like himself. It was another mild example of the Soviet belief in the controlled collective approach but on this occasion it gave me misgivings. Surely even Russian writers must quail at any collectivization of their trade? There is, for example, a remark made by Paustovsky (I quote him so often because I found him to be the contemporary writer most admired by the ordinary educated young Russians though not by the intellectuals) which reveals that he for one was deeply worried by the collective approach to writing and art. He de-scribes how the great Gorky himself once asked him to join a team of writers working on a Soviet History of Factories and Works. He refused, he says, because he was firmly convinced then as now that while teamwork may be fruitful in many fields it should not be practised in literature.

'Just as it is impossible for three persons to play the same violin,'

Paustovsky told Gorky, 'it is impossible to write a book collectively.'

Gorky winced and remarked: 'See, young man, that you don't get a reputation for being too self-confident.'

My host at this moment was calling up places as far apart as Odessa, Rostov and Kharkov with the nonchalance of an American business executive, in fact his attachment to telephoning, his air of decision and immediacy of action struck me as far more American than Russian. In between calls, quoting Paustovsky I questioned him about the collectivization of literature.

Of course, he shrugged, one must not go to extremes but more could be achieved by collective criticism and encouragement in art than by individual effort. One of their pre-war classics, *The Golden Calf* had been written by two men. I should read it because so much of its idiom had passed into current expression. Even in painting, one of my Russian companions thereupon volunteered, the collective approach could be most rewarding. For instance perhaps the most popular paintings in Russia were by a group of three men working under the name of Kukrinisky.

What sort of paintings did they paint? I asked amazed, truly shocked at this artistic polyandry.

'Socially realistic paintings of course. Pictures like the "Last Hour of Hitler",' he said.

We were prevented from going on with the subject for just then the writer brought his telephoning to an end, jumped up from his desk and with a deep laugh exclaimed, 'Now, we'll go!'

He was a big, blond, generous fellow, full of energy and purpose and he had been wounded three times in the war. He bustled us into a motor-car and off we went into the driving rain which steadily grew heavier. We drove out of Kiev for fifty miles along the west bank of the Dniepr. The river was so wide and the heavy rain had covered the flat earth with so much water that the road looked like a causeway across an inlet of the sea. Now I understood why so many people I had met told me that with such a river they felt no need to go to the sea for their vacations. This over-abundant water gave them all the sea they needed and on holiday they preferred to go to some village deep in the country. Emotionally the country, the village and the farm are still closer to the Russians than the towns and the cities. Necessity and a deliberate act of collective will drives them to the factories but their heart is always in the land and what my host told me confirmed this.

He was the first intellectual, he said, in his family. His father was a peasant and his mother illiterate. He gave me this information about his parents with obvious pride proving how much he was of the new Soviet aristocracy and how pure his descent from the suffering and enduring working-classes of the past. It is not enough to be descended from the people. The new snobbery demands that it must also be from the people who have not only worked but also suffered for suffering is romanticized in the Soviet spirit.

I asked what had become of them?

I was about to meet them, he answered, for they lived in his country villa.

Was the villa his own private property? I inquired.

Of course and why not? he exclaimed, surprised at my question. He had applied for a piece of land to the State department of land and had been granted one. Anyone who could afford it and who had a clean, responsible Social record could do the same. Sometimes if one man alone could not afford it he could combine with others to buy land and build a small apartment house in the country. He pointed out several beside the road. I would be amazed, he said, at the numbers of private houses as opposed to State apartments in the Soviet Union. Far from being against private ownership of this kind the State approved of it and helped responsible citizens by advancing money on a mortgage system. He had not needed a mortgage and all he had now to do was to keep up payment of his ground rent of about £25 a year and his property in the country remained his own. He added that recently, however, the State has tightened up on mortgages of this kind.

Had he, I asked, designed the building himself?

Oh no, he had gone to the State Bureau of Architectural Design and picked the one he liked best.

This conversation was by no means continuous for periodically our host would stop the car at shops in the villages on our way. At one he bought three large bottles of milk which he carried to the car at the double – he did everything at the double. At another he charged through the rain to return with arms full of various kinds of bread, because that hamlet baked the best bread in the land, he explained. At yet another we stopped for fish and so on until the car was loaded with provisions as if for a major expedition. At the last village, impressed by the mounting pile of food and drink, he justified himself by saying: 'Mother doesn't know we're coming and may not be prepared.'

Soon after that we came to a new world of woods and clearings and in the clearings by the road a series of country villas standing in large gardens and orchards. The villas might have been in some prosperous middle-class suburb of the west had it not been for the nearness of the wide-rolling river and the dense woods.

As we passed by one forest the writer remarked: 'We still shoot wolves in there. I often go hunting myself and if possible shoot a wolf or two. The collective farmers round about will always reward you with a suckling pig or two for any dead wolves you bring in!'

He laughed again and remembering my meetings with other writers it struck me how large a part hunting, fishing and some form of natural activity in the country played in their lives. A gun, fishing rod or better still a villa in the woods seemed to be almost part of their professional uniform. Tolstoy and even Turgenev, I expect, had something to do with the fashion but mostly it was part of the mystique about their earth which possesses all Russians.

Our host's own villa stood well back from the road. It was a two-storey little house of the kind which estate agents in Britain used to describe as a '*bijou* residence'. It was built only four years before but already the clearing around it was neatly laid out into thriving orchard, vegetable, strawberry and other plots, with eleven beehives standing among them.

'You see,' my host exclaimed with his big laugh as he quoted Yeats: 'Nine bean rows will I have there and a hive for the honey-bee.'

'The scale,' I differed, 'is not Irish but positively Roman and Virgilian.'

That pleased him. He stooped affectionately to pat an enormous wolf-hound on the head as it bounded out of a kennel to greet him: 'He is a fraud – not fierce at all – but I hope will grow into an honest wolf-hound. You see he is only five months old.'

He stopped next at a tree to explain laughing, 'This is a wild-pear tree. I have grafted fifteen different varieties of pears on it and it is now a good Soviet citizen producing more and more better pears every year.'

We stepped into the little hall of his house, to find his father and mother coming out of the living-room to meet us. She was a bent old lady in black, a black shawl around her shoulders, her face deeply creased, gentle and resigned. He was an old man indifferent to age, dressed in baggy trousers, blouse and scarf exactly as in a nineteenth-century portrait of a serf. Indeed he looked exactly like the one picture on the wall of the living-room, a reproduction of the portrait of the national poet, Shevchenko. The picture had an embroidered Ukrainian towel draped round it: 'And that,' my Russian companion nudged me, 'is the towel all the singing is about just now!'

Apart from a table and chairs the only piece of furniture was a radiogram. One of my companions immediately went to it and started fiddling until suddenly an urbane B.B.C. voice came out of the loudspeakers like a large soap-bubble out of a children's pipe. 'Miss Christine Truman was defeated in her Wightman Cup Match in the United States . . .' it began and was blurred by the laughter of my companions at the look of surprise on my face.

'Sports Round-up,' they remarked and as I still looked amazed since I had not ever heard of 'Sports Round-up' before, explained, 'It's the sports summing-up just before the general news broadcast in the B.B.C. Overseas Service. We thought you would like to have some news from your own country direct!'

'But I thought you jammed the service,' I replied.

'Only when it is too subjective and goes in for propaganda,' they told me with an air of moral rectitude.

'While you are listening to news from home,' our host said, 'I must go and help Mother in the kitchen. She has no servants.'

'And I,' said the father, 'must go and see to my bees.'

I watched the old man through the window. At his age, out there in the heavy, cold, whipping rain, he was most impressive as he set about securing the tops of the hives, making certain they were not leaking, feeding the dog and chaining him to his kennel by the gate; he looked more at home there than he had done inside. Then he removed some flotsam from the drains between the vegetable plots, inspected each item in the garden like a captain preparing his ship for the fall of night in the teeth of a storm. There was indeed something indefatigable and poignantly heroic about him. All this time it was getting darker, the rain heavier, and the water of the Dniepr in the hollow of the garden rising higher. Indeed the last thing the old man did was to make certain that the mooring chains of our host's motor-boat were locked and intact.

When he reappeared giving out the satisfaction of a man feeling his day well done, he said: 'They're a good proposition, bees. You should go in for them too. It costs me only ninety kopecks to produce a kilo of honey which I sell at two roubles eighty kopecks in the market.' He said this without asking what my profession was simply because he could not, I imagine, conceive of people anywhere in the world who did not have a stake in the land.

'There's the eternal peasant speaking,' one of my young companions, city-born and city-reared whispered to me: 'Always thinking of what things cost and how much they can be sold for.'

'I expect you pay a lot at your hotel?' the old man asked me.

I told him how much and he was filled with horror. 'They're a lot of robbers in the city,' he said indignantly and immediately told his wife who just then came in with a pile of plates.

'You should come here,' she exclaimed at once, looking at me as if I were a hurt child in need of help. 'You can live here for nothing.'

The old man went on about prices until our meal was ready on the table. No Georgian could have done better in so short a time. We had fried river fish, stacks of potatoes, masses of bread and butter, pickled cabbage, a big Ukrainian ham taken off the bone, large red peppers preserved in honey, smoked sausages, cheese and then the national dish, *Vareniki*, a kind of Ukrainian ravioli stuffed with cheese instead of meat, served boiling hot with sour cream poured over it. It was all delicious. When I complimented the old lady on her *Vareniki*, she smiled sweetly and said that she was famous for it even when a young girl. 'I could not read or write,' she told me. 'But I could make *Vareniki* and rich people from far away would send for me to make *Vareniki* for their dinner parties.'

She paused and then asked: 'Are there many of your people who cannot read or write?'

'Very few now,' I answered.

'Are things then getting better for your people?' she wanted to know.

'Yes. All the time.'

That pleased her and then some thought disturbed her.

'Go on, Mother,' her son exclaimed, 'tell him what's on your mind. He ought to know.'

She looked at her husband, shook her head, and was relieved to see him shake his. Clearly their conception of hospitality ruled out mentioning what she had been thinking, and the son had to tell me himself. It was simply that no matter where one went, even deep in the country, the great international uncertainties followed one. While helping his mother in the kitchen she had remarked to him how awful it was to feel that their little estate could go up at any moment in a cloud of mushroom smoke of a world nuclear war. Why had people to be so wicked as still to want to make war against the Soviet Union?

I could only repeat the explanations and assurances that we did not want war either and they listened to me politely without, I think, really accepting what I said. It was not only that I was a foreigner and on the wrong side. But they and their kind had long since passed the point where the reassurances of any man were important to them. Men may or may not be truthful in what they said. All they knew after thousands of years of invasion, conquest and civil wars was that somehow death and disaster sooner or later came from men and their systems. What they had of faith was in the abiding, indefatigable earth, in tending it, obeying the laws of the seasons and serving the processes of renewal through them and the begetting of children. Indeed I thought that the old lady was finding more reassurance in the sound of the rain than in what I was saying.

It certainly gave her husband great satisfaction for he interrupted us to say: 'Listen, just listen to that rain! That'll make the corn grow this season!' He broke off to ask if the rainfall were more reliable in my country than his? The droughts they got were terrible and the hot, killing winds and the short seasons.

I told him all I could over coffee which I was made to drink by taking a spoonful of honey first for every sip. The honey was thick and dark with the sugar of wood flowers and had a wild tang which, with the smell of coffee, was stronger even than the smell of rain. Whenever I stopped the old man would press me to more. 'Eat and drink up so that you need not have any meals at that expensive hotel of yours tomorrow. You'd save quite a bit that way!'

'A real peasant,' my Russian interpreter from the city whispered, 'Always thinking of prices and profits.'

'But a gentleman, too,' I answered, 'to think on this occasion of the pocket and profit of a guest before his own.'

Just then the dog began barking outside and at once the old man was out of his chair and left the room.

While he was gone his son showed me the rest of his villa. A kitchen with a gas-stove, refrigerator, table and rocking chair in it; a small cloakroom and a large double bedroom, with only a bed, chair and table. Upstairs there were two more rooms, his workroom and bedroom with the bed not yet made from his last visit. There was not a picture on the walls and it was all extremely spartan. He must have realized it because he said defensively: 'I'll make it more comfortable as I get the money!'

Yet he must have known how much better off he was than the majority of his countrymen. For at that time strictly by law citizens were each entitled to only eight square yards of floor space in the country towns, and six and a half in Moscow.

'Where do you like writing best, here or in Kiev?' I asked.

'Oh, here,' he answered. 'I do my official business in Kiev but I write my real creative work here. Writing and working on our little estate I find ideal. Look!' He held out his hands and they were the hands of a farmer.

When we returned below the old man was just coming in, shaking water vigorously from his coat. Far from being irritated by his excursion into the storm he had welcomed it.

'He just wanted company,' he exclaimed gruffly about the dog. 'He's young and it's getting cold. I wish we had some coal.'

His son explained that their coal supply had been stopped by the State on the first official day of spring. That was some days ago and it had got steadily colder ever since. But the seasons refused to be official so they would just have to endure the cold!

Apart from seeing to the dog the old man had once more done a round of the hives to check up that they were dry and warm.

'He dotes on that dog,' the old lady explained, regarding her husband with envy as he took his seat by the table again. 'I only wish I had a cat to keep me company. It is a great sadness to me not to have a cat. But we are not allowed to.'

'Why not?' I asked.

'We have so many rare singing birds in the woods around,' the old lady sighed. 'The authorities are afraid that cats will kill off their young.'

'What are you writing now?' I asked the son.

He said he was writing a book on the work of writers in their old age. It had interested him always to observe the pattern in writing. Writers would have to pause in their work after the first youthful rush of creation, and wait to discover another urge within them. Then would come another pause, perhaps so long that it seemed as if their creative powers were at an end. But then like a miracle, could emerge the greatest period of creation. It was all rather like the life of a rose. You could count on two flowerings and then sometimes just before the final fall of winter a third budding would emerge.

I agreed with him, thinking of Goethe's last book of *Faust*, and suggested that there might even be a fourth flowering?

But he disagreed vigorously. The end was but an end. There was nothing beyond and he dismissed the thought with a scornful laugh.

I wanted to ask his parents whether they agreed with him for they were both looking at him with an expression of sadness. But of course, I could not.

I asked instead: 'Have you got a title for your book yet?'

'The Third Bud,' the man replied.

Yet as I listened to the rain filling in the pauses in our conversation it was so full of the implication of eternal growth that it made our words sound like infantile exercises compared to the long arithmetic of the earth. I looked at the father and the mother. They had been unable to articulate what they were feeling but I was certain they too lived a similar meaning. That night in the villa in the woods, the sound of the rain and the next day the sight of that immense noiseless river shapeless with water yet ever making for the sea, remain in my mind as a master image of the abiding Russia.

CHAPTER THIRTEEN

TRAIN NUMBER TWO

I HAD hoped from the Ukraine to follow the black earth as the history and peoples of the Russias themselves did, and go due east towards the Pacific. But my time was running out and no permission for this had come from Moscow. I thought then of going north by river to Moscow. That I was told was not possible either, although I saw the broad steamers plying daily up and down the river before my eyes. So all I could do was to go north by road and aeroplane along the marches of Russia towards Leningrad.

The great plain, which in the south seems so level, began to undulate as we went further north. The earth itself grew greyer, towns and villages became fewer, woods, copses, forests and marshes multiplied, until one was quite startled by the sight of a factory, the TV aerials of a village, or the blue bubble dome of some decaying church spire rising above the trees. Roads were few, untarred and rough, and had a disconcerting knack of vanishing abruptly into the woods without apparently leading anywhere. Each stretch of cultivated earth, each smokeless village seemed unconnected with the other. Even here in Western Russia it was astonishing how empty was the landscape and how slight upon it was the impression of man. But there was an abundance of woods, marshes and rivers – the forest ones stained brown like tobacco juice with the essence of peat. Each smaller stream joined a bigger one over a mouth of shingle waste until round an unexpected sandy bend it found the main river, broad and smooth, filled with light and cloud and blue sky, which was to take them all on together to the sea. From the air it all looked as flat as the great southern plain. But from the ground it was full of surprises and intimate variations of clearings, rivers, marshes and lakes. Always it was a scene painted in subtle, limpid water-colours. There were no hills but occasional red sandstone cliffs startling against the green leaf-mould, or outbreaks of granite with deep ravines and gullies cut out of the gently undulating earth by water, wind and ice.

Both forest and cleared earth became increasingly green. Since I had first arrived in Moscow the spring had advanced in a rush. The flowers were vivid and profuse: wood-anemones, violets, celandine, cowslips, Solomon's seal, yellow globe-flowers and wild orchids, apple and cherry blossoms, particularly the trailing bright bird-cherry, were all bursting into flower together. I saw little children in the villages staggering as if drunk on the scent, their arms full of lilies-of-the-valley. I saw sturdy young girls with shoulders like athletes and muscles like gym instructors, walking home behind the cattle with flowers in their hair, their belts and their hands. The softness in the spirit of nature, so ready to make generous amends for the ice and snow of the long winter was most moving. I had expected the earth to be vast, rough and tough but was not prepared for such a flowering and so lush and tender a spring. Then there were the birds too, not just the small singing species vibrating like electric bells among the leaves and shadows, but game-birds of all kinds, black wood-cock, geese, snipe, the forest-fowl clucking and whirring like bamboo rattles in sudden flight through a sun-stroked patch of air, duck and geese on bronze lakes and above all the swans, their bodies white as arctic snow skimming the tree-tops, wings beating the silent air so fast that they resounded like some magic harp plucked into a passion of sound. I had never imagined that there could be such huge flights of swans outside the fairy-tales of the brothers Grimm. They would fill the dawn and twilight hours with magic and the woods with witchcraft.

I was much tempted to linger and go deeper into such country but was compelled to go to Moscow first to attend to the shape of my own journey which at that moment appeared destined to lose itself like one of the many earth roads in the general shapelessness of the earth around me. Even so the sudden transition from such a natural scene to the artificial, regimented, inflexible Moscow was so sudden and brutal that I felt almost physically hurt by it.

The only consolation was that the efficient young lady in charge of my journey had not been idle in my absence. She had got permission for me to go to Siberia by train. Vladivostok was still firmly ruled out. But the authorities were prepared to grant me permission to go to Irkutsk by rail and to Khabarovsk in the Far East by air. Why the journey between Irkutsk and Khabarovsk by rail was not allowed, I do not know. Stranger still was the news that I could not fly from Irkutsk to Khabarovsk. I would have to return the five days' journey by train to Moscow and then fly back again to the Far East. The explanation given was that the airport at Irkutsk was closed for large-scale repairs. However, I had been long enough in the Soviet Union to accept the discipline of prolonged states of unknowing. It is hard for Europeans and Americans to accept that there are occasions when one just cannot know. We are so accustomed to our condition of all-knowingness that the moment we find ourselves cut off from our normal sources of supply we rush to fill in the blank spaces with our hopes, fears, suspicions and desires. But unless I had definite hunches about people and things I left speculation alone and accepted the fact that on occasions I just could not know. I took refuge in my own experience and tried not to exceed it. In fact at this snail's pace to which even my fast journey seemed reduced by the scale of the land, I carried my days and their immediate shape around with me as a snail carries its own house on its back. In this state of unknowing I spent no more time in Moscow than was necessary to complete the arrangements for my journey. Even so it took four days – and that I was assured was working fast – before I could get myself on the appropriate train.

This train was due to leave at twenty minutes past midnight. That gave me time to go to the ballet at the Bolshoi Theatre and still arrive in time at the rambling Far Eastern station opposite the tall new Leningradskaya Hotel. I have said nothing about Russian trains as yet because this Siberian express, perhaps the longest train journey in the world, was to represent them all. But in the Soviet Union the train is not only a vital element in the country's communications but also a thing of wonder in the popular imagination. Everywhere else in the world, with the exception of Japan, the train is increasingly dishonoured. But here in the Soviet Union it is vigorously expanding and something of the excitement which accompanied its coming in early Victorian Britain still surrounds it. Until this moment always I had been puzzled by Tolstoy's prosaic description of the train pulling in at the station in *Anna Karenina*. It seemed to me a pointless descrip-

tion of the obvious. But now I understood that a national compulsion made it necessary. In all the thousands of miles I travelled
by train I never saw a vacant berth or a decaying railway station.
Even in the areas which suffered most in the war I found railway
stations either fully restored or re-designed and rebuilt on a
greater scale. Despite the demands on building resources, despite
the pattern of uniformity demanded by the obvious pressures and
urgencies of the economy, the railways are still so closely linked
with the national faith in the machine and the popular sense of
wonder which this provokes that they tend to escape the rigid
rules of standardization. Something of the same 'railway mystique' which made the Victorians build St Pancras on the lines of
a Gothic cathedral, makes the Russians too throw up railway
stations like churches.

I remember how my guide at Sochi laughed when I pointed to a
slender modern spire rising above the cypress tops and asked:
'What church is that?'

It took him quite a while to recover before he replied: 'It's not a
church. It's our new railway station!'

The stations too are built like temples. The station at Kharkov,
one of the most important in Russia because eight trunk lines
meet there, looks like a Greek temple from the outside whereas
inside it is a marble palace. The booking-hall is vast and domed,
the walls covered with immense euphoric paintings, coloured
mosaics and ceramics, and from the ceiling hangs a huge chandelier outshining anything in Versailles. Lavatories, w aiting
rooms, even restaurants, can be inadequate. But the outer shape
of the railway and the main hall express the national faith in the
machine in general and the immaculate conception of the railway
in particular.

What was most noticeable too, was the way Russian passengers took possession of their trains. In Europe and America
people travel in a train fully aware that it belongs either to a state
or a company and that their ticket grants them only temporary
occupation and certain restricted rights. In Russia people just
take them over. They move with their luggage, bundles and
children as if for permanent occupation. I saw empty trains,
newly washed and shining, pull in with great dignity to their
allotted wayside shrines. Within a few minutes they would be full

of the devout spreading out themselves, their food and their possessions with the look of rapture on their faces. Before long the train would resemble a second-rate boarding-house or a whole village on wheels. I have even seen long-distance trains with clothes-lines and washing hanging out in the crowded compartments, dropping an odd drop of water or two on the heads of the people who were eating, sleeping or playing chess below.

Architecturally the Siberian station in Moscow was not the brightest example of its kind. In some odd way the main building and its many scattered platforms had not been properly connected with one another, most of the platforms and the approaches were uncovered and in bad weather passengers could not have an easy time getting in and out of their trains. Yet in other ways this station was the most interesting and typical of the many in the city. It brought a feeling of the land and its peoples right into the heart of the capital for it was a human marshalling yard of all sorts and conditions of men and women. Night and day it was full of people camping not only in the waiting-rooms and departure halls but out in the open against the walls and barriers surrounding the station. They would sleep, talk, eat, and sit patiently there occasionally getting up, kettle in hand, to make tea at the public samovar. They apparently found nothing strange in being parked there like nomads in the heart of one of the world's greatest capitals, waiting for the appropriate mechanized caravan to take them on and out into the Siberian blue.

On my way to my train, the Moscow-Peking express or Train Number Two as it was officially called – Train Number One being I took it, the forbidden Vladivostok express – I had to pick my way carefully through the numbers of campers. When I had arrived the platform itself was empty but slowly it began to fill up with groups of twos and threes. It is rare to see people travelling alone on these journeys: and extraordinary how little baggage they carry, seldom more than a light suitcase and a bundle or two. Their clothes, too, seemed hardly adequate for few of them wore anything heavier than a macintosh, many of the women were bareheaded and at most had a kerchief knotted underneath their chins. I wore the only warm coat on the station. Considering how far we were going and how formidable the reputation of the climate on our way their attitude to the journey seemed remarkably casual.

Then suddenly a large Chinese contingent appeared in our midst. Most of them were civilians, dressed in Mao-Tse-Tsung tunics, cloth caps on their heads and the colourless raincoats of the New China on their arms. But at the centre of them marched a compact little group of Chinese military, khaki capes to the ankles and bright Staff flashes on their collars and caps. It was extraordinary how their presence altered the scene. They had the subtle, infuriating knack of making all else around them look untidy and chaotic. It is something I have been aware of ever since 1926 when I first met the Chinese in China. No matter where they may be in the world and however deeply engaged in its affairs, they have this knack of never belonging to anywhere but China. Only that afternoon at lunch a young English graduate who had just done a year studying Russian at the Moscow University had discussed this very matter with me. When he first went to the university he was greatly impressed by the way the Russian students worked. Then he met the Chinese students and they not only made his English contemporaries look frivolous and irresponsible but the Russian ones became mere amateurs. The Chinese had come to Russia to study and this they did to the exclusion of almost everything else so that even sleeping and eating came near to being hedonistic interruptions of their purpose. They did not mix either with Russian or other foreign students but living in the brand-new Chinese legation opposite the university, they kept themselves strictly to themselves. Even the Russians were overawed by such dedication to work and, he had said, were perhaps alarmed at such single-mindedness.

Watching this Chinese contingent on the platform I felt almost sorry for the three Russian officials who were there to see them off. They all three spoke Chinese fluently but with a wealth of gesture and emotion that I felt set up many barriers. The Chinese just could not respond in kind. They were circumspect and scrupulously courteous but some special Chinese characteristic kept them on the bank, rather than in the stream, of the conversation. It was as if the Russians were performers and they spectators and it occurred to me that I could not imagine two nations psychologically farther apart than these two. There was one officer among the Chinese, a Staff Colonel, who held my attention in particular. He wore his uniform with remarkable elegance even for a Chinese staff officer and had a beautiful face and head. Then suddenly he moved and the movement set something glittering below his ear. I could not resist going nearer until I could see distinctly that he wore long diamond pendants in his ears. I had hardly established this when I realized that this officer was a woman for from underneath her smart staff officer's cap a black, shining braid of hair fell right down to the small of her back. The difference between the old China which not long ago bound the feet of its women from birth to keep them small, and the new seemed infinite.

My own sleeper in Train Number Two was Russian-built but staffed by Chinese. I have never been in a roomier train, for possessing, as the Russians do, the widest track in the world their trains are broader than any others. I had hardly entered my sleeper, when the Chinese attendant brought me a cup of tea made in the incomparable Chinese way, showed me how the lights worked, asked me what time I wanted to be called, and before leaving turned on the radiogram for me. Chinese music immediately filled the air and from then on was always on tap until I left the train five days later. That was very Chinese too. The rest of the train played Russian music but all the way to Irkutsk this coach broadcast only in Chinese.

My bed was already made up on the lower of the two berths in the compartment. The blankets were part wool, part cotton, the sheets and pillows of coarsish cotton, poorly bleached but fresh and spotless. I had hardly got into bed when a middle-aged Russian came in. He gave me a friendly nod but did not speak. He belonged, I observed afterwards, to a group of four in the compartment next to ours where he spent all his time. Beyond saying good morning and good night for three days we never had any conversation with each other and yet there was nothing unfriendly about his silence. On the contrary I felt that he was extremely kindly disposed to me. But as he only used the compartment to sleep in and as I soon had other preoccupations I had no inducement to draw him into conversation. Yet at our brief meetings always he watched me intently, particularly when I was dressing and undressing. My clothes, the way I dressed and did my tie, the kind of pyjamas I wore, my slippers, all seemed to fascinate him. On his last night in the compartment he was still watching me as intently as on the first. Suddenly leaning over the edge of his bunk he looked at me, his eyes shining with the excitement of a gambler about to place his bet and remarked very slowly and deliberately in excellent English: 'Never leave for the morrow what you can do today.' With that he turned out his light and went to sleep. When I woke in the morning he had gone.

On this first night however as my watch said it was 12.50 a.m. I quickly turned off my light and my companion's went out soon after. I thought I had never travelled in so smooth a train, not even in the East-West Californian Express. I had barely time to regret that I could not travel on like that to the Russian Pacific coast and digest the irony of a freedom of movement which has shrunk with inverse proportion to the improvement in the systems of communication.

Morning came with the Volga at the window, nearly a mile wide and full of traffic. The only rivers I know that really measure up to the Russian are the American rivers. We have a few in Africa and the Nile of course which in its impact on human history and imagination exceeds all other rivers in the world. But even so the Volga was breath-taking. All told I was to cross it four times and each time it seemed more impressive. From the air it looked like a succession of lakes rather than a river. Apart from its natural size, it is the most exploited river in the Soviet Union. It has been so dammed and its waters so diverted into canals and hydro-electric turbines that men with vision in Russia have been seriously concerned about its future. The level of the Caspian, which depends so much on the Volga, is falling and the waters themselves have become so charged with the toxic waste of the factories and cities that its great fish and natural life has sharply declined. I met a young naturalist who told me with disgust that it was nowadays a river filled not with water but poison. The concern about this is so real that already Russian scientists have begun to apply the lessons learnt from their mistakes on the Volga to their new schemes on other rivers. Precautions to prevent poisoning of all the rivers have been improved not least, of course, on the banks of the Volga, and scientists say that once some of the northern rivers are diverted to flow into the Volga the danger will be over. All this does not prevent the river from looking exceedingly beautiful and the country along its banks is some of the loveliest and most typically Russian in the Soviet Union. Originally I had longed to travel all the way by steamer down to Astrakhan. I met several Russians who were ecstatic about the journey, the beauty of the country and the towns. But it had not been allowed. So I had to content myself with such views as I had on my fast-moving Train Number Two.

From the windows of the dining-car I watched a great day expand over the countryside. I was alone except for two sturdy waitresses – Siberian travellers I was to find dined whenever their stomachs moved them but all breakfasted late. I could change my table from side to side at will and enjoy uninterruptedly what I saw. It was not at all what I had expected. A light mist was dispersing from the hollows beyond the river banks and a landscape of incredible delicacy was coming into view. The woods and forests were of fine-drawn larch and birch sparkling with light, with glimpses that were pure Corot. The marshalled brick and concrete of Moscow was gone and in their stead stood villages of wood, log-cutters' huts of wood, the split wood piled high against the walls shining like gold in the sun. Everywhere in the world railways attack towns and houses in the rear where they are least protected against prying eyes so I could look into town and country at their relaxed and intimate moments. The fields were full of men and women, shawls around their heads, working side by side. The streets of the villages full of hens and chickens, ducks and ducklings and the largest white geese I have ever seen. It was a scene where nearly everything was wood and earth: nature was tender and delicate but the detail imposed on it by man was rough and casual. No street nor road was ever tarred, and all were uneven, full of mud and puddles, often ending up in bogs and ponds. The streams everywhere were as full of logs as water. Old Russian names began to appear on the station signboards, as, for instance, Nikola-Paloma – Pilgrims of the Nikola Forest – for these northern woods had given the Russians their only shelter against Tartars and other invaders. Here for centuries they were able to hide or were able to make a stand, grouped round churches and monasteries. It is for this reason that the most remarkable concentration of churches and monasteries in Greater Russia is located in the north. The domes and spires still stand, the greatest among them restored and splendid. Those within view of the railway track were rather dilapidated and forlorn like moulting hens with their last clutch of chickens around them. When I repeated Anatole France's simile to a Russian I met on this journey he immediately jerked his chin at the church in question and said in a dead-pan way, 'That's one hen that will never lay eggs again.' Dilapidated or restored, visually these churches were a vital element in the scene. As we moved east the country rolled towards the Urals but there were still no hills or mountains. The streams, forests and meadows, the animals and the men and women, were tightly drawn into a profound interlocking pattern. The villages and hamlets of wood had a natural affinity with the soil. Grey, scarred by sun and frost, the square little houses, the Izbas, looked as if they had actually grown out of the soil. There was, one felt, no break in the rhythm of unity on earth. But if the spires of the shabby churches had not been there earth and sky would have been greatly divided. Those spires raised the vast earth and lowered the immense sky into a close embrace which as the hours and the miles passed became increasingly satisfying. There are roughly two sorts of landscape, one which achieves its effects by epigrammatic and alternating statements of mountain, river, plain, forest, lake and sea. The other repeats itself on a vast scale over long sustained periods as on the high seas or in the desert. It is to this last category that the Greater Russian scene belongs. Through each window of the little wooden houses too was the same vision of lace curtains, neatly parted and gathered aside to expose the flower-pot in the centre. Flowers and lace curtains, and the longing for refinement that they represented in that immense setting was most touching. For over three thousand miles, I passed through stretch after stretch of uninhabited land but at each hamlet there, prim as ever, would be the lace curtains and the flower-pot again saluting the train, as the marks of peasant self-respect. I can vouch that from the Polish frontier to the Pacific Ocean there was not a window without a lace curtain.

I left the dining-car late but the other passengers had not appeared and the coaches behind were slowly coming alive. In the Russian cars the women attendants in uniform were stoking up the samovars, fitted in an angle of the broad corridors of each coach, and, curiously enough, not electrified. Some compartment doors were open and men in pyjamas were already playing chess with one another and sipping glasses of tea. Every male Russian, it appears, carries a portable, folding chessboard with him. It is as much part of his travelling kit as a toothbrush and razor are mine. Their radios too were full on, spraying the air with Russian sound as a revolving nozzle does the earth with water. But the moment I crossed over the footbridges into my own coach I was back in China. I found one Chinese attendant amusing a little Russian girl while her parents slept by showing her how to feed the goldfish he kept in a bowl in his quarters. The train moved so smoothly that the bowl was filled almost to the brim without spilling. His colleague at the other end of the coach had a canary in a cage singing a song of pure joy and liberation, heart-rending because as far as it was concerned no theme could have been more without foundation. It occurred to me, from the little I had seen of Russians and Chinese, that this was a train journey with a difference. The attitude of everyone on this train was that of a sailor to his ship. I might be travelling on wheels but I was in essence on a voyage.

At our first main station the train came alive with a rush. Chinese and Russian passengers tumbled out of their berths to pace up and down the platforms. The Chinese civilians – their military had vanished – were washed, shaven, brushed, manicured and neat in their Mao-Tse-Tsung uniforms of blue. The Russian men however were almost all in pyjamas though their women were dressed in neatly cut coats and skirts. I thought at first that pyjamas were worn because of the early hour of the day. But I was to discover that most of the men wore them all the time as a travelling suit. They took them off only to eat in the dining-car. Perhaps this display of male night attire was a badge of culture and emancipation, tangible proof to the outside world that Soviet people no longer slept in their clothes. Anyway the Russian officer who accompanied me all the way to Irkutsk seemed to find nothing incongruous in bestriding every platform with a measured pace clad in green, yellow and purple stripes with his military hat on his head and war-ribbons pinned on his pyjama jacket.

At this as all other main stops, too, the first people out of the coaches were the attendants, each equipped with a bucket and a mop on an extremely long handle. They filled the buckets at the station main and washed down their coaches with great thoroughness. They would do this five times a day with the result that our train glittered and shone, flashing back the sun at forests and plain by day and covering them with light at night. No train could have been cleaner for in addition to this periodic scrubbing without it was cleaned within by powerful vacuum-cleaners three times a day. I suspect that the attendants were kept so busy either cleaning or making tea for the passengers that they had no time to make our beds. That we all had to do ourselves.

From mid-morning until last thing at night the dining-car was always full and so was not much use as an observation car. People came there not only to eat but also to shop for one end of it was converted into a travelling trading post, a miniature 'G.U.M.' where passengers could buy anything from caviare and souvenirs to vodka and Ghanaian bananas and fine apples. The fruit was one of the great attractions but to me the prices seemed prohibitive. Innocently I bought a banana which cost me eleven shillings! I bought no fruit again. But the other passengers, except the disciplined Chinese, bought them in abundance until at the end of the first day all the bananas were gone and only a solitary pineapple was left like a crown jewel in a glass case. In addition to the shoppers on the train there were the shoppers from the forests and clearings who immediately boarded the train at the stations for a spending spree. The further east we went the greater their numbers became until finally the dining-car shop was so low in supplies that it locked its doors to all newcomers. But the frustrated shoppers from the land refused to take 'No' for an answer. They lost their tempers and shouted and threatened beating the train doors and windows furiously with their fists. I thought I was about to witness a riot. However, in the end, they desisted. I think not so much because the train refused to yield but because the passengers parading calmly up and down the platform in their shiny pyjamas took absolutely no notice of them. They refused to make the situation collective by even as much as a glance and in Russia no disapproval is more effective. It is perhaps a primitive characteristic that the degree of rightness of an attitude is determined by the degree of collectivity achieved. I have seen the technique used effectively by tribes in Africa. I have seen individuals dying just because their tribes formally had turned their backs on them. I remember my young interpreter telling me a story in Moscow which illustrates how deeply rooted is the collective value. Three young Americans were spending a night at an hotel feasting and dancing late because it was their last night in Russia. Just before closing-time two of them went on ahead and left one to pay the bill. He did not have enough money and my interpreter was sent for to help the waiters sort out the matter. 'None of those waiters,' he had told me, 'minded the boys not having enough money. That can happen to anyone and in the end the waiters and I clubbed together to make up the difference. But what they found unforgivable was that two of the young people could leave a comrade to pay the bill alone. No Russian could ever do that!'

In the crowded dining-car the persons I admired most were the two waitresses. They were on duty morning, day and night, and hardly ever off their feet. Dressed in becoming brown uniforms, white aprons with lace at the hems and little white lace caps like Victorian parlourmaids on their heads, they were efficient, imperturbable and always pleasant. What a western Trade Unionist would have said of their hours of work defeats my imagination, and their stamina was astonishing. They were never tired. I would see them at the double serving the last orders of night and I would think they would be wrecks in the morning. But at breakfast I found them neat, fresh and – once they got used to me – smiling. One of them even had enough energy to study English carrying an English grammar in her pocket, and after the first day she came to me for help. What complicated their work was that they had to serve two kinds of food: Russian and Chinese. We had two large '*à la carte*' menus one in Russian and one in Chinese and the food on either was appetizing enough to make me respect the chef. I would see him sometimes come out of his kitchen for air. He looked like a Toulouse Lautrec character, gaunt, hollow-cheeked and sallow to a macabre degree, but his exhausted look was deceptive for invariably I would find him taking the air and also engaged in snatching some study of physics from a primer held in a white and clammy hand.

Once I asked the waitress who was learning English if she did not find the work too much?

She found the idea so funny that she laughed out loud. 'It is nothing,' she said. 'I do this only for twenty-four days. After that I am given a good rest at home in Moscow.'

'What do you call a good rest?'

'Oh, that depends on me,' she said. 'Anything from a fortnight to three weeks.'

Throughout my journey I had always the impression that Russians instinctively prefer to work at great pressure in prolonged concentrated bursts followed by periods of protracted almost irresponsible inactivity which perhaps correspond to the rhythms their climate imposes on them.

Watching the two women working so hard I felt I ought to tip them. In Moscow when I had felt obliged to offer someone a tip my interpreter had taken me seriously to task. People, he said, were paid by the State and one only insulted them by offering them tips. Even if they accepted, it would degrade their character and I must never try it again. I had taken him at his word. But these waitresses seemed to me manifestly cast for exceptions. So I tried it once and was so firmly but courteously rebuffed that I did not attempt it again. What made it worse was that after the first day they would not let me pay for the tea which I drank since they said I was spending enough money on the train. The further we went the more they made me feel that I was not a passenger but one of the family. They would now wave and utter a cheerful greeting to the English '*Tovarich*' (as they called me) whenever I entered the car. Soon other travellers followed their example. The only people who remained apart were the Chinese. They would usually come into the car in a body to reserved tables at a pre-arranged time. While eating they would talk only Chinese. They spoke to no one outside their group and no one tried to speak to them. This separateness was all the more striking because among themselves they were obviously gay, lively, sociable and entertaining people. They were, in fact, the happiest Communists I saw on my travels and the nearer we got to China the greater their delight and the more exhilarated their behaviour became. Perhaps that is why one of them suddenly started greeting me. I thought I had achieved a real break-through, but alas!

it never went beyond an exchange of greetings which began and developed in the most ridiculous fashion. It started one morning while I was giving the waitress her English instruction. While so engaged the Chinese entered in a body. I was trying to teach her the English idioms for the Russian '*spasibo*' and '*pozjalusta*': the first could mean 'Thank you very much', the second, 'Don't mention it, please'. She was trying them out in her clear un-selfconscious contralto when the Chinese trooped out of the dining-car. Next time they entered the car, they said 'Good morning' to the waitress in Russian. Then one of them bowed to me and uttered the words solemnly, 'Don't mention it, please.'

Just in time I realized that he had mistaken the phrase as a formal English greeting so I bowed in turn and replied: 'Thank you very much!'

The next time we met he bowed and said, 'Thank you very much,' to which I responded, 'Don't mention it, please.' And so the two phrases went on reversing their natural order and intention for thousands of miles across Russia and Siberia! I always feared that he might find out the real meaning of the words but all I could do was to hope for the best and keep a solemn face. Fortunately hope did not fail me.

At all the stations fantastically long, slow trains drew up to make way for our shining express. Many of them were goods trains. Some of these were oil trains, others were made up of heavy industrial trucks or construction-material carriers. A great many were slow passenger trains filled with people and looking like villages on wheels. The traffic clearly was intense despite the fact that the line east has been doubled for some thousands of miles by a loop to the south taking in new growing industrial territory. Even so the railway looked as if it could hardly cope with the demands made on it. 'The east is to us what the west was to the Americans,' a Russian writer had told me in Moscow. 'They used to say "Go West". We say "Go East".' And so the young of Russia are going east in their thousands. With them go too the restless, the misfits, the feckless, the footloose of all ages streaming out of the more crowded west to the vast, wide open spaces of the east.

This movement east started long before the last war. There is for instance a growing industrial city of close on 300,000 people called Komsomolsk in the Far East near the Tartar Straits and connected by rail to Khabarovsk and Vladivostok. It is built on a site hacked out of dense forest. It was the work of idealistic Communist youth who started it in 1932. In those days the movement east owed much to Stalin. He saw clearly the danger of having so much of Russia's vital industry concentrated near the classical invasion routes from the west. He had taken to heart, too the lessons of the Russo-Japanese War and realized how vulnerable was a Far East dependent on a single railway link with the west. He therefore did two things. First, he developed a new industrial Russia well away from the West. On the eastern slopes of the Urals, hard by the great new fields of essential raw materials that his geologists were discovering, he did all he could to make the Far East self-sufficient, doubling the railway track and extending its capacities by loops and duplications. Had it not been for the energy and ruthlessness with which he carried out these plans Russia may well have succumbed to Hitler. But the urge to go east was there long before Stalin. Deep in Russian history and imagination the records show that the Russians were already breaking into Siberia, or Yugra as it was called in the eleventh century. But the first organized push beyond the Urals began in 1581 when an expedition under a Cossack called Yermak was sent East by the Strogonov family. Yermak routed the forces of the Siberian Khans, sent back for support to Moscow, pushed south to the foothills of the Altai and east to the River Ob. From there on torn by bloody internal strife as Russia was, the drift to the east continued with increasing tempo and success. Westward the way was blocked by Poles, Lithuanians, Baltic knights and Swedes and life made perilous and insecure by a series of frontier wars. But in the east the Russians had no such trouble since, for once, they were advancing against peoples even more backward than they themselves. In 1639 already the incredible Cossacks under Ivan Moskuitin appeared on the sea of Okhotsk. Nine years later, a hundred years before Bering, another Cossack, Semyon Dezhnev, rounded the Chukotka capes to discover the straits between Asia and America. Again the parallels with North American history are obvious and yet not superficial. As in America the Cossacks and their backers were after trade, particularly trade in furs. They were ready to do no more

than to establish fortified trading posts and to come and go indefinitely between them. But soon the matter was taken out of
their hands by the settlers. They were as in America of all sorts
and types of men who yet were psychologically at one since they
were impelled by some profound discontent with the society into
which they had been born. I know from my own experience in
Africa that in communities with a great, unknown, sparsely inhabited country around them, two sorts of people quickly emerge:
those who believe in dealing with their problems by standing
fast: and those whose instinct is to abandon all and set out into
the empty unknown. Siberia drew people of this last temperament
towards it and their numbers were swollen by the fugitives and
victims of the judgement and justice of the establishment in the
West: the escaped serfs, political prisoners and other exiles. The
country seemed to fit their temperament like a glove. Already in
the eighteenth century the exile Radischev had come to love his
house of exile so much that he cried: 'What natural wealth! What
power! As soon as it is settled, it will play a great role in the
history of the world.' Lomonosov himself stated prophetically,
'Russian might will grow as Siberia develops.' Chekhov was
moved to unusual lyricism by what he saw of the country.
Standing on the banks of the Yenesei, for instance, he declared it
more beautiful than the Volga, saying 'If the Volga is a modest
and melancholy beauty the Yenesei is a great and unrestrained
giant who does not know what to do with his energy and youth. . . .
I think of the full, wise and bold life that will in time grow on
these banks.' It sounded prophetic extravagance then. Today it is
the sober, conscious, accepted and determined vision of the
Russian people. The concentration and forced labour camps, the
exiles and fugitives may be on the decline but the displaced, the
detribalized, the idealistic, the out-of-work and above all the
naturally restless and discontented are drawn to Siberia in
greater numbers than ever before.

On this first day in Train Number Two I was already half-way
through a book which illustrated how this process goes on today.
It was Anatoly Kuznetsov's *Sequel to a Legend*. It is the story of a
young man who, profoundly disillusioned with the world and the
people in Moscow, decides to leave home and try to find himself
and a new way of life in Siberia. It is a bitter book and I doubt

if it would ever have been published did it not draw a stock Marxist-Leninist moral at the end.

'Whichever way you look,' one of the characters says, 'you see self-satisfied mugs, men of property, cynics. And their offspring are exactly like the parents. As I look at them I wonder whether such notions as honesty, a noble cause, truth and goodness really exist. This sort of good does not fetch much among our neighbours. A gorgeous villa on our right belongs to the manager of some sort of eating-place. The one on our left is even more showy in extremely bad taste too, the property of a supply director of some trust. And the last in the row is a brand-new cottage built by the beggar who makes the rounds of suburban trains with his blind wife. . . . All around me swell boys and girls in slacks dash along the streets on bicycles, play volley-ball, dance in the evening to the tape-recorder, in a word enjoy life in a big way. . . . I cannot help wondering, as I observe all this, whether it is just a bunch of desperate fanatics who play the game of honesty, doomed to die without ever knowing normal, decent life. Their life is a sacrifice. But in the name of what?' Then the hero turns his back on all this and travels East to Irkutsk in a train crowded with scores of young people in search of an answer to this and other questions. He has one advantage over them. He has paid for his own fare. All the rest are signed-up boys and girls, bound by a three-year contract. For a moment the writer lifts a curtain on the vast propaganda campaign organized by the State to get the youth of the country to go East. He talks about the advertising, posters, the agents in every town ready to draw up contracts, make an advance and give a railway ticket to anyone tempted to go East. There are also the regional committees of the powerful Young Communist League, urging, enlisting, if not morally intimidating, young people into work on the virgin soil farms and Siberian construction projects. In the train east the writer finds himself in the company of riff-raff and robbers. By the time they get near Irkutsk he decides to separate himself from his companions and to find himself work on a hydro-electric scheme. There, as a 'concreter', he finds a purpose for himself at last through hard teamwork with other young men and women serving the same machine. His friends in Moscow try in vain to get him back. 'I have no intention to stay an ordinary concreter all my life,' he replies. 'Next year I will apply to the Building Institute and take a correspondence course. I must learn to get ready quicker in the morning and do with six hours of sleep. And I must study.'

Besides this novel I had a play with me called *It Happened at Irkutsk* by Alexei Arbuzov. It was nightly reducing audiences all over the Soviet Union to tears and like the novel was concerned with a hydro-electric scheme in Siberia. It was another interesting example of how writer and playwright were drawn to idealize and advertise in the dimension of the spirit the schemes of the State. They were the contemporary press-gangs of authority. Ostensibly the play claims to be about love 'to which we attach too little significance', the playwright says. But it is a love confined and crazily mixed-up in a dialectically materialistic role. The hero of *Sequel to a Legend* finds his whole meaning in life in administering to a concrete mixer. The people in the play achieve it by serving a walking excavator. The excavator is in fact the hero of the play, a mechanical Messiah that redeems and transfigures the lesser men and women who serve it. There is also in the play another machine, a cash-register, which plays the role of the Tempter, the mechanical Satan. Walking excavators, one gathers, are good; cash-registers are bad. One of the climaxes of the play occurs when the widow of the dead hero and leader of the excavator team feels in desperation that she should go back to the only machine she understands, the cash-register, which she operated in a department store before her marriage. All the dead man's companions, horrified by the prospect, rally round and in the end she is made to see that the cash-register is evil and the walking excavator her true and only redeemer. 'I am taking Sergei's (the dead husband's) place on the excavator,' the second hero tells her: 'Every screw, every rivet there, is drenched with my sweat. . . . That machine is almost human, it has a soul and without it I don't think I could ever be happy. I shall go down on my knees to you and beg you not to let me desert my comrades. . . . Come and work with us on the excavator. . . . Forget your hurts . . . after all this is Sergei's machine, our Sergei, your Sergei.' Of course, she cannot resist such a plea and how complete is her redemption, is shown by one of her last remarks before the final curtain: 'They say there's a girl at the Volga dam who's in charge of a whole excavator crew. Is that possible?' Clearly she intends to become another such girl and one can almost hear the chorus of seraphic pneumatic drills and cherubic shovels singing 'Hallelujah' as the curtain falls.

All this linked up too with something I had just read in Paustovsky. 'You must write about machines,' he says, 'as you write about people – feeling their pulse-beat, loving them, penetrating into their life. I always feel physical pain when a machine is abused. Writers, when describing machines, must treat them with the same consideration as human beings.' On the day in Train Number Two I understood how poor Olga Bergholtz, the gallant distinguished woman poet whose agonized confession that in Soviet literature humanity and human beings were lacking so shook Russia. 'There are operators of bulldozers, and steam-shovels in our literature,' she wrote. 'There are herbiculturalists, all carefully, sometimes even brilliantly, described. But they are described from the outside.' No wonder too that Vera Inber, a poet of Leningrad, could say that nobody would read Soviet poetry as long as it was about 'the same old dam, the same old steam-shovel'. It is significant that it was not long before these and other similar voices were rebuked and warned by Mr Khrushchev himself.

I myself was wholeheartedly on the side of the poets and yet one could not help seeing how the State was trapped into feeling it had to insist on its right to determine the role of the artist in society. Dealing with a people initially so one-sided in character, so committed to a life of feeling, so disdainful of the objective and outer realities, so naturalistic and unscientifically minded, so lacking in industrial experience and tradition, the State can easily convince itself that it can only keep the nation interested and active by presenting matter and machine to them as free instruments of the spirit and the means of universal salvation. Neither Stalin nor Peter the Great with their devastating abnormalities can be fully understood without reference to this profound national indifference, this bias in the character of the Russian people. I have no doubt that the State is wrong, particularly as it has already won its campaign. Soviet Russia today is completely machine- and matter-minded. But the price the

State one day will have to pay for this suppression of the individual and subjective needs of men and women and this elevation
of the machine and technology into a national religion, daily
becomes greater. Superstition of the mind and spirit are bad
enough. But the superstition about matter and machines which
the Soviet State has put in their place, is, I believe, more
deadly.

Meanwhile, in between reading and watching the landscape, I
would see groups of hard-up young passengers from lesser trains
haggling with the saleswomen at the station stalls for anything
from stringy cooked chickens and hard-boiled eggs to bread,
butter and sunflower seeds. Unlike my travelling companions
they were not in pyjamas but in track-suits and canvas shoes from
their school and college days. For young people they were extraordinarily subdued and looked rather pathetic and overwhelmed.
Unfortunately though we had many young children in our train
we had almost no young people. Train Number Two was for the
established and the respectable not for the displaced and searching. I regretted this all the more because the population of the
Soviet Union has, I believe, the highest proportion of young in the
world and this is particularly true of Siberia. The future belongs
more and more to the young who, like the young everywhere were,
as I found from the contacts I had with them, not inclined to
accept the experience of their elders and were vaguely determined to find their own values out of their own experience.
Having finished reading *Sequel to a Legend* I concluded that it
really had no answer to the questions it asked of itself. It was not
even, I felt, representative of the young except in its initial
questioning. A young Russian whom I respected and liked, had
assured me in Moscow that, for all their national defects, Russians were incapable of hypocrisy. I think that is true in their
personal relationships but their capacity for political and intellectual hypocrisy seems to me unusually high. Therefore I would
have given much to talk to the young directly about Siberia and
their motives for going there. But in our train there were only
two young people and unfortunately they seemed to represent
those from which the hero of *Sequel to a Legend* had fled. They
were, I thought, brother and sister. They were constantly in and
out of the dining-car. They appeared to have unlimited money

and were the most expensively dressed persons in the train. Between visits to the dining-car they would change their clothes. I did not see them wear the same clothes twice. They never spoke to anyone except each other and looked as if they despised the rest of the train. The train was at first interested and puzzled but before long I was told that they were spoilt, a disgrace to society, had never done honest work and study in their lives and clearly must be the children of some powerful personage on the establishment. What was the Soviet Union coming to!

In this way we swiftly approached the Urals. A thriving industrial centre of close on 300,000 people like Kirov, as the Viatka founded in 1174 is today called, held us only long enough for watering and the train's ablutions. It was, so a friendly bank-clerk on his way to a new Siberian town told me, called after Stalin's great friend. I gathered from him that Kirov's assassination had done more than deprive the State of a dedicated and unusually gifted servant. He implied it had unhinged Stalin's mind as well and was largely responsible for starting him on his destructive outbursts. But before we could really get our conversation started we had to rush back to our separate coaches for a woman announcer was informing us over the loudspeaker that our train had just been taken over by 'Locomotiveman Ryabov, leader of an heroic team of heroic Soviet labour and himself a hero of heroic labour'. In his charge, she was sure, we would travel in comfort and safety and she wished us all possible good speed on our journey. So there we were back in the country again and it was impressive how quickly the woods and forest closed in on city, village, hamlet and clearings. By night we were at Perm right at the entrance to the Urals. Like all the cities in such an immense empty land, this town of more than 700,000 people was sprung on one by surprise. One minute we were in the country and in the dark and the next we had rounded a bend and there was a city of light with broad meshes of railway tracks and acres of marshalling yards full of trucks and coaches. Nor was there any sense of increased height for we had crossed the gentle and low ranges in the dark barely thirteen hundred feet above sea-level. And somewhere near the Chusovaya River we had flashed by a plain striped post that marked the border between Europe and Asia.

I was up at first light to watch our passage through the ranges but already the border was behind us. I found myself in the gentlest of downs looking at hills of pearl showing above woods of glowing red pine and frail filigree birch. Everywhere between the woods there were long rides, broad fire-breaks and glimpses of white brooks and flashing streams. For miles there was nothing but forest, streams, water-meadows, mirrors full of cloud and sky, a lift of land like a mist above the woods and a shy world of squirrels, foxes, wolves, deer and bear. Then suddenly would come a new clearing, a woodcutter's hamlet, a peasant cluster of wooden buildings or a railway siding with names like 'The Peak' or 'The Log-Cabin' looking lonely and isolated. Others had names that spoke of their pioneer origin like 'Pancakes', 'Candle', 'Farthest Yet', 'Naked-Boy Halt', and, my favourite, 'Studies'. 'Studies' was so small and isolated that the only reason for its existence appeared to be time and place to concentrate on the study of earth, forest and sky.

Every now and then women in felt boots, grey, dusty, worn overalls and with woollen scarves round their heads, appeared doing heavy repairs on the track. I was to get so used to this sight of seeing women working as hard as men in the Soviet Union that when on my return I visited an atomic-power project near my home in England at first sight I missed seeing women navvying on the job as they would inevitably have been doing in Russia. But on this morning I found it a mournful sight and one more example of the primitive content in the Soviet concept of life. 'Women and men,' my Russian friends had told me time and again, 'are truly equal only in Russia. Only here do they get equal opportunity of work and equal pay for equal work.' But I remembered Blake's 'one law for the lion and the ox is oppression'. In practice it seemed to me that the women, whose nature also commits them to child-bearing, worked far harder than the men in Russia. That morning the faces that I saw beside the line looking up at us as we flashed by showed their indomitable patience, and also the look of rejection which is implicit in the absence of special recognition by their men and their societies; this look I know so well in the primitive women of Africa. The wayside halts and sidings too were manned on the whole by women in worn blue serge coats and skirts and blue caps on their heads. They would turn out always in pairs, with unfailing regularity standing solemnly and holding up little gold flags as a sign that the way ahead was clear.

Where we halted, I would now find the indigenous Siberian travellers, the aborigines as a Russian official called them, appearing in growing numbers. I would find the shop, restaurant and waiting-rooms full of women in shawls, dark dusty skirts, and woollen jumpers, and men with beards dressed in blouses, faded blue trousers tucked into mud-stained boots and forage caps on their heads. The faces of both men and women were stained, creased and marked by sun, wind and frost, and they sat, as a rule, silently eating or waiting, their bundles beside them. In their midst the pyjamas of Train Number Two, particularly the finery of the rich boy and girl, seemed grotesque. Yet these peasants were oddly indifferent to us. One felt they were no longer curious about men. They were curious only about the abiding things of life, the seasons, the weather, what would come forth from the earth and the urgent harvest before the fall of their terrible winter. They saddened me greatly because they reminded me of my own Afrikaner people after the Boer War, all farmers too, poor, stricken and yet nobler by far than they are now that they have become rich and powerful. Yet there was nothing hopeless about these Russians. It just was that their hope lay in a dimension in which our twentieth century has no belief. I remembered an African proverb: 'Patience is an egg that hatched great birds; the sun too is such an egg.' That patience and wisdom lay like a clean garment upon these people. Why then did the sight sadden one? Perhaps because one was aware that one stood in the presence of people who are among the most profoundly rejected in the history of the world. The peasant in Russia has never been honoured by the State nor given the share to which his courage, endurance and labour has entitled him. Even those who understood him best and were designed to love him most, like Peter the Great, found it convenient to exploit and betray him. Spengler, for all his sweeping generalizations, uttered some inspired truths about European history. He said that Moscow had no soul, that the spirit of the Russian upper classes was western, and that the lower classes brought into the towns with them the soul of the countryside, but that between the two worlds there was no reciprocal comprehension, communication or charity. The last remark seems still to be true and the irony is all the greater when one considered that the peasants made the Revolution. The Revolution was already accomplished by the peasants and their soldier offspring when Lenin and his small band of professionals took it over. Yet their first priority was to reject the peasant. Lenin may have been a kindly person but he had no faith in or love of humanity. He loved only something called proletarian man and he and his successors one way or another have tried to change the people of Russia into this abstract image of human reality. This is one of the great differences between China and Russia. One of the first principles of Mao-Tse-Tsung's revolution was to base it on the peasant and for this, among other reasons, I believe the revolution in China could prove ultimately to be more creative than the Russian one. In the beginning the Chinese avoided this fatal 'apartheid' of the peasant which has made such confusion in Russian social and economic history. Today there may be a new awareness of the claims of the peasant, of his worth and his humanity. Several significant new concessions to farmers were proclaimed while I was in Russia and Mr Khrushchev appreciates the vital importance of the problem as no one before has done. But the gap between industrial man and the peasant is still abysmal. There is a great reckoning inevitably still to be made between these two worlds. But what makes the contemporary lack of understanding of the peasant all the more destructive in Russia is that it is unnatural. By far the greatest number of people in towns and industries in Russia are of peasant origin and with direct or near roots in the land. The Russian young are not unaware of this. One night I had met a young Russian writer at a party in Moscow. I asked him what his latest work was. His face clouded and he said: 'I don't know if I can tell you about it. It is a terrible story.' I begged him to and finally he told me at great length. It was a story about a gifted good-looking boy who comes from his small village to work in Moscow. He meets a beautiful girl of rich parents. They marry and begin life in the luxurious apartment of his in-laws. One evening he comes home to find an old peasant from the village parked with his bundles beside the hat-racks and overcoats in the hall of the apartment. Delighted, he embraces the travel-stained old man and is about to take him in when the main door opens and his wife appears. She warns him that he is not to bring so uncouth a person into the apartment so he is forced to take the old man out for dinner and find him a bed in a crowded doss-house. But that night his whole nature rebels against the deed. He cannot sleep beside his wife in their comfortable bed. He sits up to look at her lying asleep. 'Does it mean that if I am to love you I must hate my peasant Uncle?' he asks himself, 'Or because of my long and natural love of him I am condemned now to hate you?' He remembers her angry, uncompromising words and finally he chooses the peasant, dresses quickly and leaves the apartment for good. At the end the young writer exclaimed, 'It is a terrible story! I am not surprised I cannot get anyone to publish it.'

The story stayed with me not only as a parable of contemporary Soviet society but as proof which warned me that conscience is as natural as breathing to men and that nothing can ultimately prevent them from returning to a life of truth in search of greater truth. This kind of inborn radar, this natural direction-finding in the human spirit will not, I am certain, remain indefinitely denied in Russia. There is already far more self-searching going on among the young in Russia than we realize, as the latest pronouncements against the progressive artist, writer and intellectual show.

When there was time, with this and similar thoughts in mind I would leave the crowded station halls and walk into the villages and towns. It was curious how few of the passengers ever did this, almost as if they were afraid of the space, the silence and the wide earth beyond. The villages in particular tended by day to look deserted for the children would be at school, and the grown-ups at work on the land. The rough streets between the duck-boards that served for pavements were taken over by hens, ducks and geese, clucking and quacking. The clanking of shunting trains and the hum of engines behind seemed strangely foreign to the scene. The square little Izbas and their Seni straggling along the streets out into the blue with their little lace curtains, flower-pots, pig-sties and plotted gardens were even closer to the earth than one had imagined from the train. They clung to that dark earth for comfort and sustenance as an African child to its mother's black breast and seemed to me the most moving things I had seen thus far in the Soviet Union. Back again in the train one would observe them grow smaller still in their setting of sky and level plain, their beautifully ploughed, raked and tended fields laid out around them like shining wet corduroy drying in the sun. Among the prepared earth there would be these people, sometimes near enough to see potatoes falling like nuggets of gold from the hands of planters, at others so far away that fast as we travelled they changed position in relation to us at a snail's-pace. Once a horseman on the horizon despite the dust smoking at his horse's heels seemed motionless in the aspic of space around him. Although a main road parallel to the railway accompanied us all the way I never saw a truck on it and was certain it could not be used much for none of it was gravelled or asphalted to make it usable in the rains.

After such distances the towns always shocked one and the first shock beyond the Urals was Sverdlovsk, a city of close on a million souls. It sat upon the earth like a giant tarantula in a web woven of shining railway tracks and threads of copper wire sagging between the pylons. We were hardly halted in the vast, crowded, frantic station than our train was empty. It was extraordinary how a confidence, absent at halts and sidings, would return to the passengers at the smell of a city. They immediately became self-important, buying newspapers, writing postcards, drinking tea and showing off their pyjamas. But here at Sverdlovsk an additional urge took them quickly out of the train. A rumour had gone round that Mr Khrushchev was about to be heard making a broadcast! It turned out to be false but until we left it kept our lot clustered round the station loudspeakers. Suddenly I felt a hand on my arm. I turned round. It was the man I had met – it seemed in another era – in the plane from Moscow to Tashkent. I could not have been more delighted and he too seemed pleased to see me again. He said he was on his way to Irkutsk.

'But I thought you always flew?' I exclaimed.

'Yes, I do nowadays,' he answered. 'But I can't this time because the aerodrome at Irkutsk is closed for extensions and repairs.'

My first reaction was one of relief for this was the official explanation given to me in Moscow as to why I could not fly on from Irkutsk to Khabarovsk. And now I had a friend of my own in the train. From that moment the whole nature of the journey changed.

'Come on board and have some tea,' he said to me. 'There's not going to be any speech from Khrushchev!'

Yes, it was amazing, he said over tea, what a draw a Khrushchev speech had for people. He had a friend who was a highly educated and much travelled person. This friend had told him that he found a Khrushchev speech far more interesting than any novel he had ever read. He told me this as if he could not quite share his friend's interest. In fact I had the impression, as I had with other cultivated Russians, that Mr Khrushchev could never be entirely to their taste because he was too uneducated a character. But my friend fully admitted his qualities which made him a great improvement on anyone since Lenin. What he liked most about his leader, he said, was that he did care about the land and the people who lived on it. It was extraordinary that until recently they had had no proper Ministry of Agriculture in the Soviet Union. Agriculture was run as a secondary branch of industry and politics. Such agricultural experts as they had sat in Moscow or a few big cities issuing paper directives. Khrushchev had done away with all that at once. He had sent experts out into the country to assume responsibility for the application of their theories and directives. But things have been so bad that Russian crops had been planted on a theory of rotation which left a third of the land idle under mere grass. He spoke of the idle earth with a revulsion foreign to him as if it were the duty of the earth to produce ceaselessly to the fullest extent just as the worker in Russia was asked to produce. That the earth might have a way of its own in the matter did not seem to occur to him and in this regard alone he seemed to share Soviet man's profound mistrust of nature as well as human nature. Any idea that the ideal relationship between man and nature was one of partnership based on increasing understanding of the basic laws of the universe was unacceptable to him. Domination of nature by man, and of man by a single master alone made sense to him and in that sense he personified how much of the revolution was a revolt against natural Russian man.

He went on talking about his leader and his power to influence the people. For instance once at an agricultural conference a most successful chairman of a collective farm was proudly reciting his figures for wheat production.

'And what about maize?' Mr Khrushchev asked casually at the end.

The chairman went pale and said: 'I am afraid we do not grow maize.'

'Ah!' Mr Khrushchev exclaimed. 'Ah!'

And that was enough. Two years later the same farm returned one of the biggest maize harvests in the district. And then all over the Soviet Union collective and State farms had suddenly taken furiously to planting maize, often in vast areas totally unsuited for it.

Another example of his leader's power was a speech to railwaymen. 'Why produce rails only seven metres long?' he had asked them. 'Rails twenty metres long will be more economical!'

And that, my friend said, was exactly what would happen from now on. It all sounded so simple yet one look at the construction trains that we passed, their trucks designed to carry only rails seven metres long, demonstrated the complications that the changeover would produce, let alone the obvious difficulties that would arise on the tracks themselves. However, we did not talk of these things long. He had done so, I felt, more out of a sense of duty than personal inclination. His love was really for the country and he seemed happy to talk to me about it. He begged me not to judge the 1,600-mile range of Urals by the gentle, delicate waves of land through which I had come. It was true the Urals were not high and were worn down by time and ages of ice. In their centre they reproduced many of the features of the Greater Russian scene, the same trees, flowers, villages and the same pale sky. But in the north they were higher and had a stern, rugged beauty of their own, and in the south had a cataclysmic, lush wooded grandeur that was totally unsuspected. There were six railways in all cutting through the range and they all revealed a different characteristic of the hills. He had just come to Sverdlovsk from the south by way of Ufa, Zlatoust and Chelyabinsk along a track that had to twist like a serpent through the thickly wooded valleys of the Belaya, Ufa, Sima and Yurezan and on the blue day there was not a patch of sky without its eagle. Like all ancient earth it was unbelievably rich and below the cover of forest and grass existed a vast Aladdin's cave of the jewellery and lamp-oil of nature. This of course had long been known but until the thirties not properly evaluated and exploited. On the western slopes it was a world of oil, potassium, limestone and gypsum, and on the eastern, of minerals easily reached and bull-dozed to the surface; iron, chromium, manganese, nickel, copper, zinc, platinum, uranium, gold and precious stones. He wished I could see some of the areas of gold with their nuggets like hens' eggs and also the emeralds, amethysts, topaz, jasper, malachite, rock-crystal, sapphires, garnets, tourmalines and aquamarines. There was one part of the Ilmenskye Hills that was given over entirely to the mining of precious stones and the preservation of the flora and fauna of the Urals. There were mines there as bright as fire and as colourful as rainbows, and as startling as their colour was their abundance. Never, he stressed, has there been a country with such an abundance of everything as the Soviet Union. One example was the new western Ural oil-fields. There was one well, No. 100, which began spouting sixteen years ago and was still gushing as strongly as ever. It alone had produced more than three-quarters of a million tons of liquid fuel and there were many others like it. Then there were the vast subterranean fields of gas. Oil and gas were piped along pipelines in all directions for thousands of miles. For instance the Tuimazy-Omsk pipelines had already functioned for some years and soon Irkutsk itself, some two thousands miles away, would be fed by its own pipelines, thus reducing the transport costs to one-seventh of that by rail. Already heavy industry in the Urals had an output far greater than the whole of Russia in 1914. And that was only the merest beginning. The interlocking of the Ural ore regions by rail, river and pipelines with the coal and fuel-bearing areas of the south, particularly the Kuzbas, was nearly complete and the future progress compared with the past would be that of a jet aeroplane to a *troika*. Progress in the Urals could now be taken for granted and all the creative energies and planning be focused on Siberia and the Far East. Ah! Siberia, that story there would out-fiction fiction! Siberia excited his emotions as had no other part of the land. I found then that a great part of his youth and early middle age had been spent in working all over Siberia. Before Siberia could be properly developed, he said, it had first to be properly surveyed geographically and geologically. When Soviet scientists first began their gigantic task, it was fantastic how little organized scientific knowledge there was of the region. They had a terrible time for famine and civil war challenged Russian resources almost to breaking point. He had friends among geologists who could not get boats or trucks to help them on their scientific reconnaissances of the unknown and had actually gone out into the tundra of Siberia using reindeer and mules as pack-horses. Even today it was a problem getting transport for geologists because of the incredible size of Siberia, more than double the size of western Russia, twice that of Europe and bigger than Australia. Did I realize that from East to West Siberia was more than four thousand miles, and from south to north close on two thousand miles? More than three million square miles of it was covered with forest, or 'taiga' as he called it. In the *taiga* the summers were hot and short, the winters long. In winter the temperatures would easily fall to 70° below zero (centigrade). Yet they were easily borne and healthy because the climate is dry and on the whole windless. Like all Siberians he was inclined to boast of the cold winters yet he said that one Siberian summer was worth nine winters. However, surely I could imagine the difficulties of surveying so vast a country under such a cover in so extreme a climate? The amount of unbroken forest in Siberia alone covered over three million square miles. From above it was a sea of green that swept over plains, descended into valleys and broke over the mountains with equal intensity. Pines, cedars, silver-firs, larches and spruces nearly shut out the sky. Many of the cedars were 250 feet high and nine feet in diameter. The moment a cloud covered the sun the forests were dark and even in summer a poor geologist had a job finding his way around. The worst forests were the Urmans or Cherns, the black, damp coniferous ones on hilly and marshy ground. The trees among them grew in an odd way at all angles from the earth, not all straight and the space between them was littered with fallen branches, tops broken off by lightning and whole trunks uprooted by some high wind. Working in these forests how one longed for the great Siberia steppes, the southern plains

or even the bare, cold and windy tundra in the north. Yet once
out of them one experienced a powerful nostalgia, found oneself longing perhaps for the sound of a great tree exploding like a
bomb from the frost and the tense wintry silence rushing in to
wipe out the sound. Forced on one occasion to winter on a
mountain of solid metal discovered under the forest not far from
Ilymsk, hard by the Angara he told me of the delight he had enjoyed watching the natural life from smaller species like the
marten, ermine, kolinsky, weasel, glutton, squirrel, chipmunk,
and the wonderful sable up to the badger, otter, wolves and
bears. He told me of encounters with bears coming out of their
sleep in hollow trunks whence their breath sometimes rose to
hang like smoke above the stumps. He said there were thousands
of them as well as wolves, foxes and lynxes. He told me of
another winter in the north where the *taiga* declines into the open
tundra and how the reindeer and polar foxes in their thousands
moved from the open into the *taiga* fringes for food and cover.
Siberia has two-thirds of the world's reindeer population all now
collectivized and much more profitable than ever before. Already the reindeer's enemy, the wolf, is being eliminated, hunted
down by helicopter and radio-telephone and he himself had
participated in such a hunt over the tundra. He told me of a
summer by the shore of a forest lake, and of the long evenings
fishing for his supper. The woods around were full of mushrooms,
the shores red with huge bilberries and raspberries and the earth
around his camp a metre deep with pine-needles and dry moss.
Then there were the swans, 'the starlings of Siberia'. One had not
really seen swans until one saw them wild on these hidden *taiga*
waters ornamental as ever but so wild, vivid and passionate in
their ways that the swans of western Europe were shabby in comparison. Once when on an expedition and short of food a
member of his party shot a swan. All night long the bereaved
mate flew round the camp crying pitifully for its companion.
When dawn came and the dead swan still was absent, the other
flew as high as it could into the sky and then at the peak of its
flight folded its wings and fell like lead to its death on earth. It
was, he said, deliberate suicide and he, for one, had sworn he
would never again shoot a swan. Again, he told me how he had
flown over the place where the great meteorite had hit Siberia

some hundred years ago. The place from the air was unmistakable. Suddenly there was this round space in the sombre forest, a gleam of water at the centre and row upon row of dead, exploded or uprooted trees bleached like cannibal bone arranged around it in a perfect circle. It was an example to him of how remote and undisturbed was Siberia that this graveyard of a star was lying there still so unchanged and inviolate.

Into this world geologists and scientists went in their thousands. Not only male geologists but hundreds of women too, who roughed it with the men. The discovery of diamonds in Yakutia, for instance, was the work entirely of a woman geologist from Leningrad. She not only evolved a brilliant new geological theory about diamonds but went out into the *taiga* literally crawling about on her stomach for months, to prove it. And prove it she did by discovering pipes of pure kimberlite in the *taiga*. The first pipe to go into production was, of course, named the Pipe of Peace. As a result of this kind of deduction proved in practice they now had a geological map of the whole of Siberia not only on the surface but down to ten thousand feet. What they had found was staggering, coal, oil, ore, gold, tungsten, uranium, lead, zinc, copper and mercury. The supplies were truly inexhaustible. In the coal basin of the Tungska alone there were 1,500,000 million tons of coal. Some of the seams were nearly 300 feet thick. In the basin of the Lena River there was a similar coalfield, and the same went for the Kan Achinsk basin, and that of South Yakut and others. Siberia could supply the whole of the world with coal for two thousand years and still have some to spare! Besides there were the new Siberian oil-fields which promised to be bigger than any of the older ones. There were the inexhaustible possibilities of hydro-electric power since the greatest rivers of all the Soviet Union came tumbling out of the Southern Mountains to flow northward into the Arctic. The greatest European river, the Volga, carried 255,000 million cubic metres of water annually. The figures for the Siberian Ob, Lena and Yenesei rivers were 394,000, 488,000 and 548,000 millions respectively. In this connexion he begged me to go to Bratsk on the Angara to see for myself how they ordered these things in Russia. He told me of a great new gold industry developing in the Vitim and Kolyme basins. He described a nugget found on the Bodaibo gold-field which weighed 31 lb. Once the nature and extent of the resources were known real up-to-date planning had become possible in a mature, professional and scientific way. First adequate transport had to be supplied: railways extended and duplicated: the Siberian track doubled and electrified for thousands of miles and then soon the whole route from Moscow to Vladivostok would be all electric. The railway to the Lena was already built and was pushing deeper into the *taiga* and steamers now plied in summer regularly between railheads and the Arctic sea-routes in the north. The excitement, the belief in the future, which burned in him was deeply impressive. But he was most anxious that I should not think his enthusiasm naïve for he practically admitted to me that the sense of the future in all Russians was apt to be heady and dangerous stuff and could easily lead, as it had in the discredited pre-Revolution past, to neglect of the present; a newly evolved Oblomovism.* Also it could lead to waste and dissipation of energies. As an example of the discipline of the new approach he told me how after the war the plan for Siberia developed. Before the Irkutsk hydro-electric project was decided on, a Siberian plan for the future was first discussed at a conference of some 2,000 scientists held at Irkutsk. Before the next step, an advance some five hundred miles into the *taiga* north, the building of the Bratsk dam was blueprinted and a conference of some 4,000 scientists, economists and planners was again called at Irkutsk. He was there himself and he assured me it was one of the most exhilarating occasions he had ever known. I myself was to read in Irkutsk a report of this con-

---

* *Oblomov* by Ivan Goncharov, first published in 1859, was republished by the Soviet State in the twenties, mainly because the principal character, Oblomov, symbolized for it all that was decadent and futile in pre-revolutionary Russia and indeed the whole *bourgeois* world. Oblomov would go to bed with a clear vision of reform and wake up each day full of bright plans and resolutions to put right what was wrong with his estate in the country. He would lie in bed for so long warm and so rapt in contemplation of his good intentions that his power for action was dissipated in the process and, exhausted, he would postpone his departure for the field of reform until the next day. In the end, of course, he never got there at all. This inability to match thinking with doing, to close the gap between ideal and human behaviour, gave a new word to the Russian language: 'Oblomovism'. It is a tragic story, made all the more tragic by the comedy, the instinctive Chaplinesque ambivalence, with which it is told.

ference which impressed me by these very qualities. In Russia I was never certain exactly what was implied by words like 'scientist' and 'engineer'. But even allowing that many of the people at the conference were merely technicians with an *élite* of real scientists and engineers, the proceedings were like a great parliament of science and seemed to me to come nearer to democratic occasion than anything I had ever heard of in Russia. One of the great attractions of science and technology for the Russians, I believe, is precisely that it gives them a greater freedom of mind than any other occupation in the Soviet Union. Within their own fields they are permitted to speak their own minds and since Stalin's day have less and less need to fear reprisals. Judging by the reports that I saw, no one at this conference pulled any of their punches. For instance, there was one distinguished engineer who had a scheme for building a colossal power station on the Angara. The difficulty was that its capacity would depend on a discharge of water that could only be achieved by dynamiting the exit from Lake Baikal and lowering its considerable waters. He lobbied his fellow-delegates for support with subtlety and skill and the enormous output of electricity he promised must have been most tempting. But he was routed by a Professor of Marine Biology, the guardian of the fish and natural life of Lake Baikal. The professor had only to tell the conference of the damage to the natural beauty and the unique fish life of the lake for the conference to turn in a body on the unfortunate engineer. His reputation apparently never recovered from this mass setback. In a country so materialistically minded as the Soviet Union I thought the professor's victory most impressive. But it seemed to me to be a typically Siberian portent.

The one great reservation in this theme of inexhaustible abundance seemed to be agricultural. My travelling companion was obviously concerned when I mentioned this and admitted it was a problem. There was not the same agricultural abundance as there was of everything else. Yet he was convinced that with improved agricultural methods they would get over that. Already the country was building up its chemical industry as fast as possible. The output of fertilizers was improving fast and production on the land would rise accordingly. In Siberia particularly they were annually extending the area of the natural arable land by clearing the trees. That was not as rich a soil as the black steppe earth but it would add much to their food resources. Then there were the virgin lands of the south. At Novosibirsk I would see something of the impulse they had given to the national economy!

I replied that I could not accept without qualifications all I had heard about the virgin lands. Ever since I had been in the Soviet Union all the indications in the Press were of a wrong-headed scheme. Almost daily one read of chairmen of State farms, Party officials, Ministers and others being sacked for incompetence. One read of riots against shortages and mismanagement in some virgin land centres, and of dust-bowls created round others by ruthless and inexpert exploitation of the earth.

My friend dismissed these as inevitable teething troubles. As for dust-bowls, he asked me to look out of the window over the plain where each ploughed field was protected by new young windbreaks of poplars, birches and pines. This was going on all over the Soviet Union.

I admitted I was impressed by the immense protective belts of trees I had seen growing everywhere but even if they proved effective I thought the basic error was the 'factory', or 'industrial' approach to the earth and also to the people who tended it. After all the most efficient agricultural system in the Communist world was in Poland where only twenty per cent of the farming was collective and the rest individual. I suggested you could not apply 'factory' methods to the earth without courting disaster.

He was so reluctant to go on with the subject that I dropped it. He clearly had a conscience about the land and its peasants too and his reluctance confirmed all my doubts. So my conviction remains that, among the many profound reappraisals necessary before the Soviet Union will be a balanced contemporary State not merely in form but in content, the role of the land and the peasant is most urgent.

Between our long talks in the dining-car and our compartments my companion introduced me to four geologists. They were husbands and wives who had spent their married lives working side by side in the field. They all four came from Leningrad, had just been home for their vacation and were on their way back to Ulan Bator, the capital of Outer Mongolia. The two men played chess with each other most of the day and the two women, sturdy partners, sat by silently looking on. When we appeared the men stopped playing chess immediately to order tea from the train samovar and the women produced boxes of good State chocolates, and treated me as if I were a guest in their home. They were simple, unpretentious people who had found their life's work. Their initiation into applied geology had, of course, been nine years in Siberia. When Siberia became, as they put it, geologically 'tame', they had looked elsewhere. They were tempted at first by the new African states. Scores of Soviet and satellite scientists were going there and soon it would be hundreds. But they decided in the end on Outer Mongolia because it appeared a natural continuation of what they had been doing in Siberia and they were anxious to see how the two neighbours were related geologically.

But, I asked, were they related?

All four nodded emphatically and one man who loved shooting and fishing said there was nothing Siberia had that Outer Mongolia did not possess also.

Remembering the picture of uncountable geological riches pointed out to me by my friend I asked again, 'Everything?'

Yes, all four nodded emphatically, everything. One of the women added something which made them all laugh, and they explained there was one thing Outer Mongolia lacked compared with Siberia: clothes! Mongolia was not wrapped up in forest and vegetation as was Siberia. It was not a woman in furs but geologically a 'bare-bottom woman', or so they called it, and only a geologist could know what a relief that was! No crawling about on stomachs as in Siberia but an easy collection of samples of rock and earth, with geophysical readings in summer, followed by a winter of classification and evaluation of material. It was fascinating and rewarding – like reading a new fairy-tale. Did I realize, they asked, that since the brief reconnaissance of the American geologist, Morris, in 1924, nothing had been done until the Soviet Union undertook the task?

This aspect of their story saddened me as others had done from Central Asia because it underlined the sentence being passed on America and Britain for the criminal neglect of opportunity of this kind in the heart of Asia. Britain had been first in the field and had a natural basis for work of this kind from

India and China and yet had made little use of it. It needed no special prophetic insight to become aware of the vast, powerful, industrial, economic and cultural empire that the Soviet Union will, without doubt, build for itself in Asia. It seemed to me that nothing could prevent this and I found it extraordinary how blind most of us in the West were to this fact and all its fateful implications. Above all we seemed blind to the importance of having not merely a defensive but a positive attitude to this emerging great new world. Of course I said nothing of this to my fellow-passengers at the time. My friend whenever I had mentioned foreign affairs to him had already given me the answer which I believed was valid for the moment for everyone in the Soviet Union.

'What's the matter with co-existence,' he would say: 'Let us just go on co-existing and everything will one day come right.'

I do not think the answer is as simple as all that. I am not even certain that their leaders were prepared to accept and leave it at co-existence. Yet it would be stupid to ignore how much the ordinary people in the Soviet Union believe in it.

What impressed me about these conversations was their matter-of-fact and sober tone. My own friend had a great deal of the poet as well as the scientist in his make-up but the four geologists were little more than conscientious persons doing a regular job with a respectable pension at the end. They struck me as extraordinarily British in this regard, particularly when they told me they spent their leisure hunting and fishing. The wives provided the refinements, dragging their men out of the Soviet Club at night to theatre and opera with exhilarating Mongol audiences, who came riding in to town on their Genghis Khan ponies and left them tied up outside the show houses. In the intervals, one woman said, it was a thrill to see them outside under the huge crackling stars of Outer Mongolia all a-jingle and restless for their riders. Sometimes in between the sounds of music, a stallion's neigh and a mare's quivering answer would reach them even in the theatre.

What did they see in the theatre? In addition to Mongolian opera and dance they had regular visits by companies of actors, dancers, musicians and singers from Moscow, Leningrad and Kiev. They had Soviet films as well. They loved it all, even in the field. They loved their contacts with the Mongol nomads, the ruins of ancient forgotten cities and Tartar ramparts half buried in sand – there were even the ruins of medieval Russian cathedrals and settlements to remind them how long was the connexion between the two territories – and the occasional reward of a rich geological windfall of a fossil of some prehistoric animal.

I remarked how geologically the earth that was the oldest often appeared to be the richest, and I told them of the discovery in South Africa of a new diamond-field almost next door to the skeleton of a dinosaur!

They looked at one another and then announced quietly that I would be interested to know that soon the Soviet Union would be producing more diamonds and gold than South Africa. So back we were in Siberia and they expounded at length on the Siberian rivers that were spilling their waters uselessly in the Arctic and would soon now be turned around to irrigate the dry wastelands in the arid south.

At the time of our first meeting the country round the train had flattened out completely, and during the third night we reached Omsk, the town which in my imagination has always been typical of Siberia. By night it was just another busy station and even on my return journey when I saw it by day, just another large city on the Siberian plain. But both by night and day I thought I had never been to any place with so much of sky and space around it. Memorable that first night, too, were the immense thunder clouds moving out of the dark towards the sleeping city resembling, in the spasmodic lighting, fabulous swans beating towards us on hissing wings of fire. Watching the distant summer lightning from the train my friend said they had a special word for it and he would be glad if I could teach him another as expressive. The word was '*Zarnitsa*'.

'You win,' I answered without hesitation, and to my surprise he thanked me by shaking my hand. I think nobody knows, not excluding the Russians, how hungry they are at heart for some recognition of what is positive and creative in their character.

I was awake for the rest of the night and at dawn saw the first slow river of the central Siberian plain uncoiling itself like a cobra out of the dark. A faint mist drifted over the surface making the ripples caused by the rising fish look as if they were blowing smoke-rings at the sky. But my first great Siberian river flashed into view only on the afternoon of the third day. It was the Ob and I could hardly believe we were some thousands of miles from the sea, so full was it of traffic of all kinds, large passenger steamers, tugs towing barges and trains of lumber, and cargo ships. On its bank erect in a sulphur sun stood the large new city of Novosibirsk, already invested by an army of workers a million strong and its grain elevators proudly holding on to the fords and river banks like crusader fortresses to sacred lines of communication. Scores of passengers left us here for this is the strategic centre of new Western Siberia and the virgin lands, some making for the large new industrial towns, Kemerova, Barnaul and even Alma Ata and Central Asia where my journey had begun, and scores of new passengers joined the train. I found the station post office crowded and would not have got my cables and telegrams in English accepted had not a girl-clerk spotted that I was a stranger and insisted on serving me first.

Back in the speeding train I watched the big town rush by the windows, first the tall buildings and wide streets, then the factory chimneys flying flags of smoke in the breeze, then the suburbs of square, wooden Siberian houses, blurred in the spray and spume of apple-blossom, while one aeroplane after another joined in the long queue-ring over the city to land on the plain beyond. A milestone told me we were thirteen hundred miles from Moscow. The sinking sun raised a yellow gleam from a bend of the broad Ob gone bronze amid the blue of afternoon rising out of the steppe, and showed our course aimed to pass just south of Tomsk. Ahead of us I noticed a ripple on the earth which by nightfall increased to a wave. In the dying light the death of the great plain had an extraordinary personal impact on me. The earth was still black but the further we went the more the woods and trees intruded. In the fields the corn was already shooting up and the pace of the potato planting tempo increased. I saw people working in shifts and at 6.30 p.m. in one field seven big trucks discharged scores of men, women and children with spades, rakes and bags of seedlings to carry on planting through the night. Further on we entered a thick forest.

My friend sighed deeply with satisfaction and remarked: 'Ah!

A sample of the *taiga* at last.' There was, he said, another incomparable Russian word to describe the feelings one experienced in those woods, the sense of silence, breath of leaves and moss and the green twilight by day. It was '*Glookhoman*'. Did he win again, he asked and smiled as I nodded emphatically.

Deep in this forest was a clearing and there a man with a fur hat, Cossack coat, trousers and jack-boots was making camp for the night. The fire was already lit, a bright ruby of flame. One riding and two pack-horses were tethered nearby. I believe it was the first time I had seen anyone absolutely on his own in all the weeks in the Soviet Union. In that light, in that vast natural setting the man, his horses and fire all taking on the light, became a vivid symbol of all that I missed in Russia. I was deeply affected.

'You look upset,' my friend said to me.

'Just moved by the forest, the fire and the man,' I answered evasively for how could I ever explain even to him.

In the dark we halted inexplicably in a village amid one great field in the wood. The houses of wood were smaller, the village, without church, was only a long straggling row of houses beside a road of black earth of shining mud and puddles full of stars. We went into the little wooden station complete with a statue of Lenin leaning out at an angle over the gravelled station entrance. The waiting-room was barely a cell of wood raised around a stove but it had four huge landscape paintings in massive gilt frames probably once the pride of a local landlord, hung at the prescribed party angle from the wall. From here on I saw no station without the oils of a vanished era straining at their leashes on the wall. The booking-hall had no landscapes but a portrait of Lenin in oils and posters advertising the seven- and twenty-year plans of the State. The huddled peasant figures in black seemed to have no eyes for either plans or culture so framed on the walls. Nor could I connect them with the city we had left behind, so brash and arrogant on the broad river. Whenever I woke up to look out during the night I saw the lights of tractors like fireflies busy among the trees.

The morning showed a hint of change in the earth amply confirmed. We were approaching the marshes of the foothills of the great Mongolian ranges and the land now was rolling more and more heavily before us. It was Sunday and yet the clearings and fields were full of people working fast to make the most of their short season. Many of the fields were small new clearings in the wood capable of attack only by spades, hoes and horses. The thicker the forest the steeper the roll of earth; the more the frail birch declined the more pines, larches, firs and giant ferns increased. Some of the clearings had been made so quickly that the workers and their families lived in trains parked on lines roughly laid by the main tracks. They neither looked nor behaved like peasants and were here, one felt, not by tradition or inclination but by projection of the will of the State. Krasnoyarsk on the Yenesei, the fastest of all Siberian and the largest of all Russia's rivers, was there to demonstrate the long arm of that will. Big as it was, the centre of another region of new industry and transformers of hydro-electric power, it was quickly sunk like a dreadnought at sea, by a single broadside of distance in that empty land leaving no trace. In the afternoon above the red trunks of the pines, jet-green needles and Chinese fringes of fern on the crests of earth, on the pale blue horizon emerged a long line of hills of the antique quality seen rarely outside the fading canvases of the oldest masters. The women and children driving their cattle home now had flowers in their hair and hands, the clearings were bright with yellow and white Siberian bells. The sun went down as we began to wind through a deep valley and for the first time the rock below the black earth showed. I had never realized how beautiful rock can be when one has not seen it for so long. I held my breath over the beauty of the valley and, far beyond it, the glimpse of snow on the Sayan Ranges. At the station the air was clear with the mathematics of mountains and snow. The woods, my friend said, were now full of wolves, silver and red foxes, sable, deer, elk and bear.

But more memorable even than the beauty of this part of Siberia was the realization that this was my fourth day in the train. The journey I realized had been a test-tube demonstration of the Russian character. I had watched everyone in the train drawing closer together – except the Chinese. I thought of all the glib comparisons I had heard of Russia with the other totalitarianisms. Only a few days before in Moscow a foreign correspondent had said to me: 'The only difference between Russian and Nazi totalitarianism is that the Russian tramples on the individual with his left foot, where the German trampled on him with his right. Since the Russian is left-footed anyway, the result is just as devastating.' This comparison seemed odious to me in so far as it ignored the differences between the Soviet and German dynamics. The German, like the earlier Prussian model, had its origin in the thrust of a teeming people outwards. The Russian has its origin in a pull inward towards the interior of this vast, empty country. I could not see this land through which I was travelling playing any role for a very long time other than completely containing the major energies and imaginations of the Russian people. This could remain the national priority and perhaps deprive of its force and volition any aberration of ambition directed to the outside world by any abnormal statesman. This too explains why Russia has always been so formidable in defence of itself. Hitler said he went 'the way fate had pointed him like a man walking in his sleep'. From what I had seen of the Soviet Union its rulers went their way like people who never slept at all.

At dinner that evening as we pulled out of Tayshet where the new railway line to the Lena and beyond crossed ours, two young men who had just boarded the train sat down at our table. They immediately began talking and when they heard I was a foreigner insisted on buying food and drink for me. One was the chief road-engineer of the Tayshet district though he was only twenty-two and barely out of his polytechnic. That I was to find was not at all unusual for Siberia. His companion, no older, was head of public transport in the district. Their zest, vitality and open-heartedness was overwhelming. They made me promise I would dine with them in Irkutsk and were plainly disappointed that I would not get drunk with them there and then.

'You know why they are going to Irkutsk?' my friend asked me afterwards. 'To renew their driving licences.'

'But Irkutsk is more than 300 miles away!' I exclaimed.

'That's the point,' he laughed. 'We have a saying that in Siberia 100 kilometres is no distance at all, 100 roubles no money and 100 grammes of vodka no drink!'

I thought it suggested a frightening degree of over-centralization and meant to ask them about it when we met again in Irkutsk. But they did not keep their appointment for dinner with me at Irkutsk, and as this had happened to me now so often all over the Soviet Union I was not surprised.

On the morning of my fifth day the Chinese attendant woke me at five. He refused the tips offered him for his meticulous attention and took payment only to the equivalent of 5*s* for a hundred or more cups of delicious Chinese tea served to me during the journey. On my way out of the coach I nearly collided with the head of the Chinese delegation coming out of the lavatory. He bowed low in the doorway and gravely greeted me: 'Don't mention it, please!' 'Thank you very much,' I replied, bowing back.

On the platform stood the four geologists to say good-bye to my friend and myself. Touched by their gesture we waited until their train left. Then my friend and I parted on the station not to meet again. Though I have written to him and sent him some books I have had no answer. But that too is very Russian.* However, not knowing this at the time I walked cheerfully out of the station with the guide who had come to meet me to see the sun just rising over Irkutsk. The station-clerk said it was 5.30 a.m. My watch still on Moscow time made it only just after midnight. My friends in the capital would barely be getting back to their beds after an evening at the theatre.

* Since writing this I have received four acknowledgements of the hundred and more books I sent to Russia: two from individuals and two from institutions; but not from the person mentioned here.

CHAPTER FOURTEEN

SIBERIA

I STILL think that the time I spent in Central Siberia and the Far East was the most enjoyable of all on my journey. I felt more at home in a pioneering community that had many affinities with the world in which I had grown up in Africa. The people seemed freer, more independent and with more initiative than any Russians I had yet met. They tended to take the State less seriously and tragically. Moscow was not only some thousands of miles away but their instinct was to suspect authority and to rely on their own judgement and capacity for helping themselves. They were impulsive, rather reckless, open, quick-tempered and unbelievably generous. Above all they were proud of their particular achievement, the transcending of a tragic fate, and as proud as the Scots are of their country. Their pride made virtues of their grimmest necessities and they boasted about their hardships in an affectionate way. They were convinced their rivers, forests, lakes and plains had no equal in the world. Above all there were no Russians like Siberian Russians. Yet they were curiously unparochial, perhaps because the love of exploration which brought their predecessors to Siberia still directed their imagination outwards. Irkutsk, for instance, possessed an institute of geography founded some years before the American Declaration of Independence. It equipped and sent forth some of the greatest explorers in Russia's considerable history of exploration. These contemporaries were, therefore, inclined to be in love with the unknown and consequently less suspicious of strangers. In fact outside the esoteric circles of art and intellect Moscow struck me as more ingrowing than Irkutsk. The latter might not have the culture and the refinements of the capital but psychologically it seemed to me closer to the West than any other part of Greater Russia.

I had my first surprise in the character of the people within a few hours of my arrival. My hotel was still asleep. The drowsy lady, commander of the keys and captain of my floor, told us breakfast would not be served before nine. It was always like that in the Soviet Union. Hotels closed early and opened late. My guide and interpreter was all for going back to bed and promptly did so. So I bathed, shaved and went for a walk through the town until I came across a boot-black opening a sentry-box of a stall for the day. Unlike the boot-blacks of Odessa and Yalta he took me on at once. I had hardly sat down when another man came and took the seat next to me. He was very tall, had blue eyes, high Mongolian cheekbones, a turned-up nose and wide mouth. He smelt of vodka, was not drunk but in reckless good spirits after a night's feasting, and also late for work. His impulse was to insist on having his boots done first, but when he saw I was a foreigner he stared hard at me and then asked in slow, deliberate and somewhat slurred English: 'You know Mark Twain?'

'Yes,' I answered.

'You know *Tom Sawyer*?'

'Yes,' I replied.

'You know Marilyn Monroe? Marilyn Monroe sad.'

I agreed wholeheartedly. Then he frowned before announcing in a deep, vibrating bass voice: 'Kennedy and Macmillan no good!'

The thought of the iniquity of the two statesmen sent him upright out of his chair and glaring about him.

I did not know the right answer to this fierce denunciation but was saved making one for immediately his face softened, he put his hand out and said: 'You and Mark Twain good boys!'

At that moment a militiaman I had seen on the street corner some minutes before appeared at the stall and beckoned to the tall Siberian. The Siberian gave the policeman a hostile glance and ignored him. Then things began to happen so quickly that I am not sure of their right order. I believe the militiaman shouted at the Siberian demanding to know what he was talking to me about. Again he ignored the demand. The militiaman then took him by the arm to insist on being told. This was too much for the tall man. He seized the militiaman by the waist and neck and marched him regardless of the traffic to the opposite side of the street, gave him a push that sent him reeling against a shopfront and then came back to the boot-black and me. The militiaman

came after him as fast as he could but was somewhat impeded
by a crowd which had begun to collect around us. Before the
militiaman could do anything the tall man began in his most
ringing tones to explain to the crowd what had happened. Was
that cultured, democratic or necessary? he asked. No! the crowd
retorted. At this the militiaman, collectively condemned, retreated
across the street. As his back was about to vanish round the
corner the tall man drew himself to his full height, squared his
shoulders, pointed a long finger at the militiaman and exclaimed:
'That man is a very bad boy!'

After that he insisted, boots unblacked, on escorting me back to
my hotel, trying in vain to get me to sing 'Auld Lang Syne' with him.
When that failed, he recited, what I gathered was meant to be:

> 'And for a' that and a' that,
> It's coming yet, for a' that:
> That men the wide world o'er,
> Will brothers be, for a' that.'

Burns, I knew, has been so well translated into Russian by the
poet Marshak that he has become almost as much a Russian as a
Scottish possession. And for 'a' that' I invited him to breakfast.
But the sight of the time on the hotel clock made him decline and
say a quick warm good-bye.

Breakfast brought me another surprise. The young waitress,
who by her looks might have been a younger sister of the Siberian
who had just left me, was waiting to take my order. She spoke in
passable German. She had been sent by the State with forty other
Siberian waitresses for six months to study German at Tomsk.
After her studies she was attached to visiting East German delegations for another three in order to practice her German. When
I told her how impressed I was by this she shrugged her shoulders
and said it was nothing unusual. Another girl in the hotel had
been sent to study French and another Japanese in the same way.
Why Japanese? I asked. Because they got a lot of Japanese visitors in Irkutsk in the summer. Any British? Perhaps one or two
but I was the first one she had ever met and I was the first
foreigner of any kind that year. As I was interested would I like
to see her German conversation book? she continued. She
brought it to me with my boiled egg. It was called: *A guide to*

everyday conversation in German. The first sentence of the first lesson put the basic question squarely: 'Are you acquainted with the theory of the Evolution of Mankind?'

Then came the answer: 'Yes of course. We had "the Darwinism" (how much better the German "*Das Darwinismus*" sounded) as a subject at school and I became acquainted there with the theory of the evolution and origin of man. The theory of the origin of species has always possessed an exceptional and magnetic attraction for me.'

Question number two: 'Are you familiar with the writings of Friedrich Engels and in particular his essay on the role of the necessity to work on the evolution of the ape into man?'

The answer: 'Of course! Besides I have also read many other essays and popular scientific books on this subject. It is, indeed, a most interesting and important theme.'

And so it went on, with nothing to do with catering, food, hotel management or the kind of things a lively pretty young girl would naturally want to discuss. I was struck again by the profound contradiction in Soviet authority which this incident seemed to expose. Its capacity for being far-seeing in purpose and at the same time utterly unimaginative in its approach. Authority in the Soviet Union in this and other ways seemed to me psychologically to be singularly unilluminated.

'And have you really read Engels' essay on the Ape?' I asked her.

She made a face before saying with a laugh that she was more interested in essays on men than apes.

After breakfast I found my guide laughing heartily to himself. He had just been watching two men and two young hotel-maids moving a dressing-table with three large mirrors attached to it from one floor to another.

One girl teasing the other: 'Let's smash the thing on the floor.'

'Yes,' answered the other, 'it would make a lovely expensive crash. I daresay a thousand roubles in one blow!'

'They shouldn't have these things about anyway,' growled one of the men. 'They're all very well on the stage but not in real life!'

'Well, if you sincerely believe that,' the first girl proposed mischievously, 'let's smash it here and now!'

'But it's public property, we can't. If it were mine, I wouldn't mind,' the man exclaimed alarmed.

'Public property!' The girl made a noise of derision.

'Oh, these Siberians!' My guide shook his head, still laughing as he took me below to meet a person to whom I owed much. He was a writer just old enough to have been caught up in the last two years of the war. He was born in Irkutsk and assured me would die there. He wrote a great deal of poetry, film scripts, and made a film called *The Angara Tamed* which had been shown on B.B.C. television, and more recently also books for children. This last of his accomplishments interested me especially. I was continually struck by the proportion of Russian writers who have turned to writing fairy-tales. It is, I believe, part of the revolt of their talent against stifling control by the State: a return to the protection of the natural imagery and symbolism of meaning. So much is this so in Russia that even the State has become uneasily suspicious of the process, which is one of the reasons perhaps why it has become increasingly severe on the new poets and abstract artists who also traffic in the aboriginal imagery of meaning. It has come to smell danger in the process. The development of my friend in Irkutsk seemed part of a turn of the tide in the spirit of the nation.

'People,' he once said to me rather wistfully, 'ironically barricade themselves against the nature that would save them. If they would only allow themselves to know it they would find it full of wonderful things and power to help them. It is for that reason that I myself go to it and make certain anyway that the imagination of children does not lose contact with nature.'

It was characteristic of him that he was far more interested in showing me their river, the Angara and its parent lake, Baikal, than the growing city of half a million people. So we set off for river and lake by car and a chauffeur who seemed typically Siberian too. He was, my guide told me with some awe as he pointed to a coloured round metal badge on the buttonhole of the driver, a Master of Sport. Almost every male wore a badge of some kind either of his school, institute, union or some special award and perhaps they went some little way to appease the hunger of the people in Russia for some colour in their lives. It would amuse me to notice that travellers getting into a plane, ship or train would look at badges before faces. But this was the first Master of Sports badge that I had seen. One cannot travel through the Soviet Union without realizing how wholeheartedly the Russians have taken to sport. The state may have organized it for reasons of prestige but it could not have done so if the people themselves did not possess a natural love and aptitude for sport. Indeed sport has become so important in the Soviet Union that the usual national abuses resulting from popular idolatry caused several scandals while I was there. There was a university in the Far East, for instance, which passed students who had never attended a lecture merely because they excelled at sport. Or the factory which for the same reasons paid members of its football team the highest wages and production bonuses though they never worked in it at all. But the average Russian seemed to me to take his sport with due proportion rather as the English do. Just before leaving Moscow however, when the newspapers were carrying columns of reports every day on the World Football Competition being played in South America, I had an illustration of how intense is the Russian attitude to sport. A young Russian musician apologized to me for being late for his appointment because he said he could not leave until he had heard the latest result of the Russian match in the World Cup series. I hoped, I said, the result was favourable? Alas, no, Russia had lost, he answered and that was bad – how bad I would realize when he told me what happened in the Metro on his way to meet me. There, all round him, he had seen people in a fever opening their newspapers. Swiftly turning to the sports pages, he had seen them go quite still and the hands which held the sheets tremble. In that moment they died a little as he had died. That might not seem important. But when one considered that there were 220 million people in the Soviet and that they had all died a little in the same way it was serious. If the moment had only lasted five seconds then he had calculated five seconds multiplied 220 million times would amount to a loss of more than 19 million working minutes, or about 320,000 hours! Think of the loss of production that meant because this happened every time a team played an international match. However, he must be careful not to suggest that line of thought to the State lest they abolish football altogether in the interests of the Seven Year Plan! With all this in mind, I asked now of which sport our driver was a master and it turned out to be motor cycle racing. In the days to come I found that this Master of Sport was like no driver I had met in the Soviet Union.

He was full of initiative and invention and was also a gay and amusing companion with a contribution of his own to make to our excursions into the country.

We drove out of Irkutsk past the High School where my friend the poet had been educated, and he pointed out twenty-six poplars, light dripping like water from their trembling leaves. 'Twenty-six of us left from this school on the same day for the war,' he told me, 'and before we left each planted a poplar. Only five of us came back.'

He then went on to tell me how he came to be a poet. One day on the Western Front thousands of miles away during one of the great battles he had gone with a dispatch to a senior officer's dug-out. On the map-table lay an open book of poetry, face down, which had just been taken from the hand of a dead soldier. While he waited for the answer to his dispatch he picked up the book and started reading it. As he did so a great calm and sense of purpose came over him and he realized that what he wanted more than anything else in the world was to write poetry. Poetry suddenly there was more important than war and killing as it had been to the dead owner of the book.

At that moment we came out of the city on the side of a hill overlooking the broad Angara River. It was smooth and silent there because the hydro-electric barrage was built across the rapids at the head of the town below us. But before the barrage, the poet said, it had been a wild, swift, passionate river and swimming it, when he was a child, had been a hazardous business. Would I like to hear the legend of the river? Well, according to the Buryats, the Mongol hunters who inhabited this part of Siberia first and still did so, Lake Baikal, the father, had some 336 daughters. One could still see them, the bright mountain streams hanging from the forests of the mountains standing all around Baikal with their heads in the clouds, dangling carelessly like gleaming young serpents from some tall jungle-top. They were all obedient daughters and content to stay close to their father, Baikal, all that is except Angara. She was increasingly restless for she had heard rumours of the Yenesei, the bold, resolute warrior river in the West, all year long chasing alone through the nearby *taiga*. So one night when Baikal was asleep, she broke out of her mountain chains, cutting a deep cleft in them as she did so, and hurled herself in the direction of Yenesei. Her father, awakened by the noise of her flight, seized a rock and hurled it after her to stop her. But he was too late. She had gone to join the Yenesei six hundred miles further on. But to this day the rock showed above the waters where it fell in the gorge. It was called the Shaman, the priest's or holy rock because to the Buryats it became a sacred rock.

Here our road led out into the woods and the *taiga* strode right down to the broad river shore. In between the black, purple and scarlet tree-trunks, amid ferns, moss and lean woodland grass grew violets, jonquils, tulips, gentians, yellow daisies and rhododendrons.

'What do you think of our rhododendrons?' the guide asked as we splashed through the first purple tide of their colour.

I said they were smaller than the Himalayan kind, adding that they were hunters compared to the fat Indian Maharajah species.

They all laughed and the Master of Sport gave me an appreciative look. Conversation was one of the things I enjoyed most in Russia and I enjoyed it as I enjoy conversation with my African countrymen. No flights of fancy were barred. It was with them as with many primitive people I know: the word is still newborn and glistening, full of wonder and capacity for increase. The Russians, like the Africans, seemed to have a natural 'aristocracy' of the word.

Meanwhile the poet spoke to me of Baikal. Chekhov, he said, had called it 'unique and the pearl of Siberia'. He himself would slightly modify Chekhov's observation to point out that it had a twin in Lake Tanganyika in Africa. I might look amazed but though they were thousands of miles apart and one was in the tropics and the other in the cold north, yet they were identical in almost everything except environment and climate. Even their shape were similar. That was because both lakes had the same terrible parent, the same cataclysmic upheaval in the crust of the earth, so to this day they were joined like Siamese twins by the same rift that started in Siberia, cut through Central Asia, the Red Sea, Abyssinia, Kenya and ended in Tanganyika. From time to time they even had earthquakes to vouch for the fact! For instance, in the late nineteenth century a particularly severe one had killed many Buryats on Baikal. Their holy man, the Shaman, told the survivors, the earthquake had been sent to punish them for their transgressions. Promptly another tremor came, causing a fall of rock which killed only the Shaman.

At this everyone in the car, except the poet and I, laughed in the jeering way expected of the Soviet's ideological faithful when religion is at issue. Disregarding the sour little laugh behind us the poet went on to tell me that Baikal was the deepest freshwater lake in the world, in fact, 5,000 feet deep. The water entering it by river, even a drop of rain, took four hundred years to reach the exit and leave by the Angara. That was due not only to its depth and size but also a result of hot springs in the bottom of the lake which sent warm water flowing up but insisted first on drawing cold water down. Baikal was so big that if all its tributaries were sealed off the water in it would take four hundred years to empty. Even more remarkable was the fish and animal life in and around the lake. There was one fish, found at all levels from a hundred metres below the surface, which had no bones and was so transparent that one could read one's newspaper through it. Placed in our atmosphere it slowly dissolved into a unique and valuable oil. There was a delicious kind of Baikal salmon too, Oumoul, found nowhere else. There were even the Baikal seals, between 30 and 40,000 of them, of which the Buryat hunters were allowed to kill about 3,000 every year for their fur. But imagine seals thousands of miles from the Arctic Ocean, and, he believed, left marooned here by the last Ice Age of Europe! Then there were the great bears of the mountains who came down to the lake in winter, going three or four miles out on the ice to fish in the holes made by the Buryats. He would show me samples of all these things in the wonderful Baikal Institute by the lakeside itself.

No river that I have ever seen poured out of a great lake with such eagerness as did Angara out of Baikal and the river held all our attention until the road rounded the head of the gorge and suddenly we saw the lake. To the south-east the waters were blue as a bowl of Bristol glass vanishing unimpeded across the horizon as if to join the Pacific Ocean, whereas to the south-west rose the great mountains of Outer Mongolia, their outlines clear and purposeful. But hardly did we see all this when the car reached the head of the gorge and the inevitable official institute.

The Soviet may have no reverence for life in the Schweitzer way

but they have a marked reverence for science. The Baikal Institute was like a little temple with photographs, charts, maps, facts,
stuffed and bottled specimens, displayed lucidly and by a band of
staunch female votaries expert in the new Soviet testament.
Through the windows of the institute, one saw the lake itself,
indeed a pearl in colour that day. The fleets of ships which ply
up and down its shores from Buryat village to village were setting
out on their first voyage after a winter in frozen harbours. They
vanished over a horizon of pearly water that looked like an endless sea. Only at the entrance and immediately opposite us on
the far shore was land visible in the tall mountains of Mongolia
and one remote flash of snow from the giant Mongdhu-Sardik.

We drove as far as the road would take us which was, alas, only
a mile or two, because the main communications round the lake
are by water. The official *pensions* and rest-houses, rough, homely
establishments, were just opening for the season. Hard by the
shore we found a restaurant already in business and sat down to a
delicious meal of black Siberian bread and butter, Baikal trout
smoked the Buryat way, and thick fried steaks of the incomparable *oumoul*. All through lunch the poet discussed French
literature with me and asked after Paris with a curious nostalgia,
though he had never been there. I had forgotten how close the
cultural links between nineteenth-century Russia and France had
been. The Russians had turned to Britain for economics, industry,
engineering and to a degree science; Newton, Watt, Stephenson,
Darwin, Huxley and John Stuart Mill were names known to all.
The Germans had influenced the Russians politically and philo-
sophically, and the French more than any had influenced their art
and literature. Today the literature of the English-speaking world
has become even more important than that of France but in the
desperate search for continuity which goes on increasingly
among the young in Russia the France that influenced their fore-
bears is vital psychologically. The human spirit cannot do without
a past and unless it can feel itself putting its roots into its own
past rather as a tree goes deeper into the earth for every inch it
grows, it cannot move on into the future. Out of their need of a
past which the Revolution and Stalin ostensibly destroyed the
young are re-discovering their vanished links with France and
since Stalin the older writers like Ehrenburg and Paustovsky, not

so much through their own creative work as through the writing of their memoirs, are doing precisely this for the young for both Ehrenburg's and Paustovsky's own personal cultural past was profoundly influenced by France.

At the Master of Sport's suggestion the poet and I travelled home by river in one of those enormous fast jet-propelled passenger boats which are all the fashion in the Soviet Union. We went home at such a speed that even the expert Master of Sport was stretched to the limit to arrive in time by winding road to meet us at the other end. Compared to us the wild duck, geese, swan and homing wood-pigeons speeding over the river seemed slow and the women and factory girls at the end of their day of leisure coming out of the woods on the river banks, arms full of rhododendrons, seemed barely to move at all. Behind us the sun went down into a mist of pearl within its mother shell. Then at Irkutsk all the electric light was suddenly switched on. The effect by that wild river in that rugged setting was startling. I had not yet learnt to associate the heart of Siberia with such prodigious electric power.

My guides insisted that I should look into the sources of that power but the poet had no heart for it and excused himself. So next morning we went out to the power station sunk in the walls of the dam in the Angara. The engineer in charge for the day happened to be a woman still in her thirties and she showed us over the station. There were many remarkable features about it that I could neither appreciate nor follow except that the dam itself was unique in not being entirely built of concrete but had been based on rocks and gravel dumped into the powerful stream. The whole damming of the river was a dramatic story. First the quarrel between the experts some of whom thought it would end in disaster. But the optimists won and then came the testing day when the gap in the river between the concrete supports on either bank had to be closed by the new method of dumping rocks and gravel into the river. The whole of Irkutsk turned out night and day to watch the long lines of trucks driving up bonnet to tail without pause to tip great boulders into the powerful waters for the process had to be continuous to be successful. Hundreds of newspapermen and official observers from far and wide were there and the atmosphere must have been rather like the fateful day when before the Old Testament multitudes the prophet Elijah challenged the priests of Baal to a rain-making contest. On the last day the excitement was almost unbearable and then suddenly in the afternoon a lorry tipped another load of boulders in the surging waters and a head of stone showed steady above the water. Thousands of spectators held their breath. Could the stone hold in such angry water? It held. Soon there was not only a broad wall of boulders across the gap but a working bridge as well and the trucks could cross from one bank to the other. The eyes of my woman guide still shone when she spoke of it and I could well understand her pride when, deep down in the basement of the dam and far below the river, she showed us the great electric turbines spinning so fast that they seemed motionless, purring contentedly like kittens lapping up the river water as if it were so much milk. This, I gathered, was the damming method that the Russian engineers were using in the construction of the new Assuan Barrage on the Nile, for she emphasized, the Irkutsk project was a real break-through in hydro-electric construction. In fact if I really wanted to know what the building of this kind was like she begged me to go to Bratsk some four hundred miles north on the same river where the output of power was nine times as great.

Hard by the dam she showed us the new village built to house the staff maintaining the dam: comfortable stone cottages, baby clinics, hospital, recreation centre and schools. Since Irkutsk provided all these facilities next door, it seemed a wasteful duplication for a mere 200 workers but since this was the standard blue-print no one had thought of adapting it to particular circumstances. However, I had been so impressed by the Irkutsk scheme that I decided to do as the woman engineer had suggested and go to Bartsk. But I encountered difficulties. The Angara further north was not yet free of ice and the link between it and Irkutsk by ship had not yet been re-established. The only sensible way was to fly. The Master of Sport investigated the situation and declared the airport open for small local services. The tourist service in Irkutsk however said they had tried not long before to get an American senator to Bratsk and failed. The poet therefore stepped in and quietly announced that he would arrange it in four or five days' time.

Meanwhile in between telephoning and disappearing to interview certain officials, the poet helped me to see his pleasant friendly provincial city. Like all important Russian towns, he said, Irkutsk was what it was because many roads met in it. It was at the crossing of many ancient routes to China, Mongolia, Afghanistan, Alaska and Moscow. Bratsk, where he was arranging for me to go, was older. It was occupied by Cossacks already in 1623 and a small village continued to exist there until the damming of the Angara drowned it a couple of years before. But no town had so strategic a situation as Irkutsk. Hence it grew while others remained small. In his youth it was a city almost entirely of wood. I could see for myself how it had changed – he nodded at the distant factory chimneys, the new apartment-blocks and new houses on the west bank. Yet a great deal of the old remained. Personally he preferred to live in the old wooden houses. They were attractive like Hansel and Gretel dolls' houses. The gingerbread designs carved in the eaves, the fretwork, the painted wooden shutters, the cornices, the shining little window panes with their lace curtains parted in the middle and flower-pots in the centre, were charming. These houses, the poet said, would still be warm and dry inside while the new houses would be wet and cold when it turned frosty in the spring. But, of course, there were obvious disadvantages. I saw some of these myself. For instance, the inhabitants of those houses queueing up after a long day with pails in both hands at a communal tap to carry back water to their homes. The unevenness of progress is a striking aspect of the whole Soviet system. Here side by side with a revolutionary hydro-electric scheme and expanding modern industries were half the houses of the city without indoor sanitation or plumbing.

At night the poet arranged for me to see documentary films of Siberia. Thus I lived through the whole Siberian winter on the screen, saw the clearings and the *taiga* under the snow and pale blue sky of a long succession of dry, breathless winter days; the Siberian hunters trapping sable and Siberians from Irkutsk running naked across the ice in a temperature of minus 50° to swim in the only patch of water unfrozen at the mouth of Baikal! They made the cold appear almost entrancing. That, the poet said, was the difference between Siberian and Western Russians: in the west they hated their winters, in Siberia they loved them because 'they recharged their batteries'.

While we waited for the poet to get permission for us to go to Bratsk, the Master of Sport and my two interpreters drove deep into the country to look at State and collective farms. One excursion alone took us ninety miles along the only macadamized road I was to see in Siberia. The villages were few and separated by many miles from one another. The earth was grey, the *taiga* stood solid all around the clearings. The clearings were expertly ploughed and waiting only on the sun to produce its crop. The villages in between fields, clearing and sky, seemed lost and uncertain. One village, consisting of a single row of square wooden houses, each with its own plot of private earth between, was nine miles long. There I saw one of the rare individual graves I was to see in the whole of the Soviet Union, marked by a single wooden cross. I found it as moving as the single horseman I had seen from the train making camp by his fire. On one collective farm I visited the chairman told me it had three villages, ten thousand persons of all ages, and the farm was still growing. Every year, he said, they cleared another two thousand acres of *taiga* for cultivation. I regret to say I did not believe him. I had some bitter experience in Africa of the difficulties of clearing bush and forest for cultivation and I was certain he had neither the machinery nor the manpower to do so much a year. Besides, I had come to the conclusion that no statistics given me about agriculture were worth the trouble of writing down. The self-deception about agriculture at all levels was as shameless as it was fashionable. The older people might have been fooled into accepting the official picture but the young certainly were not. Back in Moscow the brilliant young poet Andrei Yosnevsky had written:

> They've got their virgin lands I know,
> Where not one pearl of grain can grow.

Here in Siberia too officials, I believe, deceived me, perhaps out of duty, patriotism, or fear, all of which I could understand. They were small men caught up in a system and forced to make a machine work which was basically of the wrong design. The officials now told me that this huge farm with its three villages and ten thousand persons was just being transformed from a collective into a State farm.

'What do your farmers feel about that?' I asked.

'They are all rejoicing,' he said. 'After all now they run no risks and get a good salary whatever the harvest.'

But I had never seen faces less joyful than those of the peasant workers hanging around the chairman's office. Besides I had only to look at the individual plots allowed to each peasant to see where their love, imagination and care had gone. It was no good pretending that these people did not feel cheated. The revolution had worked a confidence trick on them all. They had revolted in order to have the land to themselves. But no sooner was the revolution consolidated than a far more inflexible landlord, the State, had taken it away from them again in the name of collectivization. And, judging by the show pieces I saw, there were few farmers in charge of farms. Party secretaries, accountants and factory foremen were the types one usually found in positions of command. This Siberian chairman was no farmer but a mechanic. They were well-meaning men and the time would come when they would evolve a system of farming that would succeed here as well as in Khazakstan but it was idle to pretend that time had yet come. So when the chairman told me his farm made fifty per cent profit a year on the capital invested, I stopped making notes. He then ran through the farm's achievements as quickly as he could. His secretary, accountant, deputy, and my two interpreters were entranced and one of them remarked, 'I can't tell you how moved I am by the wonderful plans they have for this farm.' It is still the future, not the recalcitrant, drab present that tends to sing a siren sea-song in Russian ears, and in writing about their phoney statistics I do so not in moral judgement, but merely to point out that it is an essential part of their great scene. They have to deceive both me and themselves. It is a pathetic symptom of their helplessness. They react as an African, caught up in an alien all-powerful European system in Africa, reacts. He will always tell people what they most like to hear and those things that will not get him into trouble.

At a large experimental farm I visited I had an even greater success story told to me. The farm was lavishly equipped. The director himself showed us round and soon proved himself to be a dogged doctrinaire untroubled by saving doubts of any kind. His great speciality was artificial insemination. Even though he had the bulls (whose seed he disseminated by helicopter and plane far and wide all over Siberia), standing in sheds next door to his cows, he insisted on the cows being artificially inseminated too. The suggestion that his cows and bulls might be happier if allowed to procreate the natural way made the grey eyes behind his brass-rimmed glasses glitter. What had happiness to do with it? he asked. Hammering the desk with his fist he reiterated 'artificial insemination was best for both bulls and cows'. Clearly 'cows and bulls' were merely pawns in a master image of his philosophy of life. He had the typical revolutionary's mistrust of what was natural. Nature, for them, is a source of power but so savage that it has to be dominated without concession by man and his ideas.

Did I realize, he asked, that by artificial insemination they even got more twins than the 'other way'?

As a farmer myself I have a great respect for the value of artificial insemination but the value is relative and nothing we know of its consequences justifies us in making it the universal absolute.

'But do you think it is good for cows to have twins?' I asked, because many experienced breeders in my world believe it is not.

'A good thing?' he exclaimed as if his senses were failing him. 'Of course it is a good thing! Anything that makes an animal produce more is a good thing.'

And there we were back in Soviet fundamentals: production and more production from the earth, the animal and the peasant. My imagination boggled at what the chairman's reaction would have been to the Zen proposition of 'Action through inaction'. Here again one was up against the lack of 'fullness' in the Soviet conception of life, though the signs multiplying show that the young are increasingly aware of the vacuums in their midst.

However, the chairman, fired by the virtues of production, had gone on to ask me if I had heard of the Romanov breed of sheep developed in Southern Russia? Some of the ewes were now regularly bearing five lambs at a time, some even eight. The valuable Karakul too, fed like Tartars on mares' blood was having more and more lambs at a time. In production alone lay the state of abundance which would make perfect Communism a reality.

'But don't you have trouble applying your theories to the land?' I asked. 'Farmers everywhere in my experience are conservative people and like to hasten slowly if they hasten at all.'

Of course he had his conservatives who refused to see the scientific light, he said with a thin smile, but then he had the power to force his farmers to do what he wanted, for locally he was their State.

We looked then into his model establishment. His milking machines and dairy on the whole were admirable. I said I thought the concrete stands too long and the animals tied with too much chain, so they might get entangled and hurt themselves. Just as he was insisting the chains were just right, there came a bellow from the bull-shed, a furious rattle of links and sound of angry huffing and puffing and we found a valuable bull on his side and in danger of breaking a leg caught in his over-long chain!

I asked him about his calf-drop.

It was, he said, ninety-eight per cent, a figure never before met with on this earth. His calf mortality rate was one per cent, his cows had no contagious abortion, no mastitis, no mammitis (though I saw cows in the shed with dead quarters clearly confirming chronic mastitis), and he never had any reactors to his tuberculin tests – a state of perfection not to be encountered this side of the Great Divide! He seemed too to be over-staffed. In his cow 'maternity ward', I saw three old ladies foster-mothering a newborn calf. One cowman on my own farm did what thirteen were doing in this. Yet, on top of all this he assured me his establishment made a handsome profit and was able every year to finance more experimentation and research as well as to increase wages. This game of pretence after the hammering the peasant and the farmer have endured for forty years was not surprising. But it was evidence of the price in human material that has been exacted by the revolution in general and Stalinism in particular which no one has yet been able to calculate. Here, as on so many other occasions, contemplating the establishment, I would think of Scherbatov's terrible lines on Russia written immediately after Peter the Great: 'How could there remain any manliness and firmness in those who in their youth trembled before the rod of their superiors and who could not win any honours except by servility?' The lines seemed to me at the time as if they might have been written by one of the new young writers about their own establishment and the consequences of the national subservience to Stalin.

And the young in Siberia? A traveller has only the slightest of signs to go by. It may be true that one cannot make bricks without straw. But one of the hardest things to endure in Russia is that the traveller has to build his impressions out of bricks made of nothing but straw. The only compensation is that they are usually straws in the wind and a wind charged with change. That night in Irkutsk after a day at the experimental farm, feeling I had allowed the director's dogmatism to obscure the wonder that such an expensive, highly organized establishment should exist at all, I went with my guides to walk by the river. They were both young, one twenty-six, the other thirty years of age. In the twilight we met a boy and a girl walking slowly along the river bank with their arms round each other. My two companions stopped and turned to watch the couple.

'Would you believe it!' exclaimed one. 'How dare they do that in public!'

'Do you know,' remarked the other deeply shocked, 'I have never seen anything like it before, not even in Leningrad.'

Used as I was to seeing young working-class couples, deprived of privacy in their own homes, doing their courting in the parks of London and other great cities, I would have thought nothing of it, yet, though only a few years separated my companions from the couple, they were clearly outraged.

Then there was the scandal reported in the local Press about a woman who had appeared at a celebration in her factory in an evening dress cut too low for the taste of the committee members. Judging by the photographs her costume was demure enough for a Victorian governess but nevertheless she was ignominiously ejected from the party though the correspondence in the Press showed the public to be passionately and deeply divided on the issue.

In Russia there is a system of public praise and public correction. Boards of Honour and Dishonour are displayed everywhere in prominent places in factories, barracks, squares and at the sides of main streets where everyone can stand and stare at them. In the open the boards are enclosed in glass cases to protect the photographs of the persons chosen for honour or dishonour. Below the photograph and name of the person chosen there is a printed caption stating the reason for this display. For instance, here there was the best male barber, the best girl pastry cook, the best lawyer, doctor, truck driver, bench hand, saleswoman or factory manager, all exhibited in the glass case of Honour. People passed by this board with comparative indifference but the Board of Dishonour drew quite a crowd. Almost everyone stopped to look for any new face among the dishonoured list. The afternoon I inspected it a group of Druzhiniki, the voluntary police patrolling the streets with red armbands, paused in front of it too and contemplated it with obvious satisfaction. But on the faces of some of the older spectators I saw signs of sympathy. For what had these terrible transgressions been? One old lady her face creased and lined with three score years or more of life was there because she had sold some 'sunflower seeds' for more than she had paid for them. A young girl was there because she had worn too daring a dress at a youth café. She had a charming, eager young face yet the caption underneath declared solemnly: 'We warn Sonya D— that if she goes on dancing with teddy-boys and wearing shameless dresses that disgrace Soviet womanhood she will get into serious trouble.' There was a photograph of two young men and the lines beneath: 'We cannot prove it yet but we warn these two young men that we know them to be petty thieves and they had better drop their bad habits before it is too late.'

Clearly there was no law of libel in Russia and the individual can be thrown to the judgement and mercy of a crowd. At the same time in fairness I had to recognize that this form of public criticism has a certain innocence. It is a game played not without psychological and historical rules and the victims have some inborn immunities for it bears a marked resemblance to the mechanism of persuasion by force of public opinion practised by the primitive peasant institution of the past, the Mir. On the positive side it gives some recognition to workers whose achievements otherwise could be lost in the immensities and obscurities of Siberia. Generals, too, are honoured or reprimanded with equal impartiality as their own soldiers. Then in factories honours will be acknowledged at gatherings of all the workers, while bad workers sit in full view in chains of disgrace and drunkards are made to collect their pay at special shame booths. There was a book, the *Diary of a Soviet Criminologist* that I read while in

Russia which helped me to understand the whole thing better. The writer in his war against Russia's considerable underworld, has used this built-in prescription of public pressure through the Press and advertisements, leading to confession, and readmission to society and, according to him, it had had a miraculous effect. From all over the Soviet Union hardened criminals hastened to Moscow to confess, even the master criminal minds from Odessa which appears to hold the most active underworld.

In all this I seemed to detect, functioning like a magnet beneath the surface of Soviet life, the traditional mechanism of the Mir – the ancient village assembly of Russia. It was an institution so instinctive that few historians agree about its origin. It usually began (as the Courts of Justice still do in Abyssinia), as informal groups of men standing in an open space in the village discussing issues of communal importance. The discussion continued until common recognition was reached. An elder then translated the common opinion into a decision and thereafter no one disputed it. It has a parallel also with the way the chief and his councils of elders, the *indunas* among the Zulus, work among the primitive peoples of Africa, and not the least part of their importance to the community is that not only do they judge and punish but also have the power of salvation. Hence the Russian proverb 'The Mir cannot be judged. Throw all upon it. It can bear all.' Apart from the Mir, the Russian peasant for centuries had no meaning. And if for 'Mir' one substitutes the word 'Party' then one can see that one has in this the cordial commendment of the Soviet State. For the Russian, indeed, the Mir does something of what the Roman Church does for Catholics with its precepts of confession, atonement and absolution. 'The Mir is a fine fellow,' the Russian said according to Tikhomirov writing some seventy years ago: 'I will not desert the Mir.' To this day the State, compelling its victims by fair means or foul to confess, is functioning as a kind of Super Mir. It instinctively justifies the terrible means it employs in the assumption that it is thereby serving not only the community but conferring also grace and salvation on the errant soul. So too the uses of the Honours and Dishonour boards have to be interpreted in this traditional and psychological context.

The dilemma of the young in Russia feeling their way through these labyrinths of custom, reserves, and disciplines was to me extraordinarily moving. At one moment they would seem too conforming for sanity: at the next I would be astounded by their recklessness in a society where walking with one's arm round the waist of one's girl could be an act fraught with dire social consequences. One night already late for dinner, I rushed to my table in the dining-room, hat and coat on my arm, thinking I could leave them on one of the empty chairs by my side. But a waitress marched down on me and said severely: 'You ought to know that no one is allowed to bring his coat in here,' and I had to go all the way downstairs to leave hat and coat in the cloakroom before she would let me even have a peep at the menu. Only later I learnt that bringing one's coat and hat into rooms was the elementary breach of good manners in Russia. This discipline I saw exacted of teenagers as uncompromisingly as of generals and admirals in hotels, restaurants, theatres, art galleries and circuses.

The time passed quickly until the moment came when the poet proved as good as his word and handed one guide and myself permission and tickets to fly to Bratsk. We flew there just before sunrise on a cloudless morning in what my companion called 'a wild plane'. There was no hostess and we all helped ourselves as best we could to seats. I could find none with an unbroken safety belt. The inside of the plane looked as if it had neither been swept nor dusted for weeks. Elsewhere I might have been alarmed by this evidence of neglect but in fact I was not for I had become so confident of the Russian care given to essentials, in this case the engine.

Our route took us by way of the new industrial towns of Angarsk, Cheremkhovo, Tulun and Tayshet, all on the Trans-Siberian line. Our unpressurized plane flew low and enabled me to see in one comprehensive glimpse how the creation of hydro-electric power, or 'white coal' as the Russians call it, had enabled industry to develop around Irkutsk. Angarsk though not the biggest city was Siberia's pride. Only a few years ago little more than a few peasants with goats, consumptive cattle and a scraggy horse or two, grew potatoes and cabbages there. Today it has a population of close on two hundred thousand. An army officer in the plane proudly said there was nothing in Angarsk that was not modern and new. Why, he remarked, it had cafeterias just as in the United States and even a self-service store! It was one more example of the national appetite for going one better than America.

We landed at Tulun and after one of the best breakfasts I had had in the Soviet Union, served in a log cabin standing amid buttercups in a green Siberian field, we turned due north and left the new world and railway quickly behind. The cultivated clearings diminished until they vanished utterly to leave us with nothing but brooks, streams, rivers and *taiga* with water glinting round the tree-trunks. As mile after mile of this went by it seemed less and less credible that we could be on the way to what the Russians say is the world's greatest hydro-electric project. Other doubts too assailed a lay mind like mine. Could it be wise and indeed economical to create so great a source of power in such empty land, so far from the main centres of demand and supply? All I knew was that some thousands of Russian scientists at a great conference at Irkutsk had decided that it was. And there certainly was no element of hesitation in the way the new Bratsk had flung a dam across the wild Angara at the head of its greatest rapids and already cut itself a town of ninety thousand people out of the *taiga* as well as making the relevant roads between dam, railway and airport that were soon to be underwater when all the sluices in the dam were closed.

The schoolmaster who taught English and the editor of the hydro-electric workers' paper, *Angara Lights*, who met us at the airport were justifiably full of the achievement of Bratsk. The schoolmaster dressed in black, a camera from Leningrad slung over his shoulder, looked more like someone about to do a round of Greek temples than a young man working deep in the Siberian bush. The editor, a breezy ex-ice-breaker, appeared more appropriate to the setting. Yet both came from the west, the schoolmaster from Gorkiy and the editor from Murmansk. But what did I expect in a sparsely populated land like Siberia, they asked? Only a small experienced core of workers were Siberians, the rest come from all over the Soviet Union. Sixty-nine different nationalities worked on the scheme: the Chief Engineer was a Jew, his deputy a Tartar. They said emphatically that the only sorts of workers they did not have at Bratsk were 'slave workers'. Then as we drove towards Bratsk from the airport over a terrible road, it all came out. They railed against Mr Harriman! It had all happened years ago but it still rankled with everyone at Bratsk. Apparently Mr Harriman in a speech in Moscow had accused Mr Khrushchev of keeping him out of Siberia because he was afraid he would see for himself how much 'slave labour' was being used in the new development of the country. Mr Khrushchev immediately had said something to this effect, 'Go to Bratsk. Go now so that you will be in time to see the dramatic closing of the gap in the walls of the dam with loose boulders as at Irkutsk.' Mr Harriman left at once to witness this historic event. Meanwhile the workers had read of all his 'shameful' accusations in the Press. They were incensed. They felt such a man was not worthy of being present at the climax of their labours, so spontaneously they worked day and night and as a result closed the gap a day ahead of schedule! Mr Harriman arrived to find the dam an accomplished fact. Everyone still laughed with delight over his manifest disappointment. Slave labour indeed!

It seemed incredible to me that these two men did not know that until very recently Siberia was full of concentration and forced labour camps. Judging by a story I had just read in *Novy Mir*, the literary periodical, one of the biggest had been situated not far from Bratsk at Tayshet.* Then there are novels, too, all the rage now that the Party had de-Stalinized itself, of other concentration camps in Siberia. Some of the astonishing blackouts that Russians have of the doings of the State and their own country are genuine. I remember the Japanese ambassador telling me at a lunch in Moscow that the Russian servants at the Embassy did not know of the formidable series of Soviet nuclear tests: they thought only America and Britain did such things. Foreigners overlook the fact that it is almost as difficult for Russians to travel around the Soviet Union as it is for them. They cannot leave their districts without first getting official permission and then only as a rule for a holiday at a recognized holiday place or to visit relations.

---

* It seemed more incredible still later when I met in Moscow a Russian who told me he had served seven years in a concentration camp at Bratsk itself. All my guides told me, was that only a few Cossack families had lived at Bratsk before the barrage was built.

However, once this matter of 'slave labour' had been cleared up the two men proved delightful guides. They asked did I know what had been one of their greatest challenges in building the dam? I guessed all the obvious things which were wrong. They laughed with delight and then confessed that the greatest challenge had been midges. The Siberian midges of summer rising like smoke out of the *taiga*, stinging, biting, beating the air away from people's faces so that they came near being stifled, were terrible things. And Moscow, true to its form, had forgotten to supply the workers with nets! Work came to a standstill, people could not sleep and were near throwing in their hands when the nets arrived. Also there were bears that came out of the *taiga* and stopped the laying of telephone lines until hunters were delegated to shoot them on sight. Soon the bears, intelligent creatures that they were, saw the light and kept away. And, remarked the editor, there were those first terrible winters which, shivering in tents, the young worker from the metropolitan west had had to endure. A great many had to be sent home but most of them remained until permanent quarters could be built. I could see for myself how successfully that had been done! He pointed at the outskirts of Bratsk which we were entering. I could scarcely believe my eyes. On that dry sunny day, with dust on the road and the great Siberian pine-trees standing all around, I might have been entering a well-to-do suburb called Pinelands outside Cape Town in South Africa. Instead of the barrack blocks which still cluttered my memory I looked on a world of individual houses, each of a different design with a garden of its own.

'We call this part of Bratsk "India",' the editor said laughing. 'That is short for "individual" because it is given over entirely to people who wanted to have houses of their own design.'

We stopped at an inn at the dividing line between 'India' and 'apartment' city. Built entirely of wood, the grain inside polished to shine like good leather, the windows without lace and covered only by curtains of pillar-box red, mauve and amber stripes, it was the gayest and most attractive hotel I saw in the whole of the Soviet Union. A large double bedroom with a kitchen of its own and a bathroom was put at our disposal. Beside the bed under its bright covers was a table with a reading-lamp and telephone. I might have been in the best type of Swiss chalet.

'Wouldn't you like to telephone your home in London?' our hosts asked me.

We were some four hundred miles from Irkutsk deep in the bush and Irkutsk was more than three thousand miles from Moscow. I looked so amazed that they all laughed and insisted on my doing so! That done they hurried me out to the dam where we spent the rest of the day. I, of course, cannot pronounce on it technically. All I know is that there are today two peaks in my experience of such things which remain unequalled: the first is the Great Boulder Dam of America, the second Bratsk. The first started and the second consummated an achievement which has made the emerging countries of the world convinced that they cannot be self-respecting without similar projects of their own. Indeed these schemes have started a new kind of snobbery. Everyone I met at Bratsk, from engineers to concrete mixers, despised all other kinds of projects and pitied all other workers. And I met a great many workers that day. For the moment we stepped out on the wall of the dam rising high above the waters of the river I was told: 'Look at our slave labour! Please stop and speak to anyone and ask any questions you like.'

The first person I stopped was a girl of nineteen from the Ukraine. She was a concrete tester and although so young she already had two of the three years of her contract behind her. Standing on the wall, a cold breeze from the north blowing through her dark hair and fluttering her bright cotton dress she nodded her head emphatically when I, wrapped in a winter coat, asked her if she liked her work.

'Do they too?' I pointed at a team of young girls in overalls and boys without hats filling a grab with the concrete that she was to test.

Of course they do I was told, those who did not like it have long since departed and only those who love it remain. They are a wonderful team, she claimed.

What did she do in her leisure? I asked.

She went hiking and camping with her friends in the *taiga* in summer; in winter they had the theatre, circuses and dances; also she read a great deal and studied. They all went on studying, the schools working round the clock three shifts a day, first the children and then the workers.

And what was she going to do when her contract had expired?

At this, this young woman, nails manicured, mouth scarlet with lipstick and cheeks stained red with the fresh air, looked amazed. She would stay on, of course! She hoped to qualify one day as a hydro-electric engineer.

And these were the kind of answers that everyone gave me. Some of them perhaps were instinctively keeping up national appearances in front of a foreigner. But most, I believe, were sincere. They had picked up the hydro-electric disease and experienced a sense of superiority and satisfaction in practising the snobbery I have mentioned. More, they were joined in a common purpose with their fellow men which made the discomforts and material rewards seem negligible and gave them the greater meaning denied them in the vast anonymous environment from which they had invariably come. It was the peace-time equivalent of what men and women experience in war. In fact the community at Bratsk reminded me of nothing so much as a technological monastery-cum-nunnery applying the principles of their religion in the wilds of Siberia. I found also men who were over sixty and had passed the retiring age, and who had done nothing but work on one hydro-electric scheme after the other since they had had their first taste of such work on the Dniepr Dam. Their one fear was that hydro-electric work would give out before their death.

'But that's impossible,' I remonstrated with one grandfather supervisor. 'You have centuries of such work ahead of you in so great and empty a land.'

'It's not the lack of rivers or rapids that worries us,' he said. 'It's the lack of money and labour. These schemes cost a lot, and some people believe we already have enough of them to satisfy the nation's needs for a generation.'

'Then wouldn't you prefer to retire somewhere near your family and relax for the last years of your life?'

'I have not even had time to put my name down for an apartment in my native town,' he told me firmly. 'My wife left me long ago to take care of the children. The children are grown up and have their own life. I would only be an embarrassment in towns. Here I have my usefulness, and my friends. The work here is all the family I have left.'

The younger workers, however, tended to laugh at the anxieties of the older ones. When Bratsk was finished, as it soon would be, giving out its 4,600,000 kilowatts of power, they were convinced they would move a hundred and eighty miles further north and deeper into the *taiga* to Ust-Ilymsk, where another hydro-electric site on the same river was already surveyed and just waiting for workers like themselves. Clearly they relished the prospect as a football team does when about to play another match against a tough opponent in the next round towards winning the cup.

At the end of the day having sampled the bewildering mixture of nationalities and ages most of whom came from the crowded west, I asked a tall Siberian, foreman of a crew of seven, whether they made good Siberians. He gave me a thumbs-up gesture and said, 'Of the very best!' He had no interest in Britain but pressed on to ask about America and the Boulder Dam, not forgetting to flay Mr Harriman in the process. However, he condescended in the end to overlook the British lack of hydro-electric decency and asked me to convey to the people of Britain the greetings of all Siberians. On that note we hastened back to join our wild plane at the airport at sunset. A General and his staff were also waiting to join our plane.

'If we're not careful,' the editor remarked, 'these army types will bag the best seats. And our visitors must have them!'

When our call came they both seized me by the arm and hastened me to the plane cutting straight ahead of the military group. They had me and my guide into the best seat and were out of the plane themselves before the general had reached the steps. The last I saw of them was standing by the huge empty bus still grinning happily over the success of their strategy.

We flew back to Irkutsk directly over a *taiga*, dark and without a glimmer of light, because it was so wild and empty except when we picked up the circles of lamps of the new satellite towns that surround the Siberian capital. I realized then that if I had to make a choice of where to live in Russia I would without doubt have chosen a villa of my own design in the 'India' where Bratsk infringes on the virgin *taiga*.

The next day, I left by train for Moscow in order to catch the plane that was to take me to the Far East region of Siberia. I had tried hard to avoid so unnecessary a journey. I knew Irkutsk airport was closed to big planes but I pleaded to be allowed to get out of the train at either Krasnoyarsk or Novosibirsk and travel on by air. But permission was firmly and in the end angrily refused. So I had to go all the way back to Moscow and re-embark for the Far East from there.

So as not to lose Siberian continuity I flew at once from Moscow to the Far East. The plane was the biggest in which I have ever travelled. On land it looked so huge that one doubted its capacity to fly and once in the sky it had a tail wobble like a whale and trembled all over. We left Moscow soon after sunrise, flew for eight hours without a stop and landed at Khabarovsk at three the following morning. On the way we saw little of the tail of the Siberian earth but I came down with the clearest impression yet of the emptiness and immensity of the land. Once across the Urals I caught no sign of any of the great Siberian cities; only the essentials of land, river, forest and broken blue hills, untouched by man. Yet with melodramatic suddenness appeared the great chains of light of Khabarovsk smoking in the first monsoon rain to tell the same expanding story. Early as it was in the morning I counted ten planes as large as mine, drawn up outside the airport station and the arrival halls were crowded with people getting ready to depart. The guide who met us told me every hotel and inn was full. He had with great difficulty got me a room in the main hotel. My Russian companion from Moscow, he regretted, would have to share a room with three others.

The evidence of purpose, energy and expansion discerned dimly by electric light in heavy rain at the airport, was written large over this city of 300,000 people by day. For the first time I stood amazed at the brink of the city on the banks of the Amur River, another epic stream of the Soviet Union. It had been little more than a mirage of history in my imagination but here it was a great contemporary waterway swollen and still swelling ominously with rain. Neither Russians nor Chinese have yet been able to control this massive stream when it rains. In the monsoon it rises swiftly to the level of a five-storey building and on one occasion rose so high that a ship sailed down the main street of the town of Blagoveschensk on the lower reaches of the river. Almost as big as the Amur are its tributaries, in particular the great Ussuri which joins it near Khabarovsk. No wonder the people I met were full of plans for using this excess of water and preventing the annual flooding of the low-lying and densely populated land in the Amur basin by cutting canals to link it with the Tartar Straits, as well as the Sea of Japan near Vladivostok. My first morning in Khabarovsk the river, broad as it was, seemed burdened with traffic, steamers, barges, fishing-boats, and above all tugs towing packages of lumber tied together in shapes which earned them the name of 'cigars' and which displaced as much water as a full-sized cargo ship. Where the river met the horizon bridges worthy of those of the Hudson and Mississippi carried the railway and road on south to Vladivostok.

Yet the moment the town ended the forest stepped in to surround it. In that regard the country looked as the explorer Vladimir Arsenyev described it in his remarkable books which deserve a place in world literature for his deeply sensitive and imaginative portrayal of the Golds, the race of hunters who preceded Koreans, Chinese and Russians in the woods and valleys of the Pacific seaboard. I had just put down Arsenyev's *Ursula Dezula* and my reactions were coloured by his account of the life of the Chinese settlers, the Korean farmers, the pirates who raided their villages, and these mysterious long Chinamen who culled the forests for the '*gin-seng*' plant, the man-root, which the Chinese believed had the power of indefinite rejuvenation. We drove over abominable roads deep into the forest. So varied was the climate that the trees of north and south, cold, hot and temperate zones all grew together. It was a world of botanical miscegenation gone mad. Even more mixed up my friends assured me were the birds and animals who invested these sepulchral woods. There were, to mention only a few, the sabre-tooth, the great Siberian tiger, the leopard, black, grey and unique species of wolves, with bright red hair, the brown and black bear, an antelope with wool like sheep, tortoises without bone, elk, spotted deer, a tiny tree-fern deer hardly bigger than a rat, sable and mink; while in the rivers that flowed through the forests lived ninety different kinds of fish.

In this forest the peasant clearings looked braver than most. There was an increasing number of these because one of the prides of Khabarovsk is its scheme to make itself self-sufficient in vegetables. It has on an average 256 cloudless days a year and some pioneering spirit had the bright idea to use the sun for growing vegetation under glass. As a result an empire of collective glass-houses is beginning to advance along the valleys and probe deeper into the woods. Everywhere in Siberia I met the glasshouse tycoons grumbling over the damage that bureaucracy, over-centralization and bottle-necks were doing to their plans but the advance and the scale to me were most impressive. I thought again how Russia is fundamentally a 'marathon' country. It is not the short-distance sprints, the egg-and-spoon and three-legged races of life that catch the national imagination, but the impossible long-distance obstacle race with hope of victory against im-possible odds. They do not count the cost in time, money or human material in accomplishing the particular goal to which they have yielded their great reserves of spirit and energy. 'If only we had more manpower,' they would exclaim ruefully to me and quickly add,' But our lack of people can well be a blessing in disguise and will lead us to greater automation and improvement in mechanization of agriculture.'

Yet in this longing for manpower I thought I detected another factor. Before the war the population of eastern Siberia and the seaboard was not quite three million. Already it had risen to some thirteen million. Yet the growth is not fast enough for Siberians! Of course among the new millions are thousands of misfits who can take neither the climate nor endure the labour. But all this is trivial compared to what seems to me to be the real fear behind the longing for more people. . . . Only a few miles away are the frontiers of China as overcrowded and poor in natural resources as this land is empty and rich. There is as well a shocking history of broken treaties and pledges on Russia's part lying like a shadow between Chinese and Russians. All this area of Siberia had once been a Chinese-Mongol sphere of influence. Can the Chinese, who find it impossible to forgive a friendly India the MacMahon line drawn in the barren Himalayas, indefinitely overlook Russian penetration into this land of incalculable riches? Can they endure indefinitely having too little, with close at hand so few having too much? One doubted an indefinite acceptance of such a state and I believe in their secret hearts the Siberians doubt it too. I have mentioned before how struck I was by the western-ness of Siberia. Here in the Far East the people seemed to me more western than ever and the least Asiatic and Oriental of any group encountered on my travels in the Soviet Union. And this brought me to what was, for me, the main lesson of my probe to the Far East and the Pacific seaboard and the conclusion thrust itself upon me one day with theatrical suddenness.

A Russian acquaintance had taken us for an excursion by motorboat on the Ussuri River. We went up it until we could see where it crossed the Chinese frontier between two low blue hills, which he pointed out to me.

'The Chinese patrol boats,' he said, 'are only just around the next far bend. I don't think we had better go any further.'

I had realized China was near Khabarovsk but not that it was as close as all that. I stood up to have a closer look at the hills when suddenly I heard pronounced in slow deliberate English behind me, 'East is East and West is West, and never the twain shall meet.'

It came over me then with a dazzle of illumination that for him and all the people I had met, Siberia was the West; and China was the East. So perhaps it was not particularly strange that the great poet of British Imperialism, Kipling, who had long since ceased to speak for Britain in this regard, should be chosen at that moment to speak for contemporary Russia.

One final impression of the Far East. An old Russian writer threw open his home to me, his two-roomed apartment just off the main street of Khabarovsk. Like a true frontier outpost Khabarovsk's people were generous, informal and hospitable to the extreme. They would not hear of my eating in my hotel or restaurants. I had to have several of my main meals with them, always caviare, smoked fish, salmon, lobsters, ham, cold meats, soups, egg-dishes, pickles, cheese and several kinds of bread, butter and magnums of champagne! This particular writer was a man of over seventy and had had a mixed and tragic history which he carried without pathos or complaint. In his youth he had studied at Heidelberg University and been expelled from it for fighting with a Prussian officer who had insulted a French friend of his. He had fought in the First World War and had known Benes and the leaders of the legendary Czech legion on their march across Siberia to the sea. He had lived in China for twenty-three years but in the end he had come back to Russia. With such a history I feel it says something for Soviet authority that it allowed him back, though I think permission to return was not entirely without qualification. He was born in the west near Moscow and I suspect he lived in Khabarovsk not by choice but because it was part of the price he had to pay for his past. Yet he was from time to time allowed to visit his old home and what is more allowed to publish his books. He was just then writing a book on *The Black People* of Russia. He explained that the title was taken from the name given, in the nineteenth century, to the most down-trodden and poorest of all classes of people in Russia. He said that they had been the Russian 'untouchables', and that even in public inns and tea-houses they were only allowed to be served in special rooms called 'black-rooms', separated from the other respectable customers. 'Black,' he said, 'was the colour of social suffering and suppression in Russia'. His book was a research into the origins, and an orchestration, of this tragic social theme of the past.

When I went to say good-bye to him he had open in front of him a book of the paintings of the great Ikon painter, Rublyov, and had just been looking deep into the eyes of Rublyov's St Michael. From the peak of his seventy years, with all the tumult of his life resolved, its passion spent and his spirit now turned homeward, he begged me to say this: 'We have passed the danger point in Russia, we have crossed a terrible river. Whatever the appearances now everything will become better and turn out for the best. All will be well if only we have no more war – as all would have been well here had we not had the First World War. Work, work as hard as you can for peace, as I shall be doing here.'

I thought it almost more than mere coincidence that that very evening, after the long flight from Khabarovsk to Moscow, when I bought a magazine at the bookstall in the hotel and opened it it was to read a poem by a contemporary young Russian poet about Rublyov. The poet, too, recommended his example of faith and humility, quietly reminding the State that not everything could fit into its present scheme.

CHAPTER FIFTEEN

A TALE OF THREE CITIES

THE United States and Britain have never recognized the incorporation into the Soviet Union of the Baltic States of Lithuania, Latvia and Esthonia during the last war. Yet these States are forced to be so bound into the Soviet system that it seemed unrealistic to me not to sample life in at least one of them. I chose Latvia on my way north to Leningrad. There, superficially, the act of incorporation looked complete and final. In Riga, the capital, the streets have been renamed after Russian comrades whose appeal to the emotions and imagination of the Latvian people can hardly be great. But such considerations do not matter to the Russian authorities who believe in the magic of their official vocabulary. Thus the main street was Lenin Street; there was Gorkiy Street and Kirov Avenue. There were three districts of the city named the Lenin, Moscow, and Proletariat districts. For the first time, too, I was aware of the presence of Russian soldiers in greater numbers than I had encountered on normal occasions elsewhere. There were a dozen or so senior staff officers at my hotel alone and I saw the soldiery well represented in the streets, theatre, ballet and opera. This may have had nothing to do with the fact that we were on what is, in effect, conquered territory. It may have been due entirely to the deployment of Soviet forces in terms of Russia's reading of her overall strategic needs. None the less it was so marked an aspect of the scene in Riga that I could not ignore it.

At first glance, too, the signs of the shaping of the local economy appeared to be on the Russian model. One of the great official success stories is the Riga Fishermen's Collective, and I think there is no doubt that its material success is very real. The fishermen's cottages and apartment-houses, their theatre and concert halls, schools, clinics and offices look incredibly prosperous. Every year more and more Latvian ocean-going trawlers feel their way out of the Baltic Sea and intrude into the fishing grounds of the west and even those of Newfoundland and the North American littoral. These ocean-going crews are the well-paid *élite* of the Fishermen's Collective. The apartments in which I interviewed some of their skippers are bigger and better furnished than those of many established writers and University professors that I saw in Moscow. And all this is just a beginning. The skippers and their colleagues in the neighbouring States are determined to develop long-distance trawling in a much bigger way. They showed other signs too of having accepted the Soviet faith. For instance, in their luxurious club-hall, one official told me they had their own 'Holy Communion' services.

I asked him to explain, imagining for a moment the hall was used also as a church.

Young girls, he explained, instead of being received into one of the Christian churches came there to be initiated into the Fishermen's Collective. He showed me photographs of the girls dressed in white like 'brides of the church' for their confirmation. It was a cheap crib of the relevant Roman Catholic ceremony and the jeering laughs that accompanied the showing of the photographs hinted plainly that the parallel was not unconscious. It also proved unwittingly what they denied – how deep and indestructible is the need in human nature for ritual of this kind.

All this and much else made the Soviet conquest of the economy and spirit of the people of this Baltic State appear conclusive. Yet after a while one began to wonder. I would drive back from Riga Beach or one of the new worker's districts and see across the broad Dvina River, the city's lovely sky-line. Riga, one of the oldest cities in Europe, was founded nearly 800 years ago, and what had been beautiful or significant in the architecture over all those centuries was present in that graceful silhouette against the light blue sky. The spires of the many churches, the yellow castle walls, the gabled houses, the Assembly Hall of medieval guilds and orders of Baltic chivalry, were all there as tranquil and translucent as any of Vermeer's views of Delft. I just could not believe that all the history and the meaning expressed in that view could have been abolished. And my doubts seemed confirmed by my chauffeur who spontaneously took exception to the one postwar feature prominent on the sky-line, the University building, a skyscraper in the rigid Soviet model.

'It's wrong!' he exclaimed without fear in front of my Russian interpreter and our official guide, 'it doesn't fit our style of architecture and should never have been built. We'll not let it happen again.'

At that moment a traffic policeman blew his whistle at us and waved his arms in what seemed a most erratic way.

'He's an eccentric,' my Russian companion remarked calmly. 'What we call in Russian a *"persona"*.'

'As far as I am concerned he is *"persona non grata"*,' the driver interjected and drove on regardless.

Wandering round the narrow dark streets winding through the old city like a footpath through a great African forest, it was striking how reverently the detail of the past had been preserved. There was little evidence of iconoclasm, which is to the credit of the conquerors of Latvia and not least of all to the Soviet. For instance I found forty-three ancient churches, still intact and functioning. In one of the narrowest streets, on a wall grey with age, was carved still bold and clear the image of Christ confronting the Pharisees over the fallen woman.

In those streets too I heard more sounds of people piano practising than ever before. Riga's long tradition of culture and music clearly was still living. In that sense the city of which Wagner had once been a musical director, in which Clara Schumann was received with honours, and Liszt given an enthusiastic reception, was still an outpost of the classical European spirit. A passer-by from whom we asked the way volunteered the information to the tinkling of scores of pianos in the buildings around us that tickets for their Musical Festival were booked up on the first day for ten months ahead!

I had a haircut in an establishment run by a woman barber. She had attractive oil-paintings in gilt frames on the walls of her room, a carpet, two couches, two easy chairs and a writing-table for her clients. While she cut my hair she had a radio playing softly and apologized for not speaking to me because she felt compelled to listen to a broadcast of Latvian poetry. Barbers interested in poetry may exist in Britain and America but I have yet to meet them.

Even in the Latvian economy, after my first experience of the booming Fishermen's Collective, I became aware of important differences. The official talk was all of collective and State farming but penetrating into the country districts one could detect signs of a much greater diversification and individualism than in the

Russian scene. In the exhibition of Latvian industry open in Riga
the pig-farm brought to one's attention was not collective but
was run by one man. That year by means of automation he
claimed to have produced 4,000 pigs; his target for next year was
5,000. Again in industry, one perceived a specialization and
aptitude that could only have been the result of an attachment
to individual arts and crafts. Thus Latvia already has a reputation all over the Soviet Union for precision industry, for the
best transistor radios and automatic telephone exchanges. We
had not been in Riga long before my Russian companion, an intelligent and endearing young man, was reacting to the goods
in the shop windows as I have seen Africans react on their first
visit from the interior to Johannesburg or Durban. Before long
he had a transistor set, costing more than two months' pay,
slung over his shoulder – and with no hope, as we discovered
subsequently, of getting spares for it even in Moscow! It was all
I could do to persuade him not to buy a sports coat cut in the
individual English cavalry style out of Latvian tweed. Unable to
bear seeing another four months of his salary go on an inferior
garment, I offered him instead a real English tweed coat of my
own. The offer was declined with such a hurt politeness that I
regretted ever making it. These impressions were to be amplified
later in Leningrad and Moscow where I found the Soviet women
snatching up fashion magazines from the Baltic States as fast as
they appeared on the bookstalls. The pin-up girls who set the
fashions in their own Soviet magazines were still the collective
farm or factory girl workers smiling as if mud and coal-dust were
more becoming than powder and rouge. But the Latvian and
other Baltic magazines had a prevailing wind of change from the
west fluttering the skirts of fashion in their pages that made them
eminently desirable. And at the opera in Riga for the first time I
saw that most men had changed into dark suits, some were in
dinner-jackets and many women were in evening clothes. I think
it was this Latvian difference of approach too, that drew the
Russians to the Baltic States in such numbers and made Riga,
despite the grey uncertain Baltic summer, the most fashionable
and expensive seaside resort in the Soviet Union. Primitive people
in Africa believe that what a man eats, from a rat to an elephant's
liver, communicates something of its own nature to the nature of the

man. I believe that what nations devour by conquest, even so small a morsel as the Latvian nation of less than 3,000,000, does not fail to communicate something of its own nature to the conqueror and can set in motion changes that one day will appear more clearly.

All this sort of thing made Latvia look not only different but more prosperous than other parts of the Soviet Union. Although the prices seemed fantastic, £80 for the cheapest ready-made suit, butter 21s a lb, cheese 18s, a scraggy piece of meat 19s a lb, and tomatoes 17s yet there were no lack of buyers. The farmers' market had stalls full of equipment, furniture and manufactured goods for sale at proportionately high prices. I saw one carpet, small and very ugly, going for £500.

'What an awful lot of money,' I exclaimed to our Latvian guide. 'Surely no one can afford such prices!'

'Oh, our collective farmers are rich,' she told me proudly. 'Many of them are millionaires.' But below the matter, I felt again, it could well be another tale.

Then I met a Latvian businessman whom I had known abroad. He had migrated years before and was on one of his periodic visits to relations. Meeting him reminded me of another difference between these States, the Ukraine and Russia. The peoples of the Baltic and the Ukraine all had numerous relations abroad who helped to keep a sense of the world alive in them. Present-day Russia has no relations abroad. Only recently I read in my ski-ing journal about one of the grand old ladies of European ski-ing who said she started ski-ing because seventy years ago some *Russian cousins* had sent her skis lined with felt. But who has any Russian cousins left in these days? The only Russians encountered in the world today are officials or persons passed for outside circulation for purposes of the State, and I think this lack of natural, living bridges between Russia and the world contributes far more than is realized to the inferior quality of the liaison between the Russians and ourselves.

However, to return to my Latvian acquaintance. On Latvian soil he was a totally different person from the man I had first met. Abroad he was lively, expansive, uninhibited. But here on his native soil he was like an emissary on a delicate and dangerous mission, and so obviously embarrassed by meeting me that I did not force my company on him. But unexpectedly I did have a word with him one morning in the hotel vestibule. I remarked casually how prosperous the country looked compared to other parts of the Soviet Union.

His comment was revealing. 'Oh, it's prosperous all right but, man, you've no idea of the hatred about under the surface!'

But brighter at the surface as the Latvian life appeared, deep down there is the same old hunger in people for more colour, flexibility and variety in their lives. It showed itself most spectacularly at the ballet and opera where the costumes and settings achieve a magnificence and importance not found outside the Soviet Union. Even the rags and tatters worn by the beggars are designed to satisfy the audiences' craving for colour. The beggars and rogues of Paris in *Esmeralda* (a slanted ballet based on Victor Hugo's *Hunchback of Notre Dame*), are as colourful and splendid in their rags as Joseph must have been in the 'coat of many colours' that clinched the determination of his brethren to get rid of him to the Egyptians. This craving is so great that it is not satisfied by the repetition of standard ballet and the endless diet of Folk Costume in folk dancing on which people are fed from the Collective Farm Hall and the Factory Palace of Culture. I have a suspicion that for all the vigour and skill with which they are performed, Russians are about to become as bored with folk dances as the British are with their own Morris dances. Though it was all new and fresh to me, at the end of my journey I felt that I never wanted to see another Cossack sword dance again. Here in Riga I had my suspicions more strongly confirmed than elsewhere. At an evening of mixed ballet it was noticeable that a light ballet based on a Strauss waltz, some Mexican and Spanish dancing, performances that are clichés of the night-clubs and cabarets of the world drew the greatest applause and were received like great and original compositions.

I went to an opera based on Sholokhov's *Fate of a Man*. Originally a long short story about the last war, it has had a fantastic success in the Soviet Union and also has been made into a popular film and a play. It articulates the secret and inaudible murmurings of the male Russian soul, its predisposition to find suffering and disaster nobler than happiness and success, its tendency to regard as the heroic ultimate the capacity to endure to the end without faith, hope, or charity.

In the opera all this is overlaid by the ideological points the composer is determined to score and in one of the world's loudest compositions every trumpet and tocsin, every violin and cello pluck the national heartstrings. But the spectacle wins out even against such determined music. At the climax, the liberation of Berlin, the wide stage was so crowded with red flags, banners and pointed obelisks surmounted with twittering five-pound stars that there was no room for the singers. They were forced to do their singing in the orchestra pit and in the boxes. At one stage the unfortunate orchestra was pinned helplessly by singers against the walls of the pit and it was a wonder the violinists could move their arms at all. The soldiers in the audience applauded loudly and long. It was perhaps the supreme illustration of the growing power of the craving for colour and pageantry over a genuine love of the arts. Unfortunately the spectacle as far as the Latvians were concerned must have expressed the wrong sentiments for I saw a lot of empty seats at the end of the performance. Nor must I add would the music have been to the taste of cultivated Russians however much they approved of its sentiments. My Russian companion, who enjoyed the spectacle and presumably approved of the sentiment, said he thought the music terrible.

Yet, once all this was behind me I realized how well this Latvian excursion had served as an introduction to Leningrad. Without it, I might not have realized so clearly how European the city of Peter the Great still is. Visually, of course, one could not have failed to recognize the supremely European expression of the architecture and design of the city. But despite the Revolution and three generations of Soviet indoctrination, the mind, spirit, behaviour and inborn values and affinities seem still surprisingly to be of northern Europe. This is all the more significant because as cities go Leningrad – how ungrateful the change of a name by a State influenced so much by Peter the Great – is young. It is younger than Moscow, Novgorod or Kiev. It would hardly have had time to create so much of a mind and spirit of its own if this creation were not part of an ancient urge and indeed one of the great fundamentals of the Russian soul. And this is based on the instinctive determination of the Russian people, undismayed and undiminished throughout their hapless, tragic, random centuries, not to be separated from the rest of Europe. Peter the Great did not create but merely served and shaped that determination to a greater degree than anyone else in Russian history. Had his own vision not been profoundly rooted in the national instincts he could not have done a fraction of what he did. It seems to me extraordinary how this aspect of history has been overlooked in the distinguished books of scholarship that I have read, and how unappraised is the importance of the fact that the great Slav family to which the Russians belong, was once a vital element of the coming and going of peoples in Europe north of the Danube, Alps and Rhine, and that once, in the beginning of our histories, they even reached the mouth of the Elbe and stood where Hamburg stands today. Historians, traditions, customs, and indeed the Russians themselves, may consciously have ignored or forgotten that part of their and our common history. But by some mysterious process of metabolism it is remembered and kept alive in the instincts of the nation. In the world of these instincts Peter the Great is not a vanished historical figure but a living contemporary and compelling symbol. That accounts, perhaps more than anything else, for the extraordinary power that this terrifying, mixed-up lunatic of genius exercises over the minds of the rulers and imagination of the land. Here in Leningrad I realized that this urge is by no means expended. Indeed it seemed to me that more than any other was a vital, electric Russian terminal that kept the great internal current linked to the transformers in the powerhouse of the European spirit. More than that I felt this to be the most important impression of all the many I had gathered on my long journey. It is urgent for the world – and indeed the Russians too – to realize that in their depths they are a part of Europe. All this talk about Russians being half Asiatic and half European seemed to me valid only in externals. The Russians are basically a European people – a European people with an important difference which presently I shall try to define. But if I had any doubts on this point they would have been refuted by my memory of how the Siberian and Far Eastern Russians took it for granted that they were Westerners and were even more consciously western than the Russians along the marches of Europe. The reality of the Siberian's deep and exposed projection into the overcrowded East, cracking with the pressures of population like a ripe Persian pomegranate with seed, banished all luxury of illusion to the contrary, and removes from their minds any temptations to political and ideological flirting with Asia. I continually remembered the Russian standing in the boat on the Ussuri River and pointing to the Chinese frontier, while he pronounced Kipling's lines as if they were a text from the Bible:

> 'Oh East is East and West is West:
> And never the twain shall meet!'

The glamour of the European invasions of Russia, led by some of the most colourful and dramatic characters on the brilliant European scene, as for example Charles the Great of Sweden, Napoleon and Hitler, naturally tend to be in the forefront of European considerations and to assume an obliterating significance which is out of proportion in the total perspectives of Russian history. They have left, of course, deep scars and to this day have their reflexes. Yet it is necessary not to overlook that amid them all Russia gave as good, if not perhaps even better, than it got. That alone inevitably draws a great deal of the poison out of the European wound. But more important still these wars with Europe and these invasions by Poles, Lithuanians, Swedes, French and Germans, were brief and small in comparison with the wounds that Asia inflicted on Russia. The real trauma of history which came nearest to extinguishing the Russian will and from which the modern Russian spirit still suffers most, is that of invasion from the east and south-east and above all the prolonged Tartar domination of the land. Besides these, the wars with Europe, given their own context of time and place, are like a series of frontier skirmishes. The history of the Tartar invasion alone I find difficult to read even at this distance of time because of its sustained and unmitigated horror. All in all I suspect that, bright and wary as is the eye that Russia keeps on Europe, it is casual and trusting in comparison with that long, constant, over-the-shoulder look towards the East.

As I re-read the grim tale in Leningrad, the survival of the Russian sense of belonging to Europe seemed a miracle with such a history. Nor had it possessed the advantage of going unchallenged within the national spirit. Continuously the facts of geography, environment, and the shattering impact of external events had produced undertones and whirlpools of isolationism that made for its defeat. Yet this thin golden thread of Europeanism remains unbroken from the first dim contracts with Greek traders and Roman legions and, when Greece and Rome had crumbled, with the citadel of Constantinople itself. Even when Constantinople fell and the Turks swarmed over the Balkans to the gates of Vienna and when Christians, Lithuanians and Tartars combined to crush what was left of a national Russian identity, this continuity is never broken. Suddenly again there appears some Russian ecclesiastical or secular authority to proclaim the Europeanism of Russia; some new ruler seeks to break out of unwanted isolation and backwardness by making friends with Europe, such as Ivan the Terrible who, after destructive centuries and in the midst of his own increasing dementia, tried to conclude a military alliance with Elizabeth I of England and frightened her kinswoman, Lady Mary Hastings, with proposals of marriage.

But the real break-through into Europe came only with Peter the Great. There would be no point in stressing the harm that the belatedness of the break-through did both to Russia and ourselves in the past if it were not important to both our presents. It is important because in a sense the denial of this Europeanism of the Russian started again with the Bolshevik revolution and still goes on both *within* and *without* Russia. The external political forms of this denial and the clash of ideologies produced by it are obvious enough. The explanations fashionable in history for Europe's and Russia's many estrangements from one another are equally well known. But what are not recognized perhaps are the deeper causes of this split, and even the reasons that the contestants themselves had advanced over the centuries for the conflict seems to me to be little more than excuses and justifications invented to explain a profound, unrecognized and inner difference. This difference existed and still exists deep in the respective natures of Europeans and Russians and is the *a priori* cause of all the trouble. And the difference, as I see it, is this: the Russians are to this day still a relatively primitive people.

Anyone who knows from my writings what I feel about primitive people will know that I do not use the epithet to disparage. I have always believed that the balance between primitive and civilized values has never yet been fairly struck in any society. I see these values as two halves designed to make a great whole

and till the marriage of the two is accepted as the most urgent
task of man I see no end to the tensions and conflicts that
threaten us. As a working over-simplification I would suggest
that the primitive is a condition of life wherein the instinctive,
subjective, and collective values tend to predominate; the
civilized condition of life is where the rational, objective and individual take command. Throughout history the two have been
at one another's throats because it appears that the value of one
depends on the rejection of the other and this Jacob and Esau
theme has been played out between the nations and cultures of
the world with the reconciliation of the brothers not yet in sight.
The Russians, for me, tend to be an Esau, or primitive people. So
in Leningrad I began to understand why, on my long journey
through Russia, parallels with my own native life in Africa had so
often occurred to me. This had taken me completely by surprise.
I had expected to find life in Russia utterly new and different
from anything I had ever known. Yet I had found it oddly
familiar. I am forced to travel about the world a great deal yet
this had never happened to me before. I have three times been in
Japan yet my African past has not been much use in helping me
to interpret the profound impact that that country and its people
always makes on me. But at times in Russia without my up-
bringing and love of the primitive peoples of Africa I could have
felt quite at a loss, and I suspect that it is a whale of a red herring
to look to Marx for the origin and shape of Russian Communism. The claim of Russian Communism to be an 'objective
absolute' is necessary in Russia, firstly to keep up appearances
within the State; and secondly as a means of soliciting help from
the outside world. But the claim to 'absolutism' is false. The
Russians are naturally a communal people because they are
basically a primitive people: and primitive man is naturally collective. I know a dozen or so tribes in Africa who without the
technological dress of Soviet Russia, practise in essence a Soviet
system, because it is their natural, primitive way. The collective
value evolved in prolonged conditions of great danger is entrusted
to a powerful central tribal authority who discharges it with a
strange mixture of absolutism and deference to popular feeling,
which it continually tests and consults without necessarily
obeying it – just as in the Soviet Union. Change is imposed from

the top against the inertia and resistance of the conservative whole who naturally feel safer with the customs and beliefs that have brought it safely out of the past. Possessions are owned not so much for the individual as on behalf of the tribe: property ultimately belongs to the chief on behalf of the whole. So the phenomenon of violent change brought about from the top against popular inclination because it is thought to be in the interest of the whole, is a familiar occurrence in African history. Ivan the Terrible, Peter the Great and Stalin, complete with private obsession and personal mania, have scores of counterparts on the primitive African scene. Nor is it helpful to blame the despotism of the Russian system on the Tartars. It is a *primitive* phenomenon. The true destructive contribution of the Tartars to Russian history is that they retarded the natural evolution of a primitive society by keeping it, for centuries, a society on the run. Similarly the Arabs and slave traders in northern Africa retarded the evolution there. So, far from being the highly evolved concept of society that it claims to be, the Soviet system struck me as extremely archaic and committed inevitably more and more to far-reaching change within itself if it is to survive in the emerging world. In its primitive concept too, and not in its Marxist pretensions lies the secret of its attraction for the developing peoples of Africa. They understand and sympathize with the Soviet readily because its way is so much closer to their own both in character and purpose than ours. It is not Marxist indoctrination which makes the new African States claim the democratic right to have a vote for each man – merely to use the votes to abolish democracy by eliminating all opposition to authority and instituting a one-party State. It is because within themselves they stand at the same remote collective point in time as do the Russians. There is nothing primitive man fears more than a division within his community, within his communal self. All virtue is collective, all evil individual. What holds together is good, what divides is bad. Here is the instinctive motive-spring of mechanisms like the Mir. African societies know it well and their only way of dealing with change is to find a greater chief, an authority with some numinous surround, an all-powerful father-figure.

The Russians have always had such a figure whether called Tsar or Party Secretary. The further back in history one goes the closer these parallels become and the more dubious the surface explanations of conventional history. The terrible wars along the marches of Europe between Russia and its neighbours are explained, in part, by religious difference: an Orthodox Christian people in conflict with Catholic nations. But this overlooks the origin of the religious differences themselves. The Russians made their conversion to Christianity a sublimation of their finest primitive qualities. The emphasis was on the collective values of religion, on the unifying aspects, the capacity of 'bringing together' of Christianity. The Russian word for church of '*Sobor*' which in the first place means 'gathering', and '*Sobornost*' ('togetherness') is one of the most meaningful of all Russian words and the quintessence of what the church tried to promote. It served a vivid, primitive, instinctive sense of communion in men not only with one another but also in mystical participation with all life. On the other hand, the religion of their enemies despite its mystical roots and foundations in profound symbolism, became increasingly a conscious product of reason, a closely reasoned metaphysical and subtly argued intellectual system, selective and invested with a Roman love of discipline and order. To it what was dear to the Russian church was not only heresy but political death. Later still the dispute which rent the Church into Catholics and Protestants made matters worse for in a sense Protestantism is less primitive even than Catholicism.

The parallels too in Russian and African history are even more striking. I referred earlier on to the wars between Russia and her European neighbours as frontier wars. But they were wars fought not merely on physical but also on spiritual frontiers, and they seem, in their underlying meaning, remarkably like the Kaffir wars of South Africa fought between the primitive African invaders pushing down from the north out of their vast hinterland to clash with the small, relatively much more advanced, highly organized numbers of Europeans advancing from the south. The fear that my own countrymen to this day nourish in regard to the Africans who vastly outnumber them, is the same fear of being absorbed into a chaotic primitive horde which possessed all who shared a European frontier with Russia. One has only to travel along the Russian-European frontiers to find that the fires of these antagonisms still burn and to hear people use the same language about the Russians as a South African fanatic of apartheid will use about his black countrymen. A civilized and perceptive Pole will lose all these qualities at the mere mention of the word 'Russian', just as a gentle blue-eyed Boer will do when an African is under discussion. Many Poles speak of the Russians as 'cattle'; many Boers never speak of black Africans as anything but 'the creatures'. The parallel I find important because I believe there is unending danger ahead unless the world at large becomes aware of the existence of other kinds of 'apartheid' just as vicious as the South African variety, which is made unfairly to carry a censure arising out of an assumption that South Africa is unique and outside the forgivable perimeter of our common human fallibility.

So I could continue almost indefinitely with the list of primitive parallels between the African and the Russian way. In both there is a strange animism still found deep in the country, the superstitions among peasants about river, wood, earth and frost spirits – and their addiction, I was told, to archaic rituals and festive observances that are the despair of the bright commissars from the towns. There is the tendency, as in Africa, to be footloose and to be unable to endure for too long the cities and factories. Russians then will go on an unpredictable 'walkabout' as might an Australian aborigine, though the Russian will do so not on foot but by train, aeroplane and river steamer yet in the same assumption that always he will be at home with his own people in his own great country. There is too the Russian's love of talking for talking's sake, and his fantastic enjoyment and capacity for dancing. But perhaps the most important parallel of all is the battle between the new and the old in Russia and the new and the old in Africa.

It is this internal battle in Russia which seems to me to be most significant and likely to increase in scale and intensity as in the emergent Africa. It is essentially a struggle of men who want to live individually and specifically rather than collectively and generally. This for me is the underlying meaning of the conflict raging in Russia between the intellectual and artistic worlds and the State. It is the meaning, too, of the battle in Africa between tribal authority and the new educated Africans and explains the hatred of the new generation of Africans for their chiefs and tribal traditions who, together, claim to be able to rule over and think for the tribe. It is a battle which once joined has to be fought to the end for there can never be any return to a state of collective innocence. It is a battle, moreover, which can only be legitimately fought from within by those whose lives are committed to the consequences. I have no doubt that we have seen truly launched in the Soviet Union the struggle of Russian man, as distinct from the Russian people, to make the spirit of his nation contemporary as his country already is, technologically. Meanwhile it would be the most tragic of all ironies if we, under pressure from the extraordinary illusions and obsessions of our own fellow-travellers, assumed the shackles of mind and system which the young in Russia and Africa are struggling so hard to cast off. It would be, too, a betrayal of the Europeanism so desperately at bay in Russia. We can only prove an effective ally of this not by external interference but by giving full recognition of the difficulties of the task and by evolving what is best in our common European and western selves.

As important, of course, as the similarities between the Russian and African primitiveness are the differences. These are all implied in the fact that the Russians are European and primitive while in my country the native peoples are African and pagan. In Russia three generations of Soviet indoctrination has destroyed almost all evidence of religion, but one cannot travel through the width and depth of this country without being aware that in the behaviour and feeling of ordinary people something still remains of the primitive Christian concept. Authority daily and even violently denies it. But if the essence of Christian religion is, as Schweitzer put it, that 'Christianity is a reverence for life', then there are some signs of this in the new voices raised in art and literature in Russia. Today in the Christian world the awareness of what Christianity really was before the mind parcelled it out into systems is daily gaining ground and some years ago the World Council of Christian Churches meeting at Amsterdam perhaps recognized this when they defined Communism as 'a heresy but a Christian heresy'.

All this however did not spring to my mind immediately I arrived in Leningrad. After my long journey in the interior I was inclined to be suspicious of it. It looked such a complete, beautifully preserved European city that I thought it too good to be true. I was inclined to think it self-conscious and conceived as a cold act of statesmanship. Shelley wrote of Athens as 'a crest of columns gleaming in the mind of man' and I was tempted to dismiss this city as a crest of columns and spires rising from the will of man. Even the site of the city was unbelievably pitched in some of the worst marshland in the north-west of the country as if there deliberately to demonstrate Russian disdain of cost and their expertise in the art of the impossible. At first glance Leningrad appeared as if imposed upon the land and hardly less appropriate than a top hat on a Zulu. I suspected the foreign architects, who built so much of what is best in it, of having inflicted for riches, their foreign idiom of building upon the land.

Something of all this undoubtedly is present in Leningrad but of course there is a great deal more. As I walked around it daily I became more aware that the builders of the city, foreigners as well as Russians, had been overwhelmed by the significance of the occasion and caught the excitement of the breakthrough into Europe. Rastrelli, whose name insinuates the spinning, spiralling nature of his mind, Rossi, Quarenghi, Rinaldi, Brenna, de Thomson, Matarnovi, Tressini de Logano and Montferand (whose cathedral of St Isaac is the third biggest in the world and took forty years to build), conceived their works in a state of intoxication arising from the largeness of both occasion and place. Only one among them, Cameron, a Scot, kept his head and introduced buildings so obedient to classical proportion that among the others they look like a few lone Presbyterians determined to stay sober on a Scottish New Year's night. The imaginations of the Italians, in particular, spilled over easily like waterfalls. Carlo Bartolomeo Rastrelli designed a winter Palace on the Neva of 2,000,000 square feet with 1,050 rooms, 117 staircases, 1,786 doors and 1,945 windows. And all this was done on land cleared in dense marsh forest, the earth so soft that the building first had to be laid on piles driven deeply down, and then constructed with the labour of serfs driven there from all over Russia and so poorly equipped that in the beginning they had to scrape and dig the earth with their bare hands. The violence of the urge and the passion behind the will that raised this city can only be measured by reckoning with the immense poverty and suffering that went in to it. In Tsarskoe Seloe, now called the village of Pushkin, some eighteen miles away, Rastrelli designed another magnificent Palace 750 feet long, and others joined to equip the lavish gardens with Greek pavilions, statues of the gods, Roman

bath-houses, private eating-halls, gabled boathouses by the artificial lakes, Chinese pagodas and bridges, Moorish domes, a
marble column with an eagle on top rising from a steely sheet
of water – upon which today the inevitable statue of Lenin in his
chartered accountant's suit looks like a visitor from a world in
outer space. Inside the Palaces the lapis-lazuli, marble, porphyry,
green malachite, mother-of-pearl, amber, filigree bronze, quicksilver, gilt mirrors, the elaborate wood-carving of the panelling,
intricate mosaics on wooden floors, spinning rococo and whirling
baroque ceilings, crystal chandeliers, pillars, doors, chairs and
beds of gold, have to be seen to be believed. At the same time
Rastrelli and his followers, on the banks of the more fashionable
canals like the Maika, and Fontanka, built other palaces for the
aristocracy, the Yusupovs, Strogonovs, Galitzines, Sheremetievs
and so on, and raised some of the loveliest churches in the land.
These men brought with them a Mediterranean love of colour to
warm the cold light of this land where even the blue of summer is
grey with potential cold, and midnight is white as if with the
approach of arctic snow. The palaces and the churches are gay
with green, cream, beige, peacock-blue, white, pale blue, pink
and nigger-brown pastel washes straight out of southern hearts,
and they even covered the tallest of their most graceful spires
with gold to fire the astringent northern sky. Even the architect
of the Tartar Mosque – I do not remember his name – caught the
fever and decreed a stately dome which is covered with tiles as
blue and warm as any in Tamerlane's city.

Then the Tsars and the aristocracy filled these palaces with
furnishings and fashions increasingly lush. The Museums of the
Hermitage – in part of the former Winter Palace – and of The
Kremlin in Moscow, are charged with examples of the manners
their Tsars and masters set in these matters. Much of the frenzy,
splendour, fantasy and disregard of reality in Russian history
invest the objects burning in their glass cases with the colours of a
sunset flaming over a desert blighted with drought. As I remarked
to my Russian companion, I should have brought along my sun-
glasses! Dazed and amazed I looked at hundreds of damascene
sword blades and gold stilettos, saw a cape spangled with 120,000
separate pearls and brocaded and enjewelled dresses that took
two years to make, together with dozens of crowns, orbs and

sceptres, flashing with emeralds, diamonds, topaz and garnets. There were bridles for horses, the leather hidden by the gold and jewellery riveted on to them, and there were saddle blankets made out of thousands of peacock and parrot feathers! There were golden spoons and soup scoops, silver wine flagons some four feet high with necks embroidered in gold and emeralds, and a single set of two thousand silver pieces presented by Catherine the Great to but one of her several lovers. There were silver sets from the finest craftsmen of the London company of Silversmiths, embossed plates from Sweden, Dresden china of fairy-tale blue, and Sèvres porcelain from France. Evidence of a particular passion for clocks and watches is there too in staggering munificence. There is one Imperial Clock of Glory with an eagle on top feeding a brood of eaglets with a pearl every five seconds, music breaks out at intervals, while underneath doors open to reveal sunlight on a waterfall! There is a clock representing Bacchus and his Goddess celebrating on an elephant, with soldiers patrolling below beside a brilliant coach which moves forty feet in a certain cycle of time. There are coaches made in England, France, Sweden and Saxony, with a magnificence not seen in the lands of their origin; a French one had panels by Boucher and Fragonard. There is a sledge for the winter journey between Leningrad and Moscow, enclosed and fitted with glass windows, green baize seats and silver warming-pans on the floor. It took twenty-five horses to pull it and they had to be changed at regular intervals on the three days' journey. Then, of course, the feasts and parties given in these palaces matched their scale and endowment. The Marquis de Custine describes a ball given by Nicholas I in the Palace of Peter which was attended by 7,000 Russian guests alone, each guest, unless in uniform, commanded to carry a Venetian coat of silk over his arm. They arrived in 6,000 carriages and 30,000 people turned out to see the illuminations in the royal park. De Custine himself records that he had his purse picked and I thought how aptly Macaulay had caught the whole paradox of the Russian scene when he wrote of the Russians coming to court balls 'dropping pearls and vermin'.

The proliferation of what is false and distorted in Russian values is nowhere better symbolized than in the development of the painting of ikons displayed in these museums. Those nearest our own day are so changed that one can hardly believe the art was once linked to the medieval Rublyov. The Soviet Government has not hesitated to rob the Russian churches and monasteries of their finest ikons and to put copies in their place. As a result the museums provide a remarkably complete record of the national art. In the beginning, Rublyov is concerned only with his intense vision and experience of the imagery of religion and not greatly interested in the frame. But gradually the importance of the inner vision recedes, the frame becomes increasingly important, the pearls, gold, diamonds and emeralds take up more space, until finally they outcrowd the shape and outshine the colours of Redeemer, Virgin, apostle and saint. They chart accurately enough the course in which the national spirit foundered, and the point which the Soviet custodians want to make is made easily enough, without the help of official guides. Repeatedly one asks oneself how it was possible for so few people to have had so much at the expense of the many, for so long? The answer seems all the more remote when one sees in the paintings of Rembrandt, which the Russian rulers collected and cherished, a vision of life where beauty is not just an apprehension of the senses but a trumpet call to translate and transfigure art into human behaviour. Why did they not heed these and similar calls? One is inclined, as one is with the Nazi experience of Germany, to write it all off as a national aberration and abnormality of character – just as a Marxist will blame all on a particular system run by a certain class of people from which he is exempt. We all tend to assume that we are not subject to such evils. But the truth is that we are all still caught up, to a degree, in similar processes. The same destructive and discredited patterns, the same abyss between vision and behaviour, affect all of us. I was aware of this with a frightening clarity as I contemplated the Leningrad past. My only consolation was my hope that we in Europe have evolved some immunities to the disease of corruption and excess. But for all that we still remain gravely afflicted, and I cannot see us cured until those nations whose standards of living are high enough for decent self-respect, renounce further gain until the hungry, rag-and-tatter millions of Africa, Asia and South America have been brought to an equal level of material comfort and education.

Fortunately there was another side to the history of the City of

Peter. It had a serious purpose to its foundation despite the excess with which it was perpetuated. Both good and bad in the European spirit was funnelled through it into the vast hinterland with prodigality. Science, philosophy, education, the arts and skills of western Europe found an enduring home there. An observatory was built and a distinguished school of astronomy founded which indeed prepared the Russian spirit for the race to the stars. The first technological Russians, shipbuilders, industrialists, makers of lenses and clocks, the first great writers and intellects, the first rebels against despotism and the first believers in the freedom of the human spirit and conscience, appeared and were nourished there. At the time of the first Great War no corner of Russia needed the Red Revolution less than the City of Peter and it is significant that even after the fall of Imperial power this self-critical and highly conscious capital had no liking for Bolshevism. Perhaps one of the most terrifying aspects of the Bolshevik aspect of the Revolution is its utter lack of inevitability. History would not be so tragic if it had the objective inevitability that the Soviet ideologist claims. But history is always, individually or collectively, a confrontation of the spirit of man with a choice. The real inevitability of history is the need to choose, not what is chosen. And the choice had already been taken when, in the real revolutionary beginning, the peasants of Russia overthrew the Tsarist rulers. Among the hundreds of the people's real representatives gathered under Kerensky in Leningrad to organize a peaceful change, the Bolsheviks were a comparatively unknown minority when Lenin, smuggled into Russia in a German military train, arrived on the scene. By sheer force of knowing their anarchistic minds and sheer determination to inflict them on others regardless of the cost of life, he and his followers managed to steal the revolution from those who had already accomplished it and force it into its present shape. So the real warning of the revolution in Russia, full of fateful implications for us all, is that a small dedicated minority ruthlessly determined and professionally equipped was able to inflict their choice on millions of their fellow-men. And this too, of course, is the pattern the Communists and fellow-travellers among us most faithfully follow. Yet even to this day despite three generations of Revolution it seems to me that Leningrad tends to stand more apart, self-critically, from it. It has a pride and a self-respect, which, much as it amuses the patronizing Muscovites of the Capital, is rather impressive.

I met this pride the moment I arrived at the airport.

'How long are you going to stay in the city?' the guide who met me asked.

'About a week,' I answered.

'Oh, that is not nearly long enough,' he exclaimed with genuine disapproval before asking as an afterthought: 'How long have you been in Moscow?'

'Only a day and a half,' I answered mentioning only the length of the latest of my many transit stops in the capital.

His face immediately brightened and he patted me on the shoulder, commenting:

'That's about the right proportion.'

I met the independence and some of the fastidiousness of mind at my first night at the theatre where a mixed programme of Shostakovich's music, ballet and variety was staged. After the serious music and the solemn ballet, the audience found nothing incongruous in being presented with two comedians singing to a concertina a song called: 'But that's a detail'.

Here are some of the stanzas:

'We can send men flying out into space, you cannot buy safety razor blades in any city. But that's a detail.

'We can all rail against bureaucracy, yet there is no law to enable us to sack the fools in command. But that's a detail.

'You may have heard the doctors by the hundreds, are flying to the virgin lands. Have you heard they stay one night, then fly back again? But that's a detail.

'Do you know the wives are so anxious to get near their husbands on the virgin lands that they are flying to the Black Sea coast* to wait for them? But that's a detail.

'Have you heard that there are a hundred ticket collectors on the express to Sochi for every passenger? But that's a detail.

'Have you heard our cows started by giving us 300 litres of milk a day, then four, then five, then six hundred – until now their milk is almost pure water? But that's a detail.

'Do you know our journalists have just been to a prize collective farm? They saw some horns through a window and wrote how fine

* The luxury resorts some 2,000 miles from the virgin lands.

the collective bulls were. They were only cows. But that's a detail.'

This little breath of satire drew the loudest and largest applause of any of them on the programme.

It seemed to me characteristic also that Leningrad should have been the first to try and improve on the mean little ceremony which the system allows for marriage and to institute the first real Palace of Weddings in the land. Some of the most depressing sights of my journey were the wedding parties given in the hotels where I stayed. They might have been designed to illustrate Froissart's slanted remark about the Russians: '*Ils s'amusent moult tristement*'. The young man in his best suit, hair shining with oil; the young woman in her party frock, sometimes daring a little white artificial satin dress and a spray of synthetic lilies in the hand, would appear in our midst, surrounded by a small group of friends and relations. They would sit down at a long table piled high with food and start eating. Russians have a tendency to fall silent with awe in the presence of a feast and break out of the hypnotic moment only when the wine and the vodka have taken effect. But the silence on these occasions seemed heavier than most. I had told my Russian friends what I thought of these celebrations and how out of character they appeared to me and they had admitted there was justification for the criticism but urged me to go to the new Palace of Weddings in Leningrad for evidence of change.

So there accordingly I went one Saturday afternoon when the streets were empty of people but full of pale sunlight striking the gold arrow of Peter and Paul and the spike over the Admiralty against the surface of the sky: the 'Palace' itself stood in a row of grey-stone houses built for the vanished aristocracy and was once the home of a count. Some rather shabby taxis were huddled outside and on the river below the windows the trim cadets from the naval academy were practising their rowing. As we entered the massive doorway a busy noise like that of a village bazaar reached us. On our left several elaborate doors opened into rooms turned into shops where anything from wedding rings to umbrellas, cakes and Georgian champagne were on sale. Some of the largest rooms there and on the floor above were available for receptions and in one a table, underneath a crystal chandelier, was already set up for a celebration.

'You see how practical it is,' the Leningrad girl with us told me:

'You can come here with nothing and buy everything you need for a wedding and go straight on and be married without leaving the premises.'

It was clearly an improvement on what had gone before so I did not say that it reminded me of nothing more than a self-service wedding store or nuptial cafeteria.

'And look at that marble staircase!' The girl pointed to a wide stairway in front of us with an elaborately carved marble balustrade. Four pagan goddesses in various degrees of *déshabille* that no Commissar of Culture would tolerate in present-day sculpture, and in far from socially realistic or useful poses, looked down at us from the walls. 'An American millionaire tried to buy that staircase from us but of course we refused to part with so valuable a cultural property for mere money,' my informant added.

I was not surprised for only a few hours before in the lovely summer garden the same young woman had drawn my attention to the superb gratings designed for it by Yuri Veldten and Yegerov and remarked: 'You know just after the revolution when we were desperately short of food and trains to bring it to us, the Americans offered Lenin eighteen locomotives for these railings! But of course he refused!'

So does the American ghost trouble the Russian conscience.

On the top floor we found half a dozen couples and their friends waiting to be married. Only one bride was in white but they all seemed stimulated by the building in which they found themselves. The Commissar of Weddings called from the door and then gravely gave us permission to enter the room and attend, so as the two newly weds came out of one door we followed the couple and party of seven in at the other.

The Commissar and her deputy, both women, were seated at a large office desk at the far end of the room which still wore its opulent nineteenth-century décor and looked totally unrelated to the occasion. Both officials were dressed in sober grey gaberdine suits, thick woollen stockings and tough black walking shoes with low heels. There was no concession of colour or flowers to the business of the moment. The couple and their friends had hardly formed up in front of the desk when the senior official addressed them:

'Comrades, this is a very important day in your lives, in the life of your friends and relations, and to our Marxist-Leninist State. I hope you have reflected on the seriousness of the step you are about to take. I beg you henceforth to be good and helpful and kind to each other and to live a married life worthy of our State. If you are sure you can do that I will ask you to come forward and, in accordance with our Marxist-Leninist constitution, sign the contract of marriage.'

The young couple stepped forward and signed the document laid before them.

'I now declare you married,' the commissar said briskly. 'And will ask the assistant-deputy commissar of marriage to hand you the sealed contract of marriage.'

The broad-shouldered woman marched out from behind the desk with the step of a hockey full-back going into the attack, gave the man the scroll and wrung them each by the hand. The group of friends applauded and a loudspeaker started to broadcast from a radiogram a rendering of Strauss' 'Blue Danube'. At the same time the doors were thrown open and with an imperative gesture we were waved out of the room by the assistant deputy-commissar of weddings just as the next couple came in at the other. We did not follow the party below but went to the windows at the head of the stairs and watched them pile into two taxis which drove away at great speed along the banks of the dark river and out into that strangely impersonal and indifferent northern afternoon.

I found myself both distressed and angry about the incident. It seemed a betrayal of life and I felt the groups of young people with their open, lively, fresh faces, deserved something better. Even the most primitive of peoples make more of a show of marriage than that. It is, after all, one of the three great stages in life where man needs a demonstrable recognition of the importance of what is happening to him and I found myself thinking of Pasternak's lines in his poem *The Wedding Party*.

> And life itself is only an instant,
> Only the dissolving
> Of ourselves in all others,
> As though in gift to them;
> Only a wedding, bursting
> In through the windows from the street,
> Only a song, a dream
> A grey-blue pigeon.

Pasternak was promptly denounced for indulging in 'useless, subjective emotions' but all the same he was laying bare, as this wedding had just done for me, a whole range of experience and awareness which the Soviet system denies, and for which life in Russia is poorer than that of the aboriginal Bushman in the Kalahari Desert.

As the taxis vanished I asked the young woman with us: 'What sort of dress would you like to wear for a wedding?'

'Oh, white of course.'

My companion from Moscow smiled and said, 'She would of course living in Leningrad!'

'One with a long train, veil, flowers and bridesmaids?' I asked.

The girl blushed scarlet and said, 'No, I fear that would be excessive. I would have a short white dress – but not as short as the one we saw just now.'

'And music? Would you not prefer music and a ceremony in church?'

'Music would be lovely,' she answered. 'But no ceremony in church, thank you. I am not a Christian.'

This last remark was spoken like a lesson learned at school. I say this because I found in the days that followed that she was not as indifferent to churches as her remark might have suggested. Consciously she rejected religion as the State expected every good Communist to do and she was as scathing about it in her remarks as anyone I had met. Yet her emotions were curiously engaged by it. For instance, one day at The Hermitage, she suddenly said to me: 'I would like to show you my favourite painting of Christ.'

She took me to Poussin's tremendous painting of the crucifixion wherein the calm, classical manner and the cool lucid colours belie the passion of his perception.

'Why do you like that best?' I asked.

'Because he is painted there not as a suffering weakling,' she answered, 'but as a strong man who looks above his sorrow and is capable of getting things done.'

Rembrandt's painting of the parables, too, interested her as much and though the ideology of her country compelled her to view Christ as having been merely one of the first Communists, I suspected her and her generation of being occupied with their own reappraisal of these things. There is, for instance, the poem by Boris Slutsky, one of the three poets chosen to read examples of their work to 14,000 people in a sports stadium, while I was there. He wrote:

> Rublyov, when he took the vows
> was scarcely an unbeliever.
> He fell on his knees
> before the Word – the one
> that was in the Beginning.
> And what's the point
> of trying to turn
> his archangels into peasants?
> He was saved not by a swineherd
> (symbolizing Labour)
> but quite simply
> > by the Saviour.
> So we'll have to give up
> yet another atheist in the making;
> the spirit of the Dove, you see,
> hovered over him
> and he was meek
> and mild.
> No, he didn't wear a jacket
> under his monastic habit!*

My companion too, even had a good word in passing for Picasso. The Soviet State finds the work of this dedicated communist a considerable embarrassment. They dare not disown him because his adherence to Communism gives it prestige. At the same time they are appalled by his prolonged excursion into abstract painting and his general disregard of social realism. I have no doubt that were he living in Russia, they would make him toe the Soviet academic line. But this young lady thought differently. She saw him reaching out into something new which, even though she could not understand it she thought should be encouraged. She was also almost the first person I had met in the Soviet Union who understood why I wanted to go to church on Sunday. Many of the official guides had been genuinely puzzled by this and invariably asked: 'But why on a Sunday? Can't we take you on a Monday or Tuesday? It would be much more convenient for us and more comfortable for you.' But this girl under_

* From the translation by Max Hayward in *Encounter*, April 1963.

stood and offered to take me to the Church of St Nicholas: she
went there herself, she explained, twice a year, not for devotions
but for the music and singing. She said the Bach and Tchaikovsky
music heard in the context for which it was created was far more
moving than in any opera house or concert hall.

I had never been in a church like this green and white baroque
church, hard by a canal as tranquil as any water in the Heeren-
gracht of Amsterdam. It was packed with people, although it was
a church on two storeys. On the ground floor two quite different
ceremonies were taking place: on the left people were queueing up
and jostling one another in a feverish way, not even to be seen at
the Sports Stadium, in order to get to the font to have their babies
baptized. On the right, four old men were lying in open coffins
amid masses of madonna lilies and about to have the funeral
service said over them. Groups of relations, mostly middle-aged
and old, stood round the coffins weeping without attempt to hide
their tears.

'I warned you,' the young woman whispered to me, 'that you'd
find mostly old people in the church.' She indicated the mourners
round the coffins.

'But all those babies!' I protested. 'Besides, I saw a number of
very young couples at the font.' Indeed the crush there, I noticed,
had increased quite a bit since our arrival.

'That's only because their parents force them to do it,' she
countered.

We left the ground floor then so movingly occupied with the
rituals concerning both the entrance into life and its departure,
and climbed up a wide staircase to a floor given over entirely to
the main congregation. The floor was packed with people standing between the slender columns and the air was brilliant with
the light of hundreds of candles, the vivid colours of the embroidered satin of the priests' clothes, and the flashing of jewelled
crosses. By comparison the day coming through the far windows
was dark and I felt as if I were standing in the centre of a Rembrandt picture at some lightened Pentecostal celebration in a
medieval temple. The service, too, was being performed as much
by the congregation as the priests with whom they were like a
single orchestra of many players joined to render a single trans-
cendent chorale of Bach. In fact there was music in everything

and never have I heard such singing. The difference between the bleak, iconoclastic Protestant services to which I had been taken as a child, even the Anglican and Roman Catholic services I have attended all over the world, was striking. Here was a demonstration of a church as '*Sobor*' (the gathering of which I have spoken), made magnetic with '*Sobornost*' (togetherness), which was overwhelming and inclusive even for a stranger. For myself I have found no church services so moving as those in a country, which, like Russia, has officially abolished not only God but all the gods. In this church in Leningrad it seemed possible to recapture all the impact of the original breakthrough of Christianity which became the vital part of man's equipment if his journey on earth was to be accomplished, not perhaps without disaster and unhappiness, but with meaning.

Outside I said something of this to the young woman but she shook her head. 'I am an atheist,' she insisted: 'I cannot take part in such superstitions. But the music and the singing were wonderful.'

At that very moment a young man in teddy-boy uniform, a manifest '*stilyaga*', came running through the gates into the churchyard carrying a baby in his arms. Behind him out of breath, panting and wobbling on high-heeled shoes came his moll, the mother of his child. Neither of them looked over twenty-one and their anxiety to be in time for the mass baptism in the church could not have been more obvious.

'You could hardly call that couple old!' I teased my young companion.

Obviously taken aback this articulate girl was silent for quite a time while she stared after them. Then she shrugged her shoulders exclaiming, 'Well, what do you expect of teddy-boys anyway!'

After my visit to Riga and Leningrad I wanted to round off my journey with a fortnight in Moscow, and so as always I tried and succeeded, in getting into one of the two older hotels founded at the beginning of the century, the National and the Metropole. One is inclined to ascribe their improvements to the fact that they were smaller and so more personal and individual but I think there is a more subtle reason. The memory of what they once had been before the Revolution still hangs about the atmosphere of the establishments like the polarized needle of a compass keeping a ship on course. The Revolution, for all its claims to the contrary, has not abolished the past: at the most it has suspended it. The more I came to know Russia the more I was aware of the magnetic attraction of what was memorable in the past functioning as a growing influence below the manifest surface.

But how different Moscow now looked from my first view of it weeks before! I wondered how I could ever have thought its citizens dowdy for the women now looked relatively gay in their bright summer dresses and the men seemed almost brisk. 'You should have seen the Muscovites as we first saw them seventeen years ago,' the wife of a diplomat told me. 'The improvement in taste and variety of fashions are incredible to us, and every day the people become more demanding. Do you know I have a dressmaker, a modest woman who doesn't earn much, yet she insists on having her own special nail varnish made up for her. I have not met anything like it before – not even in Paris.' Yet I still held to my first impression of Moscow as a 'village' and still thought it a parochial capital perhaps because I was continually dazzled by the vision of Peter's great city which so utterly lacked Moscow's homely appearance. But on my travels I had picked up something of the Russian identification with Moscow which qualified this basic impression. There is no doubt that, as in Chekhov's *The Three Sisters*, all the roads of Russian feeling still lead to Moscow. The mystique of Moscow still exists.

The situation to which Moscow owes its origin and ascendancy – placed like a spider in its web at the centre of a mesh of river and other historical roads – is duplicated in the emotions of the people. I remember an able and progressive African paramount chief once vetoing a scheme for the benefit of his people because it would cut off all the innumerable little footpaths which wound through the bush like the lines in the palm of his hand.

'But they're never used any more,' I protested with astonishment.

'That may be so,' he replied. 'But the people like to feel they are there. If they were cut off from these little paths, their hearts would be like that of a young calf weaned too soon from its mother.'

It is in this deeper, instinctive sense of what a capital can mean that Moscow now impressed me. It is a central point where all the nuances of Russian character can meet. For most Russians it may be unattainable as it was for the languishing sisters in Chekhov's play, but they need to feel it is there even if only as a focal point for their misery. So when I was inclined to think of Leningrad as the head of the land I had to correct myself and realize that Moscow is the solar-plexus joined by an invisible, umbilical cord to the history which has given birth to this great family of a nation which is Greater Russia.

This impression was stimulated and maintained by the hours I spent at the Kremlin. Used as I was by now to being tossed about between the magnanimity and the pettiness of the system I was overwhelmed by the freedom with which I was allowed to wander alone, except for a guide, sometimes for a whole day, through the innermost buildings of this ancient fortress. The lights were turned on in the immense crystal chandeliers of the State rooms, galleries and boudoirs and kept burning while the two of us went slowly through the Imperial Palace, dazzled and enchanted, like men who had fallen through a pothole in the road of time to find themselves in some Aladdin's cave of history. Outwardly, the Kremlin looks an incongruous pile of shapes, styles and colours but inwardly it assumes a strange consistency as if it were not architecture but rather some geological formation of history wherein the elements that have shaped Russian destiny are deposited, layer upon layer with chronological precision, just as the formation of the earth is recorded in the strata of its rocks. Even the Hall of Congress of the Soviets, the most successful and impressive modern building in Moscow standing there behind the burning red brick ramparts and beneath the gold bubble domes no longer looked remote when we saw it again on emerging, but curiously belonging to the golden rooms of the Tsars. This effect was brought about by the absolute manner in which the shape of the building was determined by its function, a single hall in one building serving a greater number of Russians than ever before. Eight thousand people can be seated in comfort in the main theatre. I sat there twice with just such audiences and yet so right were all the proportions that the Hall did not look even crowded. The stairs, escalators, corridors and doors are so designed that in the intervals one can move easily from the ground floor to the restaurants above and, after refreshment, walk leisurely along broad promenades walled in with glass, and see, level with one's eyes, the spires of the churches, the ancient crosses, crescents, domes, five-pointed stars and, indeed, the television aerials too, rippling in the limpid light of a lucid summer evening like coral shapes in a great aquarium.

The Russians have developed a special talent for handling huge masses of people without apparent effort, as in this hall. But so too the whole of the Hall of Soviet Congress is a continuation of a political and cultural '*sobor*' which, however indeterminate it was in its beginnings, was also pursued by the founders of the Kremlin themselves. Yet perhaps the most impressive of all the buildings belonging to the Kremlin complex is the Church of St Basil, built by Ivan the Terrible. Some intuition suggested that here in bricks and mortar was a complete statement of all that was invisible and searching in the Russian spirit. I contemplated it daily as one might study some cypher for which the key was missing. My first reaction was to lose patience with the building and dismiss it as mad. Of course the imagination which decreed it was so mad that Ivan the Terrible put out the eyes of his architect in order to prevent him from repeating the creation. But that does not detract from the significance of the challenge to one's imagination presented by this extraordinary edifice, for the follies of history are so often merely a collapse of reason under the weight of a blinding vision of life experienced out of time and hence impatiently served out of season. At first glance one can read a splendid distortion of fact and a magnificent disdain or reality in the creation of the church of St Basil. It has no obvious symmetry, and its spires, domes and doorways are all of different styles and shapes. All the varied influences that had ever impinged on Russian life are present; Greek, Roman, Byzantine, Arab, Tartar and Gothic architecture is piled upon and around it. Even a hint of Babylon, Assyria and Scythia intrudes among the walls. No two domes are alike in height, shape or decoration. One is covered with gold, blue and green bands of plaster curving upwards to a single point so that it looks like a top spinning against the blue. Another remains in the shaft of its spire under the weight of a mosaic of tiles crossing it horizontally in zigzags of white and red. A third bristles with colourful greenish pointed stucco like a hedgehog. A fourth combines something of all the other three. Hard by them are Gothic spires and spits of different heights piled on varying pagan foundations. Not a single spire is of consistent

shape throughout and no two conform to the same colour scheme.
Each one seems to suggest a complete system of individual building
and appears within its labyrinthine ways and grotesquely alternating levels ill-fitted for coherent worship. But in the middle of this
wheeling, reeling system which combines all the prodigal trends
and elements of history stands one tall triumphant spire looking
like a tower of medieval Europe and ending in a round Russian
turret of gold drawn to point a single cross at the massive sky.

Gradually as one becomes familiar with this church, the apparent lack of symmetry begins to make sense and to act within
one's imagination like the impurity within the shell of an oyster
round which a rare pearl grows. Though this building possesses
no immediate symmetry it implies with passion a profound and
organic meaning. It has a firm, still centre round which all the
colourful disorder spins. Considering the darkness, horror, and
madness of the moment in which this Church was conceived it
nevertheless conveyed to me some awareness of the urgent
necessity of making whole the many and varied fragments of the
past, the boundless possibilities, conflicting trends, the paradoxes
and tensions of this immense land and its people. As I surveyed
it the past, present, and the future too, were there before me as in
a symbol so vivid that it could awake the sleeper from his dream.
Indeed the man who built it had done for Russia what the architects of the Renaissance did for Europe. This was an original
statement of a purely Russian Renaissance, a re-awakening that
has already taken many bewildering, cruel and contradictory
forms and, even so, has hardly yet begun.

But looking outward beyond the mystique of Moscow as a
whole there are two worlds around which life revolves: the first
is the area around the Kremlin; the second is the world of the
new University in the Lenin Hills where the scientific and technical faculties of the Institution are housed.

I had only to visit the theatres, ballet, art galleries, exhibitions
and bookshops, all inflexibly controlled by the Kremlin, to be continually amazed at how out of date is the mind and spirit of
official Russia. The ballet would be danced superbly. In particular
is it a joy to see men dancing with something of the primitive
qualities of which I have spoken at their creative best, for here in
Russia man dances with primitive and instinctive authority and

belief in his natural pre-eminence in the choreography of life. But the content of the ballets seem to be remarkably old-fashioned and artificial. For instance, I saw one of the more recent ballets, *Spartacus* which, with its theme of the rebellion of slaves against their decadent Roman masters, always has a special attraction. A Russian who saw it with me said: 'I feel as if I am watching something happening right in our own time and not nineteen hundred years ago.' He was drawing the moral that the State meant him to draw and it was useless to try and persuade him that, ethically, the ballet was as out of date as the music written for it by Khachaturian. For today there is not a single western European nation which has not long since taken the point to heart and is not now trying to deal with the corruption caused in its social structure and spirit by those who in the past have had the power and the glory. Indeed, we have long since passed the point of no-return in this shedding of power over less privileged classes and peoples, and the contemporary problem now is how to shed power without setting up new and cruder forms of tyranny and exploitation. The slave become Roman master is the problem that will confront us more and more squarely in the future. I said something of this sort to my companion and he sadly commented that I was as deeply soaked in corrupt *bourgeois* thinking as a piece of blotting-paper with ink! Yet I was to meet another young student for whom the ballet and its music had become a boomerang and who said that the Roman master was Stalin and his accomplices, and the slaves were the Russian mind and spirit.

Together with the ballet the theatre too seemed to be a heavy spender of the capital of its past. Old plays, even old novels and stories adapted for the theatre, seemed to make up its fare. A middle-aged Russian poet of the establishment pointed out to me the anti-Stalin theatre as an example of how free the Russian artist was to criticize. I replied that, valuable as post-mortems may be they are no substitute for diagnosis of sickness in the living body. The criticism would have been far more important had it been made in Stalin's lifetime. Living criticism is a commonplace of western societies and needs no special courage to exercise it. His reply was that Russian people were not ready for such criticism: and then he launched into a dissertation of the overriding importance of Marxist-Leninist truth over all other forms of truth.

I had no wish to denigrate the immense importance of the agonizing reappraisal of Stalinism that has now been going on in Russia for seven years. Nor do I overlook the fact that the young have given this post-mortem its contemporary point by trying to convert it into an instrument for preventing the system from ever contracting into another Stalinist convulsion of terror. The most notable example of this is in Yevtushenko's poem: *The Heirs of Stalin*, which was finally published only after the young poet had agreed to some censorship. With this and many other examples going on around one on increasing scale and intensity, I had the impression that Russia really is trying to examine and deal with this period in its history both openly and honestly. It is important also to realize that the initiative to expose Stalin came from the Kremlin itself and was political in its origin though the initiative for transforming the revelation into a genuine means of liberating the life and spirit of people comes from the intellectuals. But even acknowledging all this does not hide the gulf between what passes for criticism in Moscow and the criticism that we take for granted in Western Europe and America. The poet whom I have mentioned thought our kind of criticism morbid self-indulgence and a sign of social decay. Self-criticism, to one like himself revolving around the Kremlin, was criticism designed only to make a man aware of how he had failed the Soviet party and its system, and the papers were full enough of examples of this, factory managers, party secretaries and collective farm chairmen publicly flagellating themselves for having fallen short on their prescribed quotas. That the individual, standing fast in his differences with authority, could be of greater value to the community than the men who jumped instantly to the crack of the party whip, made no sense to him. Of course, he admitted, there could be argument – but it had to be argument ready to accept the infallibility of the Party.

The official Soviet view on art is that it has to point the appropriate social moral preferably in pictures which tell recognizable stories. The painters who have State approval remind me of the men responsible for the reproductions which crowded our nursery at home at the beginning of the century: *The Boyhood of Raleigh*, *The Death of Nelson*, and so on. But how inverted the moral. The approved Russian rendering of the picture 'When did you last see

your Father?' (the little Cavalier boy in satin breeches refusing to
answer his Roundhead inquisitors) presumably would be a young
pioneer with a red kerchief round his neck being thanked by the
Ogpu for having told them exactly where his father was hiding.
Even the vocabulary of the approved critics is curiously Victorian:
'art has to be uplifting', etc. etc. Life is divided into artistic and
non-artistic themes, paintable and unpaintable subjects, and
nothing that is not socially good can be beautiful. Not for them
any of this *bourgeois* nonsense of taking upon themselves a
mystery that is in all things and seeing in all visible and invisible
objects a paintable medium. Art as an instrument of increasing
awareness seems to them inconceivable. For them the vision is
already there, complete and absolute, and it only remains for the
citizen-painter to serve it with skill and obedience. Anyone who
tries to depart from this rule meets the savage reaction to be expected from a people who have neglected the visual arts as much
as the Russians have. The sort of immunity which a nation-wide
love and instinctive understanding of music confers to some extent
on the composer does not apply to the painter. All sorts of Soviet
Ruskins arise to denounce him and the passion and the language
they use, drawing on phrases like 'painted by a donkey with its
tail' or 'the work of gorillas aping the anthropoids of *bourgeois*
capitalist zoos' makes one think of Ruskin's attack of Whistler:
'a coxcomb with the effrontery to fling a pot of paint in the
public's face'. The great difference is that Whistler could sue
Ruskin for libel, win his case, and go on painting. The artist so
pilloried in Russia has no such redress.

Even more primitive is the spirit of the law that emanates from
this world gathered around the Kremlin. We remembered with
horror the early Victorians who could hold property so sacred
that a hungry person was hanged for stealing a sheep. Here not
only the nation's property but money itself is held so sacred that
a man can be shot for just changing a fifty-rouble note in the
black market exchange. I had a slight but significant glimpse of
the legal values of this world when I went to a people's court near
the Kremlin to see how the system of justice worked. I watched
the trial of the manager of a small food-store, accused of embezzlement. The case was so trivial that it was not even reported
in the newspapers and the trial as far as I could judge fair enough.

After the adjournment I spoke to the judge, prosecutor and probation officer (a retired old locomotiveman) who all had done their work with dignity and calm.

'Of course,' the judge remarked modestly, 'we do not deal with serious charges here. They all go to the Supreme Court.'

'What do you call a serious charge?' I asked, expecting murder or rape at least to figure among the first of his examples.

'Oh, breaches of the Currency regulations and taking part in the Propaganda war,' he replied.

Yet the background to all this provides another major paradox. In general the State has abolished private property as evil and claims that since all belongs to the people through the State, by doing this it has dealt evil itself a mortal blow. But I have never been in a country where embezzlement, black-marketeering, bribery, corruption and stealing from the State were such a feature of the daily news. In a sense everywhere in the world the government is fair game to the citizen who will tend to poach discreetly on its preserves, if only to try and smuggle a packet of cigarettes through the customs or to pay as little income tax as possible. But, judging by the Press, in the Soviet Union it goes far beyond this and the mystique of 'all-belonging' which was such a feature of the Russian character appeared not to operate as far as the property of the State was concerned. Perhaps if 'all belongs to all' then equally all is fair game for all.

What is even more disquieting and more archaic, is that the law is a major instrument of political policy. Not for it any of the British, American and Western European nonsense that the State itself is subordinate to the laws it has made. However fair, humane and on the whole disinclined to sit in judgement on one another the Russians might be, the State can and does at any moment take the dispensation of justice into its own hands and direct its course to suit a trend of policy. Thus one of the most distressing features of the cases of currency infringement which came up for trial while I was in Russia was the deliberate attempt to attach all blame on the Jews. The trouble is that systems which claim infallibility, as does the Soviet system, cannot do without scapegoats. Since it cannot itself be wrong it can only be wronged. So, like a primitive despot, it is forever sending its 'witch-doctors' far and wide through the land to smell out persons on whom it can blame the national afflictions. I fear it appears as if, within the State, the Russian Jews are cast for playing the sacrificial role which the capitalist societies play in the world without. For anti-semitism, despite the fact that it is against the Marxist-Leninist ideology, exists violently and both wide and deep in Russia.

However, in the second world of intellect and technology of which I take the university to be a symbol, it is impressive how the system is being reappraised and challenged. It is characteristic of a system so conscious of the importance of education and still smarting from the wounds inflicted by its neglect in the past, that it should have made the new university building the highest in the city. The statistics alone are impressive: over 17,000 students, nearly 2,000 laboratories, 1,500 rooms, 65 miles of corridors, 115 lifts, not to mention several cinemas, swimming pools, cafeterias and libraries full of Russian and foreign books. In such a position the new building dominates the skyline of the city, glowing from afar like a pile of new Sunlight soap. But inside away from the main staircases and behind the gilt, bronze, marble, granite, por-phyry and alabaster, it is another story. The old indifference to detail emerges again and the woodwork is rough, the staircases and floors worn away at a rate that should not have been possible. Yet one has only to look at the faces of the students as they spill out of their lecture rooms or to speak to them in common rooms to realize that if the world around the Kremlin can be compared to a power-house, then this technological and intellectual com-plex is the foremost transformer in a great system spread through-out the land, and the briefest of contacts with individual writers, artists and scientists is enough to suggest that the rigid old system is becoming more fluid and flexible. I was amazed to find how shallow was the impact of two generations of revolution on the values of the young. In so far as they feel deeply about their State it is out of love of their country and people, and not out of love of its ways and means. They were intensely patriotic and are proud of Russia's achievements with a passion that can be under-stood only in terms of inferiority over the backwardness which had haunted Russian lives for long, incoherent centuries. Meeting more and more of the new Russians I understood why they called the Second World War the 'Great Patriotic War', and ignored our saving part in it, for in that war the Russians found themselves as a people more completely than ever before in their history. Even the system, so rigid and unpalatable to me, has emerged for them as something far more representative than anything they have ever enjoyed before. I felt that the young were most fortunate in that their revolution was truly over and they were free in their minds and hearts to begin their own reformation. This may not sound as important as I feel it to be for we are apt to think of historical events as short-term happenings. Conventional history implies that the French Revolution ended with Napoleon Bonaparte's defeat. Yet I believe the French Revolution is not over yet and that events in France since the Encyclopaedists only make sense when seen as a process of change in the French spirit with which they have not yet come to terms. Lincoln, Sherman, Lee, Stonewall Jackson are all dead and the fighting ended yet I do not think the Civil War in America is by any means over. But the very remarkable thing about the revolution in Russia is that to me it does seem to be over and to such an extent that the imagination and emotions of the young now are rather bored by it. This, perhaps, is one of the reasons I think why the old writers and artists feel so bitter about the so-called 'thaw' and the new trends among the 'ungrateful' young, and why they stand at bay, like old bulls in danger of being driven away from the herd that they feel they have protected from so many dangers. In Russia the young accept fully the necessity for their revolution – but that is all. More and more they seem anxious to get away from it as if it had been some terrible interruption of their natural evolution which they want to take up again from where it left off. I thought their emerging values owed much to pre-revolutionary Russia for they love and read Tolstoy, Turgenev, Chekhov, Dostoievsky, Pushkin, Lermontov and so on with great devotion as if their sense of affinity with pre-revolutionary Russia were both real and great. Among the living writers those who seem to influence them most are persons like Konstantin Paustovsky and Nikolai Aseyev, whose lives have circumscribed the whole cycle of revolution and whose imaginations were formed in the pre-revolutionary world. The values by which nations live and have their meaning are of long and obstinate growth. They may be consciously denied and yet go on shaping the very spirits which attack them. The European atheist can reject Christian religion and yet is compelled if he wants to sleep at nights, to live an ethic which could not exist but for the faith that he denies by day. So it seemed to me that in Russia the values of the individual (not of course of the State) are those of the ancient Christian and primitive European Russia which Lenin and Stalin thought to have destroyed forever. I do not mean to imply that the Russians are 'pro-European', and that this is a political phenomenon. Rather it is a reawakening of an instinctive feeling of kinship, and a sharpening of the awareness of belonging, by right of birth, to the great complex of the European spirit. Politically the new Russian is a loyal animal and out of his almost mystical feeling of all-belonging to the great Russian complex will still surrender conscience and heart to the State. But in matters of taste, mind, and personal feelings increasingly he tries to follow his European heart. Frank conversation between his European self and others is not possible. But whispering behind the Iron Curtain is constant and intense. Already he finds it quite natural to stress the importance of an artist, scientist or writer he admires by telling his Russian contemporaries: 'His work is known in the West!' Most significant of all his interpretation of his own patriotism seems to incline to the classical European pattern. He is beginning to believe it his patriotic duty not blindly to follow the political lead but to criticize and even to resist. For instance, when Yevtushenko attacks anti-Semitism as he does in *Babiy Yar*, it is clear he does so not only out of personal conviction but for the honour and good of Russia. Nothing could be plainer than the proud conclusion:

> No Jewish blood runs among my blood,
> But I am as bitterly and hardly hated
> By every anti-semite
> As if I were a Jew. By this,
> I am a Russian.*

Similarly the scientist and the technologist whose success and efficiency depend on the regard for objective truth which so increasingly characterized post-Renaissance Europe, finds it difficult to divest himself of the habits produced in political and other non-technological fields. It is hard to imagine the contemporary scientist accepting that his science too is subordinate to the laws of

* From the translation by Levi and Milner-Gulland (Penguin, 1962).

Marxist-Leninist doctrine – as he had to under Stalin in the infamous Lysenko incident over the Mendelian law. The politician may still strive to reconcile scientific truth with his Leninist revelation, just as Victorian England insisted on scientific validity being subject to Old Testament standards and rejected Darwin's theory of the Origin of Species on pentateuchal evidence. But the contemporary scientist clearly has no further interest in the matter. The taste for the whole truth, long denied satisfaction at the front door of the System, has now found nourishment and is growing lusty on scraps fed to it at many a back-door entrance. Changes in industry and commerce too are immense, and the shedding of their abstract and ideological shackles has already gathered a resounding momentum which everywhere brings its influence to bear, even in the small foreign community in Moscow. This community consists of newspapermen and diplomats and their families, sealed off from the normal life of Moscow in the most arbitrary and merciless way. They live either in their embassies with Russian militiamen constantly on duty at the gates or in quarters allocated to them by the Soviet authorities, also guarded. In Moscow itself they can move about freely to visit one another, go to the theatre and ballet and do their shopping. They are free, theoretically, to call on their Russian friends but in practice the freedom amounts to nothing because they have no Russian friends. An Ambassador, well-liked and respected by the Russians, told me that at the end of his term he had made friends only with his Russian gardener. All their other relationships are official. These admittedly had greatly increased since Stalin's day. In Stalin's post-war days a score of Russian guests would have been counted a shower of good will. But I went to a reception at the British Embassy attended by eleven hundred Russians. Yet so deep is the political antagonism and suspicion of the outside world that the foreign community are in quarantine as if for pest. And outside Moscow the quarantine is even stricter. Diplomats are free to move at will in a radius of some fifty miles around Moscow provided they notify the Soviet Foreign Office of time and destination. I myself on a harmless excursion to a monastery near Moscow with two friends of mine from the British Embassy saw the special police on duty at every cross-road, checking the number of our car and seeing that we did not stray from the main road. No wonder the foreign community has practically developed a persecution mania and many of its inhabitants leave their posts exhausted and discouraged. Even a visitor like myself could not help being affected by the suspicion and counter-suspicion in the air. But the commercial attachés at the various Embassies seem to be, relatively, an exception to this rule. Because of the immense changes in commerce the distance between them and their Russian opposite number is not great. They meet regularly and, unlike their colleagues in the political branches, achieve concrete results. More, they have a great deal of respect for the ability and thoroughness of the men in Soviet industry and commerce with whom they had to deal. One must never forget that in the first recorded beginnings the Russians emerge as traders and this instinct and capacity persists and is an important element tending to transform the system.

In this connexion I found it significant too that among the first to pick up the scent of change are some of the descendants of the old Moscow and Leningrad traders. Forced to flee the country with their families during the revolution and take shelter where they could find it now they have discovered they can safely play a useful and profitable role as commercial travellers between the Soviet Union and the outside world. I met three such men who all assured me that they had been able to return without risk of encountering any animosity. 'Beyond the system,' one of them told me, 'the Russians have become the same people again. It's amazing how little they've changed in themselves. You'd be surprised by the numbers of *emigrés* who now regularly visit the country some, like us, to foster trade, others to get books to translate, music to publish, films to show, and to be useful to ourselves and Russia in a dozen different ways.' His great difficulty, he continued, was to get his European clients to appreciate the scale of Russia's needs and the largeness of her material vision. If she wanted machines it was never in dozens but thousands! Europe had never before been in direct touch with a market of such dimensions and would have to alter its responses if we were not to be put out of business.

I said I thought one of the American difficulties too was a certain failure to recognize the importance of 'thinking small'.

He took me by the arm and remarked: 'You never said a truer

word. I know America well and we and the Americans are in many ways terribly alike.'

That a man with his history could spontaneously talk of Soviet Russians and himself as 'we' was not the least of the many pointers I came across which indicate that the revolution is receding from Russian minds and hearts.

Then in this new intellectual world there are also painters, writers and artists. Whatever the State and Party might demand of them they have their own ideas of their duty on their art. However much Mr Khrushchev rails against the evils of abstractionism in art there are many young painters in Moscow alone who quietly go on painting their way their talent demands. Painters like Malevich, Kandinsky and Chagall are specially dear to them and they have the greater scorn for the literal painting of the social realists. One of them, at the mere mention of Serov, the Head of the Soviet Academy of Art, made a mock sign to me that he was going to be sick! Among these young, the interest in the pure form, patterns and images communicated within directly from life itself is as great as if they too wanted to start with their own vision. It is significant too that some of the most gifted young painters quietly and in relative secrecy are concentrating for the first time in the history of Russian art on self-portraiture. It is as if thereby they recognize the supreme need in Russian man to discover his individual self so neglected in the primitive practice of collective values. The agony and loneliness of such a search seemed to me implicit in the best of these paintings. Yet the beginning of all things is inevitably Euclidian: A mere point which had no size or magnitude but only position in the human spirit. Once in position, however, nothing can prevent it from growing into its own fullness in time.

There are other signs, too, of the great change firmly positioned in the Russian spirit, both in literature and drama and particularly in poetry. Here a state of open war exists between the new and the political authority. Over and over again it has seemed that the State is about to suppress the most active of the liberal spirits engaged in thawing the ice in the minds and emotions of their countrymen. At the time of the Hungarian revolution Mr Khrushchev summoned the foremost writers to a party at his villa, told them that much suffering could have been avoided in

Hungary if the government had possessed the good sense to shoot a few liberal Hungarian writers in time, and added 'his hand would not tremble' if the need for similar action arose in the Soviet Union. Yet after a while both old and new protagonists re-emerged and the war seemed to me to be still raging as fiercely but perhaps more subtly than before. There was, for instance, Yevtushenko resisting authority in his famous defence of the sculptor Neizvestny, accused of unpatriotic art.

'Neizvestny came back from the war with fourteen bullets in his body,' he told Mr Khrushchev, 'and I hope he will live many more years to produce many more fine works of art.'

'We have an old proverb,' Mr Khrushchev replied, 'that only the grave can correct a hunchback.'

'I hope we have outlived the time when the grave is used as a means of correction,' Yevtushenko retorted.

And Yevtushenko although he had become the best known of the younger poets in the west is not the only one. When in London he himself said that there were hundreds of poets in Russia today and at least twenty great ones.

'That is most remarkable!' his listener, an English poet, replied in quiet measured tones. 'You are fortunate indeed. We count a nation lucky if it produces one great poet in a generation.'

But Yevtushenko's exaggeration is understandable if it is taken as a young patriotic Russian's enthusiastic way of saying that there are more poets and a greater popular love of poetry in Russia today than in any other country. Not only is a whole edition of the work of the better known such as Yevtushenko, Akhmadulina, Vinokurov, Voznesensky, Sosnora and Slutsky sold out within a few hours of its appearance in the shops, but readings of their poetry draw immense popular audiences and have sometimes to be held in sports stadiums to accommodate all who would hear them. The reactions and the talk among the young who flock to these readings is as significant as the poetry itself. From what I myself saw of the young students and intellectuals they are passionately concerned only with the validity and meaning of human experience and inclined to reject fiercely any attempt to exploit it for the political convenience of the State. Ilya Ehrenburg, whose memoirs were appearing in serial form, and who has helped greatly to keep alive in the young the sense of their place in European literature, is criticized by them for having failed his own true experience.

'How could he write what he did under Stalin,' one young man said to me, 'when it is clear now from his memoirs that he knew all along what Stalin was like? Even now he admits he is not writing the whole truth. Such a man is no good to us. We need the whole truth and men we can believe in.'

The judgement was his, not mine. I can only hope we shall never be tempted so cruelly to suppress the truth as Ehrenburg must have been. I felt this all the more keenly as I watched the pressures of the State forcing artists, writers and poets to recant their living faith as even Yevtushenko was forced to do, and I felt certain they were being driven to recant by a belief that it was patriotically necessary, and because the umbilical cord between their newly born individual modern selves and this ancient, primitive European mother Russia had not yet been cut. I thought too that the time was coming when someone would refuse to sacrifice the truth of his own living experience for the convenience of the State not only out of courage but out of conviction that it was the greatest good he could bring to the State. For such men one of their main protections is the interest of the outside world in their fate. I think the violent reaction of the outside world to the treatment of Pasternak and his mistress and daughter made a profound impression on Soviet authority. The Soviet pretension to be the foremost exponent of the highest philosophy of which the human spirit is capable is maintained as the chief means of obtaining support in the outside world. This makes it vulnerable to criticism, as it is of paramount importance that the State should remain intellectually respectable. It is even possible that the ageing Valeriy (Tarsis) author of the satire *The Bluebottle* and a member of the Soviet Writers' Union, who was sent to a lunatic asylum, was released some weeks later because of the revulsion of the outside world at the news.

It is not a pretty sight to watch the Soviet establishment coercing persons whose work implies doubt of the Soviet absolutes. Russian poetry has an heroic tradition and it seems natural that today the poets' freedom of utterance should be as unwavering as that of Pushkin and Lermontov who are so honoured. One cannot help therefore feeling acute dismay at seeing them come to the political heel. But for me this is not half so sinister as the sight of the non-Russian Communist abroad, subject to none of these pressures, enjoying freedoms that the abolition of the society they hate would immediately bring to an end, dancing ardently to the Kremlin tune against which the new poets in Russia are rebelling. Pasternak was the first to break through the sound barrier between Russia and the outside world and to resume communications with the rest of the world in the ancient and classical meaning of the word. I am ashamed to say that in my own world where we still take communication of this kind for granted I had not fully appreciated the greatness of his achievement. I had to go to Russia, to experience the power of the State and the Establishment, the immense primitive insistence on 'likemindedness' and 'togetherness' as the greatest of all values, to appreciate what he had done. His achievement was all the greater, too, because it was a reluctant achievement. If he were the first Soviet saint and martyr (as the new Russian writers regard him), his saintliness was made pure and capable of true increase by its reluctance. This element of reluctance is of the very quintessence of the matter, for the saint or martyr who seeks his fate with eagerness as a deliberate policy of his spirit never rings true. There is an abnormality in it which reduces the power of the example to influence and heal. Only those who grow into their role and reluctantly bear their bitter fruit (as, for instance, Thomas More) can change the destiny of the human spirit. This I believe Pasternak did and because of him Russia will never be the same again. It was significant to me how much he is discussed and what emotions he still arouses. The severest criticism I heard came from members of the Party and amounted in the main to the charge that he had been unpatriotic in publishing his book abroad. Only one, an unpleasant young Komsomol leader said: 'What do you expect of a Jew!' But even at these political, non-literary levels I was amazed by the numbers who said to me as a young Communist did: 'Both sides were wrong in this matter, Pasternak was wrong to publish without permission and particularly to publish abroad. The State was wrong to refuse him publication. If it had happened now, I am certain *Dr Zhivago* would not have been suppressed.'

I went with a friend one week-end to the place where Pasternak is buried at Peredelkino. We had no difficulty in finding the place for we met a woman who seemed to know without asking why we had come, and pointing said: 'You'll find his grave over there.' The grave was apart under some tall pines, carefully tended and covered with fresh flowers. There at last I found an individual grave of a life individually cared for, mourned and remembered. It seemed to me that Pasternak, in his separateness, belonged more to the country he loved so deeply than any persons in their collectivity of life and death. I also feel that until Russia has developed this 'belonging through separateness' among its people, it will continue to be as backward in spirit as it once was in knowledge and technology. Yet I felt also that such a development was inevitable among such a people, though it could take many years – more years than the world and peace could afford – unless we all stand firmly and without excess of aggression in the values Pasternak tried to communicate to his people. Let a young Russian poet speak for me as he speaks for the whole of the new world within this old, old world of Russia. His name is Andrei Voznesensky and I quote from the translation by Robert Conquest published in *Encounter* in April 1963. This is what he wrote of Pasternak:

> They bore him to no entombment,
> They bore him to enthronement.

And this is how the same poem ends beside Pasternak's grave:

> Above, the forests loose
> Their leaves, but out of sight
> In the soil fivefold roots
> Are twisting, tough and tight.

So I came back to a Moscow full of the fever of summer. Spring had definitely gone and the summer firmly established a great restlessness seemed to fill everyone in the capital. It was not the restlessness one experiences in the capitals of Europe when their tired inhabitants are straining to get away from work for a holiday by the sea, but rather the kind of unrest I have observed among the aborigines of Australia, or the Bushmen and Hottentots of Africa, who can endure only for a time the conscious, applied, European way and, when the rains come, are compelled to abandon it and go for a long 'walk-about' in the manner and the country of their fathers. Almost everyone I met in Moscow was

preparing to leave the capital and go for such re-communion with
the natural spirit of their vast land. Young men and women with
a new light in their eyes spoke to me of their holiday plans. As
always the mass exodus was being superbly organized for all age-
groups. Even in the foreign community some people had caught
the fever and I met parents who were happily planning to send
their children to Soviet Youth camps in the woods, which they
declared were 'superb'. On my journeys by car in and out of
Moscow I found the woods, meadows and river banks full of
picknickers.

The last night of all I went with a young Russian to a Youth
café in Moscow. So popular have these institutions become that
we only got in at eight in the evening because his girl-friend had
stood in a queue from four o'clock in the afternoon to get a
table for us. The café was run by a committee, a small Soviet
elected by its patrons, and the waitresses and other servants all
were young, mostly students working their way through Polytechnic or college. When we arrived, some of the young people
were eating at their crowded tables, some drinking coffee, tea,
wine or beer – the café served no spirits. Others were playing chess
or just talking with great animation and obvious enjoyment and
some dancing to a jazz orchestra of young players under a young
conductor. I heard nothing but jazz all evening, and a good deal
of it taken straight from tape-recordings of American, British and
French broadcasts. Some of it too was original and composed by
persons in the café. At one moment in the evening I was introduced to a sad-faced, ascetic young man, who looked like an
Aubrey Beardsley drawing. I was told he was the best jazz composer and conductor in the country. I asked him to play for us.
He shook his head and whispered: 'I am not composing or playing just now. I found I was becoming repetitious and trying to go
ahead of my experience. So I have given up music for the time
being and am working in a factory to get in touch with life again.'

The three of us had hardly ordered our food when many young
people started joining us at the table as if they already knew us.
Before long we had a crowd so big that they sat in a circle wide
enough to fill a wing of the café. We talked about many things and
between times danced every kind of dance. One young woman
wanted to know all I could tell her about Princess Margaret – but

I soon found she knew more than I did! A young man wanted to know if I knew Benjamin Britten's music, and when he learned that I was a friend as well as admirer of the composer himself showered me with questions about him. Others asked me about Hemingway, Nkrumah, Galsworthy, Logical Positivism, the British Health Service, the state of marriage, birth control, Existentialism, automation, T. S. Eliot, and so on. Every time I came back from a dance I found new questions awaiting me. Without exception they all seemed full of hunger for direct news and contact with the mind and ways of the outside world. When asked if I knew how to dance 'The Twist', I replied 'Yes', and they insisted on my doing it for them at once. I pleaded in vain that it was against *their* law. They made a derogatory noise and forced me to dance it for them. Half-way through the evening a young man, a medical student, took his place by the piano, and recited one of his poems to a quiet, attentive audience. It was about a girl whom he had seen every day for years and who had always appeared to him to be an ordinary girl. Then one day suddenly he looked at her again and she was no longer ordinary but full of mystery. This poem drew a long round of applause.

'It's strange about women,' another young man began to tell me as I listened carefully – for I always wondered about the quality and texture of relations between the sexes in Russia, so matter-of-fact, almost coarse-grained, did they appear on the surface. 'Once I met a girl at midnight by the Moscow River. She was a stranger, beautiful and limping. I wondered why, until I saw she had on only one shoe.

' "Hullo, Cinderella," I exclaimed. "You've missed your coach, and lost your slipper!"

' "Oh no," she answered, "I'm just an ordinary girl walking home. After work all day in a stuffy office and an evening of night classes I was enjoying the fresh air and moon so much that I foolishly kicked my foot out and my shoe shot off into the river!"

' "Just wait," I told her and I dashed away, got a taxi and took her home. . . . She was really beautiful!'

'What's become of her?' I asked.

'I do not know,' he answered gravely, 'because I never saw her again.'

'Why on earth not?' I exclaimed. 'Didn't you like her?'

'Of course I liked her,' he answered. 'But you see something rare happened to us both that night that belonged only to that moment. I would have spoilt it all had I tried to see her again. It is all right if the ordinary girl becomes mysterious and beautiful, as did the girl in the poem. Then you *must* go on. But how wrong to let the beautiful and mysterious girl become ordinary! It would be a kind of murder. Have you ever thought why Dante did not follow up his vision of Beatrice's face by trying to get better acquainted? Why, if he had, he would never have written *The Divine Comedy.*'

That story, I felt, put Russian metaphysics fully in their place.

Finally about twenty of them walked back with me to my hotel arm-in-arm and singing aloud in the night of the silent, deserted Gorkiy Street. I watched them vanish into the underground and looked across the square at the golden bubble-domes, gilded crescents and crosses and red five-pointed stars of the Kremlin. The whole of Russia was for me at that moment in that evening and that view.

The next day, before I left, the Soviet authorities suddenly decided to bury someone in the Kremlin wall. They threw a cordon all around my hotel and the squares nearby. I could not get out to say good-bye to my friends at the British Embassy, to one of whom I owed fifty roubles. At the airport I asked a young Russian with me if he would be good enough to take the roubles and a note to the British Embassy for me in my car on his way back. He blushed with humiliation at a system which forced him to refuse a friend so obvious and easy a service but said firmly: 'I am afraid that is quite out of the question.'

And that too, I thought, as I sat down in my seat in the British *Comet*, was Russia. I fastened my safety belt and looked up to see the English faces of the crew calmly doing their work about me. I thought I had never seen happier and more resolved expressions: like the girl in the poem formerly ordinary, they were now suddenly full of the mystery for me, the mystery of a freedom as yet unknown in Russia. Suddenly too I felt myself to be so much lighter that I was almost giddy as with lack of ballast. Until that moment I had not known what a weight on my spirit had been the Soviet system.